A SHOT IN THE DARK

BOOKS BY SANTE D'ORAZIO

NONFICTION

A Shot in the Dark
Sante D'Orazio: Polaroids
Barely Private
Gianni and Donatella
Pam: American Icon
Sante D'Orazio: Photographs
A Private View

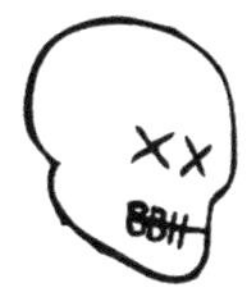

A SHOT IN THE DARK

A Memoir

SANTE D'ORAZIO

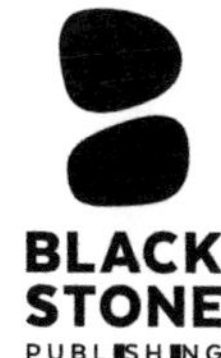

Published in 2025 by Blackstone Publishing
Cover design by Alenka Vdovič Linaschke
Book design by Joe Garcia

Some names and identifying details have been changed to protect the privacy of individuals.

Printed in the United States of America

First edition: 2025
ISBN 979-8-8747-2769-7
Biography & Autobiography / Artists, Architects, Photographers

Version 1

Blackstone Publishing
31 Mistletoe Rd.
Ashland, OR 97520

www.BlackstonePublishing.com

I dedicate this book to those who crossed
the River Styx and made it back to tell their story.

*With a special thank you to Diane,
who has always kept this boat steady.*

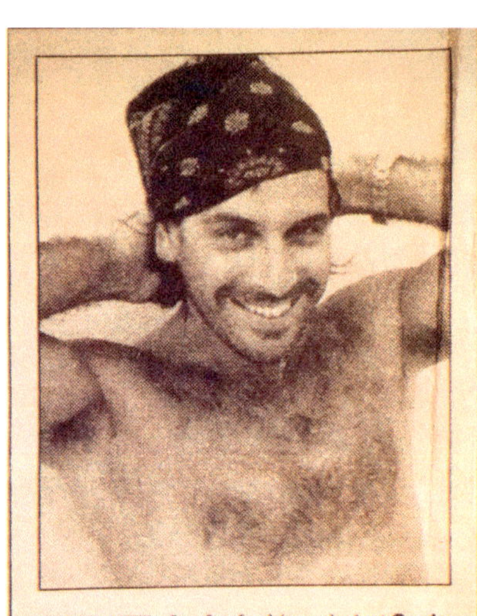

SUITE LIFE: Cry for fashion photog **Sante D'Orazio** *(above)* when you get a chance. He spent yesterday afternoon in the Manhattan Suite of the Four Seasons Hotel with **Helena Christensen**, who was in bra and panties. Relax, it was for the next Victoria's Secret catalogue. . . . **READ**

Sante D'Orazio, *New York Post's* Page Six

FOREWORD

Picture, if you will, a lavish circus tent and, inside, celebrities, hustlers, entrepreneurs, and the most glamorous girls in the world running wild. D'Orazio, the ringmaster, recording every detail, each exquisite manic moment captured in his heat-seeking lens.

This book is an authentic insider's view of the world of international fashion and celebrity as it existed in the '80s, '90s and beyond, a brief exhilarating period of personal and sexual liberation, long before "cancel culture," COVID, and strict political correctness.

The truth you will find here is Sante D'Orazio's truth, related with honesty and humor by someone who was in the room when stuff happened. These unembellished tales chart an Italian American boy's stratospheric pilgrimage and progress from Brooklyn to the pinnacle of the fashion heap. Scenes from the goldmine in which he cavorted with the boldface names of the time, epic days and nights photographing and partying with the beautiful and the damned.

Max Blagg

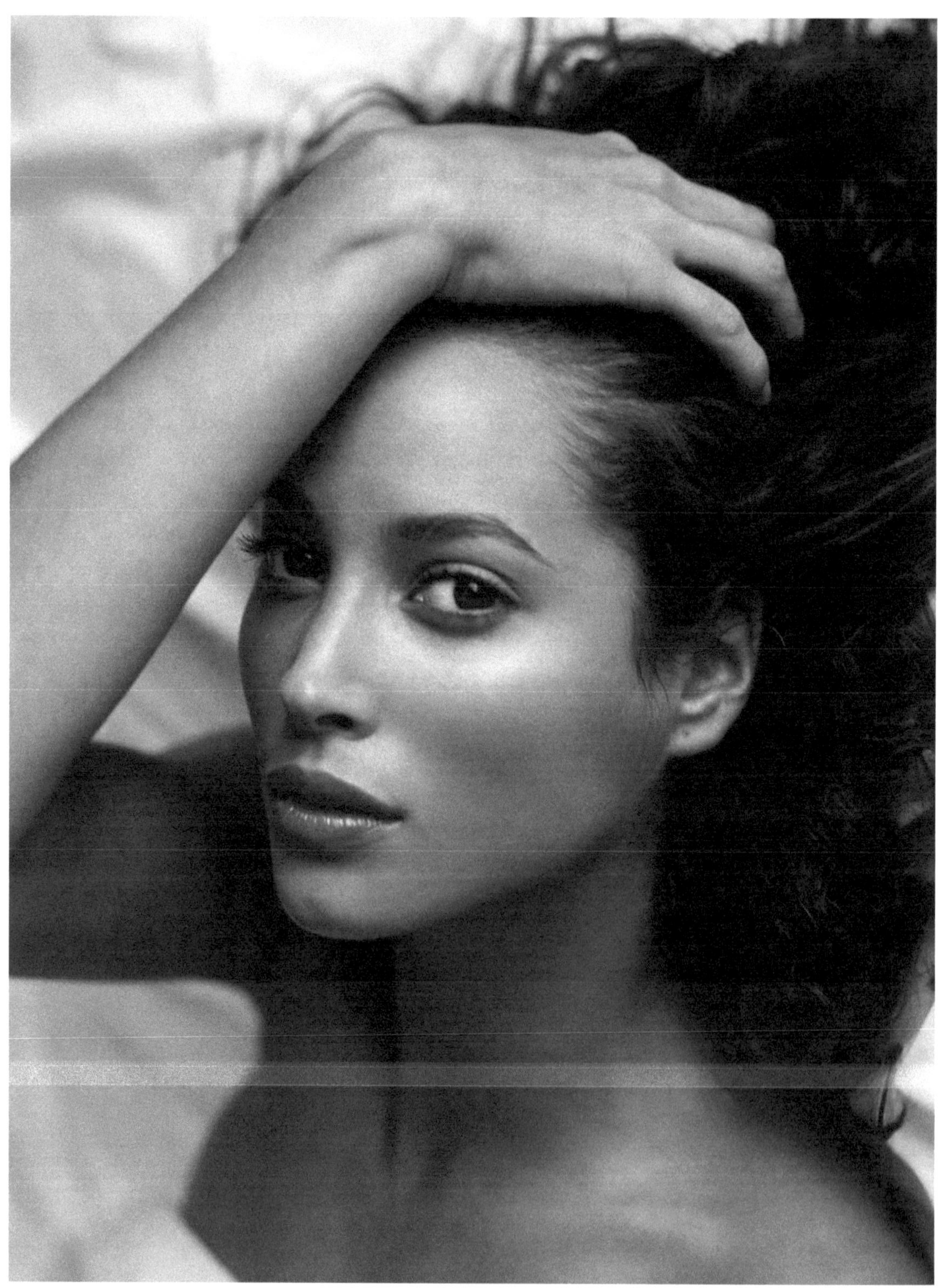

Christy Turlington for Italian *Vogue*

INTRODUCTION

These tales I write of are my truth, nobody else's. Whenever I drop a boldface name or two, it's not at their expense but only to paint a picture in an insightful, endearing, and entertaining way. Otherwise, I've changed some names to protect those individuals for the sake of, and value of, telling my personal story without spilling other people's secrets, only my own.

I never recall any of the funny or tragic stories coming to me in any particular order. They seem to flow with a will of their own, without my doing, yet they sum up a poetic dialogue within me as fragments. And so as fragments here, I've chosen to leave them.

Everything I've written is how I remember it—what I saw and what I came to believe. Someone standing next to me may have seen it differently, but I'm not going to worry about that. How I perceive the world around me becomes my truth.

I've been telling stories my entire life. I write the way I speak, with the accent of a New Yorker from Brooklyn. I speak in the vulgar dialect, in every sense of the word, of the neighborhood. The way I speak is also the angle from which I see the world.

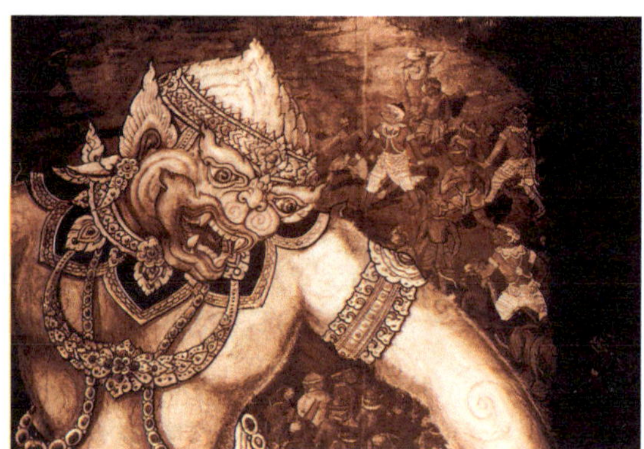

Detail of a temple mural, Phuket, Thailand

1

Working for *Vogue* magazine sometimes meant traveling the world to unknown and unexplored destinations, as well as working with the most talented people in the fashion industry. Hair and makeup artists, editors with great designer clothes from Valentino to Versace. Superstar models, as well as unknown models, soon-to-be superstars. *Vogue* had top priority over every other magazine in the world, and some locations offered them exclusive first rights before any other publication. The coverage for everyone was priceless, in terms of prestige and exposure.

On rare occasions, two of their magazines from two different countries would collaborate and piggyback a team and any expenses into one glamorous trip, like the one that sent us to Thailand, courtesy of British *Vogue* and French *Vogue*. These high-profile magazines could eventually turn beautiful foreign locations into popular tourist attractions, so the tourist board of the Thai government rolled out the red carpet for us.

My crew and I arrived in Phuket, then unspoiled, now a major tourist destination. The models on this trip were Tatjana Patitz and Kara Young. Tatjana and I had dated for four weeks, three and a half of which she was out of town for, so we soon agreed friendship was a much better idea. Kara, at the time, was my new girlfriend. We stayed at the magnificent, newly built Amanpuri resort and hotel, located on a bluff above a pristine beach. The British *Vogue* shoot was first; our location was in and around the hotel and beach, very easygoing. The PR for the hotel basically paid for our stay for the next two weeks. Tatjana was our model for that shoot. Then, she took off on another trip somewhere else for another magazine.

The second leg of the trip was for French *Vogue*, and we would shoot around the Phuket area. The PR for that was covered by the Thai government and tourist board. We were assigned a driver who was also our guide. We scouted locations with him for two days and planned out our schedule. He was a really nice guy who also happened to be an ex-Thai kickboxing champion. He invited us to attend a match, and although I had never been to any kind of fight before and wasn't one for any kind of violence in general, he was so excited and proud that I agreed to go to a bout. Plus, the guys on my crew really wanted to go.

We had front row seats. The ex-champ's younger brother was competing in one of his first big fights. He must have been sixteen or seventeen years old. The ex-champ was excited, and we all leaned over on the tarp to watch. Almost immediately the brother's opponent landed a kick to the kid's face that broke his nose in I don't know how many places, and his blood splattered all over us. *Fuck this!* I left my ringside seat, blood all over my face, and went to clean myself up. The ex-champ took it in stride and laughed at me, and so did my crew. That was the end of that!

We started shooting the next morning in a beautiful location. The clothing was elegant: Dior, Givenchy, light and summery, some transparent, some silks, and embroidery. Kara looked exotic in clothes that matched the environment. She had already gotten some sun, and her skin had a beautiful bronze tone. The place was perfection, with palm trees, clean beaches, and green-blue waters. We shot the whole thing on the beach with simple, clean backgrounds. The following day I met up with my editor Barbara Baumel to look at the Polaroids, to see if we liked the entirety of the shoot. They looked really good.

We finished shooting in two days, which gave us a couple of days to just take off and hang out. I was looking forward to going to the beach. The boys in my crew had managed to get some weed and some hash, and we laid out on the sand, drinking rosé wine and fruity drinks with umbrellas in them. Perfection! While we were enjoying our drinks, my editor came to me with the Polaroids and pointed out something that the magazine had mentioned to her. There were no images that specifically indicated we were in Thailand.

The town wasn't pretty enough, and we weren't allowed to shoot at any of the temples because of the strict religious laws. In fact, when we visited the temples, we were warned that nobody would be allowed to enter unless they were dressed appropriately. The women especially had to be covered, no shorts or bare shoulders. Also, if we happened to encounter any of the young children training to be monks, we were not to pat them on the head; it was an offense. The top of the head was where the soul transcended out of the body or something, so don't touch! Apart from the town and temples, there wasn't much else, other than the beaches. We had covered the hotel for British *Vogue*, so I was at a loss.

Then, I remembered that, as we were driving, I had seen a beautiful tree with colored ribbons tied all over it not too far from the hotel in a small patch of forest. There were nice rocks and broken statuary scattered around as well. Maybe we could go there and get one shot off that would cover us. There's always one shot that you feel is maybe your weakest image, that you can reshoot. I pulled that Polaroid for the reshoot. It was an important designer, a big advertiser who the magazines always loved to feature editorially as a gesture to a loyal client. In that shot, Kara wore a gorgeous Givenchy burgundy outfit with sheer leggings and gold embroidery and a matching top. Our guide and driver had already left; we'd dismissed him, having thought we were finished shooting, but we had the van, and it was one shot, something we could handle in less than an hour. So we got up early and found the location, which was just fifteen minutes away. No one else was around, so we set up the shot, with Kara leaning against this beautiful tree with the ribbons and broken statuary; it looked divine.

As I was starting to shoot, I noticed an old man squatting nearby and watching. I nodded hello; he nodded back. Then, a little distance away, another man was watching, and then another. I nodded again to them. One gave me a thumbs-up and smiled. I did the same but started feeling a really bad vibe. I finished off one roll of film, but the situation didn't feel right. I told the crew to pack it in, that we should leave. I put the roll in my pocket and, as always, loaded the camera with a fresh one. Next thing I knew, the cops arrived and surrounded us. They were openly hostile and rounded us all up. None of them spoke English, but we were clearly under arrest. They put us in our van with one officer, and we headed for the local police station. Still, no one spoke English. They had confiscated my cameras and the passports we carried with us. We had no idea what was going on.

On the ride to the station, I sat in the back of the van with one of my assistants; he discreetly signaled to me that he was holding a big bag of weed! *Holy fuck!* With the window open and one eye on the cop in the front, he started taking weed from the bag and sprinkling it out the window. He didn't want to fling the whole thing because there was a cop car following us. He managed to get rid of it all. That was the last thing we needed!

At the police station, we couldn't get any information as to what was going on. It took hours to get us a translator. Finally, a woman from the tourist board arrived. She started to ask what was happening. There was a big commotion between her and the cops, and then she turned around and looked at me in a state of shock. She was speechless. *Now what?* She told us we were under arrest for desecration of the Buddha by putting a naked girl against a sacred Buddha tree! *What??* They had the one empty roll I had given them from my camera. My Polaroids, however, were in my camera bag, and I was able to show them that Kara wasn't naked. That was a twenty-five-thousand-dollar Givenchy outfit she was wearing. And how the fuck was I supposed to know that was a sacred tree?

"No," they said, "you could see her legs and breasts."

In fact, the top and pants were sheer, so . . .

We managed to get the hotel manager on the phone. He was an Aussie and a nice guy, but I could hear the panic in his voice as he spoke with the translator. He was going to call the American Embassy in Bangkok. In the meantime, he asked if I had anything in my room he should know about because they may go through my stuff. I told him I had some weed the boys had given me. He said he would go in and throw it out for me.

Kara and I were sitting together inside for a while. The cops said everyone else should leave. My crew went back to the hotel; it was just Kara and me under arrest.

One cop pointed to Kara and said, "You jail, very good, ha-ha, very good jail!"

"You cocksucker!" I said. He obviously didn't speak English.

Then, they separated us and put me in a cell with a guy with a shaved head in an orange jumpsuit who was literally cuffed to a ball and chain like in those old movies. The iron ball was the size of a bowling ball. I found out later he had killed his wife with a hammer. I also found out that his crime was considered less serious than mine. In one of the British papers, I read about an English husband and wife who had been arrested and put in facing cells. Two guards and a prisoner raped the wife and then tried to bribe the husband to keep his mouth shut. It was no fun getting arrested here; that's for sure.

As usual, I was wearing my Rolex, the silver one with the red and blue dial. One of the guards—the same guy who had pointed to Kara and said, "You jail, very good!"—spotted it and pointed to it and then pointed to himself. I was thinking, *Fuck you, man!* I said, "You, you like New York, New York you come?" I pointed to me and pointed to him, and he nodded yes. I made the sign of writing on paper, and I said, "You come visit, yes?" He nodded in agreement, and I said, "Yeah, because if you're in New York, I'll give you a tour of the East River!" I smiled, and he smiled back. That seemed to distract him because I couldn't believe he actually went and got me a pencil and paper. In the meantime, I put my watch in my pocket. I still have that Rolex by the way.

Ten hours later, our Aussie friend somehow managed to get us out, on house arrest at

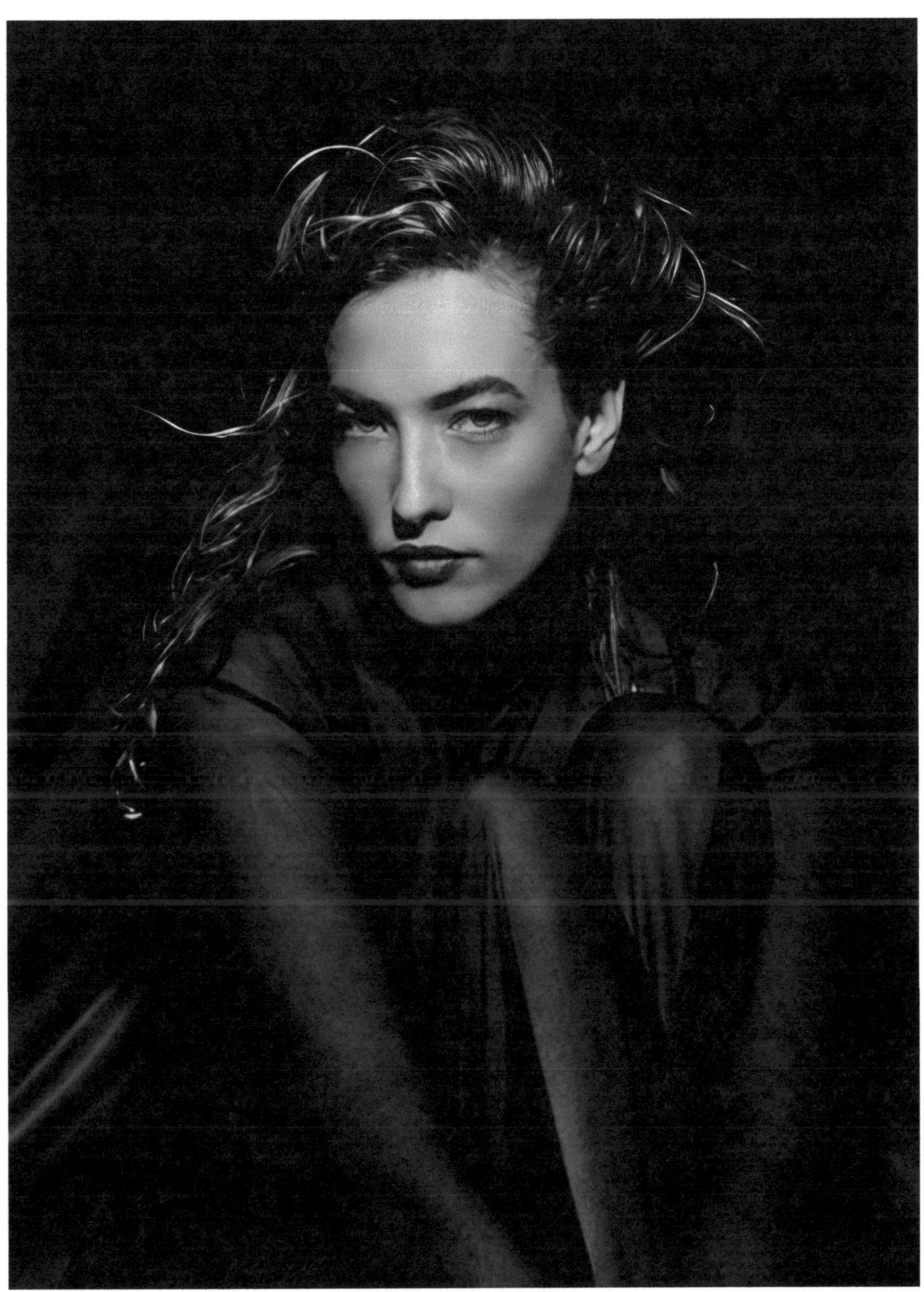

Tatjana Patitz for German *Vogue*

the hotel. They had our passports, so we weren't going anywhere. Except for my editor Barbara Baumel and makeup artist Laura Mercier, everyone else had packed up and gotten on the next plane home. No reason for them to stay.

Finally, some guy came down from the American Embassy, who wasn't even American, and did some investigating. Barbara, our French editor, had gotten in touch with French *Vogue*, and they were going to do everything possible on their end.

This schmuck from the American Embassy, whose title I still didn't know, came back late the next morning to give me some news. He said we'd be charged with desecration of the Buddha, a seven-year mandatory prison term. We had a fifty-fifty chance of going away for seven fucking years! Kara naturally freaked out, but I managed to calm her down.

Barbara had heard that French *Vogue* was in touch with the French Ministry of Foreign Affairs, and they advised us not to talk to the Americans, who were bound to fuck things up—especially because the Thai government wasn't on good terms with the United States. We would find out in the morning if they would release us.

The morning came and went, so maybe that afternoon, we'd know something. That afternoon, there was no word; maybe tomorrow morning, we'll hear from someone, and again nothing. This torture continued for seven days. Every morning, we held onto the hope for news that we could go home, and we'd wait. I made calls to people I knew back home. Someone was going to send a plane and have us smuggled out of the country, but that plan got too complicated to risk.

Meanwhile, my editor informed us that the French Minister of Foreign Affairs was in contact with the Queen of Thailand's office, and to stay put and wait. Kara finally cracked and lost control by panicking and babbling hysterically and wanting to call her father back home and making no sense. I had to shake her to snap her out of it. I couldn't blame her; I was ready to crack myself. Next thing we know, our story was all over the Thai news, and now the locals were up in arms. Then, CNN got hold of it. In their version, Kara was butt naked on a sacred tree! This didn't help at all. I envisioned myself in an orange jumpsuit with my head shaved and the word "bitch" tattooed on my forehead in Thai!

On the seventh day, we were told that we would be sentenced and given probation, but we still had to go to court, and it would be up to the judge. We met with the DA the next day. This guy had graduated from the University of Texas. Finally, someone who spoke English. He seemed like a reasonable guy I could talk to.

"Sir, I never intended any disrespect to anyone. My mom is very religious, and I myself have gotten a much better understanding of Christianity through my extensive reading of Buddhism (This was true.). Please allow me to make an offering to the temple. I would never intentionally disrespect the Buddha or any religion, for that matter."

But his answer was harsh. "You Americans have no respect for anything. You drop bombs indiscriminately and kill innocent people without any concern for innocent lives."

"Oh, fuck." Kara jabbed me with her elbow.

I should have kept my mouth shut right then and there, but no, I decided to mention the fact that, a week earlier, someone had offered me a virgin for a hundred dollars, and like a typical New Yorker, I had laughed and jokingly replied, "A virgin, ha, what is she, ten years old?"

The guy said, "Yes, I get you ten-year-old virgin."

I was horrified—the pimp had been serious.

I asked the DA, "Sir, where is the desecration of the Buddha? Innocently leaning a model against a tree or taking the virginity of a ten-year-old girl? That's a desecration of the Buddha if you ask me."

"And your bombs take hundreds of ten-year-old lives with no second thoughts," he replied.

I figured this guy must be on the local take to say shit like that, even if it was true.

Thank God, he changed the subject. Kara gave me a dirty look, and all I could do was shrug my shoulders. After all that, the next thing he did was hand me a hundred-dollar bill; then he wrote down the address of his alma mater in Texas and asked me to mail it to them as a donation. I have no idea why.

Meanwhile, French *Vogue* had arranged for a lawyer to come down from Bangkok, and we had a court date the next day.

Kara and I, Barbara and Laura Mercier (God bless those ladies for staying with us the entire time), and our lawyer were sitting in the back of the court. In the front row sat half a dozen ladyboys, all excited and giggling; they seemed thrilled to be going to jail. They kept turning around and looking at us, pointing their fingers at me and giggling as if I were on the menu! When it was their turn, the judge just hammered his gavel without even addressing them and sent them off to jail. One of them blew me a kiss as if to say, "*See ya later, honey!*"

According to our lawyer, we were still subject to the judge's discretion, so we were still unsure. We finally got in front of the judge, and I kept my mouth shut. The judge handed us a three-year suspended sentence. We walked out of the courthouse and were met by two undercover dicks who escorted us to the airport and onto the plane and even checked that I had fastened my seat belt. They waited till all the passengers had boarded and left just before the doors closed. It wasn't until two hours after we were airborne that I started to relax, but even then, I felt edgy. When we finally landed in Paris and got off the Thai Airlines plane, I bent down and kissed the ground. Eight hours later, we arrived in New York, and I finally felt safe. A sense of patriotism came over me like I'd never felt before in my life!

God Bless America, as my father would always say!

Thirty-some-odd years later, I still haven't gone back to Thailand.

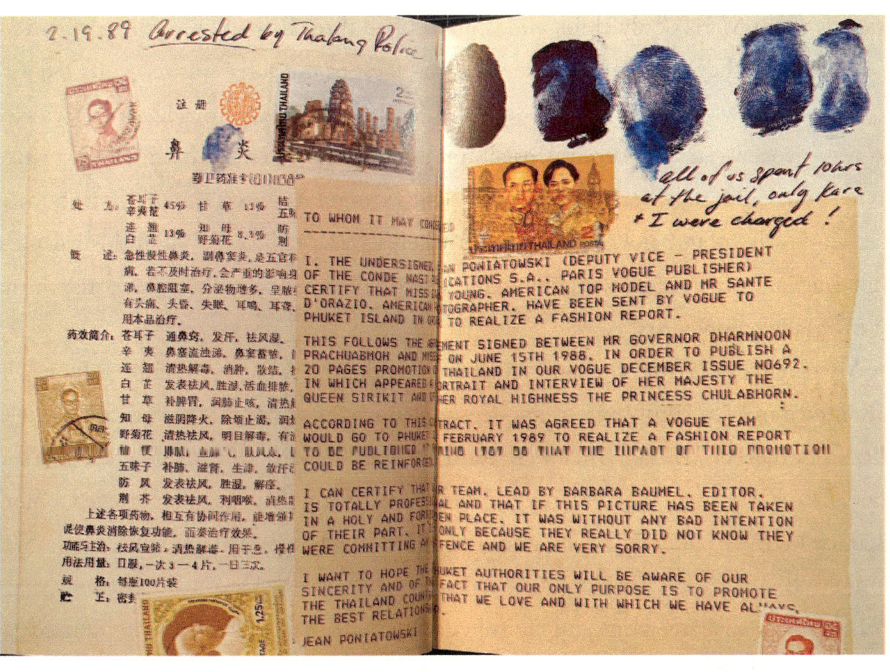

Sante's diary page from French *Vogue* to the Queen of Thailand

2

I was my mom Maria's only child, and though I had three half-siblings from my dad's previous marriage, they were much older. The youngest of the three was ten years older than me, so as a kid, I was alone a lot. My dad, Nicola, spoke English with a heavy Italian accent, and was preoccupied with survival, as all immigrants were. He had been working since he was ten years old as a barber. There were no books around; there was no one to help me with homework. My mom barely spoke English when I was a child, and all of this led me to a lot of drawing, which came naturally to me, eventually making me the class artist throughout my grade school years.

My parents were from the same small town, Valenzano, Bari, in Southern Italy, where, with interconnected family ties, everyone was a cousin of some sort. My parents knew each other from their childhood. They were third cousins, which may explain why I was such a mook. Theirs was an arranged marriage of necessity on my dad's part. He needed a mom to help raise his three children. My mom resisted marrying him at first, knowing him as well as she did, but the families pressured her, and she finally agreed. Deeply devout and educated by the church, she later went and consulted with Padre Pio (a latter-day canonized saint) who was pissed off with her for wasting his time, considering she had already, from heavy family pressure, made the decision to accept and go. Through a friendly intervention from her parish priest, who had made the introduction, Padre Pio came around and helped her to see the marriage as a blessing and spiritual mission to raise my father's children. She was in her early thirties and, up until then, had devoted herself to the church.

As a teenager, my mom was discovered to have a unique operatic voice from her singing in the church choir. This got the attention of local voice coaches who offered their services for free, and soon she started training, and later performing, at major venues in Bari, Naples, and Verona. She saw the beginnings of her career take off and then fall apart because of World War II. It took everyone years to recover from the war, especially those in the south.

In comparison, my dad had left for the United States when he was twenty years old, long before Mussolini signed a pact with Hitler, and by the 1930s, his entire family—both parents, two sisters, and three brothers—had already immigrated to the United States. They were not educated in any formal way, and the boys started working at a very young age. My father and his five siblings were always fighting among themselves, and as children, they were fighting for their mother's attention and love, which she didn't freely give. As a result, my father was not an affectionate man. They were hardworking immigrants who forged their way in the new world, and money became, at times, another source of their mutual hostilities and petty jealousies. They were not generous people among themselves, and even I, as a teenager, grew distant from them with time.

When my mom came to this country in 1953, none of her family members were living here. Her family was mostly in Italy and spread out over the immigrant trail in Venezuela, Canada, or wherever they were granted entry. Instead, she was surrounded by my dad's dysfunctional family, who made her feel like an outsider. My mom instilled in me all her prejudice, her solitary pain, and all her disapproval of my dad and his family.

She suffered from depression. Unfortunately, she continued to suffer from it throughout her life and couldn't help passing it on to me; I was basically a *mookie* kind of kid.

Carl Jung said, "One great source of depression is the loss of dreams." So she placed her hopes and dreams onto me, her only son.

My mom raised my father's three children as her children as best she could—Marie, John, and Mike. Marie, who, as a woman, later became one of my mom's closest friends and confidants, was the first to marry and leave the house; then two years later, the second oldest, John, followed. The most devastating thing to my mom and me was when both Marie and John moved to Florida. It felt as if they were forever gone. I loved them very much. I was closest to the youngest, my brother Mike. We shared a room during my childhood, but by the time I was around ten years old, he was married and out of the house. I was, again, devastated.

My psyche, by now, had begun the process of building walls of defense and detaching from the people I loved leaving. Due to all those circumstances, my mom became overbearing and oppressive at times, and after my dad died, she clung to me as her only lifeline, her only reason to live as she reminded me every freakin' day of my life.

She smothered me with what she claimed to be all her love, and I believed everything she said. She made me feel different from everybody else. It was me and her against the world since we both felt left on our own.

It took me thirty years to learn she was wrong, but by then, the damage had been done.

I was alienated from my father when he was alive because of his and my mother's differences, and for the next twenty years after he passed away, I was angry at him for dying on me. I wouldn't even acknowledge him in my life. Between that, my siblings moving out while I was young, and being left alone to care for my mom, I didn't realize the complexes and sense of abandonment I had developed or the sense of isolation that came with it.

The realization of who our parents are when we are young never occurs to us. As kids, the world is always about us.

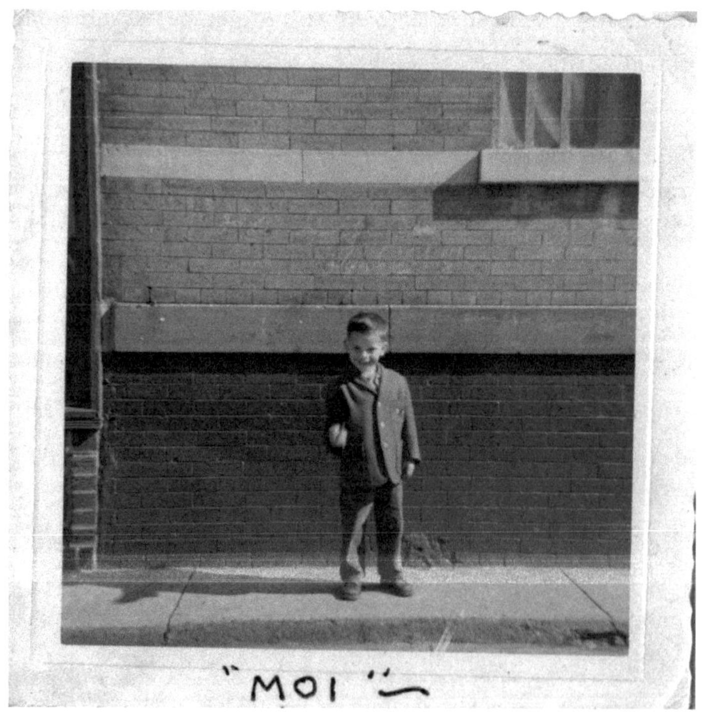

Sante, giving the middle finger

3

Art can come to you from many directions, from different sources, influences, or just from unexpected and sometimes funny places. Enlightenment is your psyche's response to a jolt of awareness from out of the blue.

When I was five or six years old, my two cousins from New Jersey, Nicky and Johnny, would visit Brooklyn. They were around my age, and together, the three of us were tiny terrors. Our families referred to us as "the coyotes." At family gatherings, news that the coyotes were coming would be greeted with alarm. We were terrible and very mischievous when together, but at the time, we saw it more as being creatively curious. We had an unscientific approach to our creative mischief, always posing the question, "What would happen if we did this . . . to that?" Which later on I learned was the same method all artists use in approaching their subjects.

By instinct, I quickly understood that all the Arts were related, and at five years old, I had already been drawing for at least half my life. I'd also become interested in pop culture and modern dance. I learned how to do "the Twist" by watching Chubby Checker on *American Bandstand.* His record topped the Billboard charts in 1960 and again in 1962, and the dance stayed popular for years. I mastered it in no time and began to perform solo at family weddings—and my family had a lot of weddings when I was a child.

I lacked one piece of essential equipment: Twist shoes like the ones Chubby wore. They were the low-cut pointy shoes that were in vogue during those early years of the '60s, with one critical difference: the laces were placed diagonally on the side of the shoes. I constantly badgered my parents for a pair. When they refused to yield, to everyone's dismay, I quit dancing at the weddings in protest. I sulked so much that, finally, they gave in. On our next Saturday trip to visit my coyote cousins in New Jersey, we made a stop at the Robert Hall clothing store on Bloomfield Avenue in Bloomfield, New Jersey, and for the princely sum of seven dollars, I got my twist shoes.

Chubby Checker was constantly on *American Bandstand*. He was even on *The Ed Sullivan Show*. I knew he was going to be on television the next day. I woke up early that Sunday morning, still in my pajamas, proudly walking around the house in my twist shoes to break them in, until performance time. When Chubby and "The Twist" came on the screen, I debuted my shoes by dancing and twisting like a dervish. My brothers and sister applauded and cheered me on. It was beyond a performance; it was center stage! I felt great!

That same Sunday, Nicky and Johnny were coming over for a coyotes' day to spend with the family. The day before, my father had just finished painting the garage in the backyard and tarring its roof. He had wedged the paint and tar cans up against the doors so we couldn't go in and warned us not to even try.

When the boys arrived, I showed off my twist shoes, no way was I taking them off. The boys showed off their new suits—most parents would dress their kids in their "Sunday best" back in those days. My cousins were jealous of my shoes, and I was jealous of their suits. We ended up in the backyard, where Nicky and Johnny began opening the cans of paint and started repainting the garage. I told them to stop, but they wouldn't listen. So, inspired by Moe, Larry, and Curley, the Three Stooges, I grabbed a brush and started painting on their suits, laughing all the way. Then we decided to look inside the garage. We climbed on the heavy cans of paint and tar my dad had stored against the doors and peered into the windows about five feet above ground level. As soon as I stood on the top of the can, the lid gave way, and my feet sank up to my ankles, all over my brand-new twist shoes. I never even got to perform at a wedding in them!

Naturally, we caught a freaking beating for the mess we had made. My twist shoes, tarred and stuck together, were relegated to the basement. It took a while for them to harden. They eventually resembled bronzed baby shoes, but in black, the laces still tied. As time passed, I would visit them in the basement. They began to take on another dimension and acquired a sort of magic and mystery. Using a box as a pedestal, I put them on top of it as a personal display. I wasn't quite sure what I was doing, but I felt somewhat possessed when I would stare at them. I didn't realize, at the time, that this was my first venture into sculpture. The visual memory remained lodged deep in my psyche, a kind of totem. They took on a life of their own. Those tarred twist shoes sparked a lifelong pursuit of an object as art and its poetic mysteries of something sacred yet unknown.

I often wonder what became of those shoes. I guess it doesn't matter as they still live inside of me, as all meaningful art should. It took a can of tar and a whooping of my hide to shift my perception and prepare me for the "twisting" road to becoming an artist. I was fresh out of kindergarten.

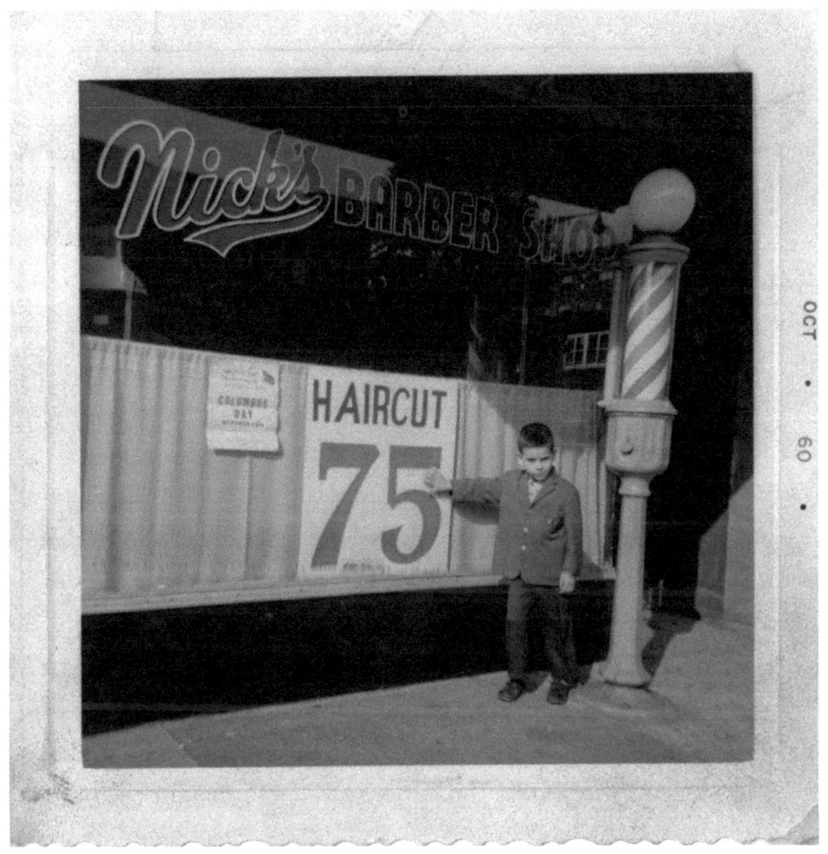

Sante, punished with an unwanted crew cut

4

In the summers, we vacationed in Italy. Though most of our family was in Bari, we'd always visit my mom's brother Frank and his family in Verona. While we were there, my mother would take me to Verona's ancient Arena, a first-century Roman amphitheater that is still in use today for opera, equal in prestige to La Scala in Milan. My mother was a gifted mezzo-soprano who had sung there many times when she was young. My mom didn't talk about it much at home, but over time, I began to realize her operatic history. Her voice was later compared by her conductors and opera contemporaries to that of Marian Anderson, the renowned American contralto.

Prior to the war, the Fascists had imposed strict laws on women working, and Mom, being a young girl from the south, could never travel alone. She had to travel with her brother Michele who also sang opera. He was a soprano, which unfortunately meant his voice was less in demand. Then, a motorcycle accident ended his career and, with it, his ability to chaperone my mom for her to continue singing in places that meant travel. She stayed local and sang at the Petruzzelli Opera House in Bari, and always at her church, where she felt the most comfortable. I got to hear her sing only a couple of times. Her rendition of "Ave Maria" impressed me—her voice was almost overpowering; I couldn't believe that was my mom. Today it's hard for me to hold back tears when I hear that beautiful song. I'm very Italian that way.

As for my father, his musical talents also had to take a back seat to life's circumstances—survival. But singing and playing Neapolitan folk songs were his great pleasure—and hearing that music always evokes his spirit in me. Years ago, when I was in my mid-thirties, I was at a restaurant in Naples, Italy, with my then-wife, Kara, and three musicians were playing many of the songs my father used to sing as he played the guitar, accompanied by his brother on the mandolin. I'd hear that music played almost every Sunday around the dinner table while growing up. In that restaurant, while hearing those musicians play, a sadness came over me, followed by tears with a mixture of joy. I cried a lot, being the Italian mook that I am! My dad was long gone, but at that moment, he was in the room next to me, reminding me of the joy he felt singing those songs with family and friends.

The upside of my mom's suffocating love was my gaining an acute sensitivity and love toward people and nature. As a kid, I would sit in silence and feel everything around me as I drew. Drawing came very naturally to me. I almost took it for granted. Everything was felt, like the curve of a tree branch can evoke an emotion: a line, a tone, the atmosphere. Things had to feel *like* the object, not necessarily look exactly like it.

When my class in P.S. 179 in the 1960s put on plays, I would be in charge of painting backdrops and sets. On the day of the performance, I'd insist on being the curtain guy. I never wanted to be onstage and preferred to be hidden, invisible. That training came in handy when I later turned to photography, especially street photography and reportage, which required that invisibility.

I don't remember when or at what age I first realized my feelings for art. I just remember always drawing and responding to it instinctually, almost as if recognizing my home. Teachers were constantly advising my parents to send me to art school. I can still see my father looking at my mom and saying in Italian, "What, is she crazy?"

My parents' generation had lived through World War II. They'd left their homes and their families to search for a better life.

"Artist? She's out of her mind!"

So that was that, but it didn't stop me from reacting to images and paintings whenever I saw them and drawing whenever I had the chance.

I went through my school years doing all the things kids do in Brooklyn: stickball, football, baseball, softball, and basketball. I was athletic and on my school teams. Art classes weren't available to us in any serious way. The art that was taught at my high school, which was rated as one of the ten most violent schools in the country, was the art of dodging bullets and flying objects! The history of art and artists were not a subject on the curriculum. No one ever talked about Leonardo, unless you meant the pizzeria down the block.

When it came to exposure to fine art, our summers spent visiting family in Italy impressed and taught me the most. Art in Italy is like trees in a forest—it's everywhere. It's valued, respected, and taught in school at an early age, along with history, poetry, and philosophy. My mom, the former opera singer, was proud of her artistic heritage. She answered all my questions as best she could. There were also other relatives in Italy involved in classical music, painting, poetry, and of course, looming over everything was the church. They were more like great museums of art, and we visited them wherever we went in Italy: Bologna, Verona, Venice, Bari, Naples, and Rome. We had friends and relatives practically everywhere.

In Padua, I was fortunate to see the Arena Chapel with Giotto's frescoes, masterpieces of our Western Civilization. The chapel was cool and quiet, away from the summer heat and commotion outside. I was eight years old, and my eyes immediately gravitated to the vaulted ceiling with Giotto's starry sky, rather than to the figurative paintings of Jesus's life

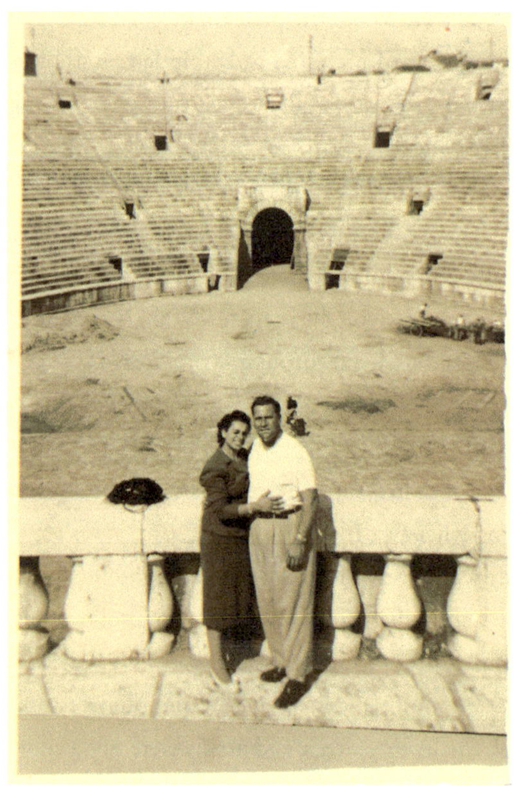

Sante's mom and dad in the Verona Arena, Verona, Italy

that wrapped around the chapel walls or to the depiction of Heaven and Hell on the wall behind the altar; I was too young to grasp its formal innovations. The deep blue sky and gold stars filled me with pure awe—those frescoes still conjure up a fairy-tale fantasy of staring into heaven. Looking up at it was a sensual experience, a chance to lose myself in the space between the stars. In Giotto's night sky, I could connect with the mystery, feel the artist's sense of the Almighty. I remember that feeling as if it were yesterday.

At the Basilica of St. Anthony of Padua, I roamed around the gigantic space freely on my own. I'd skip out on my dad, whose buffoonery I tried to avoid, like his having a picture taken of himself in the catacombs sharing a *cannoli* with a human skull—a perverse humor I realized later I had gratefully inherited. Instead, I'd sit with my mom in a pew and watch as she'd take out her rosary, lean forward, and make the sign of the cross. I'd follow along, and when she'd begin to silently move her lips, I'd sneak out of the pew and explore, reading the plaques beneath every painting and sculpture and, sometimes, go down to the crypts where I would find the really creepy stuff. This was a routine of mine in every church we visited, and one she was quite used to. One time, I came across a skull in a glass case, lit by a candle from below. The plaque read: *I was what you are, you will be what I am.* I had nightmares about that skull for years.

The skull motif is called a *memento mori*, Latin for "remember death," so that you live a purer life. The Buddhists, as well as many other cultures and religions, always observe that same symbol in one form or another. Monks, for example, are meant to own only one possession, their begging bowl for offerings of food. Traditionally, the bowl is the top half of a skull or cranium, turned upside down. Our pop culture has come to glamourize the skull. I always have a skull on hand. I've done some great pictures with skulls as props. Artists throughout history, along with contemporaries, like Andy Warhol and Damien Hirst, have done the same.

I learned my art history from those family summer vacations in Italy, thanks to my mother forcing us to visit every church in every town and city we visited. Rome was the biggest treat of all, with the Vatican and its museum, but I wasn't allowed to explore on my own. They knew I'd get lost.

My father was my mother's polar opposite; the church was not for him. While Mom prayed, he would go off with visiting relatives and hit the cafés. He loved his pastries, Strega liqueur with his coffee, and ice cream. And while my mom talked about things in metaphors, about God and Jesus Christ, the only utterance of "Jesus Christ" from my father was right before he'd smack me one for something I had done to piss him off.

He loved telling dirty jokes, leafing through girly magazines (which I'd find in the basement), and making everyone laugh. He also loved a good prank. Occasionally, I'd be subjected to my father's public spectacles, all done for a photo or a laugh or both. The man didn't give a shit about anything. His behavior would mortify me and my mom—like the time he jumped in a sarcophagus at the Vatican Museum, waving his camera in hopes of having his picture taken. The guards needed two stepladders to get him out because the interior was deeper than he thought; afterward, they walked him, or I should say *us*, out of the museum. Things were looser back in the '60s—a few years later, they would have cuffed him, for sure. I always tried to pretend I didn't know him.

But as I got older and farther away from living at home with my mom, and long after my father was gone, I began to appreciate his antics. I realized my mom's bias had me shut him out and how unfortunate that was. I now understood why people loved having my father around. He brought laughs and entertainment, along with some of his rather embarrassing points of view.

He once argued with a Roman taxi driver because he couldn't understand why the city didn't just knock down all those ruins in the Roman Forum and replace them with skyscrapers like we had in New York. "That's why Italy is so backward!" he said. I wanted to get out of the car and hide.

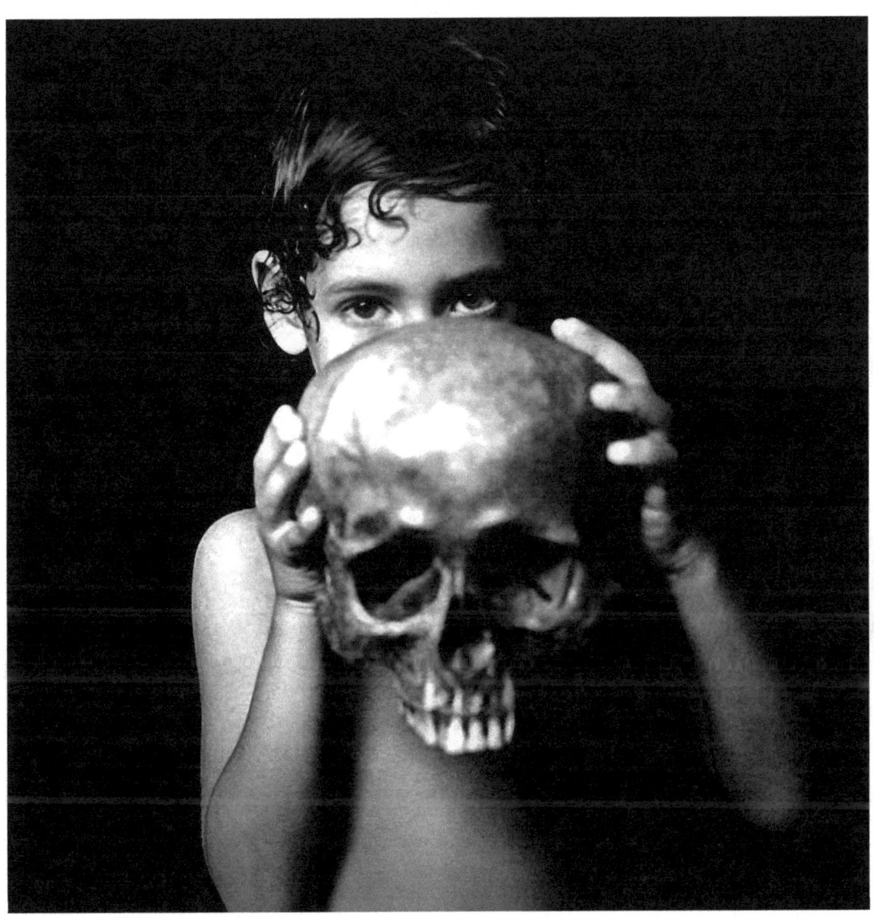

Portrait of Sante's son, Nick, with skull

5

The first time I fired a gun with real ammo, it was in Tommy Momo's basement. I must have been twelve years old, and Tommy was about seventeen. Tommy was considered one of the older guys. He told me to shoot at the wall, and like a jerk, I did. *Ping! pang! ping!* Who knew where the bullet went, but it scared the shit out of me, and I never wanted to hold a gun again. I'd almost killed both of us.

Tommy was a wannabe tough guy—that's the worst kind. He'd do the most stupid things to get the attention of the really tough guys who weren't much smarter than him and to show them he had nerve to gain their acceptance and approval. He was small in stature, with narrow eyes. He could easily pass for one of us in size and liked hanging out with us younger kids so he could show off and impress us. Tommy looked normal on the outside, but then again so did many people who were nuts—except maybe Mikey Aiello. (We'll get to him later.)

Tommy liked collecting sick guns. One time, he got ahold of a bazooka. Don't ask me how. We cut school, and a bunch of us went to Prospect Park to watch him test it out. A couple of rowboats were tied together on the other side of the lake. It was early and during the week, just before summer break, and no one was around. He aimed at the boats with the bazooka and missed, but he blew up the rental cabin fifty feet away. Everyone cut out in different directions and met up later back in the neighborhood. I didn't want to see him again for a long time after that—what a nut job!

I lived in what looked like a quiet Jewish and Italian neighborhood. You'd never think sick shit like that was happening. Nobody had guns—the Jews certainly didn't—only a couple of guineas or jerkoffs like Tommy and Mikey Aiello.

Mikey, known as Mikey Bear, was an animal unto himself. He had about ten years on me and hung out with a bad crowd. He lived around the corner from me and also hung out with my cousin Joey.

My beautiful cousin Joey was one of the best-looking young guys in the neighborhood, and one of the most sensitive. If he had grown up in a nurturing and loving environment, he would have been an artist, a poet, or a writer. Instead, he lived with constant physical abuse from his father and was truant from any kind of education, sheltering in hard drugs and violence. In his early twenties, his face was repeatedly slashed and disfigured in a gang attack. During his long and painful convalescence, he found a god who he understood and a god who understood him. He swore off violence and also found the good in everyone, including his boyhood friend Mikey Bear.

They were once partners in crime, but now things had changed. Mikey wanted to be somebody. He didn't know what, but he wanted to be *somebody*. He was good with his dukes and not very bright. What made him even crazier looking was that he had two lazy eyes. One eye always looked left while the other looked right, so when he talked to you, you didn't know which eye to look at, especially when he'd say, "Look at me when I talk to you!"

Every one of us feared Mikey, even though we knew he liked us. You'd never know with him, and the worst part was that he was always on drugs.

On the next corner from where Mikey lived were our neighborhood stores. Leo's grocery store, Pop's candy store, Sal the butcher, who'd always give me a slice of bologna when my mom shopped there. There was Tony the Tailor, Gin Lee's Laundry, Harry the Beautician, who did all the Jewish ladies' hair—purple, blue, and a strange shade of orange. There were Bob and Joel at the pharmacy, and my father in his barbershop next door; their adjacent stores shared a tiny bathroom whose walls were covered with my father's pinups. The shopkeepers were Italian or Jewish, except for Gin Lee, who had the only laundry shop in the neighborhood; he was Chinese.

One day, I was sitting in the kitchen having lunch with my mom when five or six gunshots went off in front of our house. I heard the sound of screeching tires from a car taking off. I told my mom to get down and stay there, and I went to look and see if the coast was clear. From my porch, I saw a van speeding away. In the middle of the street was a guy I couldn't recognize, lying face down in a pool of blood. I ran inside and called the cops. I stayed with my mom to keep her calm. After the police, ambulance, and even the fire department came, cleaned up, and left, a crowd still mingled around, but no one had any clues. I'd never seen anything like that before.

I found out the next day from my cousin Joey that it was Mikey Bear Aiello who had gotten shot; he had taken three bullets to the face and head and two or three to his body. He lived for two days and then died. The guys who did it were never caught, but I discovered much later on what most likely happened. Seemed that Mikey had gone to all the neighborhood stores where our parents shopped, having decided that everyone should pay protection money. The shopkeepers were like, "Protection from who?" and Mikey responded, "Protection from me." I told you he was stupid.

Soon enough the old-school Italians, with certain unspoken connections, put their money together, and they organized a crew. Whoever it was—and it was someone Mikey knew because he had voluntarily gotten in the van to take a ride—put a few bullets in him and threw him out of the van right in front of my house. Rumor had it that maybe, just maybe, the trigger man might well have been none other than Mr. Bazooka himself, Tommy Momo.

Soon after the shooting, after living in the neighborhood his entire life, Tommy relocated to Vegas without saying goodbye to any of us. Word had it he wanted to move back after a year or two away, but the thought of it was met with some disapproval by people in the neighborhood. I heard he eventually moved to a small plot of land in the desert instead . . . really small, if you know what I mean.

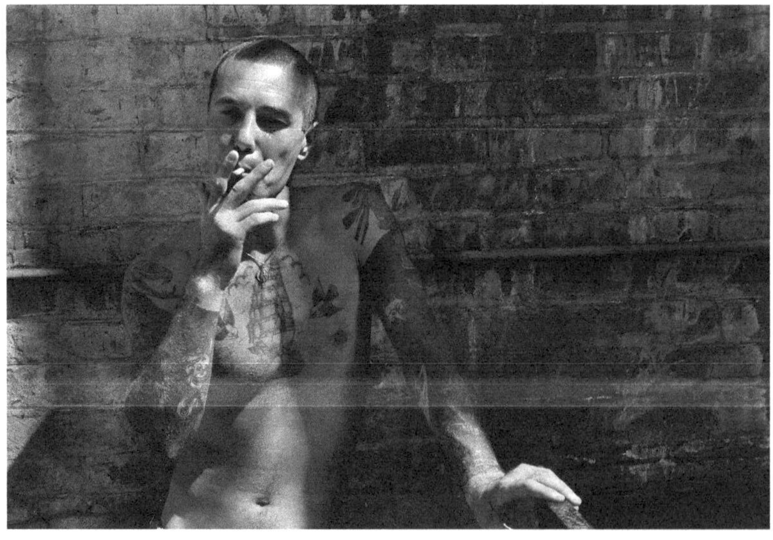

Sante's cousin Joey, photographed in Brooklyn, New York, in 1975

6

The neighborhood I grew up in is now referred to as Kensington, but I always knew it as Flatbush. It had a great mixed bag of people. Almost all were good family people, hardworking blue-collar, Italian, Jewish, some Irish, and other minorities spread around.

Then, there were pockets of low-level mobsters—guys on the lower end of the mob totem pole mostly, with a few others who reported to a bigger boss. As a little kid, I'd steer clear of them, but they were also the guys who'd buy me ice cream when I was little. They owned scrap metal yards, auto body shops, construction companies, etc.—usually businesses their parents or grandparents had started. The more idle family members were pinkie ring–wearing good-for-nothings. When I'd ride my bike by the social club, they'd call me over and joke with me or even ask me to take a package to someone else I knew, like the butcher.

For those of you who don't know, a social club was usually an ex-bar, restaurant, or storefront on the ground floor, street-level, with the windows blackened out, and where *members only* could gather among themselves. Usually, it was barely furnished, with a backroom for the boss and the front for the muscle playing cards or scheming. The basement would be used to temporarily store stolen goods or to hang a guy by his feet and smack him around if he had broken some rules or disrespected a senior member.

On the outside, their wives or moms had known you since you could remember and would ask you to go buy them a loaf of bread from Leo's, and you'd pocket fifty cents. Once in a blue moon, someone would ask you to make a delivery into another neighborhood that would earn you twenty to fifty dollars. Simple street sense told you not to ask any questions or, God forbid, open their package. They were always good for a full day's pay for a half-hour bike ride, and in the '70s, twenty dollars was a lot of money to a sixteen-year-old. In return, they'd have your back if there was trouble around, and you'd be the first to know if something *fell off a truck*. In other words, if the cops ever stopped you with a stolen item and asked where you got it from, you'd answer, "I don't know. I happen to be there when it fell off a truck!"

Everybody knew everybody, and most guys got their haircuts at my father's barbershop. But just one or two blocks away was sometimes considered an entirely different neighborhood, and no one in my 'hood knew anybody from the next 'hood over. But since I rode my bike everywhere, I knew everybody from every neighborhood. Some days, I'd hang out with one group of guys, then the next day another, always touching base with my own neighborhood. I was social, non-threatening, and liked by most people. I was a weaver, weaving in and out of every neighborhood. That's why I knew everybody.

One day, when I was around sixteen or seventeen, I was walking by the social club, and one of the old-timers called me in to ask if I could help him and his buddy out. Someone had supposedly hijacked a pharmaceutical truck, but if you asked me, the haul looked more like they had hijacked a minivan. I didn't know who was involved, and I didn't ask. They had acquired a large assortment of pills. There were bottles containing anywhere from one hundred to one thousand pills: barbiturates like red and blue Tuinals, red Seconals, Nembutals, black beauties, etc., with a street value of a dollar to a dollar-fifty for each pill. They knew what most of them were, and I identified the ones they didn't recognize. I knew about pills because, at sixteen years old, I was going out to the clubs every week, and everybody was smoking pot and popping pills. These guys were old-timers in their sixties, and alcohol was their thing. They'd never think of popping pills. I didn't want to get involved and was about to leave when one of them asked me about one more item.

He pulled out a box, opened it up, and I couldn't believe my eyes. Two fat bottles, one thousand pills each, each pill stamped with the number *714*. Quaaludes! The motherlode! He didn't even know how to pronounce it. Quaaludes had just started appearing in clubs in the city.

"What the fuck are these?"

"Well, the Tuinals, Seconals, and stuff are worth a lot more. Nobody I know is really into these." I had to restrain my excitement. "I might know someone, but they can't be worth much. How much you want for them?"

"Get me two hundred dollars each bottle."

I told him, "No way. Maybe two hundred for the pair? If I'm going to take them and ask around, I need to put something in *my* pocket."

Deal! I got two large bottles of one thousand—that's two thousand pharmaceutical Rorer 714 quaaludes—for one hundred dollars a bottle. In the clubs, the pills were going for two dollars each. That meant each bottle was worth two thousand dollars! I put them in a paper bag and told the old guys I'd give them the cash if I found anyone interested, and I got out of there.

I walked four blocks, to the house of a dealer I knew. He was eighteen or nineteen years old. He lived with his mother and looked like a scientist. His eyes almost popped out of his head when he saw what I had. He gave me seven hundred dollars for one bottle. Minus the two hundred dollars for the old-timers, whom I paid right away, I had just made five hundred dollars by walking four blocks and dropping off a package.

Nobody believed that I could get pharmaceutical 714s. To put more cash in my pocket, I made ten baggies of one hundred pills each from the other bottle of a thousand pills. I kept one baggie for myself and my friends; the rest were to be sold. But no way was I going out on the street and selling them. There were a bunch of guys who would be more than happy to do the job . . . including my high school English teacher, Mr. Schiano. He dispensed them in front of the 9th Circle, a gay bar in the West Village, and at Le Jardin, a club on West 43rd Street. Mr. Schiano sold everything out in minutes, and I gave him one hundred pills. Everyone was happy!

It was a fun summer, going out to the clubs. I now had a lot of cash in my pockets and told my mom I'd sold some paintings and contributed to whatever was needed at home. A thousand dollars was a fortune for a kid my age in the early '70s. As my friend Frank once said, "We had to do a lot of bad to do good." But that's just the way it was.

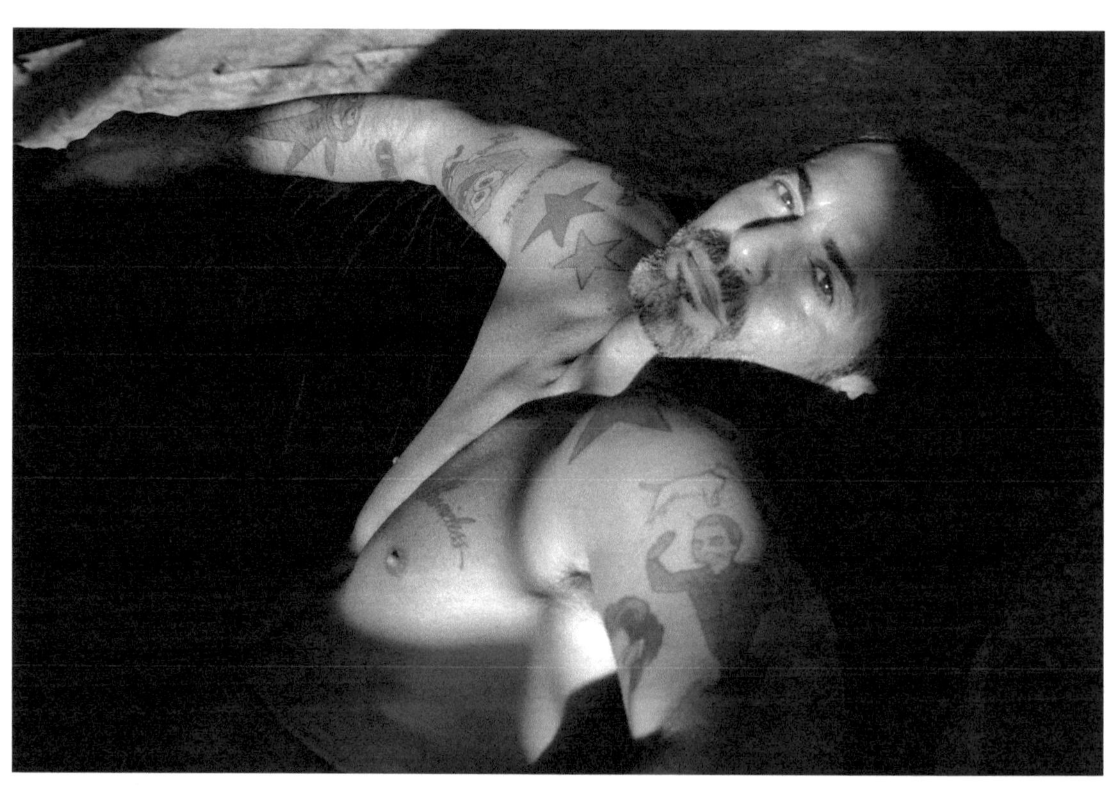

Sante's studio portrait of Marc Jacobs

7

We knew all sorts growing up the way we did, and the guys in the social club knew everyone in the neighborhood. We stayed out of their business, and if they asked something of us, we would accommodate them if we could. If something fell off the truck and they earned a buck, they were happy. They would never ask you to do anything that was out of your capacity to do, and usually they took care of you. We were kids, and we would never go to them with our problems. I was never a tough guy type, but I met a lot of tough guys in my life; some of them were really dangerous, too. It led me to excel in track and field. I learned how to run like hell when needed. I also led my Little League and H.S. baseball teams in stolen bases. I basically could tear ass!

Another mode of protection in the street could be to wear a mask that read "Don't fuck with me," but that could also backfire; then, you could really get your ass kicked! Track and field was a much better option for me. I know, because I took a few unnecessary blows when I didn't have to at thirteen to fourteen years of age. I never wanted to hurt anyone. I wasn't a violent kid, but in turning the other cheek, as my Mother Superior counseled, I got my ass handed to me one too many times. I was still a novice at being saintly, so in the early '70s, my heavenly guides were my pair of Adidas, the white ones with the trinity of black stripes on either side that would save the day for me. As two eighteen-year-old goombahs with gold chains around their necks and a baseball bat approached me in someone's driveway, my mother's words came to me: "Turn the other cheek." I did better—I turned both cheeks and ran like a motherfucker. I'd leaped over three garbage cans, up and onto a chain-link fence, onto a garage roof to an adjoining garage roof, down that driveway to the next block, through an alley, over another fence, to my friend's backyard three blocks away before they could say "fettuccini alfredo!"

I also learned how to bullshit bullshitters, and my success at it became a form of talent. All my friends had older brothers, but in the street, I was on my own. I was fortunate to be fast on my feet and street smart, and my sneakers had wings! I also learned how to turn around dangerous situations. When some big jerk is about to break your head, throw him the fuck off and flatter him. Tell him how great that shirt looks he's wearing and ask where can you buy one just like it.

When I made it through school, I applied the same approach to getting somewhere out there in the workplace. There was always somebody looking to cause trouble outside while I was shooting pictures on the street, someone who wouldn't get out of my background, even when asked politely. I'd go up to him and tell him how good-looking he was and do a portrait of him with my Polaroid camera, then gift it to him. My friend for life! Easy, just be nice. Just stay on your feet and keep moving.

And when someone did me wrong, that was their problem, their karma. I could take the blows and move on and not close myself up emotionally. As a photographer, I realized that, to get someone to open up, I had to open up first. As an artist of any kind, you have to expose your feelings raw. If you can't do that, then you're bound to fail. I've met plenty of people who wanted to write or paint. They had the wit, the smarts, the perception, but they feared failure and only failed themselves by allowing that fear to stop them. Jackson Pollock couldn't really draw well academically, and it frustrated him, so over time, he developed and invented his own visual language to express himself—that's genius. Art is the expression of your experiences and perception, including your fears. The rest is all craft.

Naturally, you have to steady yourself against the blows and rejections. Who cares if you fail a number of times, as long as you come back and figure it out. I used to tell myself they were the assholes for turning me down—fuck them! At least I showed up and rang the bell many times! My first job in a professional photo studio was cleaning the dishes and mopping the floors. I didn't know the first thing about strobe lights or meter readings. Five years later, I had my first *Vogue* cover.

The emotional mask of being tough may serve you well when you walk into the wrong neighborhood, but it does you no good if you want to be an artist. Here lies your greatest and toughest teacher. My definition of being tough is having the courage to fail. Tough shit? Chew harder!

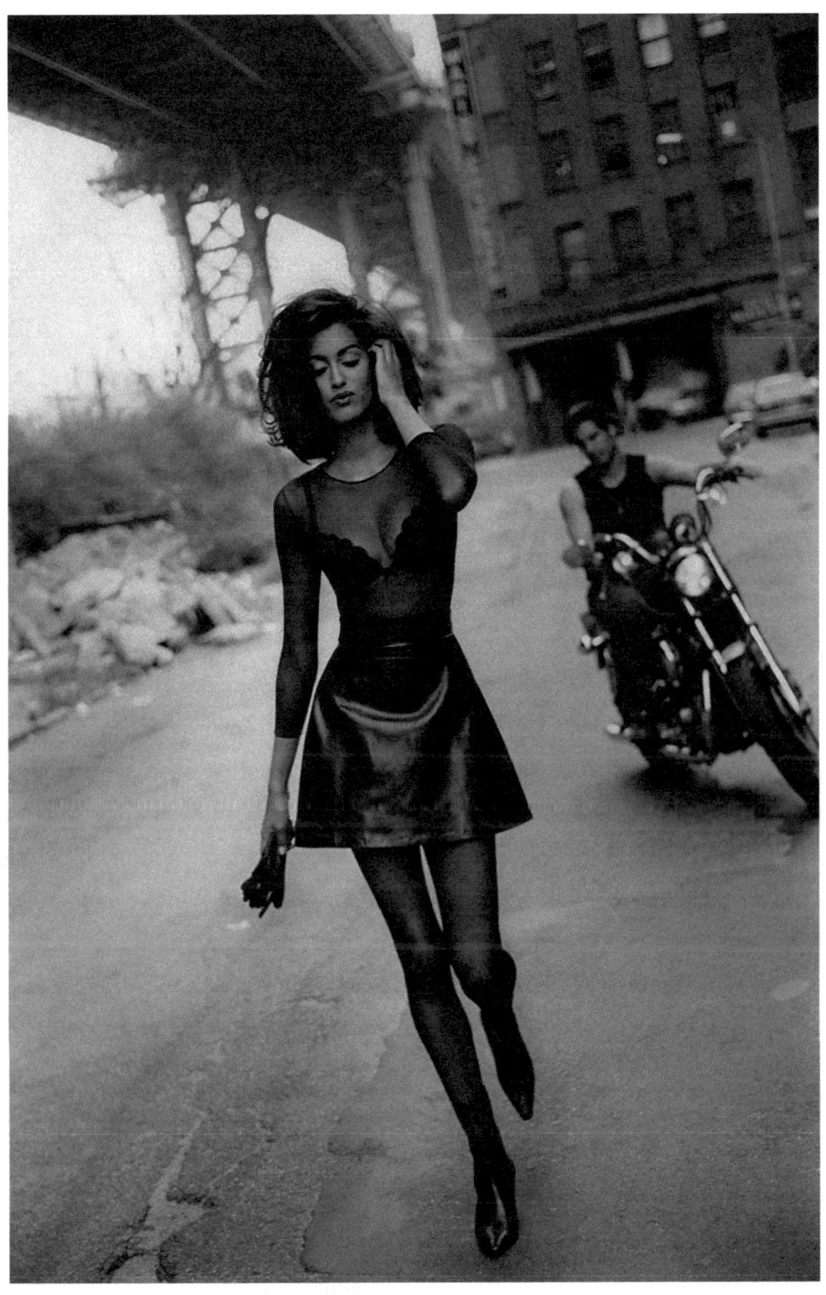

Yasmeen Ghauri for British *Vogue*

8

At seventeen, I went to driver's ed and got my license. We had a 1963 Chevy Impala, so on Saturdays I'd drive through the neighborhood, pick up a friend or two, and just ride around. On one of those weekends, I was driving with my friend Tommy when we encountered a funny scene while stopped at a red light. Across the street were two guys we knew—Jimmy and Sally, whom we knew from grammar school but rarely hung out with anymore—both nodding out as they stood at the bus stop. We were laughing, and I pulled over to the side and said to Tommy, "Let's watch these yo-yos and see if they get on the bus."

A bus pulled up, then pulled out, and the two dummies were still standing there, heads down, doing the lean. (The lean, which you may have seen on your city streets, is performed by dope addicts who appear to be sleeping while standing up. They have this uncanny way of leaning forward, seeming to defy gravity until they get so impossibly far, snap out of it, only to catch themselves and start the lean routine all over again. It's sometimes hilarious.) Another bus pulled up, left, and they were still leaning forward there ("on the nod," as they say). We had already smoked a joint and were laughing hysterically, tears running from our eyes.

The buses kept coming and going, and finally, we couldn't take it any longer. "Let's pull up and scare the shit out of them." I started the car and pulled up next to them. "Yo, you're under arrest!" They barely budged.

One of them saw us, recognized me, and said, "Yo, Sandy, man! Whad up, man? We're waitin' for a fuckin' bus! Can you give us a ride to Newkirk Plaza? I gotta buy something for my mother at the drugstore."

I let them get in the car and drove them to Newkirk Plaza.

"Thanks, man. Gimmie five minutes, just two minutes. I gotta get back home real quick. A minute! Don't even turn the engine off. I'll be right back."

"All right, hurry up."

The two of them got out of the car, and I was sitting there laughing with Tommy while they went inside the drugstore. I was facing Tommy, and Tommy was facing me and had his back to Newkirk Plaza. Before I could react, I saw the two jerkoffs running out of the drugstore holding bags. Sally was also holding a gun. They jumped into my car. Now I was the getaway car and driver! Tommy turned white, and I just took off out of there because no one was going to believe me. At the next light, Tommy jumped out of the car and left me with those two.

I was pissed. I wanted to kill them both. Sally wanted me to drop him off at his house. He said, "Come upstairs. I need you to help me count what we got. I'm too whacked . . . I'll take care of you, I swear."

I parked the car and went up with them. Luckily, no one was home. They unloaded the bags of pills they had just robbed onto Sally's bed, and we started to separate them. By the second opened bottle, the two of them were out like a light, heads back, mouths wide open, gross. I counted out all the individual pills. Half of them were useless on the street; I left everything on the bed. The good ones I counted, "One for you, one for you, and six for me . . ." I let myself out with my share and went directly to visit a guy I knew in the neighborhood and handed him my take. He handed me a wad of cash, and I went home. It was the kind of situation I always tried to avoid, but sometimes you just walked into it, like I did in this one. I never heard from those two again. Turned out the drugstore they robbed was where their parents shopped. Jerks.

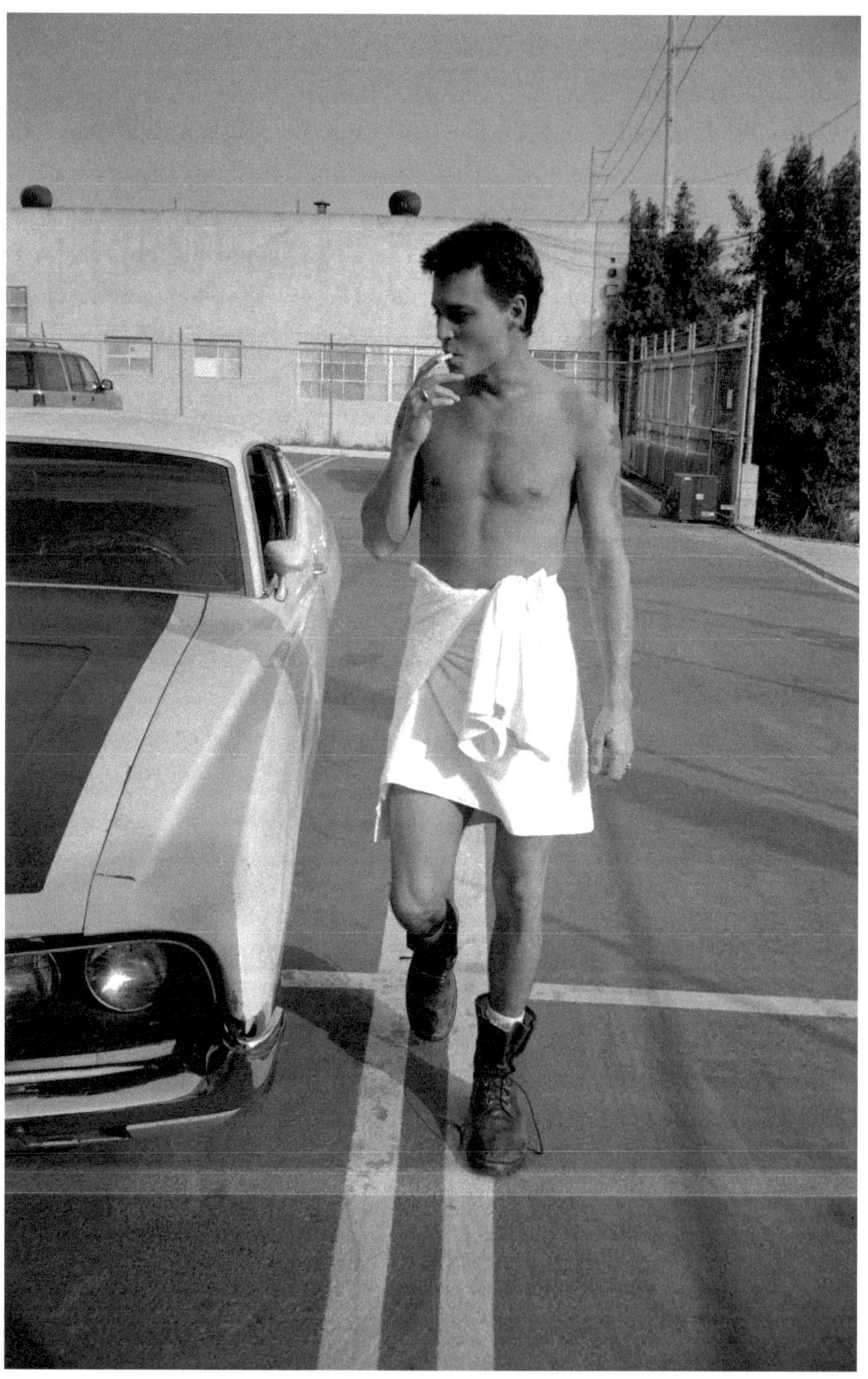

Johnny Depp, Hollywood, California

9

When I was fifteen, I met my new neighbor, a Cuban kid named Noel Naranjo. He was my age and smoked pot. His father was the new super in the building next door to my house. We started hanging out, and he introduced me to his friend, Perry, and to weed. We lived on Avenue C, while Perry lived on Avenue N, a twenty-minute bus ride up Coney Island Avenue.

That winter, the three of us were inseparable, and we would always meet up at Noel's apartment next door. In their living room, next to their TV, his parents had a life-size Madonna statue of the Virgin Mary in a black wig on a pedestal. It towered over us and freaked the bejesus out of me every time I'd walked by it, especially after I had smoked some pot. Of the three of us, Perry became like a brother to me. We had a chemistry I never had with any other friend, and we hung out during the most important years of my early life. He introduced me to the soul music station on WBLS FM, then disco, and later to the clubs in NYC. I had been a straitlaced kid up till then, still parting my hair on the side. That first winter together, we started going to school dances where Perry always tore it up on the dance floor, and I did my best to keep up. We bought short, thin leather jackets on Orchard Street in Manhattan, then platform shoes. It was the time of *Saturday Night Fever*, and we coiffed our hair into DAs, ducks' asses—which meant the back of your hair was cut into a V-shape down to your shirt collar, like a duck's ass, and the front had to be blow-dried using a round brush so it rolled back in a bouffant and then sprayed with half a can of hairspray until it was like a helmet. In the middle of the winter, we'd freeze our balls off in our thin leather jackets and jump on a train or a bus and go to the school dances. Many times, we'd have to walk for blocks, and if the wind was blowing from the right, we'd walk straight ahead with our heads turned to the right so as not to mess up our hair. God forbid if the wind was blowing from behind, we'd have to walk backward all the way!

Noel always had the pot, which for me was like doing heroin. I had grown up with a relative whose life got messed up by drugs. I wasn't going down that road! I could never do that to my holy mother, never mind myself.

Two winters went by. Noel moved to Florida, leaving me and Perry as the dynamic duo. Our DAs were replaced with shag cuts. My cousin John D'Orazio was a hairdresser for all the top hair salons in the city—from Kenneth to Pierre Michel to Suga—and he told me stories of models and movie stars and all that glamour. Perry and I bought our clothes from Jumping Jack Flash, near Bloomingdale's on East 59th Street, the coolest boutique in the city, where supposedly Bowie and Jagger bought their outfits. The heels and platform shoes were getting higher. Disco was about to kick in big time. I was attending Erasmus Hall High School, and I knew the WBLS (Soul and R+B) crowd, and Perry went to Madison High, where he was friends with the Bowie-influenced androgynous crowd.

The club scene in the city became our getaway. Whether it was the Garage or Le Jardin, Studio 54 or the Mudd Club, the crowd was always mixed, which was what made the clubs so great; it introduced you to the creative world: Warhol, Liz Taylor, Halston, Mick and Bianca Jagger, and Diana Ross, along with graffiti kids; rich, poor, black, white, brown, yellow, green, blue, gay, straight, trans, all dancing and drinking and doing everything else together. So cool. There was no class or racial structure. It was cheap and fun. The best dance clubs were gay all the way. We were fit, good-looking, and just seventeen! The gayer the club, the hotter the girls, and the girls loved us!

Half the crew Perry introduced me to were gay or about to come out. Perry was straight, but based on the way he'd started dressing, you'd never know it. Wearing the tightest lamé pants that needed him to lie down to pull them on, eight-inch platform shoes with ten-inch heels, and a tiny sequin jacket à la Bowie and Jagger. Perry's friend, Danny, was even more extreme, both in dressing and in getting high. Once or twice, he went to Le Jardin with us, high as a kite on Tuinals, heavy barbiturates—it was a dance club for Christ's sake, why downers!

One time, Danny was so stoned, he tripped and fell in his eight-inch platform shoes in the middle of Fifth Avenue. We were so pissed off we left him there. His pants were so tight, he had to crawl to a lamppost to pull himself back up on to his feet—that was his punishment for getting sloppy-stoned before we even got to the club! Sometime during that year, he decided he was gay but couldn't bring himself to make out with a guy. His remedy was to eat three Tuinals (one was enough to knock me out), and later, we'd find him making out with someone in a dark corner. After that, he just went on a roll.

Danny came from an Italian family. His father was a sergeant in the NYPD, a real old-timer type of guy who wore a white wife-beater T-shirt around the house and at mealtimes. All of us Italian kids had fathers like that, though our dads would never beat their wives. He came from the He-Man generation, so father and son avoided each other at this stage of Danny's development.

Danny also had a buddy, a gay apprentice in training, who copied whatever Danny said or did. Danny was cute, skinny, and a good dancer. His friend was short and squat. On him, the sequin tops and lamé pants didn't really work, but if Danny wore them then he wore them too. And looked ridiculous. They both lived in Marine Park, close to the south shore of Brooklyn, way east of Coney Island, near Flatbush Avenue. One night, the two of them got so messed up on Tuinals they didn't want to leave the club, so we bailed before they were ready to go home. Later that night, fucked-up as they were, dressed the way they were, and in full glitter makeup, they took the train home, nodding in and out of sleep as they checked for their stop. They woke up at what they thought was Marine Park, but it was Prospect Park, located in central Brooklyn near the Brooklyn Museum, which at that time was a no-man's-land. As kids, we'd never venture that way without an armed escort. Those two got out of the station, didn't know where they were, and decided to just go to sleep on the grass. When the cops woke them up, it was daylight and they were both naked—someone had stolen their sequined bolero jackets and lamé pants (which must have been a struggle to pull off), their platform shoes with ten-inch heels, socks, drugs, and whatever money they may have had. Left them butt naked, except for the glitter makeup!

The cops gave them blankets to wrap themselves in and drove them to the police station. They called Danny's father because Danny, still stoned and pissed off on account of his entire wardrobe being gone, including his brand-new bolero jacket, started yelling at the cops, "Don't hassle me! Do you know who my father is?"

I can't imagine what may have happened when his father, the police sergeant, picked Danny up at the station house. I didn't see him for months after that, and when I did, he was wearing a new bolero jacket and was too stoned and couldn't give a shit to talk about it.

Years later, I heard Danny moved to Miami and became a weightlifter!

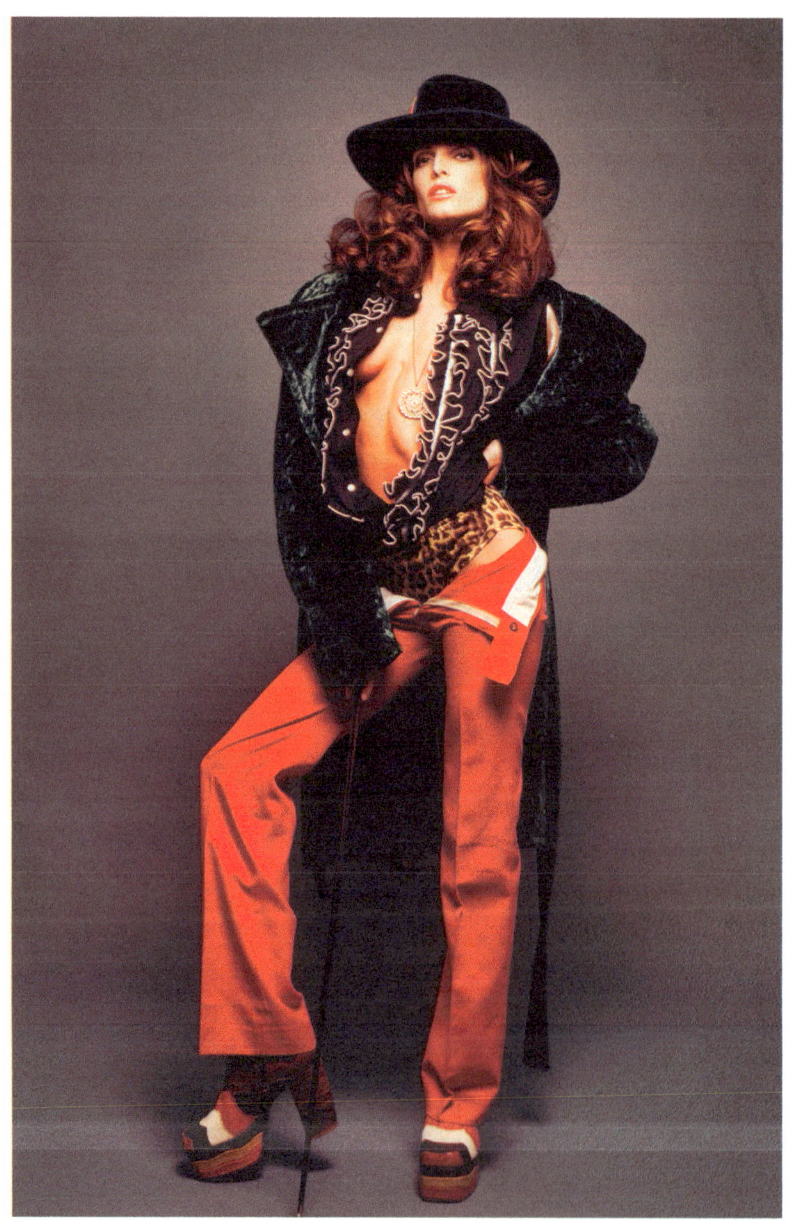

Stephanie Seymour for *Esquire* magazine

10

Quaaludes were basically muscle relaxers and, by definition, a sedative-hypnotic. I wasn't aware of any hypnotic effect, and the last thing I wanted to do when I took one was sleep. I wanted to dance! It was a touchy-feely drug, like ecstasy; it definitely loosened you up and made you think everybody was your friend. It was a lovefest, and you could move on the dance floor like nobody's business.

First manufactured in 1965 by the pharmaceutical company Rorer, they were the drug of choice on the club scene in the early seventies. I had a T-shirt that was almost identical to the Alka-Seltzer kid (known as Speedy) T-shirt, which was an image of a stick figure with an Alka-Seltzer body, with a smiling face wearing a hat, but his body was a Rorer 714 tablet, which resembled an Alka-Seltzer instead. That logo was the legit authentic stamp of approval, euphoria for up to six hours. We never went clubbing without them, and we'd go to any extreme to get them.

One time, me and Perry were trying to figure out how we could get our hands on some quaaludes since we had no money to buy them, to get in the clubs, and to buy drinks and all that.

Perry told me he had an idea; he knew this guy on 77th Street on the Upper East Side. Not somebody I knew. Our friend Danny had introduced him to Perry. The guy apparently sold everything, every drug imaginable. I agreed to drive Perry into Manhattan.

Perry called the guy. When we arrived at the guy's building on East 77th, the doorman let us in. In the elevator, Perry reminded me, "Listen, let me go in the back and talk to him. Maybe I can sweet talk him into giving me two for nothing; he likes me."

"Whaddya mean 'he likes you'?"

"No, no, we get along. He thought I was nice and told me to come over anytime and all that. He even gave me and Danny a few for free."

I said, "Okay, guess it's worth a try," but I wanted to get back home in time to watch the end of the Yankee game. If they won by two runs, I'd make some good money tonight!

So Perry introduced me, and we made a little chitchat. He seemed like a decent guy, a little frumpy maybe. When he went to the kitchen, Perry whispered, "I'm going in the back to talk to him about you-know-what, just wait here in the living room."

The guy's apartment looked like an old lady's, white sofa with a doll sitting on it, white carpet, and tchotchkes all over the place. I was sitting on the sofa with the doll, just looking around. I waited, I waited, and I waited, and from somewhere, I could faintly hear the Yankee game. I was all ears, but I had no idea where it was coming from. I was dying to find out the score. After more than half an hour, Perry came out smiling, and we said our goodbyes and left. In the elevator, he opened his hand, which was holding six 714s! I couldn't believe my eyes. We began jumping up and down in excitement.

"He gave you six just like that?"

"Yeah, I told you! I had to sit there and hang out a bit. I couldn't just ask him straight out."

"Wow, man, that's really cool!"

A week went by, and we tried our luck again. Back up to East 77th Street we went. Again, Perry went to the back bedroom to talk to the guy—I figured that's where he hid his stash—while I sat on the white sofa with the doll. There was a fake fireplace with a collection of white doilies on the fake mantle. And again, I could faintly hear the Yankee game, coming from where I still didn't know. Eventually, Perry came out from the bedroom, and we got out of there. This time, because there were people in the hall and the elevator, he waited till we got outside and away from the building to open his hand. He had *eight* Rorer 714s!

"Wait a minute, wait a minute. What's going on? What the fuck you up to? Don't tell me he's giving you all these pills for nothing!"

"Yes, I swear!" Perry said. "He's lonely, he likes me, he likes the company, I swear."

"Then why do I have to wait in the living room and sit there with that fucking doll?"

"Forget about it. We got the pills. Let's go out," Perry said and changed the subject. "Everyone's gonna be at Le Jardin tonight!"

Two weeks went by before we went up there again. Same routine: the sofa, the stupid doll, and the faint sound of the Yankee game. *What the fuck is that about?* I heard a door in the back open. Perry appeared and didn't say anything. There were people in the hallway and the elevator, and I could see Perry was trying to keep a straight face. We walked out of the apartment building and presto! Eight Rorer 714s. He was jumping up and down, laughing and all happy. We got halfway down the block, and Perry gave me four pills and said, "Ya happy now?"

"I'm happy, I'm happy," I said, "but we ain't goin' anywhere until you tell me what the fuck is going on. And don't tell me it's because he likes you. I can tell how much he likes you, eight fucking quaaludes' worth! I want to know, now!"

"Okay, okay. How do I put this? Basically, what he wants me to do is just sit there while he lays on the bed and jerks off. You happy now?"

"Oh, shit, you're kidding me!"

"Yeah, he lays down. I don't have to look at him. I sit on the edge of the bed and watch the Yankee game. What do I care? Eight quaaludes while the guy jerks off. Think about it, big fuckin' deal!"

"You sure that's all that's going on?"

"I swear on my mother, and I never swear on my mother! The guy lays down, drops his drawers, I turn on the game, and everybody's happy, right?"

"Yeah, I guess so. What was the score?"

"Yanks up eight to four, bottom of the eighth."

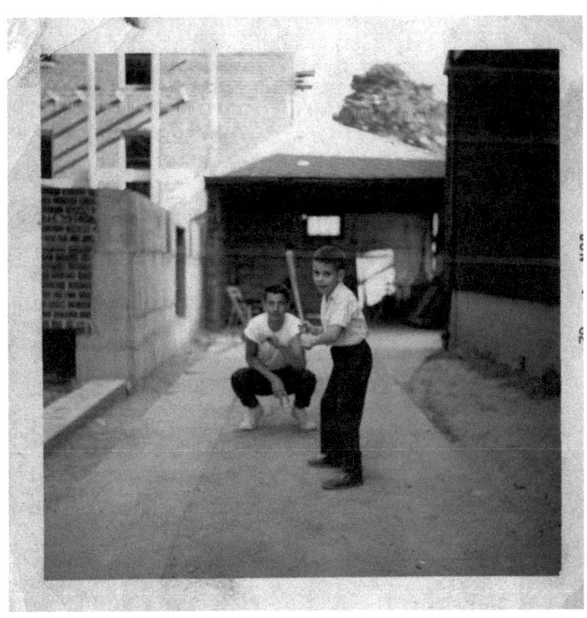

Sante, at bat with his cousin Mike in his parents' driveway

11

Mostly it is the loss that teaches us about the worth of things.
—Arthur Schopenhauer

Time moved slowly during my junior high and high school years. I was always in the moment, never looking too far ahead. Everything was new, everyone was awesome, and we were the smartest and coolest—or so we thought.

But in my sophomore year, when I was sixteen, my father passed away. He was a diabetic and went into a diabetic coma, and in three days, he was gone; he was fifty-seven. We were all shocked, and I didn't know where to turn. After the funeral, everyone went back to their normal lives, except me and my mom. My most urgent need was to tend to her; she seemed more in shock than I was. She then fell into despair and depression. We were broke, so I took some odd jobs after school, but as long as I remained in school, my mom could collect social security from me being a student; it wasn't much, and it wasn't enough.

By my senior year in high school, I needed to make choices, pick some direction. I knew it had to be in the arts. Unfortunately, the New York City public school system made my high school years a farce. Classes with forty-plus students—some just beginning to learn English, no connection to teachers, no room for any individual needs, and a system that focused on moving the overcrowded student body through and out as quickly as possible. I never read a single book!

I didn't know at the time I had dyslexia, along with attention deficit disorder. Back then, kids struggling with learning disorders were simply considered stupid. I made it through school on my athletic ability, especially in baseball. I firmly expected to play for the New York Yankees. But art also came naturally to me, and when I thought about it, art was the obvious direction for me.

Once I got out of high school, I increasingly became a loner and an introvert, even though I loved being with people. I knew I had to get serious, and I was feeling the weight of responsibility since I was now the head of the house. I needed answers, and art led me to look inward. At eighteen years old, certain metaphysical concepts made me feel at home and put me on a path far removed from the friends I had grown up with; they were moving on as well. I started going to museums on my own and began reading artists' biographies, even if it took me months to read them. I took drawing classes at the Art Students League and the Brooklyn Museum.

What I had learned from my travels was an unschooled understanding of what it took to become an artist. I thought that the first requirement was learning how to draw and paint the figure. That seemed to be the common denominator among all the artists, from Ancient Greece to the Renaissance, to our contemporary times. Phase One: Start with the nude. Phase Two: Become an apprentice or assistant to an artist whose style you could learn from, an invaluable job for a beginner. As a student, I tried to imitate or copy the works of artists I admired, to try and become them, even for a brief period. I was learning by the book, and it became the only source I knew to get somewhere.

Early on, I found myself responding more and more to abstraction, which means creating a language, a landscape all your own through the use of lines, shapes, and forms, and responding to that composition in a way that moves you. Music without lyrics is the closest description of what abstract art means. There are harmonies, tones, lights and darks of lines, shape and form within its composition, all moving you in a manner without the use of literal descriptions. Music then becomes the most abstract of all the arts that everyone has an immediate response to. It's the same with painting and sculpture, except our visual training has forced us into literally describing what we see, just as lyrics in music tell us why and what to feel. I would dabble in abstraction while in my teens, while sticking with the figure, thinking I needed to master the nude first. I didn't know any artists. I had no guides, except the history of art and the books I read.

During this period, I was putting myself through school, and the one thing they never taught you was how to make money and earn a living. Now when I say putting myself through school, I don't mean paying tuition and all that. I managed to stay in school plus four years of college, while apprenticing with mentors in both painting and photography. Most of my friends had dropped out of school, gone to work, and had one, if not two, working parents. My dad left us with no savings. My mom, through the grace of God, got a job on the kitchen staff at my old J.H.S. Working for the Board of Education meant, for her, a lifetime of insurance and benefits—that made me secure to go to college. Up until that point, I had made it through on my wits, tenacity, and dreams.

No matter how bad things got, and though she had missed her own calling, my mom gave me constant encouragement and support. She was determined never to let happen to me what had happened to her, the lack of support from the prohibitions of living in that Southern Italian culture, or in my case, that immigrant culture of only applying yourself to the family trade and to what's practical. She said, "You have to knock on every door, and eventually one might open. If it's not exactly the one you want, step in anyway; it may lead you somewhere closer." I didn't have many options, so I took her advice and followed every lead. I learned to adapt, and it became my yellow brick road.

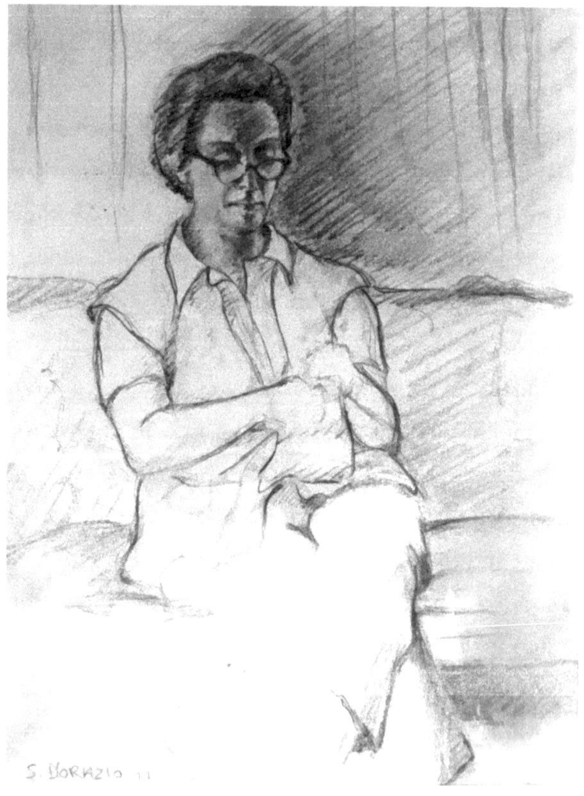

Sante's drawing of his mom knitting

12

As a kid, I had to hustle to make every nickel and dime. Occasionally, when I was very young, I'd get twenty-five cents from my mom or some change from a neighbor for running an errand. When I was ten, I'd go to my dad's barbershop and sweep the floor for a dime. He was making seventy-five cents a haircut in the early '60s yet managed to buy a house and own a car, without my mom working. He was always grateful to this country for that. Out of nowhere, he would suddenly exclaim, "God bless America!"

On birthdays, I might get a dollar, maybe two, if an uncle was visiting. By sixth grade, I had a bankbook at the appropriately named Dime Savings Bank. If we wanted to go to the movies, we kids would put our money together, enough to get one of us in. The other ten kids would go around back to the exit doors and wait for whoever had gone in to open the door. We'd all run in and slam the door, so the theater stayed dark, and we'd scatter before the ushers arrived, then regroup when the coast was clear.

One hot summer day, we pulled this stunt and made it in. *A Man for All Seasons* was playing—too grown-up and boring for us, and from the looks of things, for a lot of other people too. The movie theater was almost empty, so we were easily spotted and thrown out. A few of us managed to escape via the same exits we had come in.

You learned to do whatever was necessary to earn money and get somewhere; the risks got higher later when survival kicked in. At fourteen years old, my first real job was at a large mob-run catering hall next to a cemetery, which seemed appropriate. I got to see a lot of crazy shit, from a stripper at a Bar Mitzvah to an Irish wedding where the groom had a fistfight with the father of the bride—and the bride got clocked by accident when she tried to break it up and left with a black eye. The boys in the back room broke it up. I got a twenty-dollar tip from somebody for getting ice bags for the bride, groom, and bridal party. I was so happy!

Perry and I hustled everything and anything we could get our hands on. We learned from the best, Perry's father—he was a big guy with a big head and hands the size of catcher's mitts. A real hustler and a gambler, he sold everything that fell off the truck, including the truck. On weekends or during the summers, he'd organize a bunch of us kids to go up to the Hunts Point Market in the Bronx. First, we'd help him load his truck with boxes of various kinds of fruit; then, we'd set up in different areas of the City or Brooklyn to sell the shit.

At sixteen, we started selling the fruit on street corners in Manhattan or downtown Brooklyn. He'd set us up with boxes of oranges, strawberries, you name it. Once we got planted, no matter the weather, we weren't going anywhere till Tom the Bomb or one of his partners came to pick us up at the end of the day or night—by then, I would have around eight hundred singles in my bulging pockets. They'd load us into the back of a truck, along with whatever was left of the fruit, and head to Carroll Street in Brooklyn to drop off tribute money to whoever their boss was, but not before they'd lock the truck's back door because they wanted to make sure we animals stayed in our cages. We were known to hang off the back of the open truck and throw strawberries at people as we drove by. We were kind of wild at fifteen, sixteen.

It was hard to cheat those guys, but we did our best for extra cash. The only time we were able to skim off the top was during strawberry season. We'd shake up the plastic baskets and the loose strawberries would fall out; then once we made a sale, we'd drop the strawberries in the bag but keep the basket. Then we'd refill the baskets with the loose strawberries we had already shaken out to create extra baskets and pocket the money from those sales. All nickel and dime stuff. I did this on weekends or whenever I had days off from school.

Occasionally, something different would fall off the truck, like Tupperware, or better yet, cheap digital watches. We'd go out in pairs with someone who could drive. We made sure to go where no one knew us. It was the first time I saw a digital watch; they were so cheaply made that they'd stop working two hours after we sold them. They went for ten dollars each, and we'd go to the beauty parlors and stores in new neighborhoods, and we made sure to never repeat a visit.

One time, they put me and forty boxes of fruit on a corner in some unfamiliar Italian neighborhood in Brooklyn. They introduced me to Jimmy, who owned a pizzeria half a block away. Jimmy said, "Any problems, you come to me, and I'll take care of it."

I said, "Okay, thanks."

I usually never had any problem, but no more than twenty minutes later, I see this old-time Italian guy staring me down from across the street. He was a thin guy, looked like a switchblade, and had a pencil mustache; he was wearing a Borsalino hat, like the hats my grandfather had. He came walking right at me, and in a thick Italian accent, he said, "I wanna you outta ear nowwa. I owna the fruita store onna the corner. Get the hell outta ear!"

I said, "Mister, where am I going to go? I got forty boxes of fruit, and they weigh a ton."

"I no giva sheet. Getta hout. I come backa in ef an hour!"

I closed the boxes and ran over to Jimmy at the pizzeria.

He said, "Don't worry about it. Go back to your stand."

I then saw Jimmy walking across the street to the fruit store, in and out in less than five minutes. Fifteen minutes later, the guy with the pencil mustache was walking toward me from across the street, and I braced myself for anything.

He said, "Why you no tella me you friend of Jimmy? You stay as longa you lika. You need a more fruita, you calla me, okay?"

"Okay, thank you!" Guess Jimmy had some pull around there.

Later, it started raining lightly, and Jimmy came over and said, "C'mon inside, kid, and eat something. Don't worry. No one's going to touch a box. They know you're with me."

Jimmy brought me into the pizzeria and led me to a door in the back. Inside was a room with a big table and about ten old men sitting around it, some wearing hats, eating and smoking. One man got up and brought me over to his chair and told the others to get me some soup. He patted me on the back. "Nice boy!" he said. It was like a retirement home for old mobsters. They were so friendly and kept on feeding me till the rain let up. Then, I went back to my stand.

I got picked up early that day by Perry's father, the guy with the big head and hands. He was with two buddies of his and was in a rush and threw everything in the back of the truck. Perry was also with them. They took whatever cash I had and left me and Perry to take the train home. "They didn't even pay us," Perry said. "They're heading to the track. They took all the money without even counting it!"

One of Tom's many vices was gambling. This wasn't the first time I saw him drop everything and run to place a bet. Perry's father would sometimes come home on payday and take everyone's cash, including his wife's, then blow it all at the track. Sometimes they couldn't even pay the rent because of his gambling.

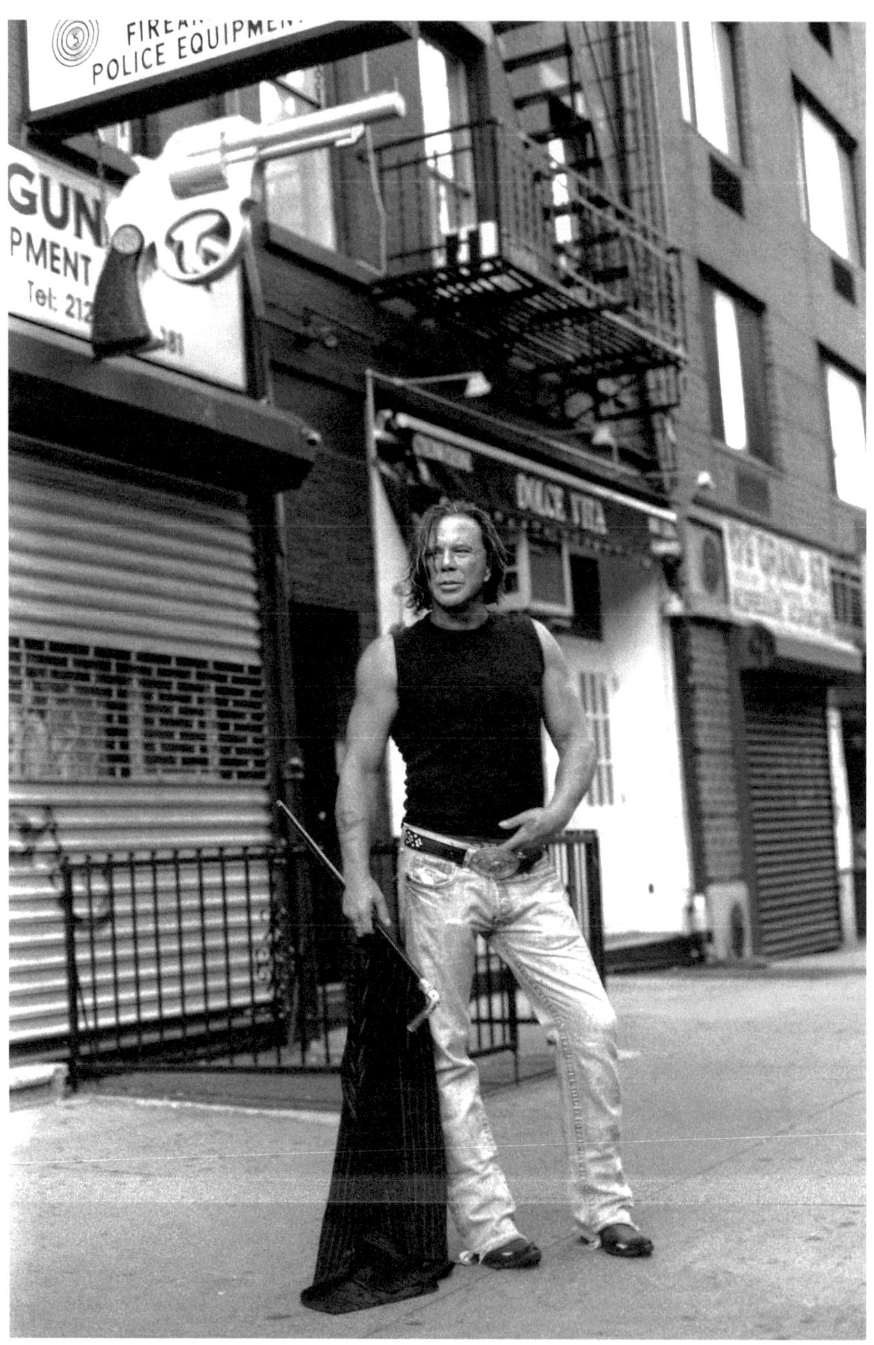

Mickey Rourke on Grand Street, Little Italy, New York

Perry repeated again, "They took everything. We don't even have money for the train home."

Then, I remembered I had taken all the big bills, the fives, tens, and twenties, and put them in my sock in case anyone tried to rob me. Two hundred dollars. I split it with Perry, and we enjoyed it twice as much as we would have if they had paid us. The jerks never noticed the two hundred dollars that were missing!

Growing up was all about a hustle, always trying to find a way to make a buck, taking care of things at home, and trying to make something out of myself.

13

After graduating high school, I needed to figure out how I could support myself and my mom. I decided to go to New York Community College to train in art direction. By the middle of my second year of a two-year degree in commercial art, I hated what I was doing in school. I finished the course to get the degree, then transferred to Brooklyn College to pursue fine art, and my first year there was pure heaven. I knew it was where I belonged. I was finding my way and figuring it out.

Brooklyn College didn't have a full-time art program, but they had great artists teaching, like Philip Pearlstein and Lee Bontecou. I majored in the "humanities" and took courses in philosophy, literature, language, and art history, along with studio courses in anatomy, painting, and sculpture. While at Brooklyn College, I was also exposed to theater, film, dance, all the arts. The school was the best-kept secret in the New York City public university system.

As I said earlier, I came from a household where English wasn't a first language, and I didn't read much at home on my own for the same reasons. My mom spoke to me in Italian, and I would answer in English. The books I began to read in college were always on art, art history, or artists' biographies. I managed to struggle through dyslexia with my reading list. Because I recognized myself in what I read, I became obsessed and devoured everything that had to do with art. By nature, I recognized the language of reading objects, shapes, forms, and colors—their emotional dynamics. It was all very real and alive to me; I had just never been formally introduced to it before. I also went to work on my hardcore Brooklyn accent—my teachers insisted on it. Those couple of years there were my best school years ever.

During my time there, I ran into a friend's brother who was into modern dance. He was tall, black, lanky, and very feminine. I already had many gay friends by then from the club scene;

plus I grew up with a gay cousin whom I loved, no problems there for me. Until then, he and I weren't well acquainted. I knew him as Archie, but he had changed his name to Donnell. His brother, my friend Vinny, was straight and very much a ladies' man. He worked at No Problem, a hip clothing store on Church and Flatbush Avenue that featured platform shoes and lamé pants, and all the girls loved him. We knew each other from grade school. Archie/Donnell, on the other hand, belonged to a dance company in the city. By this time, I had a few friends in the arts whom I could relate to, and Donnell and I eventually talked about collaborating on one of his choreographed pieces. He took me to some performances, and I started to get familiarized with dance. Sometimes we would meet at the studio in the city where his dance company rehearsed. I began making notes about lighting and costumes. I loved all these various disciplines.

One day, I ran into Becky, a beautiful Latina girl from Marine Park, Brooklyn, a friend from my club days a few years back. Becky told me she was into modern dance, and I said I was just starting to get into it too. She invited me to see her perform and gave me an address on Canal Street. At that time, Canal Street was no-man's-land—at night, you needed a bodyguard or to carry a weapon. I couldn't imagine any dance companies on Canal Street, and 10:00 p.m. was kind of late for a modern dance performance.

When I arrived at the address, I discovered it was a strip joint, and Becky had saved me a front-row seat, so I could lean on the stage. I was mortified. I was still so fucking stupid and naïve. I felt like a schmuck. I had never been to a strip joint before, and five minutes after I got a drink, Becky came on and did her thing. I told her she was great and quickly escaped back home to Brooklyn. I loved Becky as a friend and kind of felt bad. I didn't see her again for about a year, by which time she was turning tricks in Midtown and missing a front tooth. That was the last time I saw her. I realized I had to start asking more questions first.

Meeting people in the arts became important to me, and Donnell encouraged me to take part in the dance rehearsals and stretching exercises at his classes. I resisted for the longest time—I just couldn't see myself in leotards. Eventually, I finally bit the bullet. We all lined up facing the mirrors, arms out at our sides. We were meant to step, turn, lift one leg to the side, and turn again. Somewhere around the second or third lift, I lifted too high, farted, slipped on my ass and somehow split my leotard. Earlier, I had observed a beautiful girl do the same and was shocked after she farted, and she continued like nothing happened—no one seemed to care. I thought maybe I was the only one to notice it, but I was new at this. I abandoned the exercise, changed in a hurry, and left. After that episode, I just focused on lighting, scene design, and costumes. I figured I should stick to what I know best.

14

Perry was my best friend through my teen years. He was and still is a sweetheart of a guy, and I'm still in touch with him forty years later. I love him and his sister, Eileen, who was my teenage girlfriend. Their loving nature is in sharp contrast to the terror they grew up with in their home.

Their father was ruthless, ignorant, cruel, almost savage at times. His nickname was "Tom the Bomb." He looked like the guy you would call to break someone's legs and chew their head off. He never had a steady job; he was always gambling and selling what fell off the truck, but he may well have broken legs and arms as a side job for the mob, who knows? Perry and his three brothers were deeply affected by him, but you would never know it from knowing Perry and Eileen. I remember when their father found out that his oldest son—Perry's brother—was taking heroin. He freaked out and got himself a gun and went out looking for him. He said, "Fuck him. He's not going to do this to me! If he's going to take heroin and kill himself, I might as well go shoot him now and get it over with."

For two days, the fucker went everywhere looking for him, but thank God, he never found him. Eventually, the boys couldn't take it; their habits got worse. After a short few years, three of the boys—the two oldest brothers and the youngest brother—overdosed and died, leaving just Perry and his sister.

I was sixteen and Eileen was thirteen when we let our feelings be known to each other. We were young and innocent, and it was puppy love. But if Tom the Bomb had found out, he would have strangled me with his thumbs and buried me at the dump past Plum Beach off the Belt Parkway. Perry wasn't even allowed in the house alone with his sister. Tom was a sick fuck with a sick mind.

In the meantime, as I said before, the club scene was the best. From the Mudd Club to Area to Studio 54, to the Palladium, and everywhere in between. The crowd was always mixed, and that's what made it so great. Warhol, Liz, Halston sitting along with graffiti kids, rich, poor, black, white, brown, yellow, green, blue, gay, straight, all dancing and drinking and everything else together. So cool. There was no class or racial structure. It was cheap, it was fun, and Perry and I were out all the time with our crazy, fun friends.

Perry had a wild-child girlfriend named Liz who had a body to die for. She came from Queens, and I would fool around with Liz's sister from time to time. We never had any money, and Liz would disappear and come back with a handful of quaaludes and what have you. This was a time when we had platform shoes and heels, high-waisted pleated pants, short tops with our midriff showing. We were all very cute. People would always be buying us drinks, and we didn't have a care in the world. Our club friends were a fun motley crew. One couple was married; he was gay, and she supported them by turning tricks. Some were artists, dancers, strippers, and in those four years—from when I was fifteen to nineteen—Perry and these characters provided me with a lifetime of genius memories.

When I was seventeen, I would pick everyone up in my Mom's 1963 Chevy Impala and head to the city. At the end of the night, I'd take whoever was ready to leave back to Brooklyn. The last person with me was always Perry. Sometimes, I'd park in front of his house and we'd laugh about the shit that went down that night. One fucked-up night, around 4:00 a.m., Perry was sitting with his back to the passenger door as I was on the driver's side. Behind him, I saw his father charging at the Impala. I couldn't even get a word out before his father opened the door and started beating the shit out of Perry, landing solid punches to his face and head. It was so violent; Perry just had to get out of there, away from his father somehow.

Liz, Perry's girlfriend, had moved to Puerto Rico, where she had family and was making good money working at a casino. Perry called me one day in November and asked me to drive him to JFK the next day. Liz had bought him a ticket to come stay with her. She also had a studio apartment at a condo on the beach. When I picked Perry up, half his face was still swollen. He was carrying a paper bag. "Where's your luggage?" I asked.

He had a toothbrush, two pairs of underwear, a hairbrush, and twenty dollars in his pocket.

"No time to pack," he said. "Get me the fuck out of here."

About three weeks later, I got a phone call from Perry. "Liz wants you to come and visit, stay for a week or as long as you like."

I had never been to Puerto Rico. I bought a round-trip ticket for $150 and flew to San Juan. When I got there, I couldn't believe my eyes. He looked like a million dollars. Perry was tan and wore powder blue swimming trunks and a terrycloth jacket to match with tan wedge platform sandals. He even had a newspaper under his arm, as if he was keeping up with his funds in the stock market or something . . .

"Wow, you're looking great," I told him.

"You're going to love it here," he said. We took a cab to the condo, and, fuck, it was a brand-new beautiful building right next door to the Fairmont El San Juan Hotel and Casino, overlooking the clear blue water. We spent the whole day there with a beach bar and drinks with umbrellas. Perry paid for everything with a big wad of cash in his jacket.

"Where the fuck did you get all that money?" I asked. "I dropped you at the airport with a paper bag and twenty to your name."

"Liz gave it to me. She's got a great job at the hotel and the casino."

"Doin' what?"

"These cocktail waitresses make a fortune."

We got wasted on piña coladas and fell asleep on the beach.

When I woke up, the beach was empty and I was fried on one side. Perry said, "C'mon, let's get back up to the room."

We smoked a joint on the balcony and had some beers later.

"Where's Liz?" I asked him.

"She went to see some family and is going straight to work. She won't be home till like four o'clock in the morning."

I went to pull out the blanket and sheet, but Perry stopped me. "Sandy, I gotta tell ya something. I have a confession to make." (They used to call me Sandy because, in Brooklyn, San-tee became Sandy because of the way we talk. Besides, as a little kid, I hated my name. I wanted to be like everyone else—why wasn't I Frank or Joe or Mike? Anyway—) "I know I should have told you earlier, but we were having so much fun . . . Liz is turning tricks in the El San Juan next door."

"Oh, you're fucking kidding me!"

"No, I'm not, and she brings the johns here to the apartment if they don't have a hotel room."

"So how are we supposed to sleep?"

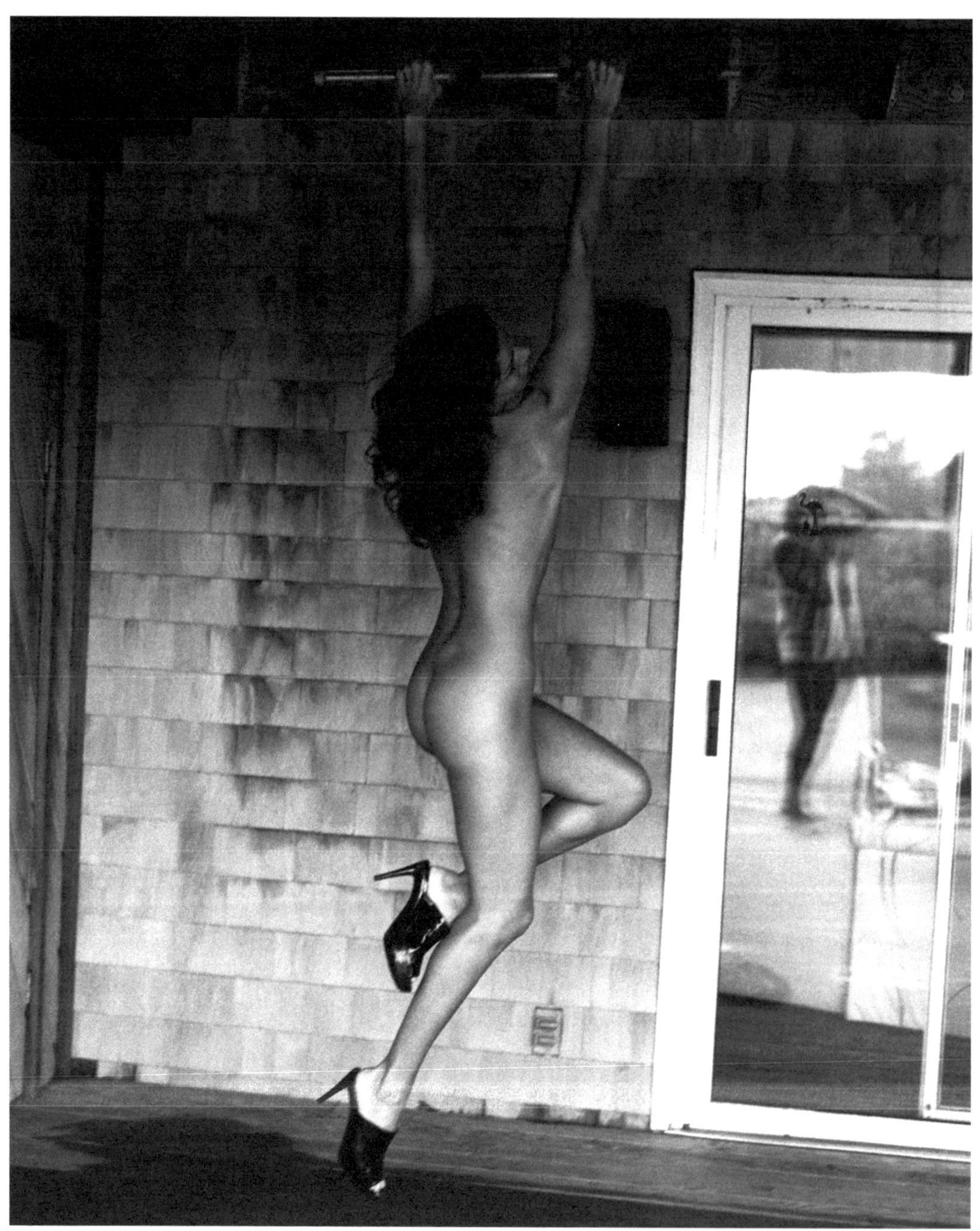

Tahnee Welch, Sagaponack, New York

"After they use the bed, we can sleep in it."

"Oh, man!"

"No, Sandy, listen, it's easy; we got a plan. We sleep on top of the sheets and keep the place neat. Then, if she needs to come here, she'll press the buzzer three times, and we get the fuck out for a half an hour, an hour. C'mon, Sandy, it'll be funny."

So we fell asleep on top of the made bed in our clothes. It's hard to sleep under these circumstances, no matter how tired you are. So by 3:30 a.m., I said, "Let's just get under the covers and go to sleep. She hasn't been here all night, and you said four o'clock."

"Yeah, you're right," he said.

So we zoned out under the sheets in no time. Then, the buzzer rang at who knows what time. We jumped out of bed and tried to make the bed and get our stuff into the closet before she made it up the elevator. Too late! When we heard a key in the door, we jumped into the closet. In the Caribbean, the closet doors have shutters, so we got to be witnesses to the whole fucking thing. We couldn't move because the closet was two feet from the bed.

After they did the nasty and we heard the door close and lock from the outside, we slowly moved out and managed to find something to cover the sheets with and went back to bed.

I fell sound asleep but was awakened suddenly by the sound of a vase smashing against the wall. Liz and Perry were fighting. She was in a rage because she knew we were in there. She grabbed a bag of her stuff and said, "I'm leaving!" and slammed the door behind her.

Good, I thought. *Now, we can get some sleep.*

The next morning, Perry was worried because Liz hadn't come back. I said to him, "Where's she gonna go? This is her apartment, and her shit is still around. She probably went to her uncle's or something."

But later, he confessed, "She ain't got an uncle."

Liz left for New York, and her pimp threw us out after we bullshitted him for two days and told him she went to visit her uncle. We were on the beach with our suitcases. Perry had a wardrobe by now. We slept on the beach for one night fully clothed. Fortunately, the next day, we ran into four girlfriends of ours because they knew we were down there. They let us sleep on the floor in their hotel for three to four nights. We had very little money, and Perry didn't have a return flight.

Since I always carried my paints and brushes with me, I ended up taking everyone's T-shirts and painting scenes of the beach and sunsets in Puerto Rico on them. We put them on the beach and sold them for ten bucks each. We made enough to get a ticket home for Perry and a steak dinner for us the night before we left. When we got home, Liz and Perry made up. Then, we hit the clubs.

As time went on, we all needed to move on. I stayed in touch with Perry, though there were long stretches where we didn't see each other. Liz remained a wild child, and a stunning and beautiful one at that. Years later, Perry told me she'd married a real mobster from an old mob family, but her old habits didn't die. One day, she was found with a bullet to the head. *What a shame*, I thought. I really liked Liz. That news was a real shocker and a bummer; at the same time, it didn't totally surprise me, very, very sad.

Me . . . I went to school and was the first in my family to get a college degree. Once I found my calling, I left the other life behind. But it had well prepared me for the life and the career to come—only it would come with better clothing and better pay.

15

It is by going down into the abyss that we recover the treasures of life.
Where you stumble, there lies your treasure.
—Joseph Campbell

Ever since I can remember, I've had this sense of other things happening from the invisible world. I'd have premonitions and feel myself silently spoken to both in my waking hours and in my sleep. It was always something comforting, always protective and guiding.

My Southern Italian heritage came with a belief in spirits and the otherworldly. I didn't necessarily fear visitations in my sleep; I had often heard of these occurrences while growing up. Even while I was awake, I could sense a lot of things that weren't there in front of my eyes. Being my mom's only child left me with a lot of alone time, and that's when I was most sensitive and in tune with the invisible, especially in nature.

My mom was very religious; she prayed three times a day. She never pushed or imposed anything on me, and because of that, I became more open to the metaphysical. If I had questions, she'd answer them as best as she knew how. She interpreted my dreams as signs to be deciphered.

As I got older, I never mentioned my beliefs to other people. To each his own—things were between me and the universe only. No one needed to know. Anyone who brought up ghosts or spirits or religion would prompt a joke or two from me. To admit my ideas might weaken my sense of connection.

This psychic part of myself remained intact through most of my childhood and adolescence. But the more outside of myself I was after my school years, the less the invisible came to me.

For me, Italy was the land of spirits and mysticism where I encountered the gods daily. On our summer trips there, my mom would reconnect with her past semimonastic life that she had led prior to her marriage. Her close friends were Sisters of the Church—not nuns, but women dedicated to working for the church and leading a spiritual, ascetic kind of life. Celibate and loyal to God. This only bothered me when I was forced to go visit them. As a child, I found it dull as hell and one of the few times I felt more akin to my father being, in my mother's eyes, a heathen and a heretic.

Once, when a group of these ladies came to visit New York, my dad gave them a tour of the city and took them to 42nd Street and Eighth Avenue as a prank—this was late '60s–early '70s. That's when the place was filled with XXX theaters and peep shows, along with pimps and hookers. He had a good laugh. They were mortified but thankfully cried laughing when they got home. Coming from the same village, my father had known all of them and their families, and the women were familiar with his practical jokes.

On a more serious level, I was more solitary in this land of spirits, where it was easier to connect with the invisible. That's when I met Padre Pio, a known healer and saint. On his hands, feet, and ribs, he was marked by the stigmata—corresponding to the wounds Jesus received when he was crucified on the cross. (It's all based on faith. There are no facts when it comes to miracles, even if you think you saw it with your own eyes. To the faithful, his life is documented, as are the healings for which he's credited. Each of us has to discover and believe, or not believe, things on our own; it's not for me to convince anyone of anything here.) My mom's parish priest had taken us to visit Padre Pio. He laid his hands on my head and hugged me. I must have been eight or ten years old.

In retrospect, I feel fortunate to have been blessed by him; it left an impression on me. Padre Pio died in 1968. His body was exhumed in 2008, and it now lies in a glass coffin in San Giovanni Rotundo, constantly visited by thousands of his followers, many of whom still claim to have been healed through prayer by his visitations. Believe what you will.

My father died suddenly at the age of fifty-seven, when I was just sixteen. He had gone into diabetic shock, then fell into a coma, then hemorrhaged to death, details of which are now in my remote past. My world turned upside down.

Now I feel a need to explain the unexplainable. It started with a visitation in my sleep two nights before my dad died. Two healers came to me and said they needed to take my father with them. I pleaded with them, and they did their best to comfort me. They were Cosmas and Damian—two brothers, healers, doctors, saints—whose basilica in Alberobello was a pilgrimage site for my mom, not too far from my parents' hometown of Valenzano. This is how our subconscious speaks to us, with signs and symbols, comfort and the familiar.

That next day, visiting my dad in the hospital was tough on all of us, but no one thought he'd die. Then the next morning, at 5:00, the phone rang. To this day, if the phone rings at that time of night, I know it's never going to be good news. I answered and the hospital asked for the family to come; they wouldn't say why. I called my brothers, Mike and John, who lived nearby, and the three of us went to the hospital. He was gone. We had to identify our father, then go back home to tell my mom and the other family members that he had passed away. I felt perfectly calm. The visitation from the two saints had prepared me for this. But my mom went into shock. I lifted her and carried her to her bed. On her dresser was a picture of those brothers, Saints Damian and Cosmas. I didn't remember seeing it there before.

Things were about to change for me, both for the good and the bad. I had to learn who I was by finding out first who I didn't want to be. I had to embrace those invisible forces within and around me, ask for their help. It took a while for me to find them. They say the road to Heaven leads through Hell, and that's where I was headed. Alone at sixteen, I crossed my personal River Styx, the East River, via the Brooklyn Bridge, downtown to the Ninth Circle!

Into the den of thieves, drugs, and clubs. I got lost, and I didn't want to be found until fortune sent me my guides.

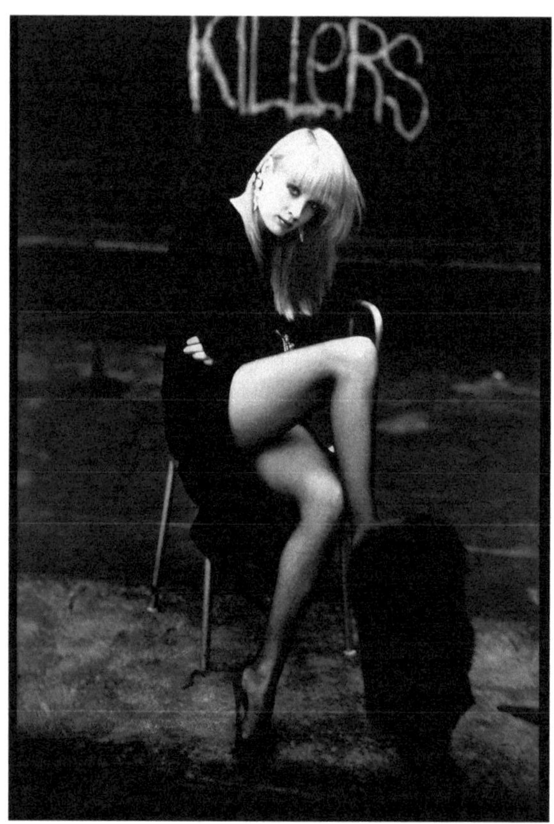

For Italian *Vogue* on Sante's SoHo rooftop

16

At nineteen, I began privately studying photography with Lou Bernstein, a professional photographer and my neighbor whom I'd known since I was a kid.

That fall, I'd started attending community college, studying commercial and graphic art. I went to school during the week, and on Friday nights, I went to Lou's. He held a photography class in his apartment with three or four students. I became very single-minded and into my studies around that time.

I still wasn't sure where I was going. I'd inherited my mom's depression and began experiencing it more often than not after my father passed away, causing me to isolate frequently. At the same time, I had become my mom's keeper, watching over her as she battled her own fears and depression. I had made the basement into my den and studio, but when my demons came out to haunt me, I had nowhere to turn. I felt trapped and alone. Most of my old crew had either moved away or had been put away.

That year, Lou became my mentor and only friend. He was sixty-five years old; I was nineteen. The philosophic and photographic lessons he taught me were crucial to my development as a photographer and a man, and still resonate with me to this day. Most of all, he had a good sixth sense about me, much more than I realized. There were moments that I wanted to die, just disappear; I didn't know enough about how to cope with depression, and it was hitting me hard. When I entered that desperate headspace, Lou always managed to call. He could hear it in my voice and would immediately say, "Grab your camera. I'm coming to pick you up."

I wouldn't want to move, but Lou insisted. He'd show up with his car, and we'd drive to Coney Island. Lou saved my life a few times, and eventually photography saved me as well.

Lou's philosophy was based on his sixteen years of studying with the philosopher Eli

Siegel and his Aesthetic Realism movement. To put it in very general terms, it was based on the balance and harmony of opposites, in both life and art, which ultimately are one and the same. I understood the philosophy and adapted to it quickly from my interest in Tao and Zen Buddhism, which I began studying after my father passed away.

Within the first six months of studying at school and with Lou, I took to photography naturally. Outside of school, I wasn't as social anymore; I spent most of my time focusing seriously on my work. By the end of that year, I encountered new struggles, aesthetic issues that interested me and tested Lou's flexibility. Lou's approach to art, in general, was based on a poetic Social Realism, an approach to photography that began in the 1930s and laid the foundation for the New York Photo League, which Lou belonged to. What we came to know as "New York Street Photography" initially captured the intimate, social, and political relationships of "The People." On the other hand, my own personal journey, by that point, had led me inward to the abstract, more in line with my Eastern studies and with post-war painting.

The post–World War II years introduced translations from the East on Buddhism and Zen, with concepts of the Void. The death toll and near annihilation of Europe forced many artists to flee to America, with most landing in New York. The Surrealists with their theories grown out of Dada and Symbolism transformed the new generation of American art with the likes of Rothko, Jackson Pollock, and others, the Abstract Expressionists. A sense for the Almighty through nature is the underlying force of Romanticism and Abstract

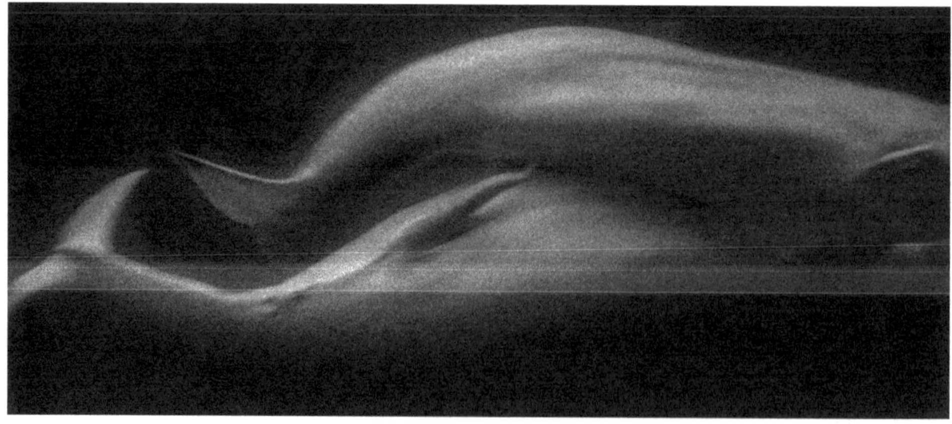

White beluga whales, New York Aquarium, Coney Island, Brooklyn, New York

Expressionism. East and West were united, and it's where I began to feel my aesthetic and spiritual home.

My first photos showed evidence of Lou's approach and my own sense for abstraction—for example, my photographs of two white beluga whales I shot while standing alongside Lou at the Aquarium in Coney Island. His teaching method sometimes involved us taking pictures, side by side, of the same subject. Shooting through the large glass into the tank, these two large mammals intertwined in a sensual act of copulation. In Lou's pictures, you see the whales relating to one another emotionally, as two human beings would, as in a caress or what resembled a kiss. In mine, you see them as two white abstract forms in a blackened void of space. In the darkroom, I had painted with light by taking a board with a small hole in it, creating a narrow beam of light, to use like a paintbrush, and exposing it to the light sensitive photographic paper—"burning in," it's called. I darkened the tank around the whales, creating a black space contrasting their massive white abstract forms. Their forms related in a sensual manner. Lou was pleased with my photographs and proud of me.

But when the time came for me to bring in my abstract paintings and drawings, he was very discouraging and dismissive. It made me angry at times. He would insist I was going to become a photographer, not a painter. I had no one around to support this important side of myself. Eventually, I resented him for it because it left me second-guessing that work. To this day, I don't believe in dismissing anyone's desire to explore mediums.

Only much later did I realize that my early, undeveloped ideas were way ahead of the game, and that the abstract was just not a part of Lou's language. It took another thirty years and a lot of drama to bring me full circle and define that part of my identity as an artist. For all the good Lou did for me and my rapid development in photography, that continuous discouragement toward my painting and abstract work created a chasm between us. It's what forced me, three years later, to leave his mentorship.

After graduating from community college with a two-year degree in commercial art, I transferred to Brooklyn College for fine art. I decided to pursue figure painting and the nude, which led me to Philip Pearlstein, who was teaching there. Philip was a leading figure in the realist movement at that time, focusing on the nude. His concept was to use the classical nude as a means of arriving at abstract compositions. His studio lighting was bare and severe, almost sterile. He was as far from being a Romantic as one could get, and far from the Romanticism I was practicing at that time. That suited me well because I needed to get out of my comfort zone. The Romantic Movement I had been interested in was that of the metaphysical in art.

By the '70s, I found myself searching for answers in the metaphysical. My upbringing made the invisible available, and my psychic experiences affirmed to me that something was out there in some invisible, intangible form, and generally speaking, unperceivable to our limited human nature. I had experienced death up close and around me many times while still a teenager. I'd read books about psychics, and I'd experimented with automatic writing just as the Surrealists had done. Carl Jung was my hero. I'd had some profound experiences in the pursuit of the invisible, so I was naturally attracted to the Romantic movements of the last two centuries, which emphasized the connection of man and God, whether through nature or the abstract. The latest version being the Abstract Expressionists of the 1940s-50s, with the likes of Mark Rothko and Jackson Pollock. I worshipped those guys and their work.

Artistically, I knew I needed to explore the other side of the emotional coin. I had to better understand what it meant to have a more detached perspective of making and looking at art. Philip Pearlstein became the artist who could help me with that, while at the same time allowing me to continue my studies of the nude. He consciously stayed detached from any emotional expression in his work, focusing instead on the construction of his compositions as abstractions. Most of all, I could learn to avoid any traces of sentimentality—the kiss of death.

Within a year, I became Philip's first and only assistant. I would go up to his studio on 88th Street and paint alongside him, and for a while, I became part of his family.

I love taking photographs, but it's so much different than brushing paint onto canvas. There's something primitive in the process that, for me, evokes ritual and sacred mystery. In photography, I go to the outside world and bring it in. With painting, I go inside and bring it out. I can't do without either one. Art is the life you bring to the object; the medium is merely the tool.

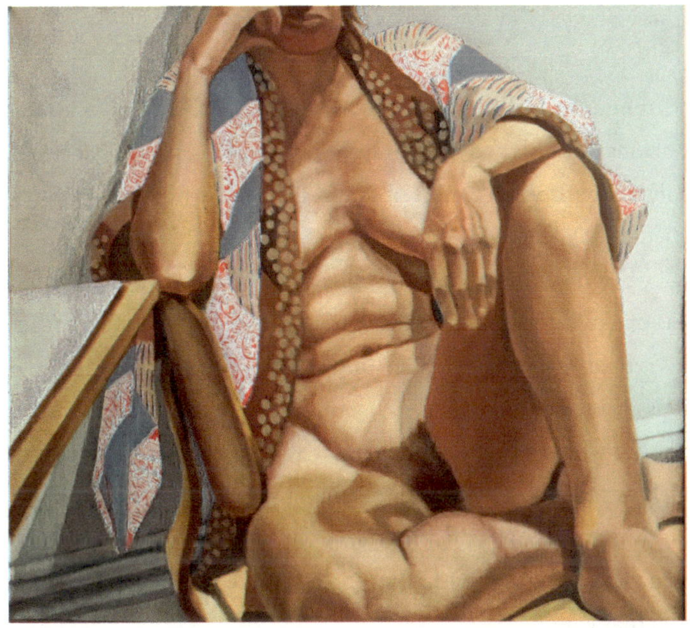

Sante's painting while apprenticing with Philip Pearlstein in his studio

17

At New York Community College, there was a lounge area where everyone hung out between classes; the cool kids, the girls and guys, and the beautiful people, all had their sections. Like my former high school, Erasmus, most of the students were from the projects, from Crown Heights and Bed-Stuy.

At the age of eighteen, I looked like Serpico, the famous NYPD undercover cop of the '60s. Occasionally, I'd visit my Jamaican friend, Rex, in the projects near the Brooklyn Museum. Kids would run when they saw me walking toward them, some of them dropping nickel bags of weed.

One time when I rang Rex's doorbell, someone blocked the light coming from the peephole, which was followed by a lot of rumbling and voices in an incomprehensible language—Rex and his friends were from various islands in the Caribbean and sometimes I couldn't understand a word they said. Then, an eye came back to the peephole, and I heard Rex say, "Sante, that you?"

"Yeah, Rex, you told me to come over around this time."

Rex opened the door, laughing, and said out loud to someone behind him, "It's Sante, *mon*. Don't flush anything!"

"Rex, why is everybody runnin' from me?"

"Sante, when you walked here, did you see any white people?"

"No."

"That's what I'm saying, mon! Plus you look like that Italian cop in the movies, mon. What's his name? Serpico!"

Then, the other guys started laughing too. One guy sitting on the bathroom floor was laughing but also sweating bullets; he had been about to dump a whole pound of weed into the toilet, along with various other items. After that encounter, those guys would always introduce me to their friends as Serpico. (*Mon* is the Jamaican form of saying "man," as in, "Hey, man, how goes it?" It translates as, "Hey, mon, how goes it?")

My mom never blinked an eye whenever I brought home someone of a different race or color, as long as they ate her food, so it always felt natural to me—although that was simply not the case in most communities. I once brought home an Irish friend of mine who was going into the seminary to become a priest. He made the big mistake of not wanting to eat something my mom cooked. After he left, my mom was worried about what kind of friends I was hanging out with; she warned me about him. "Be careful," she said.

During the first few months of school, I made a couple of new acquaintances down at the lounge, but basically, I didn't know anyone. I was somewhat of a shy loner, especially about asking girls out. When you're hanging out in school, your eyes will always be checking out the good-looking people.

There was one particular corner where the best-looking girls congregated, and every guy was giving it a go. Occasionally, I'd catch one of those girls looking my way and sometimes whispering to her friend; then both would be smiling at me. I wasn't that cool or smooth back then, maybe never. These girls were black and beautiful, and the most popular girl—and by far the most beautiful girl in the school—was named Lena Horne (not the famous actress, singer, dancer, and civil rights activist, but her namesake who was much younger). My Lena Horne was an absolute stunner. I would always sit as close to her as I could, hoping a seat near her would open.

One day, one of the girls came over to me to introduce herself and invited me to meet her friends, Lena Horne among them. They told me that, for a while, they had been expecting me to come sit with them. Lena was especially nice to me. It took another couple of weeks for me to get up the nerve to ask her out to a movie. She said yes right away.

I picked her up in Bedford-Stuyvesant where she lived, and we went to the movies on Flatbush Avenue. Afterward, we made out in my mom's '63 Chevy Impala, then finally in my basement makeshift studio. At one point, she turned to me and said, "What the hell took you so long?"

We continued to see each other, cutting out the moviegoing after a while and heading straight to my basement where the stereo was always tuned to WBLS.

Lena was hot stuff. Her girlfriends would see me at school and give me that look and smile. Fortunately, I was in great shape because Lena Horne wanted to do it all the time—to the point where my johnson started to burn. When the burning persisted, I decided to go get a checkup. My doctor was an old man, around eighty years old.

I dropped my pants, and he squeezed and said, "Yup, you got it."

"You mean?"

"Yup!"

He gave me a prescription and told me to lay off the sex for ten days, and I should tell my partner. I guess Lena was more popular than I thought.

When I saw Lena in the lounge, I took her aside and gently told her. She was grateful for my honesty. After our quarantine period ended, we started going out, mostly to my mother's basement. At the end of that school year, she graduated, and I never saw her again.

What can I say, I went out with Lena Horne, and she gave me the clap. It was wonderful.

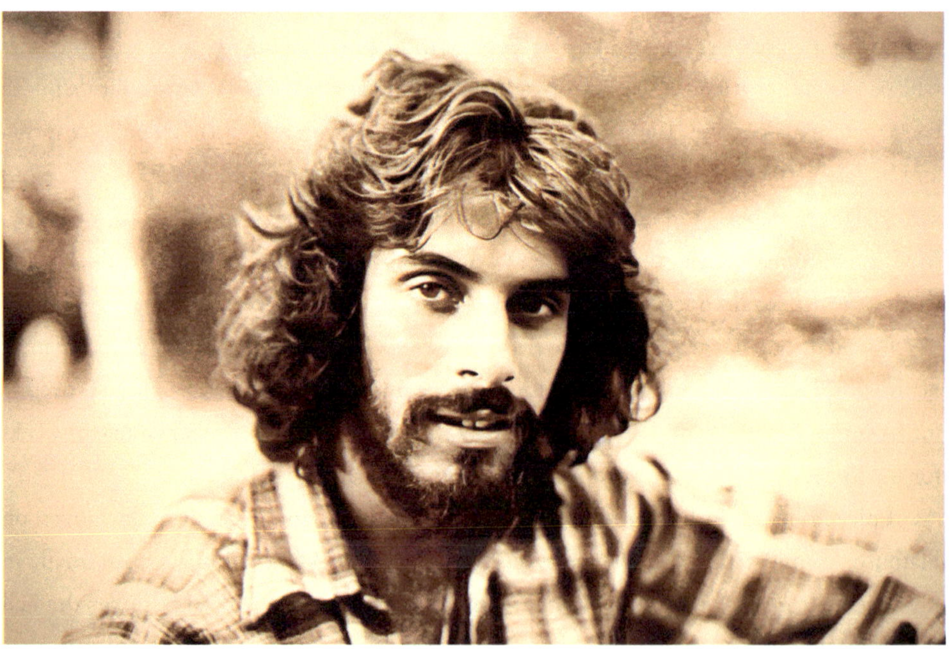

Eighteen-year-old Sante, painting in Provincetown, Cape Cod, Massachusetts

18

Where your fear is, there is your task.
—Carl Jung

After I graduated from Brooklyn College, I supported myself with an assortment of odd jobs while I painted for a year in my mom's basement, which I had already converted into a love den during my college years—hanging beads, Barry White, and incense. It wasn't a stretch setting up canvases to paint and putting together a makeshift studio.

But the universe had other plans for me. I had to find a job first. My mom didn't want me to feel the pinch, but I felt it, even in my own pocket. I had to bring in a real income. My cousin, the one who was a hairdresser who worked in many of the top hair salons, had been telling me glamour stories for years about the city. He pointed out that, since I'd been studying photography for some years now with Lou Bernstein, why not let fashion photography become my direction? He was right, and the thought was scary at first.

The day I thought I was ready, I took to the city streets with my portfolio. With no appointments, no experience in the job market, and no one to guide me, I began knocking on doors, hoping one would open. I managed to get the addresses of the only fashion photographers I knew of. My first stop was Richard Avedon's studio. I didn't get past the front desk! One down!

Next on my list was Irving Penn, and they wouldn't even open the door for me. Why didn't I think of calling first?

Soon after that, on the day a blizzard hit the city, I took the train from Brooklyn to try Francesco Scavullo's studio. I had to walk some blocks from the station to get there, waves of snow coming at me ninety miles an hour. I rang the bell and was buzzed in. The first person I ran into was Scavullo himself. "Who are you? What do you want?" I told him I wanted to be an assistant, and he said, "Get out! And what's with the hair?" *What is he talking about?*

As I turned to leave, I saw myself in the hallway mirror. The snow had piled up on my sprayed hair, making it seem like a foot tall, and the weight of it was splitting it down the middle with a wide part; the snow was on top of both sides of the part. What the fuck! I went home to rethink my approach.

I finally got a start as a second assistant to an advertising photographer, making seventy-five dollars a week cleaning the studio, the kitchen, mopping the floors, and being a general gopher assisting the first assistant. But I was in!

The thing I learned first was that I knew nothing about commercial photography. I learned quickly, and as time went on, I made friends with other assistants, and I occasionally would work freelance for the photographers they worked for. At the same time, when things slowed down, each of us would put together small test shootings for our portfolios, where everyone involved—from the model to the hair and makeup people—got new photos for their "books," as we called them. It usually meant working with people at a similar stage of development, who needed to expand their own bodies of work.

One assistant I befriended and worked with a lot was Tommy Peters, who assisted an editorial photographer who worked with great magazines and top girls. Tommy was a cool guy, and he happened to be going out with Kim Alexis, one of the top models at the time, a precursor to Kate Moss or Christy Turlington. One year, I remember she must have had about eight of the twelve American *Vogue* covers, French *Vogue*, British *Vogue*, *Elle* magazine, and the best advertising internationally. This was in the late '70s, and Tommy and Kim occasionally invited me out with them and other top industry girls to places like Studio 54. I would assist Tommy on his tests and his infrequent paid shootings. We were in our early twenties.

I was always happy for my friends when they were getting somewhere. I was trained as an artist and as a photographer, but that didn't mean much if you weren't connected professionally and socially. Tommy was connected; plus, he had a good personality which counted for a lot—but I felt he couldn't take a good picture to save his life! It was easy to mistake a good picture with an ordinary one, a photo of a top model looking beautiful didn't mean you had taken a good picture. Her looking beautiful and you taking a good picture were—and are—two different things.

By this time, Kim was turning down *Vogue* covers because she was in such great demand. But she did Tommy a great favor by saying, "I'll only do it if my boyfriend shoots the cover." It was a no-brainer; having Kim on the cover would generate sales, even if my mother took the pictures.

Tommy's method for a cover shoot was a popular approach at the time. He would have a 300mm lens on a tripod, and when Kim was camera-ready with hair and makeup, he would press the trigger and with the motor drive on rapid, shoot off a roll of thirty-six exposures in seconds, and throw another roll in. Maybe shoot ten to twelve rolls, change outfits, and repeat. He would then hand in practically all the film after a quick inspection. Tommy, at twenty-two years old, had a portfolio of the best girls in the industry from all the European *Vogues*, plus the *Elle* magazines. Professionally, he was light-years ahead of me, no competition.

In fact, I had a meeting with an art director for an Italian fashion magazine published by Mondadori; I had about ten pictures in my portfolio, so I didn't even consider myself in the running for any work. I thought of it as a good "getting to know you" since he was in town, staying with a friend. Tommy's name came up because of how young he was with all of those covers and who his girlfriend was and, of course, that he was a friend of mine. He asked if I thought Tommy would consider going to Milan and doing some assignments for his magazine. I told Tommy about the job and offered to go with him to assist. I spoke Italian and half my family still lived there—we'd have a blast.

We set a date for a trip to Milan at the end of June, and I gave notice to my job and my other freelance connections. I had saved fifteen hundred dollars—a fortune for me—and bought the cheapest possible tickets on Swiss Air to Zurich. Then I'd take a train down to Milan. Everything was falling into place. Tommy and I were excited about it. I was packed and ready two days before the trip. I had two large suitcases my father used when we'd go away to Italy for months at a time. Obviously way over-packed, but hey, ya never know.

The night before we were to leave, Tommy called and said, "I ain't goin'!" *What?? Why?* No excuses. In retrospect, I think he chickened out! He had it too good here at home with his top model girlfriend, staying at her great apartment, with all the creature comforts to go along with that, and getting invited to all the best parties. Sometimes, it's a bitch to have it real good; you lose your hunger. After I hung up, I panicked. What was I going to do? One of the things Lou Bernstein ingrained in me was that "the unknown is friendly"—it became a mantra of mine. I decided to go. If worse came to worse, I'd see some people maybe, then just get on a train and go visit relatives like I did every other summer with my parents, so fuck it.

The next evening, I got on the plane, then the train, and I made it to Milano Centrale with my two-ton suitcases. I had thirteen hundred dollars in American Express traveler's

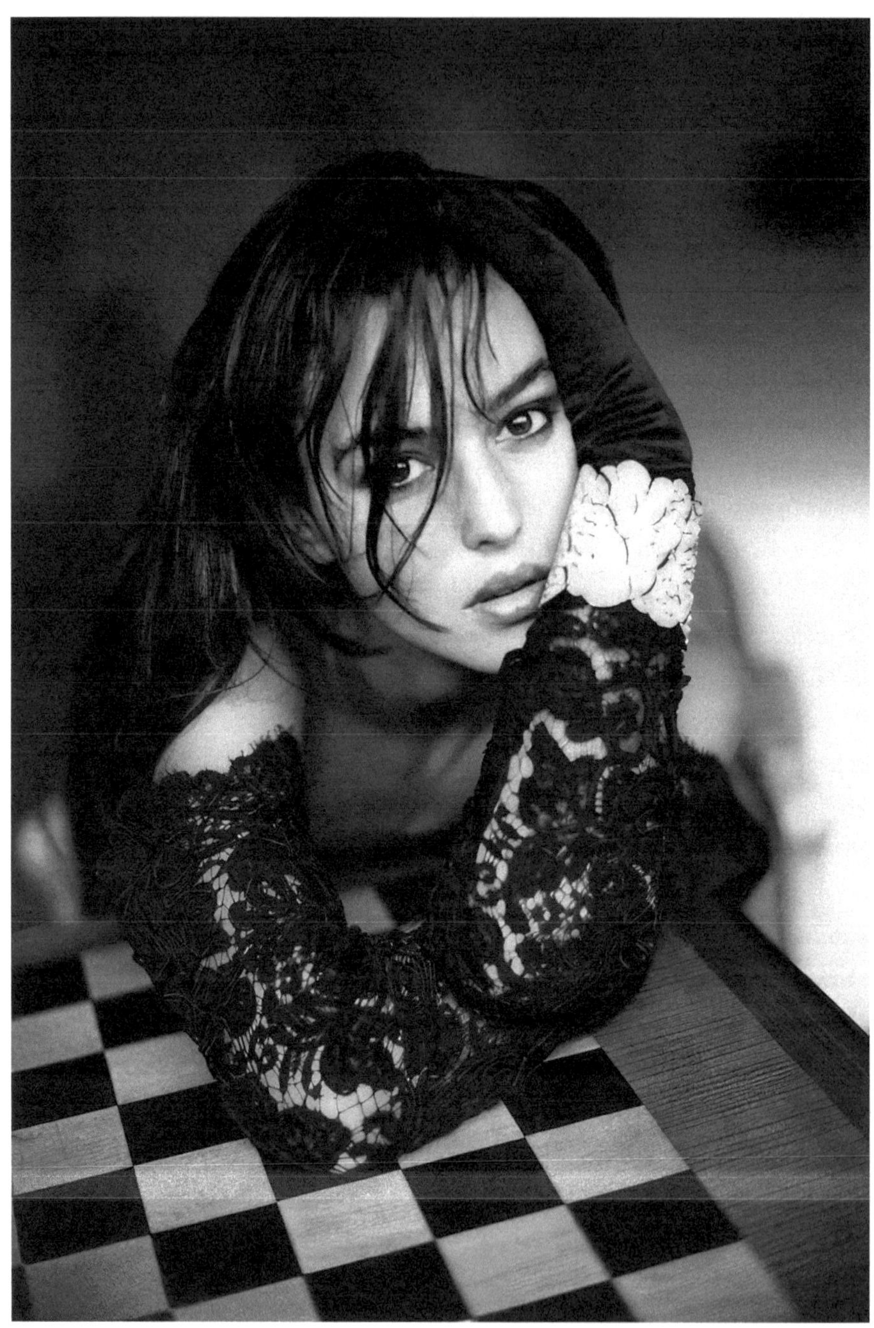

Monica Bellucci for French *Vogue*

checks in my money belt and two hundred dollars in cash and the name of one hotel that Tommy had mentioned. I didn't even have the addresses of the magazines or the model agencies. I was supposed to be here assisting Tommy, not looking for work as a photographer.

I took a taxi to the hotel that offered long-term stays of a month or more. I was sweating bullets because of the luggage and the concierge told me there were no rooms. It was 1981, no cell phones, no Google, and I had no credit card. It was scary, and I was nervous as hell. I asked the concierge if he could recommend anywhere affordable, and he mentioned a place. I went there, but they had no room, either. Now I was shitting myself. Finally, I asked a taxi driver if he knew of any place, and he took me to the Arena Hotel. The street was wide enough for the car to go down and for the door to open. The place was a dump. I got a room with the neon sign out my window like something out of film noir. I said to myself, "*What the fuck? I can't even go home now.*"

I made a long-distance call home to my mom and let her know I was safe and sound; otherwise, her neurotic voodoo vibes would have kept me up all night. Though we could hear each other well, we were talking loudly, as if we're talking through two tin cans and a string. All the Italians from the old country would do that; they'd call Italy and yell into the phone.

I had to get out. It was around 9:00 p.m. and starting to get dark outside, so I went to an outdoor café at the nearest piazza, ordered a pitcher of beer, and started drinking with the intention of getting shit-faced. I'd never been to Milan before, and I noticed immediately it wasn't beautiful like the other Italian cities I was familiar with: Rome, Florence, Venice, or Verona. It looked like I had taken a twelve-hour trip to Newark, New Jersey. Most of the city had been bombed during World War II, and the only remaining monuments were the magnificent Cathedral and the castle where Leonardo da Vinci lived for about eighteen years, Castello Sforzesco. Leonardo had designed the great castle's moat and the canals for the city, and he had painted the *Last Supper* somewhere close by. Some stark-looking fascist architecture made things appear bleak, but I would discover that Milan was a city of elegance and interiors.

I already had a buzz going when I saw a familiar face pass by—Lane Pedersen, a photographer from NYC, whom I had assisted a few times on catalogs. Lane was in his forties and friends with a stylist ex-girlfriend of mine. I was so happy to see him; I jumped on him like a drowning man. He was equally surprised to see me. I explained I had just arrived and didn't know anyone, and that where I was staying—which he knew of—was a shithole. It was a Thursday night, and he was leaving the next day with his girlfriend for Portofino on the Italian Riviera. He invited me to come along. I could leave my luggage at his hotel for the weekend and check in as soon as we got back Sunday night. I was going to the Italian Riviera my first day here after arriving. God was looking out for me!

The next morning, I met him and his girlfriend at their hotel, overlooking the giant Castello Sforzesco. We had breakfast, and they held a room for me. It was basically a model's hotel, one of the places the agencies would have their models and young photographers stay at. I had a wonderful weekend. Clear, beautiful waters, the best pasta and seafood, and most of all, a feeling of security.

Lane gave me every name and number I needed to know: magazines, editors, model agencies, and people to see there. I could not have been luckier!

The one discouraging note: he'd been in Milan for three months and there was no work. He said he was leaving to get back to his business in NYC. He was really disappointed and had been hoping to get some editorial work, after spending his entire career doing catalog work for money.

Creatively speaking, catalog work is the most mundane, uninspiring work a creative photographer can do. If it weren't for the money, you might end up putting a gun to your head after a few years, or even months, of doing catalogs. Editorial, especially in Europe, is where photographers have creative control and artistic license to make images that become their visual style and trademark, where they make a name for themselves; it's the closest a photographer comes to becoming an artist in the fashion industry. The problem, as in Lane's case, is that your eye has only developed and known twenty years' worth of catalog photography, which makes it hard to break out and start doing editorial in your forties. Exceptions can be found, but those individuals developed their editorial work from the beginning of their careers, alongside their commercial work, and even that is a long shot.

Also, once you establish a catalog career making steady money, you simultaneously create a lifestyle you want to keep, with a studio, home, and maybe a family to support. When you're just starting out editorially, you have nothing to lose because you have nothing. Plus, there's the social side of the business, going out and meeting people, and growing up with contemporaries, people of your own generation that know each other. I'd meet most of my contacts at parties and clubs between the hours of 10:00 p.m. and 3:00 a.m. The kiss of death is going right into catalog work after assisting—you're trapped before you even get started.

I was thinking, *If Lane is right about the lack of work, I'll find out soon enough by going to a couple of top magazines and some modeling agencies.*

Sunday night, I checked into the Hotel Bruxelles. Nicola, the concierge, was from Naples, and he sort of took a liking to me. A real character in his Neapolitan way, he asked if I was a photographer like Lane. I told him, yes, and I needed a cheap room for I don't know how long. He had a perfect room for me on the top floor, with a skylight and overlooking the Castello, at fifteen dollars a night. The skylight was a small plastic bubble that you pushed up, and it leaked when it rained. The bathroom was down the hall, but there was a sink in the room. At fifteen dollars a night, I wasn't complaining.

In the morning, I met Lane for a café latte and brioche. On Mondays, nothing got started till after 1:00 p.m. I didn't come to Milan to show my portfolio around, but I did bring some pictures. My hotel was at 13 Piazza Castello, and Italian *Vogue* was at 27 Piazza Castello. For many years, Italian *Vogue* was the cream of the crop; only the who's who of fashion photographers worked for them. I went upstairs to my room and took out the portfolio of pictures, which consisted of nine photographs of white beluga whales I shot at the Aquarium in Coney Island with Lou Bernstein, ten life drawings of nudes I did while at school, and twelve fashion test pictures that looked like twelve different photographers had taken them. I was far from having developed any semblance of a photographic style. What was I thinking when I put these together?

But that was really all I had. Once, again, I said, "Fuck it!" I'd walk over to Italian *Vogue* with what I had, and when they said no, I'd pack up and leave. Again with no appointment, I went over to No. 27 on the next block, went up to the second floor, and asked if I could meet the art director. I sat and waited.

Alberto Nodolini, *Vogue*'s art director, strolled out and asked if he could help me. I asked if I could I show him my portfolio. He said okay but that I had to wait for when he had a minute. An hour later, he strolled back out to get a coffee—I think he had forgotten I was waiting for him. He then let me wait in the art department, where they were laying out the magazine. I stayed there for three hours and got to see the newest images coming in from photographers like Helmut Newton, David Bailey, Arthur Elgort, and Denis Piel. It was a major *wow* moment for me. I was a kid in a candy store. These were new pictures by some of the greats. And there were other images tacked to the walls, a virtual fashion photography hall of fame.

A couple of hours later, Nodolini looked at my book. I was a nervous twenty-five-year-old kid from Brooklyn. I told myself, "All he could do is say no." I felt I had already scored just by being there. He closed my book and told me to wait; he wanted the beauty editor to see it. Another hour passed, the editor came in, and she and Nodolini looked at my book. They said a couple things back and forth. Then, they turned to me and said, "*Va bene*."

They took a chance on me and gave me two double-page beauty nudes to do for Italian *Vogue*—basically, two double-page nudes that they could credit one of their beauty clients for skincare or a fragrance. To their credit, they recognized a passionate kid with elegant photos of white whales in a black space, along with beautiful nude drawings done with sensual lines, and other photographs that showed I could handle the lighting technically.

On my first day out, I got my first job with Italian *Vogue* Beauty. You might say I was lucky, but you could also say I made that luck by showing up. I made the trip. There's always the chance that they might say yes, but ya have to show up!

I was ready to start shooting that day, the next, or at the end of the week; instead, they scheduled it for the next month. I was naturally excited and very anxious. I stayed busy and productive as best as I could. I made appointments with other magazines and art directors, and I got to make friends. I met model agents and agency staff, had dinners with them and with models, with hair and makeup people. A sweet young girl I sat next to at dinner one night was a young Italian Canadian girl by the name of Linda Evangelista. We bonded at that drunken dinner party and have remained friends throughout our careers.

That trip to Milan was the beginning of a wild ride. It was the call of adventure, an adventure with no guarantees, no security, no insurance, and, basically, no net.

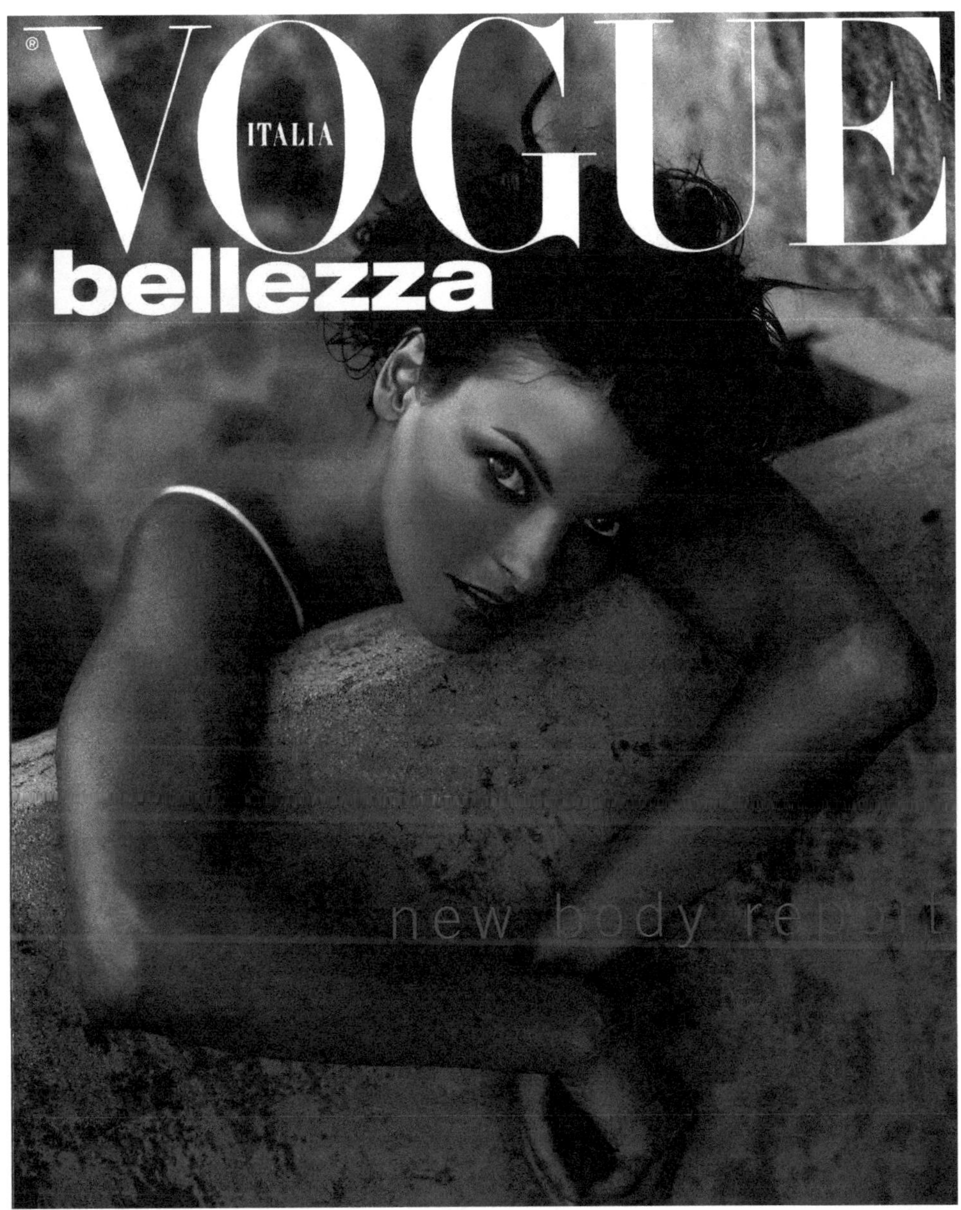

Linda Evangelista for Italian *Vogue*

19

I always considered myself a late bloomer sexually. I'm pretty sure my mother stunted my growth with all the Roman Catholic shit hitting me left and right, always with the sins. My father didn't live long enough to take me under his wing, and even if he had, my mother would have come down on him like Hail Mary full of grace.

As a kid, my parents' bedroom was next to mine. Whenever I'd hear the latch on the door, it would only be a minute before I'd hear my mom saying, "Nick, no, Nick, no!" I never knew what was going on; I was eight years old.

Now I understand why I'd find all those dirty magazines in the basement, and I can feel sorry for the poor guy. It reminds me of a Rodney Dangerfield line: "I think I married a nun—I get none in the morning, none in the afternoon, and none at night!"

I had to learn about sex in the streets of Brooklyn, and that was kinda worthless, too. Everybody bragged about shit they didn't do. When I was in junior high school, if a girl called the house for me, my mother would freak out and act like Satan was on the line. If he was home, my father would smack me on the back of the head before he even knew what was going on. Then he'd grab the phone and say, "You no colla ear no mo, *vaffanculo*!" and hang up. All just so he didn't have to hear my mother. Then, she'd go in her bedroom and pray for me! I'd be mortified and have to go to school the next day, not knowing how many people the girl had told. And I used to wonder why I was awkward with girls when I was young.

When I got to college, things slowly began to change. Fast-forward to me when I began to get professional assignments as a photographer. The floodgates opened when I had *Vogue* magazine covers and editorials published with my name all over the place. *Fuggetaboutit.* I became a chick magnet; I was worried I'd go blind.

Years later, I got into a serious relationship, meaning something that lasted more than a year, and I realized it constituted a threat to my mom somehow—or I should say she made me realize it. She had this psychic sense of knowing just when to call to put the old cock-block on, even if I was in another country. As soon as I was with any girlfriend and about to hit a home run, no matter what time of day or night, the phone would ring, and it would be my mother. I could see the phone ID by the bed that said "MOM," and my ship would sink. Years later, when I got married, my mother wore black to the wedding—though she claimed it was a dark navy blue. She just didn't want to give me up to any other woman, plain and simple.

As a response, I tended to lean toward girls who were the complete opposite of my mother. For example, my girlfriend (let's call her Karina) who was living with me at the time was very outgoing and fun and sometimes kind of wild. She grew up in the suburbs of Americana, where all the real crazy sexual shit went on. She was tight with the hottest and wildest girls in the modeling business and was the leader of the pack. They flocked to her—and from her to me and my loft. I got a fast crash course in what I had missed by not growing up in the suburbs. We were all young, but I was no match for most of these girls. I mean, I looked the rogue part, but I still had a tad of the Catholic mother/whore thing clinging to me. I'd probably never shake it off completely, but I did my best.

Since I didn't want anyone thinking I was conservative, I went along for the ride. Girl on girl, girls on girls, this and that, that and this. Things began to get out of hand. There was one particularly gorgeous sexual seductress whom you couldn't help but love, who needed to be wanted, and whenever she was in town, trouble of some kind always followed. Once, wearing just a trench coat and heels, she schemed to get on the same plane as her gynecologist; she thought he was sexy. She even charmed her way to switch seats and sit next to him on an overnight red-eye flight to New York. When the cabin lights were turned down for sleep mode, she opened her trench coat, where she was completely nude, to turn him on. Another time, she answered the phone and even though the caller had dialed the wrong number, she started a conversation with the caller and eventually met up with him later in a Denny's parking lot. Then the cops caught them in the act in the back of her car, still parked at Denny's. She was so beautiful and twisted, I miss her.

We all walked on the wild side for years. Maybe I did it just to spite my upbringing. It all became a sexual circus, and I was the kid in the front row with the lollipop. What I didn't realize was that my girlfriend was the ringmaster, in the top hat and tails. It was like clubbing in the '70s, with all these girls and me, the difference being that these girls were superstars, making tons of money. We took it past the limit; at least, I did, and eventually, I was flying high on the trapeze with no net, with my bollocks swinging in the wind for all to see. Crash, sooner or later, life doles it out to everyone. Money, drugs, family. Then came payback time. I got fucked all right, literally and figuratively. From infidelities, jealousies, backstabbing, sometimes pregnancies, rumors, breakups, and lies, I've never been the same since—but I'd most probably do it all over again just the same. It was too much fun.

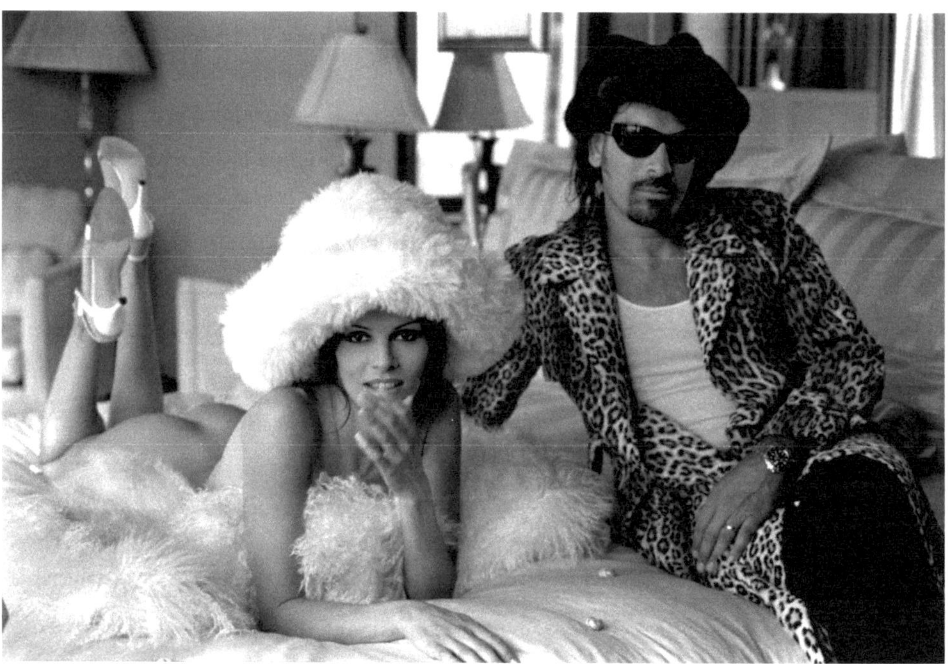

Sante and Tahnee Welch for *Playboy*

20

It doesn't make much difference how the paint is put on as long as something has been said. Technique is just a means of arriving at a statement.
—Jackson Pollock

I read somewhere that Jackson Pollock had the uncanny ability to locate large stones below the surface of his property just by using his sense perception—the way a water dowser uses a forked stick to feel for that invisible downward pull. Pollock used his sixth sense to locate these stones—you can say he felt the vibe—and apparently, he was quite accurate. Having had many psychic experiences when I was young, I'm a believer. Pollock was an artist who worked from the gut, from his sensory perception as opposed to theories and concepts. He used that same sensory perception to lay down paint and compose his canvases. I gravitated toward those artists and those methods.

When taking a photo, it's crucial for me to feel my subject's energy, their vibe, and I make sure my subject feels that invisible something coming from me. I can direct them with just that silent action of energy. I couldn't tell you how to reach it for yourself, but what I can say is that it's all sensory. I use it in other ways as well. For example, if I have to look for some misplaced item in my home, I will close my eyes, empty my thoughts, and tune into it; my senses will lead me there, almost every time. It's a non-thinking, all-sensory process.

In art, sensory perception is critical in composing a picture, a musical score, a movement in dance, or any other form of expression. It can tune us into anything we allow ourselves to be conscious of. I believe ideas are in the air the same way electromagnetic waves are; they travel through us, and we can pick up on them—or not.

Carl Jung believed, as Nikola Tesla did, that ideas were picked up by individuals tuned in to receive this invisible source of knowledge ("it's in the air"). That kind of awareness became a defining asset for me as an artist. I realized, later in life, that I developed this awareness due to being dyslexic; I couldn't rely on written words to guide me.

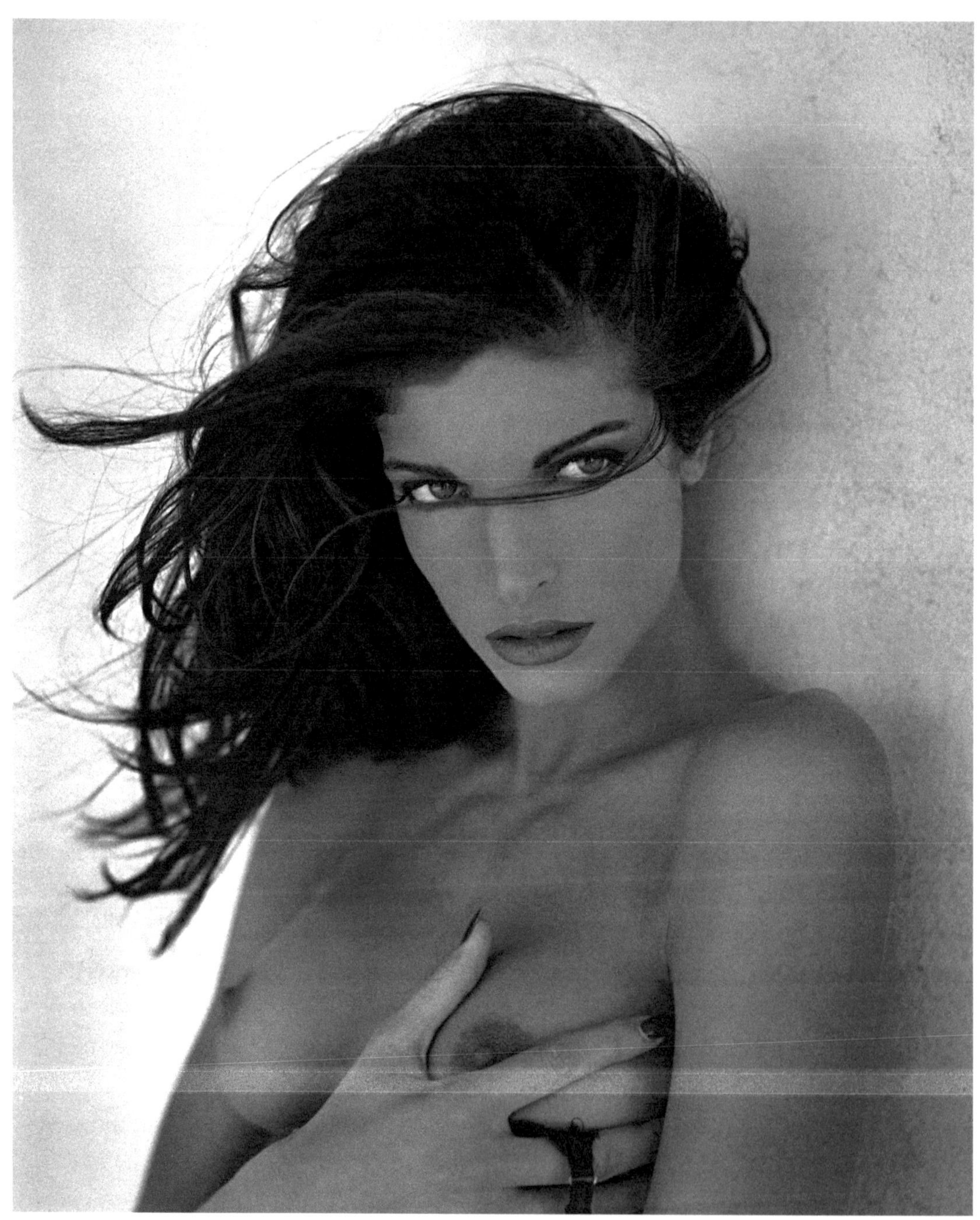

Stephanie Seymour for *Playboy*

This ability to sense things with any accuracy is what I go on—it stems from an intuitive nature that primitive man survived on. We don't always trust it because it's not reinforced outside of ourselves, and it's only when we don't listen that we learn our lesson the hard way—when we find ourselves saying "I knew it" or "I should have listened to myself," for example.

In Pollock's case, his work grew from ideas that were "in the air" at the time and discussed among artists, along with the Surrealists, who experimented with things like automatic writing and chance, exploring the subconscious through dreams, abstraction, and mythology—intuitively tapping into something unique, through an "eyes closed" perception. Pollock was seen by some as a wild drunken cowboy, lacking discipline and self-control, and he wasn't known to be a bookworm—I read somewhere he was probably dyslexic, too. Whatever the case, he used his perceived disadvantages to his advantage, and in his belief in following his sense perception, he invented a language all his own. In the process, he revolutionized the visual language of twentieth-century art.

Another great example was Barbara Rose's description of Robert Rauschenberg, in an article she wrote for *Artforum*: "Rauschenberg suffered from acute dyslexia, which made reading, following instructions, and retaining textual information extremely difficult." Recent studies have shown that dyslexia displaces intelligence from the strictly verbal mode to a multidimensional sensory perception. In certain cases, one's focus is diffused, taking in an entire environment rather than an isolated word or object. Dyslexics think in pictures rather than in words.

According to Carl Jung, the language of the subconscious can only be interpreted through images and sensory perception, the language of artists. Interpreting dreams and symbolism was not only critical to Jung but to art and artists in general, a dialogue through images that goes back to our first ancestors. Myths and mythology have given us paths to follow and guideposts for our lives. Those invisible ideas that travel in the ether can only be picked up through our senses and transcribed in images.

I needed these things reinforced when I was young to help me validate my approach to art and to life; it's never taught in school. After college and my school years in general, I lost touch with that sense of perception for a while; it was dulled by a bombardment of survival needs, anxieties, and the pressure to secure my family's financial well-being. I lost that inner quiet, and I listened to too many outside voices that drowned out that psychic channeling I had received so clearly as a kid. I didn't realize, at the time, that my sensory perception was the source and wellspring of my talent, which did not come from technical mastery, but from the ability to perceive and express myself through forms, from "catching the vibe."

21

Hearing someone say out loud that they're spiritual makes me want to smack them one. I always thought that side of you should be kept between you and God, and announcing it at lunch makes you a fraud to me. If you don't believe in God, keep that to yourself as well. I grew up that way; actions are what's sacred, not the mouthing off about it. If you have to tell people you are spiritual, then it's likely you're not. I kept things like that very close to me. If someone asked, maybe . . . but most times, I'd laugh or brush it off. Keep it to yourself; it has more power that way; besides, there are many different definitions, and I don't need to hear it. My mom, a devout Roman Catholic, taught me at home that it's a personal and private matter, but never did she push it; it was up to me to observe and investigate on my own. My father, on the other hand, was a very funny, outgoing guy, a blast for his friends to hang out with; he didn't give two shits about faith. I believe in that, too. Mom and Dad were two opposites you couldn't imagine together. It was an arranged marriage. My mom was pious, talked about things in metaphors, about God and Jesus Christ. Again, the only utterance of "Jesus Christ" from my father was right before he'd smack me one for something I had done to piss him off.

My life revolved around the drama that was my mother. I didn't realize at the time that my mom was emotionally handicapped and raising me to be a choirboy, and it was something I resisted for the rest of her life; she held onto me as close as possible, desperately at times, oppressively at other times, yet always lovingly. If I got a fat lip from playing in the schoolyard, she would wail with grief and make a scene—you'd think the mob had put a bullet in my head. And if my father was around, she'd freak him out so much that he'd smack me one because I got a fat lip and freaked her out. I got smacked a lot back then, all us kids did; it was the '60s.

The moment I was about to leave the house, the wailing would begin again. "If anything happens to you, I will die! I love you always! Remember I love you; I can't live without you!"

"Mom, I'm leaving for school! I'll be back at three o'clock!"

The pathos of this Mediterranean mourner seemed normal to me until I got older. She made me feel permanently responsible for her life and constantly guilty about her emotional well-being.

My father could hardly put up with her. If he left the house, she couldn't give a shit, but me? Her son and only child, holy fuck!

While pregnant, some mothers knitted socks, some made sweaters and blankets. My mother began making buttons, the type that would affect my nerves for the rest of my life. When she wanted attention, she knew which button to push. When she wanted more attention, there was another button. There were a lot of buttons.

When my father passed away in my sixteenth year, Mom played those buttons like they were keys on the organ at Yankee Stadium in mid-July. She had a psychic grip on me. I could feel those buttons even from across the ocean. I'd be in Europe starting my career while in my twenties and get depressed out of nowhere and couldn't understand where it came from, and then it would dawn on me: Mom was sending me a message. I'd call home and hear her depressed voice, and I'd ask, "Ma, what's wrong? What are you doing?"

She'd answer, "I do nothing, I do nothing. I sit by the phone and wait for you to call!"

It would drive me up a wall. A lot of times, I'd start screaming at her. My friends would ask who I was talking to.

"My mother!"

"Oh, okay," they'd say, like it was normal.

Years later, a psychic warned me to be careful: "When she dies, she's going to try and take you with her!"

I'd be like, "Fuck you!" Then I'd feel guilty and get more pissed off.

Mom would tell me she prayed to Padre Pio for me and everything would be all right. She was such a devotee to Padre Pio, the saint and healer who had laid his hands on me and given me his blessing as a kid. Unexplainable things would occur when she prayed to him, and it was sometimes difficult to doubt her.

One day, my mom came to my loft downtown in SoHo by car service from her house in Brooklyn. She often came by to bring me food, babysit my infant son, or feed me and my friends. She'd stay a few hours, and when it was time for her to go home, I'd call her car service to come pick her up. I'd help Mom with her coat and scarf and whatever bag she carried, along with some Tupperware from her last trip over, and I'd take her downstairs to put her in her car and wave good night. That was our routine for years.

This time—she was probably in her late seventies at that point—the car was already there, which was unusual. The driver was standing outside and opened the car door.

"This is for D'Orazio, right?" I asked.

He said yes. Mom got in, and I waved goodbye. I went upstairs and waited for her to call to say she was safe at home. Not even five minutes later, the phone rang. It was my mother's car service, letting me know they were downstairs.

"Say what? I just put my mother in the car."

The car service guy said, "That's not possible. I got my driver on the radio, and he's in front of your apartment. The driver confirms he hasn't picked her up!"

Holy shit. I just put my mom in somebody's car and have no idea where she is and no number to call. I can't do anything but sit and wait. Finally, after fifteen minutes, the phone rang. It was Mom.

"Mom, where are you?"

"You never believe! When I get in the car, I see the driver has a picture of Padre Pio on the dashboard, and I say, 'I pray to Padre Pio every day.' He says, 'I know, and all my life, I pray to Padre Pio too.' He says he was driving around and was not far away when Padre Pio came to him and said, 'Go pick up Maria and make sure she gets home safe.' When we get home, he open the door, and he walka me uppa the steps and says goodbye."

"What? Can't be . . . Oh, yeah, and how much did Padre Pio charge you for the ride?"

"He charga nothing, he no wanna taka my money."

This is the kind of stuff I grew up with. There was always some kind of mystical something going on in my house. I could never explain it. It's still hard for me to believe, but it happened; my mom wouldn't lie; it's a sin. God is always watching . . .

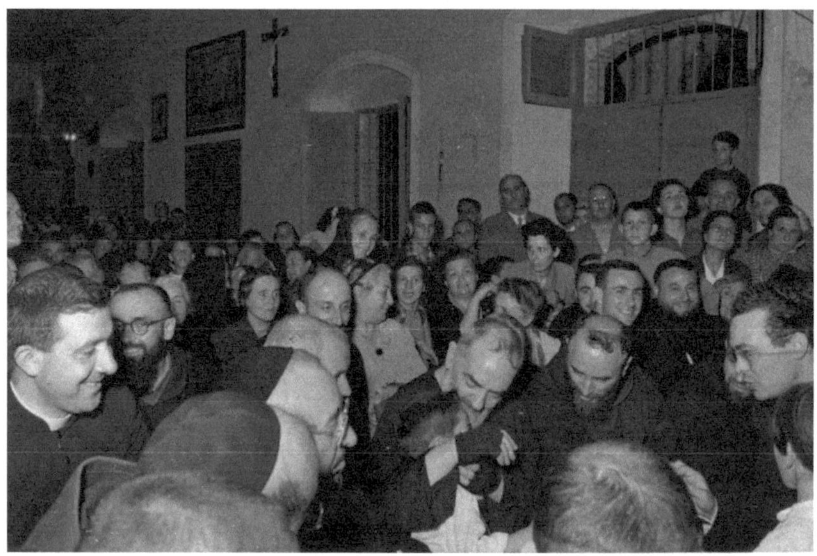

Padre Pio, friar, mystic, healer, and canonized saint, San Giovanni Rotondo, Italy

22

Depression is a flaw in chemistry, not character.
—unknown

It always began with a certain unpredictable change in my physical chemistry, then turned into melancholy that grew darker by the hour. Once I felt it coming on, I'd employ everything I had in me. I'd be my own coach, my own guru, my own priest. I'd remind myself over and over again that it would pass. Let it move through me, let it go, and it would be gone. Instead, I always tried to fight it. I had the therapeutic tools, and when they didn't work, I had the pills. If I had to be out in public, I'd do my best to conceal it, but people could read it in my face. I'd keep my shades on to hide my eyes. I hid it well enough behind the camera. Strangely enough, I'd always come through with great images. It's what saved me . . . most of the time.

I'd only fail if the client I was working with threw in every obstacle and tried to tell me how to do my work. It was worse still if they had hired me for my growing reputation but really needed a less invested photographer, or if the clothing had no relation to my visual style. I found it hard to detach personally from my images, and under those circumstances, it would cause me to produce mediocre work.

Then, the melancholy would turn into full-blown depression. It even affected my physical strength. It was not a place I wanted to be, but it was in that darkness that I found my ability to connect and where I was able to feel everything in a most profound way.

The drink, the pills, the powder, what have you, were the only quick relief for me. When I got high, I would be the life of the party. I didn't give a shit, loved taking risks, loved entertaining, and making my friends laugh because I knew I was always within an inch of that dark place. The paradox was that I worked with light, but emotionally, I lived in darkness. Being around people always saved me, but I could never be around anyone like myself—their pain would unleash mine, which came from being raised by an emotionally handicapped

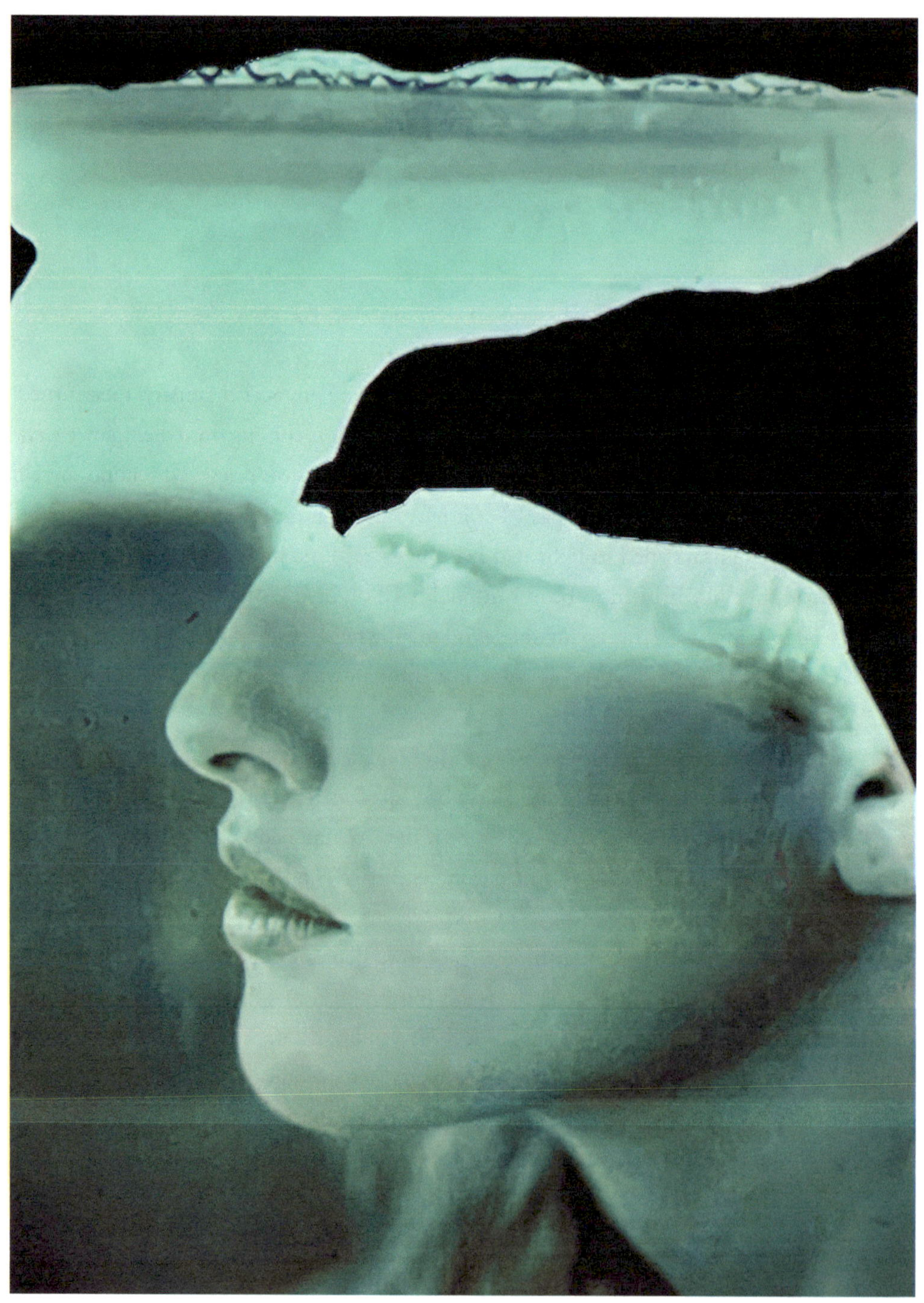

Tatjana Patitz

person. I had to run from people who were like me. I had spent my life with the emotional mania that was my mom. When she suffered breakdown after breakdown, whether it was real or fake, it would disable me. I promised myself never to give up on her. She was my mom. But I almost lost my life for it, and many times, I would have welcomed that.

I lost many people I loved because of my depression, first and foremost, my wife and son. It was scary and hard for an adolescent to deal with a parent dealing with depression—I knew that all too well. Friends I loved also took offense at my disappearing on them. They weren't aware I was in need of help and would take it personally when I'd isolate and hide myself out of pain and the shame, sometimes for months at a time. The longer I stayed out of touch, the more embarrassed I was to call. I was ashamed of how I was failing to deal with it. It was much easier to hide in the dark, take drugs just to cope with each day, then watch it turn into addiction. I overcame it, but it took years.

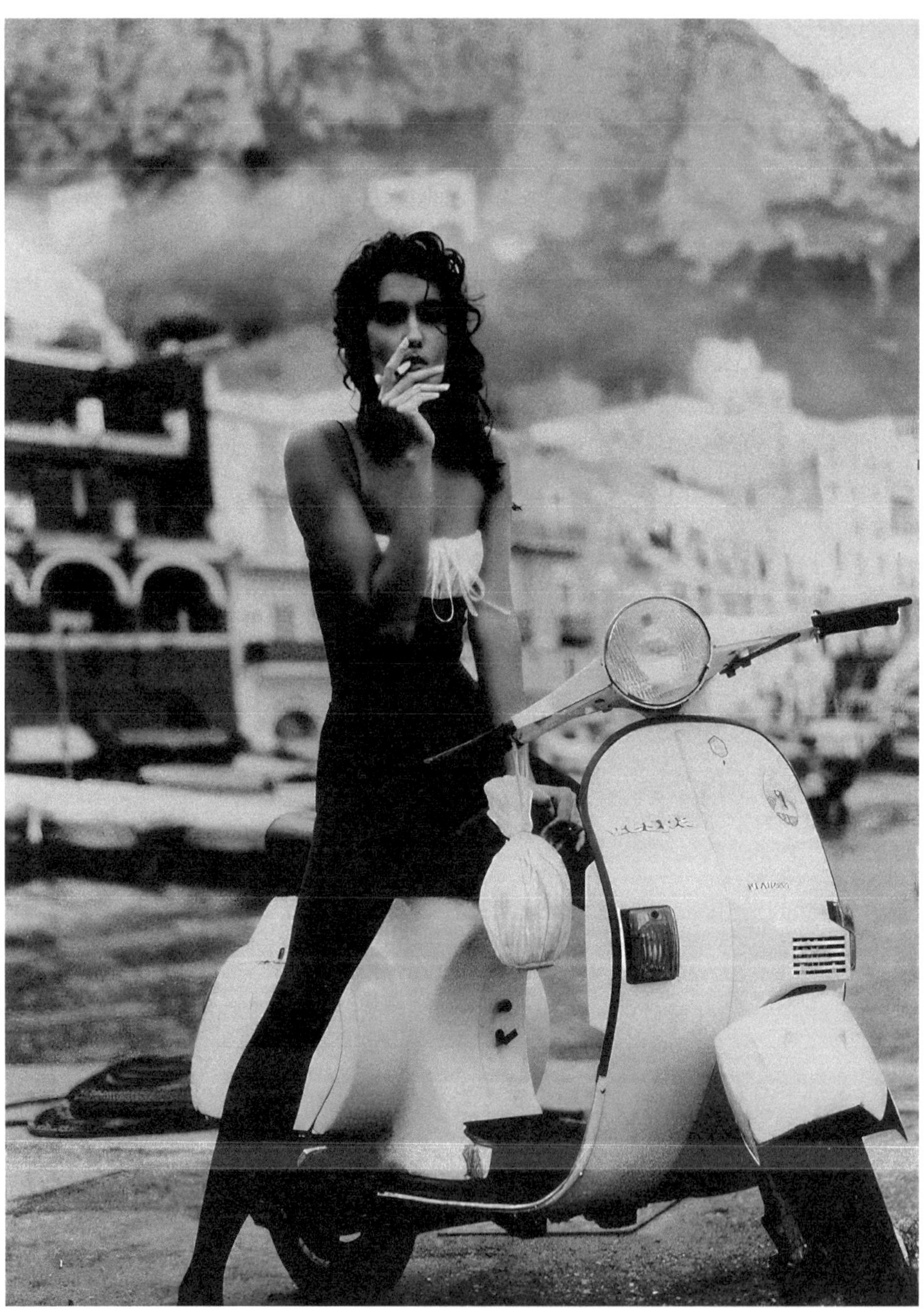

Yasmeen Ghauri for French *Vogue*, Capri, Italy

23

After my first trip to Milan in June 1981, I returned home in August. In Europe and especially in Italy, practically the entire country would close down for summer vacation, so there was no point in sticking around. Besides, I needed to make some money.

I picked up where I left off, this time as a freelance assistant helping out all the other assistants I had come to know in the years before, including my old friend Tommy. In the meantime, I was also anxiously awaiting my Italian *Vogue* tear sheets to come out in the September issue, which wouldn't arrive in New York till mid-October. Besides saving up some money for my next trip, I could also start shooting more tests in order to build up my portfolio and apply what I had learned in the short amount of time I'd spent in Italy. If anything, it was both inspiring and confidence-building that I could definitely do this. I was secure with what I knew, where to go, who I could call upon, and what I needed to do, and I had made friends.

In New York, I started working freelance in different studios with different top-notch guys. I started earning more money by building sets for advertising shootings, applying what I had picked up from working with a girlfriend who styled sets for advertising shoots a couple years before. I knew all the prop houses, lumberyards, and carpenters. Photo sets were easy because they were shot from one direction, so one main wall was what you needed, plus different props to change the scene—not much to it for me, but building sets tripled my daily income.

Of all the really good editorial photographers I got to work with, believe it or not, I learned the most about studio technique and lighting from the guys at Abraham & Straus department store in downtown Brooklyn. They had the latest of everything in equipment times ten—sometimes to the point of driving me crazy because they couldn't see the aesthetic moments; the good shots were just passing us by. But truthfully that's not what A&S wanted; aesthetically, that's not what most commercial photography wanted. They needed clean, sharp illustrated product shots, nothing too fancy. I didn't know it yet, but that fact would later become my undoing when I had to shoot very commercial work for money, and I'd hate myself and everything commercial. I fought an uphill battle mostly because I was trained differently as an artist and needed to be back working in Europe where they appreciated more forward-looking images.

In February 1982, after being home for six months, I made it back to Milan. I got my same fifteen-dollars-a-night hotel room at the haunted Hotel Bruxelles on 13 Piazza Castello with the leaky bubble skylight and the bathroom down the hall. Even though I slept in my down jacket most nights, I was happy to be back.

I went straight to Italian *Vogue* at 27 Piazza Castello to see the same art director and editor who had given me work the previous June. I showed them what I had done up to then, expecting to be greeted with open arms. Although they welcomed me into the office and allowed me to see what was coming in—I was obviously impressed with the likes of Helmut Newton, David Bailey, Denis Piel, Barbieri, etc.—there were no hints of anything coming my way. I was disappointed.

In the meantime, I made my rounds to all the modeling agencies. I got invited to dinners, parties, and clubs. I took more tests, met some advertising people. When I saw nothing was going on at Italian *Vogue*, I made an appointment with Italian *Bazaar*.

Harper's Bazaar Italia was owned by a private family who made their fortune in textiles and sold fabrics to many in the fashion field. The wife's family ran that end of the business and the husband, Peppone della Schiava, ran *Bazaar*. Peppone was known as somewhat of a Playboy type, sort of. He was definitely in it for the babes. He didn't know much about fashion photography, but he hired the right people. He had an ex-model, Lizzette Kattan, as director and Joe Eula as his illustrator—yes, that Joe Eula of Halston days! Great character, great talent, tell you more in a minute, but both Joe and Lizzette were terrific. They, in turn, had Albert Watson, Patrick Demarchelier, Jimmy Moore, and Eric Boman as their main photographers—an all-star crew if you ask me!

They also owned *Cosmopolitan Italia*, and Lizzette hired me on the spot to shoot for *Cosmo*. This may have been about a month or three weeks after I arrived back in Milan. Both Lizzette and Joe Eula (who was not only a great fashion illustrator in the '60s and '70s, but he was also later creative director for Halston) took a liking to me, and after a couple of successful *Cosmo* shootings together, they gave me a shooting to do for *Bazaar*. Joe became my coach during my time at the magazine, and I learned a lot from him about fashion. The photographers I mentioned that worked steady for *Bazaar* were all out of New York. They used all the great models, from Kim Alexis to Kelly Emberg, from Nancy Donahue to Kelly LeBrock to a young Brooke Shields. It was a hot magazine, and I was about to become the new kid on the block at the age of twenty-six.

Because *Bazaar* was privately owned by a textile family, they preferred all the shootings be done in studio where the fabrics could best be illustrated. They allowed their photographers carte blanche, but it was all studio work only. Once they found that I was pulling off shootings to their liking and living in Milan, Peppone realized he could use me to save production money by shooting in town, instead of flying teams in and out of New York. The top photographers like Albert Watson still did the featured work with the big-name girls, whereas I shot in one of *Bazaar*'s makeshift studios in Milan, with local hair, makeup, and models, plus his sometimes girlfriends. His advertisers could save on production costs, too, and buy more pages in his magazine. These same clients were buying Peppone's family's fabrics, too. They had a racket going on, Italian style. But I was shooting in good photographic company, in a high-profile magazine—that's all that mattered to me.

Eventually, I got booked for two weeks straight, every day for Italian *Bazaar* at fourteen pages a day—practically a catalog house, but what did I care? My work was coming out in the same issues as some of the best guys in the business. Granted, the girls weren't top names, but I was holding my own. Fourteen pages a day for fourteen days at a time, I had to come up with ways to light in order to make each of the shoots look different. My A&S department store training came in handy. I started putting the light everywhere I could except up my ass!

Then, I begged Lizzette and Joe to help me out. I needed a top girl to shoot, please, please, please. They understood, but we were in Milan. I didn't know that the family also owned French *Bazaar* until they took me to Paris. That's where I stood a greater chance of getting a great model. Paris was synonymous with fashion!

French *Bazaar* was located in a large apartment on Rue de Richelieu (close to the Palais Royal). That's where we set up a photo studio, and I was told that I was going to get some great model to shoot. I didn't get my hopes up, but when they told me who, I couldn't believe it. They had confirmed Iman!

I was so excited. I was pacing around as my assistants were getting the set ready and the stylist was having clothing arrive and was setting up. Hair and makeup were arriving. The place was tight. Remember, it was an apartment, and now the doorbell was constantly ringing, people coming and going. At one point, I was standing near the door when it rang, and I opened it myself. There stood Iman. She walked right past me, waved her hand, and said, "Get me a cup of coffee!" She headed toward Joe Eula and Lizzette, with big hugs and kisses, and the same with hair and makeup, and then asked, "Where's the photographer? I want to meet him." I was standing behind her, and they pointed to me. She was mortified. I was holding her cup of coffee, not knowing if she wanted milk or sugar. Everyone started laughing. I was so nervous I didn't know what the big deal was.

I loved Iman—we're still friends to this day. She told me that, when she first came to New York, she went to see Halston to audition for his runway show. She was new to this business and its lingo, and the types of people involved—the story about her being discovered by Peter Beard in Africa is true—so when she met Halston, he said, "Darling, can you walk?" He meant on the runway, of course.

She answered, "Of course I can walk. How do you think I got here?"

Iman was the first of the top girls I got to shoot, then came Janice Dickinson, and from there things took off because Italian *Bazaar* sent me to Rome a couple of times to shoot couture, which are the featured high-end (alta moda) fashion shows showcasing Italian designers. (They've since transplanted these shows to Milan.) It was an important editorial profile for a photographer to be doing.

Working for *Bazaar* in Rome, we all stayed at the Grand Hotel, which was styled somewhat from the late nineteenth century, and each photographer was given a large dining hall to set up as a studio. Some, like mine, were curtained off salons, but still very elegant. Within that space, backdrops, lighting equipment, electrical wires, including a makeshift hair, makeup, and dressing room, were all included. We would wait till after the shows that took place that same day, get the clothing rushed over to us—usually by then it was evening or already night—and shoot into the early morning hours. We were done maybe around two or three in the morning, sometimes later. Afterward, we'd be too jacked up to go to bed. We'd have some drinks and walk wherever the streets took us, and we'd have the place to ourselves, no one out at that time, desolate and magical as in the scene in *La Dolce Vita* with Marcello Mastroianni walking behind Anita Ekberg with the white cat her character, Sylvia, finds. They turn a corner to discover the Trevi Fountain, the dawn light barely coming up, and Sylvia, fully dressed, walks into the fountain for an ecstatic stroll. For me, a fledgling photographer just finding his way in Rome past midnight, familiar with Italian Neorealism films of the '50s and '60s, it was awe-inspiring.

I was with *Bazaar* from 1982 to early '84. I grew sick and tired of shooting in the studio, especially with all these great locations around. Not to seem ungrateful, I kept my mouth shut and would only make suggestions, from time to time, for us to shoot on location. But I was talking to deaf ears.

The other thing you have to know is that, because I was the youngest member of a team filled with all-stars, I wasn't getting the nicest fashions to shoot. I found some of the clothes hideous. Nevertheless, I was grateful to be at the bottom of the totem pole of a great group of photographers at that time.

Then one day, out of nowhere, I got a phone call from Italian *Vogue.* Not only did they want me to shoot for them, but to shoot the collections in Rome and on locations of my choice!

Vogue vowed to give me the aesthetic choices I needed to do my best work possible with the best fashions available, suitable to my taste and theirs—not their family business, and not who the boss was sleeping with. I was about to be given four to six pictures a day at the most, and as much time as I needed with a team of my choice, a location of my choice, within the parameters of certain designers of our choice. You couldn't shoot for both magazines; they were fierce competitors. Italian *Vogue* was considered the best magazine of the fashion industry then, and for a long time to come. If I appeared in six issues a year, it would appear to the industry that my work was everywhere because the magazine was aesthetically the fashion photography bible. I was thrilled because I preferred Italian *Vogue* for the quality of their images and the fact that they allowed their photographers greater freedom to express their style. I was also honored to be included in such illustrious company as Avedon, Hiro, David Bailey, and Helmut Newton.

Italian *Vogue* housed us at the Villa d'Este Hotel at the top of the Spanish Steps—total glamour. On nights off, I'd be invited to large dinners at Nino's, hosted by Eileen and Jerry Ford, I got to know many of the great girls. I bumped into a sixteen-year-old Christy Turlington in the hallway of the hotel; she was there with her mom, shooting with Hiro. We've been friends since. It was all new to me, and I knew it was special as it was happening. I went to all the shows and soon became familiar with the models, designers, and editors.

Soon after, I was called to shoot my first-ever cover for German *Vogue,* which was followed by shooting spreads and covers for French *Vogue* and British *Vogue*, both considered great magazines as well. I was getting choice assignments with each and every one of them, as well as the respect that came along with it. They were happy with the choices I handed in; my work was never in question, and I was working with the best girls of my generation, soon to become superstars.

In time, I came to know a lot of people in Rome. There was this one beautiful German model I knew from New York. Her name was Frauke, and she had a Roman boyfriend, Icaro, who knew everyone in town. He had introduced her to an astrologer who lived in Trastevere—across the Tiber on the Vatican side of town; it was known as the artists' quarter. Frauke knew I was into astrology and asked if I wanted to have a reading done. The astrologer's name was Mariangela and she could read your astrological chart, as well as your Tarot cards. We called for an appointment, and she asked me for my birth date, time, and place.

We met the following night. She was a good soul, a very kind person. Mariangela laid out my Tarot cards and was accurate concerning things in my past and quite accurate about the direction—what I aspired to. The Arts were all over my chart, as they were with other readings with other astrologers, each having one specific piece of information the others didn't have. When the reading was done and the cards were still spread out, she stared at them, then back to the chart of my planets. She said, "I have a friend in New York City you should meet. I think you two would make great friends, a lasting friendship of a very long time, with a past life connection. He's an artist. His name is Francesco Clemente."

I knew of Clemente. Just that past winter I had seen a magnificent show of his work at the Mary Boone Gallery on West Broadway. His work has a mysticism that attracted me. He was becoming a superstar and a darling of Andy Warhol. "Call him when you go back to New York," she said and gave me his contact info. I'm used to people being so guarded about giving out phone numbers, especially of anyone known to the public, but this was Rome, and Mariangela just read me my chart and felt she now knew me.

When I landed at JFK, I walked past a newsstand on the way to collect my bags and saw Francesco Clemente's photo on the cover of *Time* magazine! What a strange coincidence—or was it? The signs couldn't have been more obvious. I waited a couple of weeks before I called. Francesco picked up and invited me over to his studio, not far from my loft. We had coffee and began a long friendship, as Mariangela predicted. He's been family to me for the last thirty-five years and is also my son Nick's godfather! Thank you, Mariangela, and Rome.

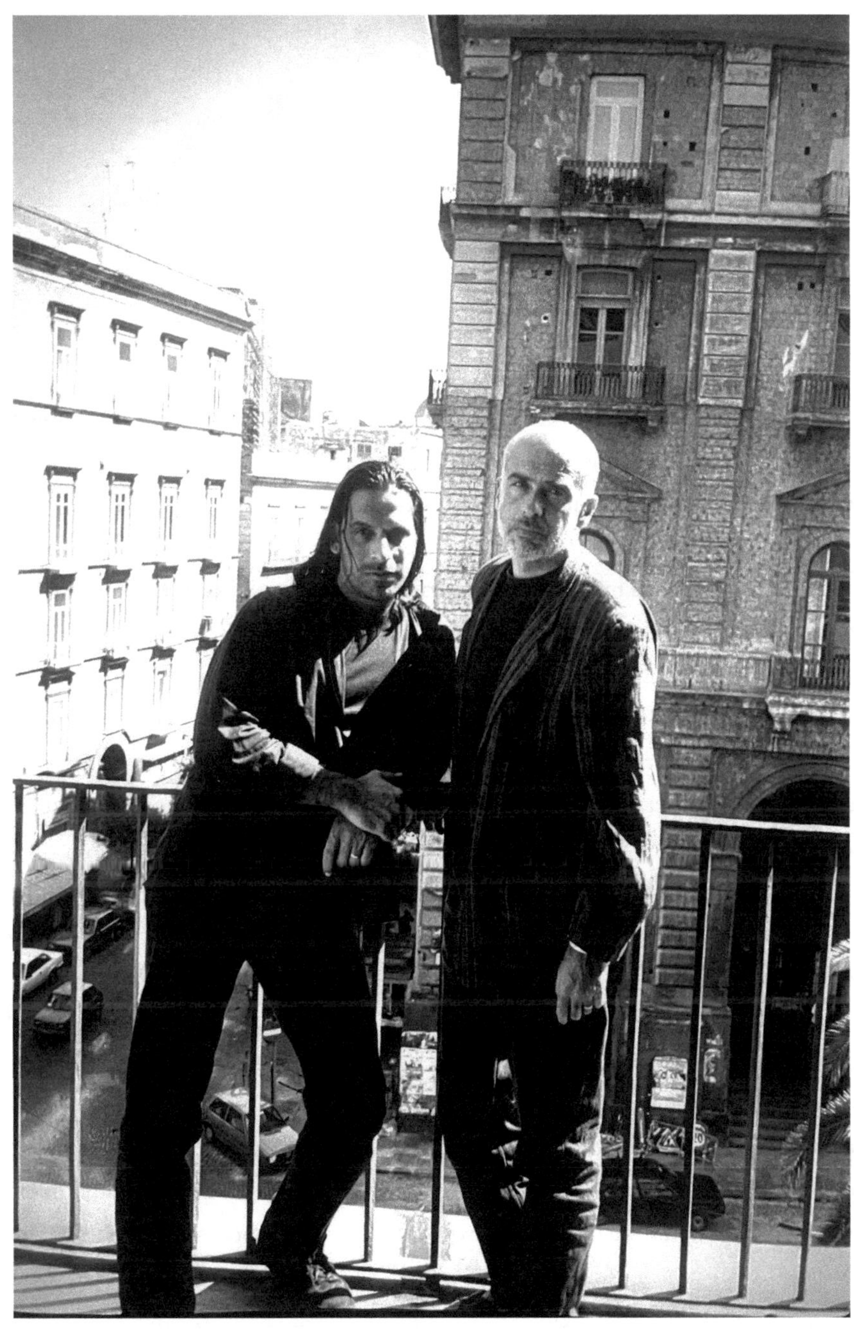

Sante and Francesco Clemente, Naples, Italy

24

Along with some friends, I made my first trip to Paris in early 1982. One of the first things on my to-do list, after visiting some modeling agencies, was to go to French *Vogue*, even though I only had the two double-page tear sheets from the Italian *Vogue* Beauty story I had shot the previous summer.

Pictures published in a magazine were referred to as tear sheets because you literally tore the sheet or page, with your pictures and your name on it, out of the magazine. There was a long wait from the time you shot the pictures until they appeared in print, and the differences between the magazine page and a print you had made and put in your portfolio were obvious. On the tear sheet, there was always some kind of text, even if it was just a brief description placed in the corner. If you were lucky, your picture remained untouched with just your name in the corner, which usually meant the facing page featured twice as much type. These were not photo magazines; they were fashion magazines designed to sell clothes. European editors, in general, had a higher regard for photography than the American consumer magazines, including *Vogue*, whose audience, according to American editors, needed literal guidance to be persuaded to buy.

In general, both clients and magazines were always impressed with good tear sheets, especially covers from a *Vogue*, *Bazaar*, or *Elle*. That *Vogue* logo over the cover shot of a famous model was your seal of approval, your five-star Michelin trophy. What it really meant was that someone else had initially taken a chance on you with great confidence. If you shot for one of those high-profile magazines, it was guaranteed that everyone in the industry, both in editorial and in advertising, would see it. Your star would rise as more of those shootings got published.

Way before that lucky star shone on me, I had to schlep my portfolio around Europe.

When I first went up to French *Vogue*, I heard the same old riff that everyone would repeat, "Nice work, but come back when you have more tear sheets." *How am I supposed to get tear sheets if you don't give me a chance?* I'd get a smile and a pat on the back, and a "don't let the door hit you on the ass on your way out."

It became annoying. I had to figure out how I could get them to see my pictures in a different light, how they might be visually convinced that my pictures were good enough for their publication. It took a while for me to grasp the fact that everyone, including art directors, needed to see my images in the context of their magazine. It was wrong to assume that, because "art" was somewhere in their title, they knew anything about art or had the vision to recognize it. The top talents in art direction could design to enhance your pictures, but 90 percent of them simply didn't have the imagination. I had to get creative and come up with a way to convince that 90 percent.

Looking through the magazines, especially the European ones of the 1980s, I noticed that many great spreads would have a picture on the right-hand page, along with a romantic story on the left, written in the most beautiful calligraphy. If it were about Dior, for example, the *D* would be extra-large in a wonderful script followed by the story that would fill the page. Since I had a degree in art direction and—looking back—the balls, I decided to recycle those beautiful calligraphic pages from whatever magazine I found them in, mostly French and Italian *Vogues*. Since everyone wanted to see tear sheets, I inserted these elegant calligraphic pages on the left-hand side in my portfolio and placed one of my photos on the right. The mocked-up double-page spread now resembled the beautiful layouts in French and Italian *Vogues*, only with *my* picture on the facing page. I then interspersed several of these spreads throughout my portfolio.

Months later, I went back to French *Vogue* to meet with the same art director, with the calligraphic pages in my book that I knew he had designed—because most were from that year's issues. He looked at them, and when he looked up at me, I smiled and said, "Ya, see, we already worked together and look what a great job we did!"

He started laughing and said, "That's great. I like you. Let's talk." He showed my book to other people in the art department, and they all gave me a thumbs-up. That started my career at French *Vogue*.

Everyone was super impressed when I got back to the States with that same portfolio. It helped that most people couldn't read French or Italian. I still had a lot to learn in general, and I absorbed everything I could through every available source.

My first *Vogue* cover assignment was for German *Vogue*. I was twenty-seven years old. The model, Hanna Schygulla, was a celebrity, and we would shoot in Paris.

"That's fantastic. I can't wait. I'm so excited to meet her. Oh, my God!"

When I hung up the phone I was like, *Who the fuck is Hanna Schygulla?* I immediately did my homework. Hanna Schygulla was the muse of director Rainer Werner Fassbinder, one of Germany's great post-war filmmakers—she was a mega star! I mainly remember what a nice and unpretentious person she was. I wish I had taken the opportunity to better educate myself beforehand. I tried never to make that mistake again.

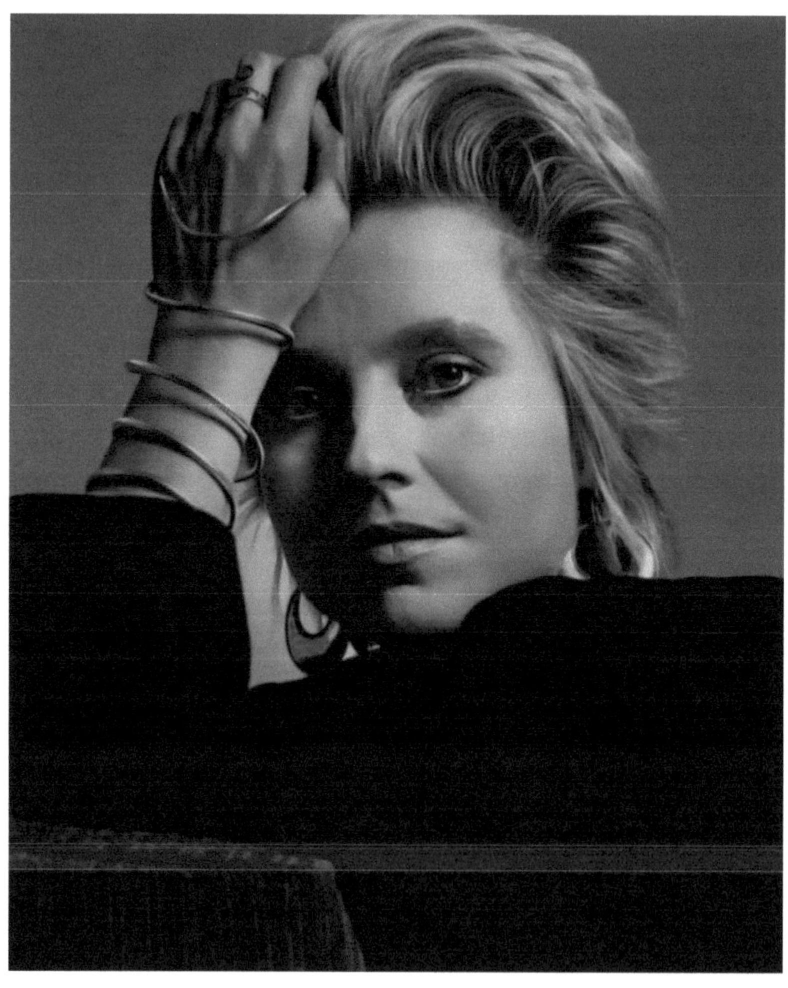

Hanna Schygulla for German *Vogue*

25

When I was seven years old, I had to go to church every Sunday with my mother to prepare for my first communion—my first rite of passage into the church, whereby I'd confess all my sins and symbolically receive the body of Christ in the form of a wafer at Mass. Christ offered bread to his disciples at the Last Supper to remember Him by. The sins of a seven-year-old were simple, like throwing snowballs at your grandmother (She was not a nice old lady!). After that, I would continue religious instructions toward my confirmation at the age of thirteen.

By thirteen, I'd already had years' worth of preparation (Confirmation is the equivalent of a bar mitzvah and the Catholic rite of passage to becoming a man in the eyes of God and the Church.). Again I confessed my sins, which were much worse than a seven-year-old's. For discipline, the church unleashed their more sadistic nuns on me. These were the nuns that lobbied for the return of the Inquisition.

I was now a man, and one of my first acts as a man was to stop going to church. I would sometimes attend Mass, on certain Holy days, out of a sense of obligation to my mom. Being an only child came with an invisible force field of guilt around the house, so I had to go to family dinners on Christmas, New Year's Eve, Thanksgiving, and the rest. I was too young to go out partying with friends, and I never had money anyway.

By the age of sixteen, these obligations increased tenfold with the passing of my father. I became the man of the house and was expected to accompany my mom to family gatherings. By this time my siblings had already moved out. One brother to Staten Island, where he was absorbed into his wife's large family. My sister and other brother had moved to Florida with their families. All those large family gatherings dissolved, and I was left with my uncle Dominick, my mother's brother, his wife, Anita, and their three very young children.

At first, we'd alternate homes for the holidays; then, it became my uncle Dominick's house in perpetuity. My uncle was the silent type, and he, his wife, my mother, and I would sit around the holiday table like four mooks. Uncle Dominick liked having the TV on at dinnertime, which was obnoxious to me, but the one time I asked to shut it off, the silence was so depressing that I turned it back on.

At weddings, it was me and my mom; funerals, me and my mom. Holidays, me and my mom. This went on forever, and sometimes, I was embarrassed by it. If I had a girlfriend, she wasn't invited because she wasn't my wife. I began to feel like one of those distant cousins I would occasionally meet: forty years old and still living with their mothers, real mamas' boys. I started hating the holidays, especially Christmas and New Year's Eve!

It might've been August but if someone mentioned Christmas, I'd immediately get depressed. I'd have anxiety attacks at the sight of Santa and his reindeer, no matter what time of the year it was. With the days getting dark at 4:30 p.m. and the cold weather, I'd start feeling lonely by the first of November and was ready to go into full mook at the sight of a turkey!

My personal breakthrough came years later, when, on a cold December night, I had dinner with friends at Raoul's. Everyone was talking about their plans for the Christmas and New Year's holidays. I started drinking more heavily. The only thing that saved me from despair was the stunning girl sitting across from me. She had come with my friends. I had never met her before. Her features were strikingly beautiful, but I couldn't make out what part of the world she was from. Maybe Scandinavian—or Siberian? I was mesmerized. She was fairly quiet, but I switched seats with a friend sitting next to her and started chatting her up.

Her name was Tatjana Patitz. She said she lived in Sweden but was German—although she looked more exotic than that. She had arrived in New York City not too long before that night. Tatjana had the reserve of a Garbo mixed with the beauty of an extraterrestrial. I couldn't guess her age, which turned out to be nineteen, but she looked like a woman. We hit it off. I was in my late twenties, and my career was just taking off. Hers was about to go through the stratosphere.

Women her age were already making far more money than me, jetting around the world as often as I took the F train uptown. Jumping on a plane at the last minute was part of the job description.

I asked her what she was doing for the holidays. She said she was going back to Sweden to spend Christmas with her parents; after that, no plans. "Same here," I said, "Christmas with my mom and family, then nothing much." Everyone I knew was leaving town, either for vacation or for their homes visiting family. "I'd love to go somewhere warm for a couple of weeks, maybe Jamaica."

She perked up. "Sounds great!"

"How about we go to Negril after Christmas?"

She enthusiastically replied, "Yes! I'm leaving for Sweden in two days, so let's plan it before I leave." We got kind of giggly about it.

Three weeks later, we met up at JFK for our flight to Kingston, Jamaica. Once there, I rented a car, and we drove for about two hours to Negril. In the mid-1980s, it was mostly country roads, and it was beautiful. All my holiday blues and anxieties were gone. I had found the cure—no more mook for me!

Negril, at the time, was a down-to-earth place, consisting of small and family-like beach hotels, and just a few larger ones around. I was lucky to get any accommodations at all—it was high season, and everything was booked. I got one room for eight days with two beds side by side; it seemed like the last one available in Negril.

When we finally got there, I had to check the address twice—this couldn't be it! We were shocked and ready to cry. It was a real back-alley, shantytown shithole, with rusted tin siding, trash cans littered about and two beat-up cars, making it look like a junkyard. I only realized later that the only spot available for my car was back behind the kitchen where they threw out the garbage, which made things look ten times worse.

After we checked into our suite, I saw the lighting fixture was a simple bare light bulb hanging down in the middle of the room. I put down my bag and acted like this was a cool place with lots of charm. I unpacked my swim trunks, and when I turned around, I saw Tatjana in front of our closed door. She was holding her bag to her chest like it was the last life preserver on the Titanic. She looked terrorized.

"C'mon," I said, "we can tidy up, put a sarong around the light bulb and make the place our own. You have to look on the bright side."

I thought I'd give her some privacy and told her I'd be right outside. The beach was gorgeous. I put my trunks on in the bathroom and headed out for a swim.

The beach calmed us down. Clear water, clean sand, swimming, and the sun—it couldn't have been better. The hotel did have charm and looked much better from the beach side. That evening, we had a good dinner of barbeque jerk chicken and Red Stripe beers. Not so bad, and the locals were really friendly. We found our comfort zone until it was time to go to bed. Once we got in the room, she looked at me like a sheep going to the slaughter. Oh, boy! I quickly separated the beds, almost using sign language to make things clear. I said I was going for a walk, so she could have some space, use the bathroom, and get ready for bed.

"Let's just hang out, and I'm not expecting anything but that. Besides, I didn't need to come all the way to Jamaica to get laid." That got a big chuckle out of her, and she lowered her guard. As I went out, she said, "Hurry back. I don't want to be alone."

The next day at breakfast, I was getting the silent treatment and the cold shoulder. I had no idea why, and so much so, it was starting to piss me off. We went to the beach and ran into a bunch of people we knew from the fashion business.

What a relief. In no time, a joint appeared, then drinks, then more joints. Some people had mushrooms. They told us about Miss Brown's Ganja Shop down the road, where you could get anything you wanted to smoke or eat—she was famous for her brownies. I was warned that the brownies could get you really fucked-up. I thought, *Really fucked-up? I can do with really fucked-up right now.*

After an hour or so went by, Tatjana wanted to go to Miss Brown's. "Why not?" I said, so off we went to Miss Brown's, and I bought some ganja. Tatjana was fixed on getting mushrooms and brownies. We went back to the hotel and smoked some Jamaican gold and ate some mushrooms. Back at the beach, I went for a swim, then lay in the sun. It took a little time for the mushrooms to start coming on. I was beginning to feel outside myself and observing everything around me, but then things were beginning to look weird, and I was afraid it was going in the wrong direction!

I started to feel nauseous, so I went back to the room in case I spewed, which I did. Once done, I closed the bathroom door and started feeling really good and began seeing colors and auras. Then, I made a big mistake and looked at myself in the mirror. My face was moving independently of me, and it freaked me out. I started holding my face so it wouldn't go anywhere. Tatjana walked in; she needed to use the bathroom, and that was the only thing that got me away from the mirror.

She, meanwhile, was feeling great. "The sky so blue," she said, "the water soft and nurturing" and a bunch of other new age-y stuff. She was really feeling it. After a while, she grew tired and decided to take a nap, so she got into her bed. By now, I was really tripping. "Don't leave me alone!" she said. I stayed through her entire nap, in a corner of the room where I could hold up both walls.

Tatjana woke up in a very dreamy, peaceful state, while I was glued to the walls. She described a dream in which they tested her blood and found it contained a chemical substance that could cure every disease in the world. "I was the only one with that blood," she said. "Imagine . . ." Her focus was so clear, and she said again, "The only one in the world. I was standing on a tall mountain when I saw this." She also told me that, at nineteen, she was way more intelligent than me. She was obviously flying high.

I put on my Carl Jung hat and began to access the symbolism of her dream. She's on a mountain, which meant she's above it all. Her blood being the only blood that could save the world told me she thought she was unique. All that silent treatment was contempt for me because she's smarter than me—that had to be it!

I spent the rest of the day on the beach coming off the fucking mushrooms. I needed to get away, so I made a right on the beach when she made a left. I lay on my back on the sand with my towel over my face, hoping it would stop the hallucinations I was having. I don't recall how long I was there, but when I woke up, the front of my body was burnt, and my face was white.

We met back at the room. She had had a great day, and she wanted to do more mushrooms. *Fuck you,* I thought! But since I was a schmuck, I said, "Yeah sure, why not."

She took out the brownies. I ate a very small piece; I wanted to stay mild. She ate an entire mushroom, and half a brownie. *Oh, boy!*

An hour later, missy was having a bad trip and feeling sick. I went out and got her a pizza—that's what helped bring me down earlier. She ate some pizza and wanted to lie down. I started laughing. Ten minutes later, I felt something coming on. Damn, I had eaten a tiny piece of that brownie, and I was starting to get fucked-up all over again.

A while later, I was standing against a wall, facing the toilet. I don't know how I got there. The color of the room was a tropical blunt green, and the toilet was looking at me, and there's the light bulb hanging from the ceiling that was painted red. When I looked down, the floor was black but seemed like a void to me, like outer space. I managed to get out of there after having struggled with the bathroom door—pushing and pushing until I finally pulled, and I was out. Why was I not supposed to leave the room? Then, I remembered that I was on guard duty; Tatjana was frightened to sleep alone. It was 7:30 p.m., and I was meant to wake her at 8:30. At 8:20 p.m., I poked her with my finger a couple of times, and she didn't respond. I saw that she was breathing, so I let her sleep.

Back in the tropical blunt green room, I again got sick and violently threw up while trying to gargle. I opened the door—Tatjana sat up, screamed, then fell back to sleep. I closed the door.

I woke up in the morning, sitting on the toilet with my head against the wall. My legs and ass had fallen asleep. Tatjana needed to go to the bathroom, but she didn't realize I had spent the night in there. I put on my trunks and grabbed some coffee and some toast with more coffee. We were both still feeling the effects. We headed for the beach, and I told her I'd catch up in a bit. I grabbed another coffee and went and sat next to this Jamaican guy I had met the day before.

He said to me, "You hangin' out with the finest woman on the beach."

I told him never judge a book by its cover.

He commented again on how good-looking my woman was—best on the beach! "But why she look so scared all the time, always covering up, looking frightened? She must be young, but she looks like a woman."

"Yeah, that must be it . . ."

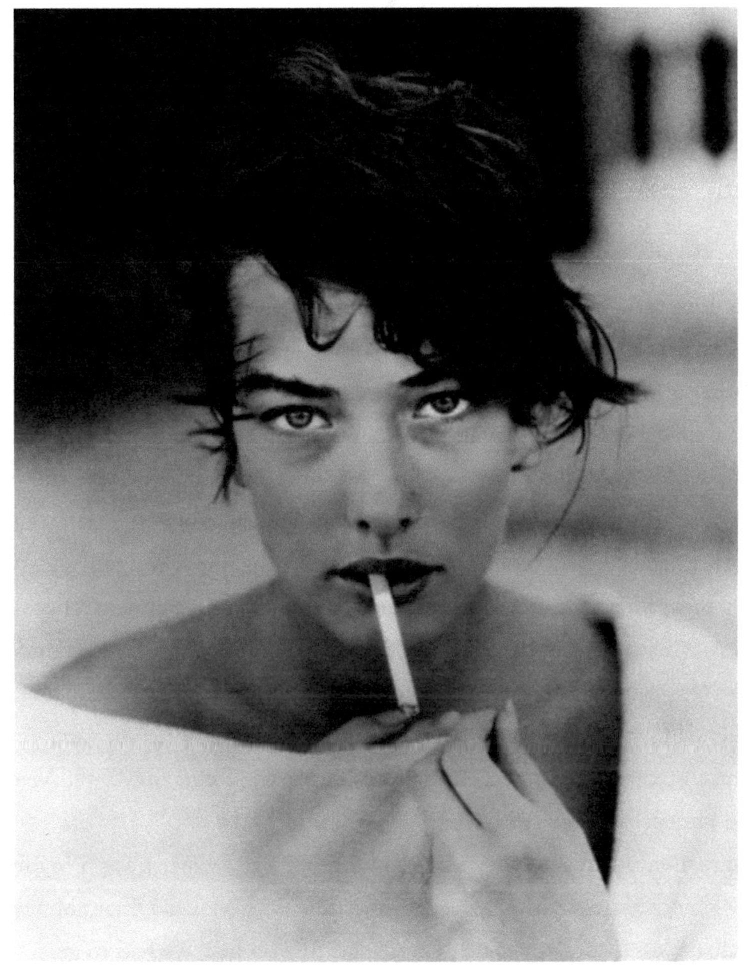

Tatjana Patitz, Negril, Jamaica

26

After a couple of years spent on and off in Milan at the beginning of my career, I came back home to New York in the mid-80s with my German girlfriend, Martina, who was a model and somewhat of a tomboy by nature.

Before we left Europe, we visited her family in Hamburg, and out of nowhere, she decided to buy a BMW 650 motorcycle—only she didn't buy a spare helmet; they were out of stock in my size. We rode around the city, and she taught me how to ride.

Her father had been a doctor in the German army during WWII and a POW in a Russian camp for five years after the war. He loaned me his old army helmet. When it came time to go back to Milan, she suggested taking the bike on the train to Switzerland and riding through the Alps, with me on the back. I couldn't wear the German helmet for obvious reasons, but her dad gave me an old American football helmet, minus the face guard. Europe and the Alps in January, I don't recommend it—I froze my nuts off. We survived that ride to Italy and returned to New York City for the summer.

I told my mom I had a girlfriend but had forgotten to tell her I was bringing her home with me. My mom almost fainted when I showed up with Martina unannounced—and on a motorcycle no less. Mom acted as if I were cheating on her. We had to get a place of our own ASAP, so we soon found a loft to rent on Greene Street in SoHo.

After we had settled in, I made an appointment with the art director of Andy Warhol's *Interview*. The magazine's office was in a former Con Edison building on East 33rd Street at the time. There I met *Interview*'s art director, Marc Balet. I had great tear sheets in my portfolio from Italian *Bazaar* and Italian *Vogue*. He called in Kate Harrington, the magazine's stylist/editor; both Marc and Kate loved my work. Immediately, we started planning fashion shoots for the magazine.

Kate also showed me around the offices, and of course, I was impressed. At some point, we bumped into Andy Warhol himself. He had been painting in another part of the building. Kate introduced us, and Andy said, "Gee, that's great." I was besides myself meeting him; I shook his hand and said something like, "Ne, ne, ne, nice to meet you."

This was my first job in New York. Both Marc Balet and Kate Harrington are still friends of mine today.

Andy would occasionally take a small group of us young, good-looking kids out with him to restaurant openings, to galleries, or to places like the Playboy Club. He always had his camera and tape recorder at the ready. One night a week, Andy, his associate publisher and close friend Paige Powell, and the writer Tama Janowitz would organize blind dates for themselves. Tama would set up Andy; Andy would set up Paige; and Paige would set up Tama. I somehow made the list twice. The first time, I was Tama's date, and we all went to the Playboy Club on 59th Street for some event, then back downtown to a gallery opening, onward to SOB's (Sounds of Brazil) on Varick Street. We spent some memorable nights there.

One day, Kate asked me to accompany her to Andy's townhouse uptown in the Sixties near Lexington Avenue to pick up a package. I was really excited to visit. When we walked in, I don't know what I was expecting, but I was surprised to see traditional nineteenth-century furniture. There were cardboard boxes of all sizes everywhere—what Andy called "time capsules." He would drop into a box anything he'd picked up that day or week, whether they be drink tickets from Studio 54 or a magazine or a random toy. The box would then be sealed and put in storage, not to be opened till a specific date in the future. Like a hundred years from then. That was roughly the idea. I remember seeing a Cy Twombly painting and other artwork hanging in a room that was kind of dark, but none of Andy's work, and wondered why the lights weren't turned on. Maybe Andy hadn't paid the Con Ed bill—he was rumored to be cheap.

Kate then brought me upstairs and showed me Andy's bedroom. There was a nineteenth-century four-poster bed and a standing crucifix on the side table. A beautiful little painting (on the side table? Or was it on the wall?) depicted a Madonna and child; from its style, it appeared as if it could have been painted anywhere from the late Renaissance to the nineteenth century. Andy had a strong religious background, and I naturally related to it, since I had been raised by the Virgin Mary herself. Kate told me later that Andy stopped by a church to light a candle and say a prayer each day on his walks downtown to work. Kate also had that Catholic thing going on—Irish Catholic. She had met Andy through her adopted godfather, Truman Capote. Truman was close to Kate's father, his lover to be exact, unbeknownst to Kate at the time, and they came from a family of NYC cops. We all shared that strict Catholic upbringing, yet we were all connected in such an unconventional environment.

Kate and I put together lots of fashion shoots. Once, we shot at the Palladium on 14th Street, which, at the time, was *the* hotspot. Studio 54 had closed because its owners, Steve Rubell and Ian Schrager, had been jailed for tax evasion. When they got out, they opened the Palladium. Like 54, it was in an old theater built in the 1920s, and like 54, it was run by entrepreneurs. When I was sixteen, the Palladium had been a music venue where I had seen Cheech and Chong and the Grateful Dead, too.

Rubell and Schrager did a great job of transforming the place into a nightclub. One of the main lounges was named the Mike Todd Room. Along the wide bar, slightly above and behind a row of bottles, was a long, narrow Jean-Michel Basquiat painting. I remember the black, red, and white colors. There was another large Basquiat on the center wall; it was gorgeous. Francesco Clemente had painted a beautiful mural on the domed ceiling, and Keith Haring had created a mural on the huge stage wall in front of the dance floor. It was 1985. These guys were way ahead of the curve.

We shot in one of the rooms that had dining tables with candles on vintage candelabras, with wax dripping down. The walls were distressed; the ambience was sexy. It was one of my more memorable early shoots for *Interview*—everything shot in black and white. All I did was bring one tungsten light on a stand; I used their lights to fill in. One camera, one lens, one assistant. Always kept it simple, as with my street photography. People often asked, "Where's all your equipment?" I'd show them my one small camera bag. "This is it."

Years later, one of my favorite photographers, Helmut Newton, told me how he would show up at an advertising shoot needing four pictures that the client had requested. He used a Rolleiflex camera with 120 Tri-X film that had twelve frames per roll. He'd shoot all four setups on one roll of film consisting of three frames per shot! "However many rolls you shoot, you will have to edit them later, and that's a job unto itself. Shoot less, work less later!"

Another assignment that came through *Interview* was a trip to London in 1984 to do portraits of an award-winning designer, just graduating from Saint Martin's School of Art and Design. That was John Galliano. We shot him in and around his first studio. I remember he was highly influenced by the Japanese designers who were revolutionizing fashion at the time. You could tell he was going to be great.

One of Andy Warhol's mottos was, "Give them what they don't know they want yet." He may have gotten that from Diana Vreeland, the famed grand dame of fashion editors in the '60s–'70s and the editor-in-chief of American *Vogue*. She would even show up to Studio 54. But magazines like *Interview* were on the cutting edge, discovering great new talent way before anyone, like Galliano in this case.

In those early Palladium days, New York City was an exciting place to be. As long as you handed in great work, it didn't matter how you got it. Anything went. Lots of room for experimentation and lots of respect for the photographer. I always had fun working with Kate, and for *Interview*. It was a great time to be a photographer.

A mere three years later, in 1987, Warhol was dead, and one year after that, Basquiat.

You realized every day was the end of one era and the beginning of a new one. This was the beginning of mine, and as a photographer, I conceived of my role as a witness of my times, using the most poetic means possible. That was and is the responsibility I gladly took on, and seeing it that way gave my work more meaning.

I've come to recognize that no particular era is better than another. We just have less of a perspective when we're experiencing events in real time. Every generation creates its own icons and has its own heroes. With the past, things and people have already been identified for us and belong to that generation that experienced it. Our current icons are walking around, and the current generation will base their identity on them; they're being discovered as we speak. I've tried to stay in the present and live it, compare it to nothing and witness it all. Otherwise, as an artist, you will easily lose sight of the moment you're in.

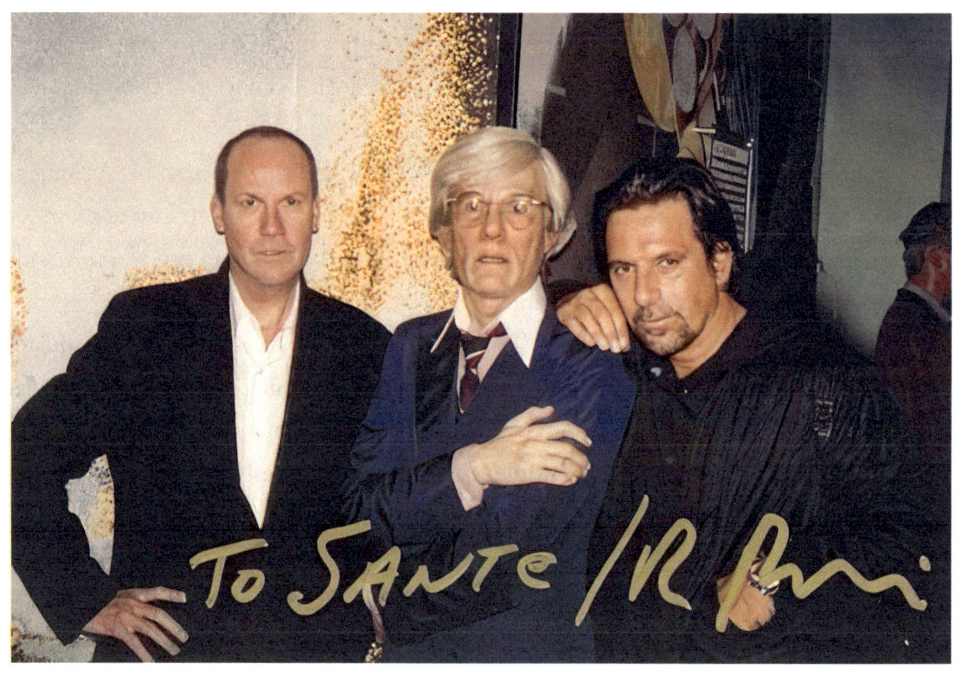

Richard Prince, Andy Warhol (wax), and Sante at Madame Tussauds for German *Vogue*

27

One time, British *Vogue* sent me on a shoot to Russia. Back then, it was still the Soviet Union, and St. Petersburg was called Leningrad. We booked Helena Christensen; I'd always wanted to work with her because I loved her look. On the first day, for the first shot, we scheduled a double page of Helena in the vast plaza in front of the Hermitage. I normally preferred closer, more intimate shots, but it was understandable doing this wide shot as an opener. It was an iconic location, and we had a small window of time before the streets got busy. I figured out my angle while Helena was getting her last touchups. I explained to her that she would walk toward me and I would shoot; plus I gave her some other basic directions. She was barely acknowledging my existence, but I knew she was a pro, so that didn't bother me. I walked her to her starting point, ran back to my spot, and gave her the *Go!* sign. And she just stood there, not reacting, arms folded and looking off in the distance, totally ignoring me. Okay, I figured she didn't get my instructions, so I ran up to her and explained it all over again. She spoke perfect English, so no problems there; I didn't understand what there was not to get. I politely asked if anything was misunderstood, was anything wrong?

She looked me up and down, and in a somewhat snotty tone, said, "Oh, please, I know all about you. You fuck all the models."

"What the fuck? I don't even know you. How could you say something like that?"

With her arms still folded, she just looked away.

"Helena, what the hell? We have a shooting to do here! Let's get to work."

People were starting to gather 'round, and they were going to get in my way. *Let's shoot and get the hell out of here.* I repeated my directions to Helena. I ran back to my spot and gave her the signal to go! She looked away again and did not move.

The editor asked, "What's going on? Is there a problem?"

"Nothing," I said, and asked Bob, who was my friend and the hairdresser to come and help me out.

We went over to Helena, and she said to me, "I know your type. You got a big mouth and a small dick."

I looked at Bob, and he looked at me, and we were both like, "What???" Both our jaws dropped, and I thought, *Wow, this girl must be fucked up*. "Bob, talk to her please."

Bob didn't know what to say.

I left him with her for a couple of minutes to tease her hair. After a few blah blahs, I was back, and she pulled the same stunt again! Now I was seething, and I went right up in her face, teeth clenched, and said, "Listen, I've fucking had it with you. Try it one more fucking time and I'll embarrass you right here in front of this crowd! Got it? Don't test me, goddamn it."

My little speech must have given her either a scare or a hard-on.

Bob said, "She's obviously into you, man. She's going to throw that at you until she gets what she wants. Some girls like to play that game!"

"I don't know what the fuck you're talking about."

"I'm telling you, mark my words."

We eventually got the shot after that mini-nightmare and left for the next location. That was only the first shot, with four more shots scheduled for that day, on the first morning of a four-day shoot. This turned out to be one of those iconographic shootings for us all, visually memorable with plenty happening!

Some of the best work comes out from the most twisted scenarios. It's when things are running too smoothly that something goes wrong, and most likely, the pictures are crap. Not a rule, just an observation.

For those who might be wondering what kind of camera or lens or film I used, my answer is "Who gives a fuck! Any camera will do; it's what happens in front of the camera that counts."

Try to imagine capturing the sexual tension alone on that first shot. Get the moment, I say, and the picture will compose itself. If the exposure is wrong but you caught the moment, well then, that's the shot, and you're a genius. That's my method of photography—and FYI, I use a normal 50mm lens, so I can be close enough to hear my subject breathe . . .

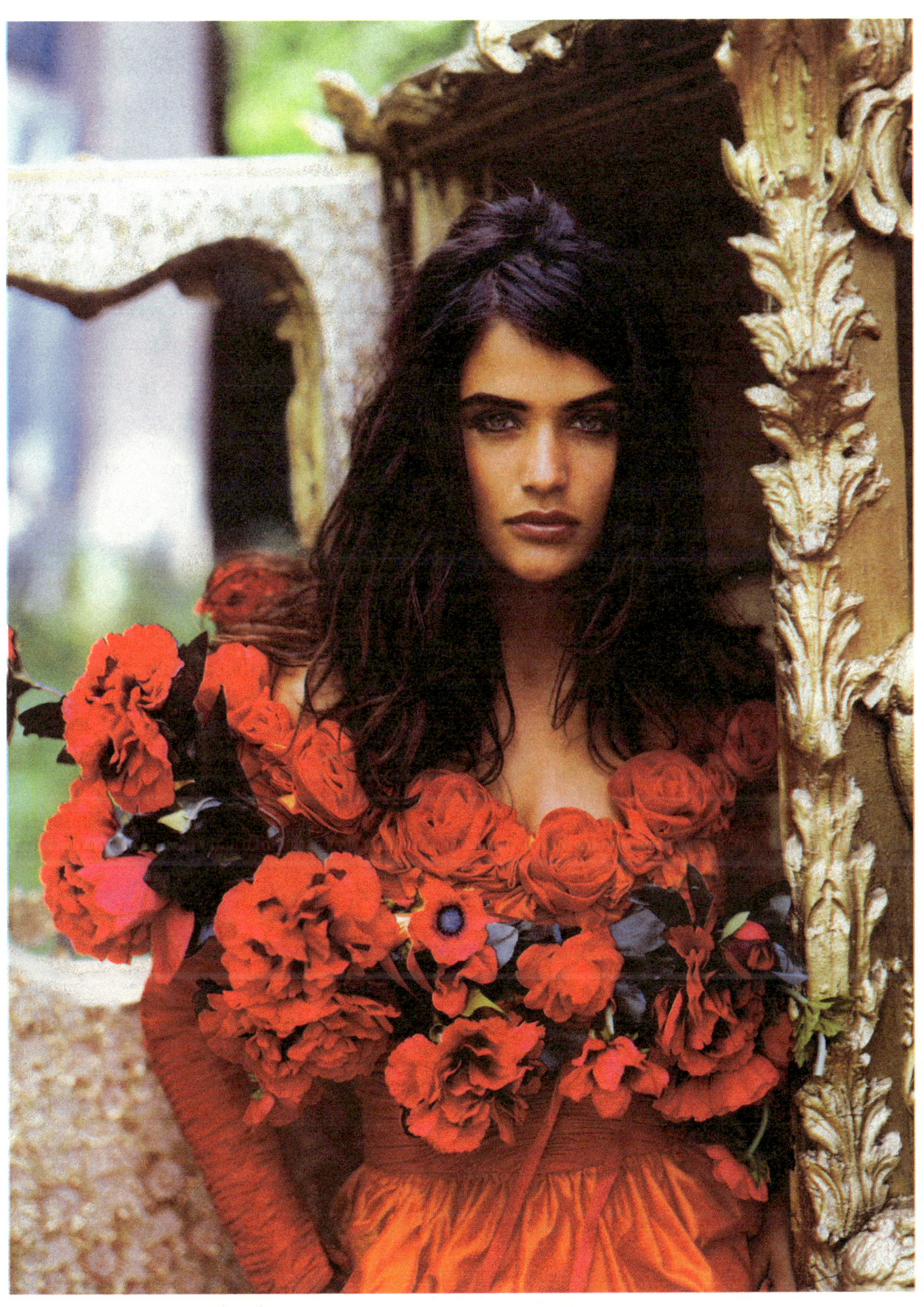

Helena Christensen, Pushkin Palace, St. Petersburg, Russia, for British *Vogue*

That night, Helena decided to join Bob and me at the bar before dinner. We ordered a round—the drinks were strong—then we went to eat. This was Russia during Soviet times—dinner wasn't gourmet; it was inedible except for the boiled potatoes. And that wasn't tap water they poured in our glasses before dinner—it was straight vodka! So every night, for the rest of the trip, we got shit-faced, and there was no being uptight about anything. Either you got wasted every night at dinner for lack of proper food or anything better to do, or you went to bed very early! Most of us chose the former. That's all I remember, sort of.

After dinner—I really can't remember which night; we were all very drunk—we noticed some pretty girls hanging out outside the hotel. Bob and my assistant Jonathan went to talk to them. There were three of them. They said they were students, and only one could speak broken English. I told Bob to invite them in for drinks, but he said the hotel wouldn't let them in. Instead, the girls invited us to go out with them.

I checked with the concierge, Viktor, a friendly guy, and asked him if it was okay to invite the three students inside for drinks with us.

"Ha! Students? Then, you and I har professor! Ha-ha! *Nyet* student, my friend. Hotel not allow. You see big vuman outside? She drive truck daytime; she crush balls with one hand but nice lady, dee utter skinny one her daughter, graduate Polytech University, she drive truck too. Go out vit dem, nice people, iz okay, show you good time, take taxi from hotel, no problem."

"Thanks, Viktor!" I gave Bob the OK.

Helena had overheard everything and said, "I'm coming with you."

"Sure, why not!"

I ran upstairs to grab some rubles, and we jumped in the convoy of mini-taxis. We were already shit-faced from drinking that table vodka, and soon, we stopped at a bar with our new *student* friends. When we walked in, everybody waved hello to the girls. It seemed they were regulars. I got a better look at them: they were still pretty, but they certainly were not students. I slurred something to that effect, and Helena just looked at me and said, "You're so stupid."

Bob was all giddy, and my young assistant—a science student lookalike—now looked more like a kid in an ice cream store. Helena latched onto me like we were lovers, and the girls ordered more drinks.

A bit later, Bob came over and said the students wanted to take us back to their place.

"Bob, these girls are prostitutes," I said.

"No way! They're students."

I looked at him. "You're so stupid."

Now my gang was egging me on, and Helena really wanted to go to their place as well. The girls loved Helena—you could see how they were checking her out. I didn't blame them; she was smokin' hot!

I paid for our bottle service, though I never saw a bottle, and we left. But before we took off to their apartment, I needed to talk to Bob.

"Bob, as fucked-up as I am, I ain't fucking any of these girls. Who knows where they've been?"

Bob said, "Come on, let's just have fun."

"Yeah, that's all I'm saying."

We climbed into the taxis again and off we went. By now, it was around 10:30 p.m., and in the summer, it never got dark; we were so far north that midnight looked like dawn or dusk. Out the car window, I could see we had left the city proper and were driving through the woods. Helena was squeezing my arm, and then we started making out in the taxi, with one of the Russian girls watching us from the front seat. That came out of left field, but I guess Bob was right.

The woods were getting thicker now. No idea where the fuck we were; no one's going to find us out here. Then we came to a clearing, and all around were blocks and blocks of housing projects, really ugly Brut architecture. All the lights were out, except for one ground-floor apartment with a red light glowing in the twilight. It was their apartment. More vodka, music, and dancing. It's a party in our own private red-light district apartment!

Once inside, I saw Bob talking to the girl who knew ten words of English, and making hand gestures; then, he came over to me and said, "So what should we do?"

"What ya mean, what should we do? We agreed we weren't doing the sex."

"Yeah, but we gotta do something. They want to do something."

"I don't know. Maybe they can dance around naked and just have fun. We'll still pay them for the time they spend with us."

Bob went back to the translator, who shook her head from left to right. Bob came back and told me the answer was no. We were to fuck them or nothing. No dancing naked, capitalists they weren't.

One girl who looked like a wrestler—maybe she was the mother and daytime truck driver Viktor the concierge told me about—grabbed my skinny assistant in a headlock and dragged him into a room and closed the door. We were drowning ourselves in vodka, and things started spinning. Another girl had her eyes on Helena. Then, Bob disappeared with our translator. That left Helena, me, and the third girl, who kind of reminded me of a bouncer. I was so drunk by then that I couldn't even begin to describe her.

Later on, I might have been hallucinating, but I thought I was having sex. When I came to, I was halfway under the kitchen sink, and my pants were around my ankles. My shorts were still on, but my ass was exposed. One of the Russian girls, the bouncer, was leaning against the cabinets, puffing on a cigarette, staring down at me while I adjusted my shorts; she seemed really bored. Helena was sitting on the floor opposite me, rubbing the back of her head as if searching for a bump. I couldn't make sense of anything, and my ass was getting cold from the kitchen tiles. Then, Bob walked in and said we had to get back before they closed the bridges into town. Apparently, they raised the draw bridges between 1:00 a.m. and dawn, some medieval fortress-like tradition. We had to get our asses moving pronto! The translator called the same taxis, saying we only had a few minutes, so we got ourselves together as quickly as we could and said our goodbyes.

I tried giving them some money, at least for the alcohol, but they wouldn't take it. I discreetly left two hundred dollars by the eggs in the kitchen. I think they were eggs . . .

The taxis sped us homeward, and when we got closer to the city, I could see the red lights of the draw bridges flashing while the taxis flashed their signal lights. We made it over in the nick of time.

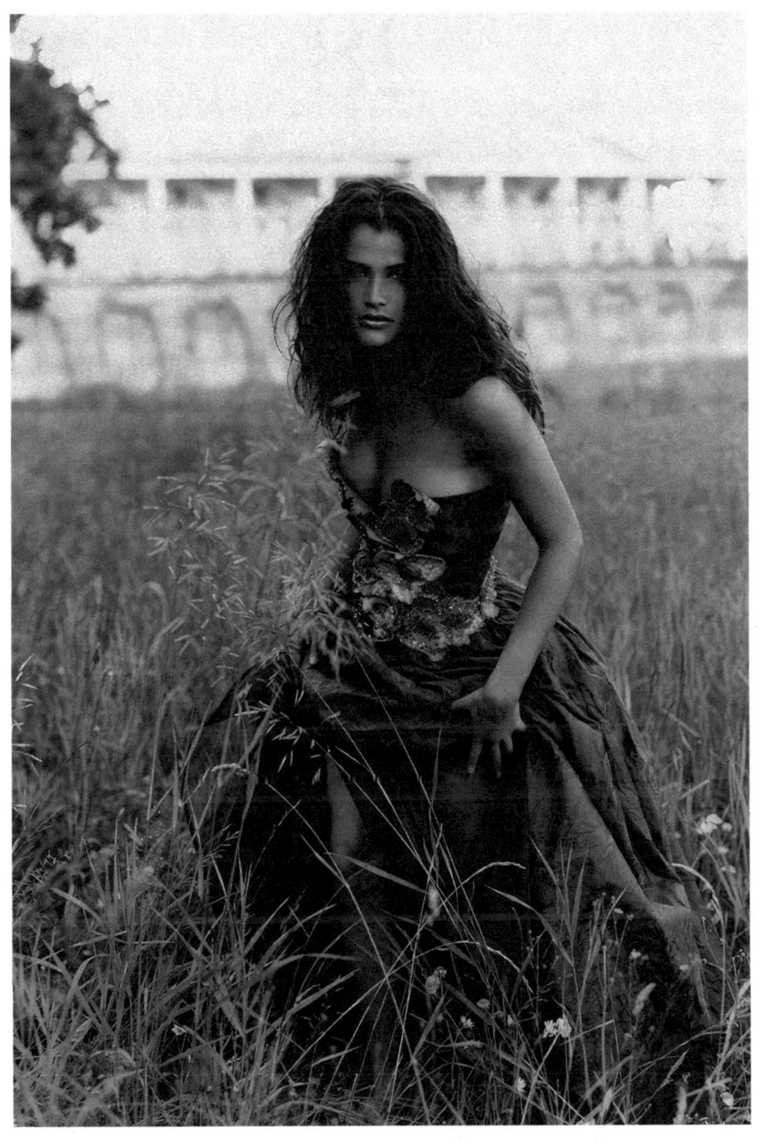

Helena Christensen, Pushkin Palace, St. Petersburg, Russia, for British *Vogue*

28

I began working for Italian *Vogue* in the early to mid-80s. My first big assignment with them was in Rome to shoot the collections, *alta moda*, as it was called, or high fashion. Most of these shootings took place soon after the runway shows, and if those were in the evening, our shoots went way past midnight. Afterward, at 3:00 or 4:00 a.m., I'd take long walks alone, just to unwind. We were always put up at the Villa d'Este Hotel above the Spanish Steps. On one of those sleepless nights, I walked down that beautiful cityscape and followed Via Condotti toward the French Quarter.

I'd always be somewhat buzzed from the combination of being on a set for ten hours, with all the models, the drinks, the crew, and the general lunacy of a fashion shooting, and so my imagination would come out to play while sightseeing alone at this time of night.

I began to sense I was being accompanied by the many whispers, echoes, and voices carried on the winds of this ancient city, knowing full well no one was there but having a good time answering the imagined voices back with a laugh. I was in my late twenties, and I romanticized about how much this city had seen. It was the center and heart of the Western World for hundreds, if not thousands, of years. Walking Rome's ancient streets, which bear the footprints of all who walked here, was unavoidable.

I found myself at Piazza Navona, a Roman racetrack from antiquity, whose oval impression is all that remains, surrounded today by cafés and fountains. Then I remembered, just around the corner was Palazzo Madama, home to Cardinal Del Monte, during the late sixteenth, early seventeenth century, Caravaggio's first patron, and where the painter lived his first five years in Rome. This was his neighborhood, and this was the time of night that he and his friends would be prowling around. I'm sure I was walking in his footsteps. Yards away was the church of St. Louis in the French Quarter, or la chiesa de San Luigi dei Francesi, housing three of his great paintings in the Contarelli Chapel, one masterpiece being my all-time favorite: *The Calling of St. Matthew.* The doors of the church were locked. The hour was not yet day, no longer night. The pale blue sky was signaling dawn was approaching; it was time to turn in, catch some sleep, and come back tomorrow. It was important for me to see these paintings.

In Rome, the Church was making money hand over fist. Selling postcards and trinkets by every door, candles that you could light up to save your soul, donation boxes for every saint. When I went to visit the Caravaggios the next day, on little sleep, it was a very hot summer day, around noontime, and the chapel was closed. That really pissed me off. I went back later in the day, and it was still closed. I started cursing out loud. I needed to see this painting, all three paintings!

On my third attempt, another blistering hot hell of a day, the church was open. There wasn't a single person around, not inside or outside, no one to even keep an eye on these masterpieces. At the end of the hall, the Contarelli Chapel, where they were housed, was in darkness. I could barely see the paintings. *Where the hell are the lights?* I was fumbling for switches, even asked out loud, "Is anybody home?" Nothing.

Then I found a little sign that said *Insert 100 lire to turn the lights on*. I didn't have a hundred-lire coin, the equivalent of a quarter. I just sat there in the dark, my lips moving as if I were praying like Mom, but I wasn't saying the rosary. I was cursing like my father instead. I sat there in the dark for a while, and finally, a young couple entered the chapel. They must have come to see the paintings because they immediately put a hundred-lire coin in the box. They hadn't noticed me sitting there, and when the bright lights came on, my presence scared the shit out of them. I kind of looked like Caravaggio at the time, or maybe a murderer—or both!

Caravaggio was a genius, but he was also a street brawler, a known troublemaker who would pick a fight with anyone who looked at him the wrong way. Our only records of him are police arrest reports. Always dressed in black, with black hair, a goatee, dark penetrating eyes, and always carrying a sword, which was illegal in Rome. He was an excellent swordsman, but this was his undoing. He was challenged and killed a pimp in a duel over a woman-friend he was standing up for. Wanted for murder, he became a fugitive, and went on the run throughout Southern Italy, from Malta, through Sicily, to Naples, wherever he could find a patron to hide him from the papal police. Everywhere he landed, he left us a masterpiece, until the authorities caught up with him. He wasn't arrested or killed; instead, they slashed his face as a mark of dishonor, most probably by the Knights of Malta, where he escaped jail from, for dueling with a knight. Physically wounded, and again on the run, he met his end under mysterious circumstances, malaria they said, at the age of thirty-eight. The heights of Caravaggio's creativity were equal to his self-destructive nature, his inner light and darkness were reflected equally in his paintings.

He reminded me a lot, in talent, attitude, and potential, of the guys I grew up with, the few that made it and the many that didn't. I don't say they were equal to his genius, but yes, he was one of us, a kindred spirit. Caravaggio's hand was guided by the heavens; his poetry with a brush was supreme and beyond compare. It changed the direction of painting and gave birth to later painters like Rembrandt and Velázquez. The life he chose to live was as Lucifer's friend, but in contrast to others, his work possessed the light of God.

After a minute, our lights went out in the chapel, but this young couple had a handful of coins and kept feeding the meter. The church had a racket going on over here—nothing new. It was worth coming back for, as many times as I did. I got to take in the magnificence of these three masterpieces—more intimately than in a museum, and to stand where Caravaggio himself most likely stood when the paintings were installed. From that time on, to this day, every trip I make to Rome, I make a pilgrimage to this church. Not to pray, but to worship Caravaggio.

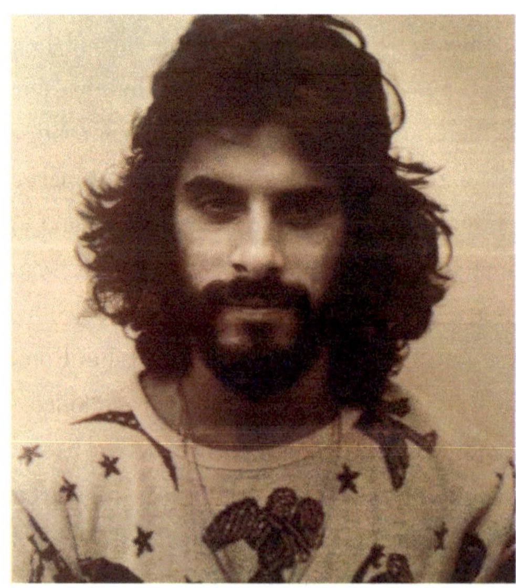

Nineteen-year-old Sante, photographed by Lou Bernstein

29

Jean-Paul Sartre has this phrase called "The Against"; if you're an artist,
you're in a position to challenge the fucking status quo. That's where I'm coming from.
That's the job of an artist in society. It's not to paint pretty pictures.
It's to say something even if it's just, "Fuck You!"
—Richard H. Kirk

One night in New York, I went out to the Rose Bar drinking with friends, and I ran into Mickey Rourke. We had a drink together with some chitchat, and we left off agreeing that we wanted to shoot some pictures together sometime soon. We had done some great pictures in the past, and by this point, we had known each other for about fifteen years or so. I liked Mickey; we're kindred spirits, and I understood him—he's an artist. I said goodnight and went home and got into bed around 2:00 a.m. I got a phone call at 5:00 a.m.

"You have your cameras?" It was Mickey.

"Yeah."

"Let's take some pictures.

"Mickey, it's five a.m. and still dark outside."

"C'mon, we'll go have a coffee first! I'm in Little Italy, in front of Ferrara's pastry shop."

"Okay, I'll be there in fifteen minutes."

I lived about six blocks away, so I grabbed my camera and threw a bunch of film in my bag and met up with him. He was wearing a mismatched suit, but it looked cool, and he was also carrying a cane.

Little Italy was silent and empty. Nowhere to get coffee, but there was a hint of late-summer light coming out; it's dawn on a Sunday morning. There's Mickey knocking on the window of Ferrara's, though it's obviously closed. I didn't even say hello. I just burst out laughing and thought, *Look at us.* I started taking pictures; then we began walking toward Mulberry Street. The lights were still up from the San Gennaro Feast, creating a series of arches over the street. I gave Mickey some direction, and as I shot, we kept talking and laughing, all with the camera close to my face. I was crouched and walking backward as he followed me.

At Grand Street, Mickey stopped for a cigarette under the John Jovino Gun Shop with its famous sign of a huge gun hanging outside the shop. It's famous in New York City's visual history. Everyone from Weegee to Berenice Abbott took pictures there. It used to be behind the police building, and Weegee's apartment was right over the gun sign. That's where he lived and took all those pictures of people getting out of the paddy wagon in the early hours. He knew what time the police would book people from that night, and since he slept in his clothes, he'd run outside, take the pictures, then go back to bed.

Mickey took off his jacket and was wearing a black sleeveless muscle T-shirt. He lit up a cigarette, and we then walked north on Mulberry Street to Spring Street. I saw where he shot scenes from his film *The Pope of Greenwich Village* more than twenty years ago! The area hasn't changed all that much. Mickey was very familiar with the neighborhood. I could see something shift in him, maybe an awareness of this someone else within him or a feeling of being free, at home with no one around.

We switched T-shirts. I was wearing a white tank top under my shirt, and Mickey put it on; he looked like he belonged there. Walking at me but looking past me, past my camera; he had that look that said someone's about to get their ass kicked—it was great.

At Prince Street, we went by St. Patrick's Old Cathedral. Mickey stopped to light up again, and he was peering around the corner of that famous wobbly brick wall of the graveyard. His whole demeanor had transformed. He was no longer Mickey Rourke, my friend—he was someone else he'd invented for me and my camera, someone who belonged there at that moment who I no longer knew. He was staking out a scene where something was about to go down, something risky, even dangerous. It was as real as could be. I personally had been in this place as a teen, and it was the wrong place to be, at that time of night, and the realism Mickey portrayed scared me. I never wanted to be in that place again in my life.

I became invisible to him—I let him lead me. I felt the power of this someone else walking at me, past me. It was amazing—something performed, yet this was lived, made alive in front of my eyes. With my camera pointing at him, he brought out the great actor for me to witness. He's a tremendous artist with the gift of perception and transformation, and the ability to communicate what it is to be in another's being. An artist guided by a deeply intuitive light, yet equally plagued by self-destructive tendencies. This paradox sometimes seems to be the nature of such brilliance: the light and the dark doing constant battle from within.

Those last twenty minutes of our rendezvous in Little Italy were pure genius. I had it all on film. All this took about an hour, just me and him. The first rays of the sun were starting to appear, and the mystery of that ambient light was turning into day; we were done. Like vampires, we gave each other a hug and said goodnight. Mickey went back to his hotel—I'm sure to close the shades—and I went home and back to bed.

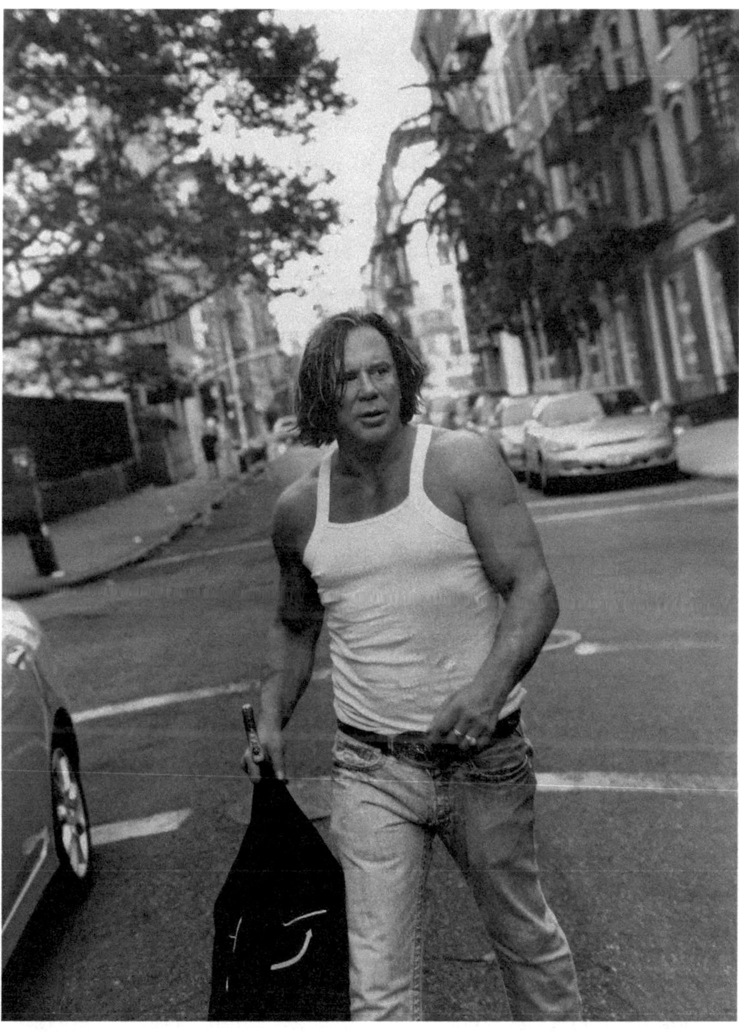

Mickey Rourke, Little Italy, New York City

30

God forbid I didn't call my mother regularly. Sometimes the obligation would annoy me so much I wouldn't call at all, in protest. I'd soon regret it because, being the Mediterranean mourner that she was, she would call everyone else and act as if I had been kidnapped. They, in turn, would be annoyed to have to call me and tell me to call her. Wasn't worth it. So many times, I was traveling on multiple assignments, enjoying myself, hanging with girlfriends between shootings or whatever fun I was trying to have, and I knew if I called her, she'd piss me off, push some button, and freak me out over nothing. I was the caretaker in her cuckoo house. She'd sometimes call hysterical, saying, "I'm going crazy! Don't send me to the crazy house! I don't want to go to the crazy house!"

"Ma, you're already there—it's me we gotta worry about!"

Then, I would call the live-in aide and ask, "What is going on? What's up with my mother's voice? She sounds possessed!"

"Nothing's wrong. She was upset you didn't call. She was fine before you got on the phone and happy after. That voice she puts on special for you. When she hangs up, she speaks normally."

I was in therapy for years because of her. One therapist explained why she was able to push my buttons. Because she made them the moment I was born. The shrink said, "Just remember to stay calm and realize these are her problems, not yours. You have to detach yourself and live your life." *Easy for him or her to say!* My mother has been "dying" since I was a little kid. She'd say things like "Don't do this, don't do that, or else I will die right away, and you will never see me again!" I was six years old at the time.

When I took my therapist's advice and "detached," soon enough someone would call and say, "Hey, your mom's in an ambulance! She's on her way to the emergency room!"

I'd sometimes have to leave in the middle of a shoot if no one else could get there. I'd find her in the hospital bed, dying, rosary in her hands, and a picture of Padre Pio by her side. The doctor would come in, and I'd ask what's wrong. "Oh, nothing, she's healthier than I am! She was a bit constipated and needed to pass gas, so we gave her an enema and need to monitor her overnight." So basically, my mother was full of it and needed to let one rip, and now she's okay. Motherfucker!

I left a Cindy Crawford cover shoot for this.

I warned my mother that crying wolf all the time would be her undoing. "One day, when it's real, no one is going to believe you."

The next day, I'd have to make up some story to explain why I'd left work. This routine had stopped being funny a long time before that.

When I was twenty, the rest of the family wanted to send her to an institution after she had a nervous breakdown—not her first. I wouldn't let that happen. I was her only child, and although Mom was close to my sister who lived in Florida, I always wished I had a younger sister closer to home who could help out. I was mostly alone and on my own having to deal with her.

I finally found a psychologist who spoke Italian. He was able to translate certain psychiatric states of mind in religious terms to her and prescribe her medications, according to the book of Revelations, but that only lasted a year because he lived and worked out in Freeport, Long Island. Luckily, my aunt and cousins lived nearby in Merrick, and they offered to lend a hand; she could stay with them for a week at a time. But when my mom had recovered and my aunt needed help, Mom refused to help her, saying, "Who is going to feed Sante?" I was close to thirty years old at the time and not living at home. I was mortified, and my cousins were stunned, rightfully so.

My mom saw me as the replacement for my father. Whenever I got into a serious relationship, she acted like a jilted lover. Every primitive society knows that, at a certain age, the mother must let go of her son and allow him to become a man. It's not healthy otherwise. But those societies weren't from Southern Italy! Being an only male child, I lived in a Southern Italian hell!

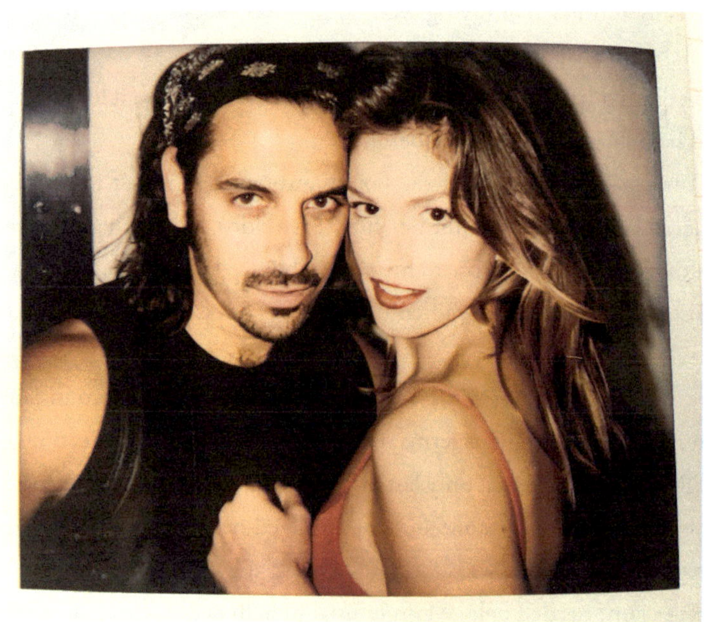

Sante and Cindy Crawford in the studio

31

When I started working in New York back in the early '80s, one of my first steady clients was Bloomingdale's. They put together some great trips that sometimes lasted two weeks, traveling from one city to another, or from one country to another. Three or four models, hair and makeup, and my crew, tons of clothes, tons of fun!

One memorable trip was through the Mediterranean, accompanied by Christy Turlington and Kristen McMenamy. We started out in Sicily: Palermo for a couple of days, then the town of Cefalù for a beach day and some shots, then on to Taormina. All these towns and small cities that have an ancient past, going back to the Greeks who first colonized Sicily, followed by the Romans, Byzantines, Normans, Arabs, the French, and Spanish, everyone leaving their mark culturally and architecturally. I got a history lesson from walking these ancient paths. It was a grand tour of Sicily and in every Grand Hotel—Bloomingdale's spared no expense. It became such a great education for all of us.

In Taormina, we stayed in a thirteenth-century monastery converted into a hotel with extraordinary views of the active volcano, Mount Etna, and the gardens surrounding the ruins of a Greek amphitheater, still in use today for concerts and performances. They recently shot the HBO series *White Lotus* there—it's been renovated since our trip, but the views are the same. After a couple of days, we packed up and drove to Agrigento, a hilltop city known for its great ruins and some of the best-preserved Greek temples, dating back to 570 BCE. And after Agrigento, we returned to Palermo and flew to Athens, then took a boat to Santorini, the Greek island.

Santorini is a semicircular-shaped volcanic ridge left over from a huge volcano that is thought to have erupted thousands of years ago. It caused so much destruction that it ended an entire Mediterranean civilization—supposedly Atlantis, according to Plato. It's how we imagine the Greek islands to be: whitewashed dwellings, some clinging to the cliffsides, contrasting with deep blue skies, and that bluest blue of the Aegean Sea.

As beautiful as everything was, the trip was also an exhausting traveling circus. Luckily, we got a few days off. I had to return calls to my office, which I always dreaded. There was always a problem to solve and a decision to have been made yesterday. And there were messages to call home: *Your mom took the wrong medications . . . went to emergency room; a neighbor brought her there . . . where are you? . . . she was back home yesterday and fine; please call, urgent!*

I knew this trip was too good to be true.

I asked my studio manager if she would hold all messages from my mom until I got back. She had a way of always getting on my nerves and ruining things, even from the other side of the globe. My shrink told me to never respond to her; those were manipulations. But of course, he didn't have to take her calls!

While taking a break after our shooting in Santorini, we discovered *ouzo*, Greek tequila in terms of getting inebriated, and I needed one! We'd found a restaurant and had dinner, instead of going back to the hotel, and that's when the drinking commenced! The ouzo got everyone wasted, and after dinner, our location bus resembled a typical frat house party—or maybe more like the one in *Animal House*. Somehow, I ended up wearing a green sequin dress with full makeup and jewelry. I honestly have no idea how that happened. With my facial hair, I resembled one of those bearded Southern Mediterranean women—not a pretty sight.

Like any ouzo boozer, I couldn't recall exactly why, but Christy and I had a full-on drunken fight and a bit of a go at each other. She thought I was taking my photography work too seriously! "It's not brain surgery, ya know!" was one phrase I remember her uttering. She was probably right, but I had a lot of shit to deal with. My mom was foremost on my nerves, and not everyone on set would get it, nor would I want them to know; it was embarrassing that, at thirty-two, my mother still had me by the horns.

Then, there were the calls from the client's New York office, canceling good pictures already shot because of new advertising coming in; other shots canceled because of some minor detail—wrong earrings, etc.—and other calls doubling the workload. The photographer always got blamed for everything. If there was an earthquake, it was my fault; if it rained or if the boat sank, somehow it was my fault! I'd be in survival mode on most of these big budget shootings, so it might as well have been brain surgery for me! Still, I'm sure I needed a chill pill.

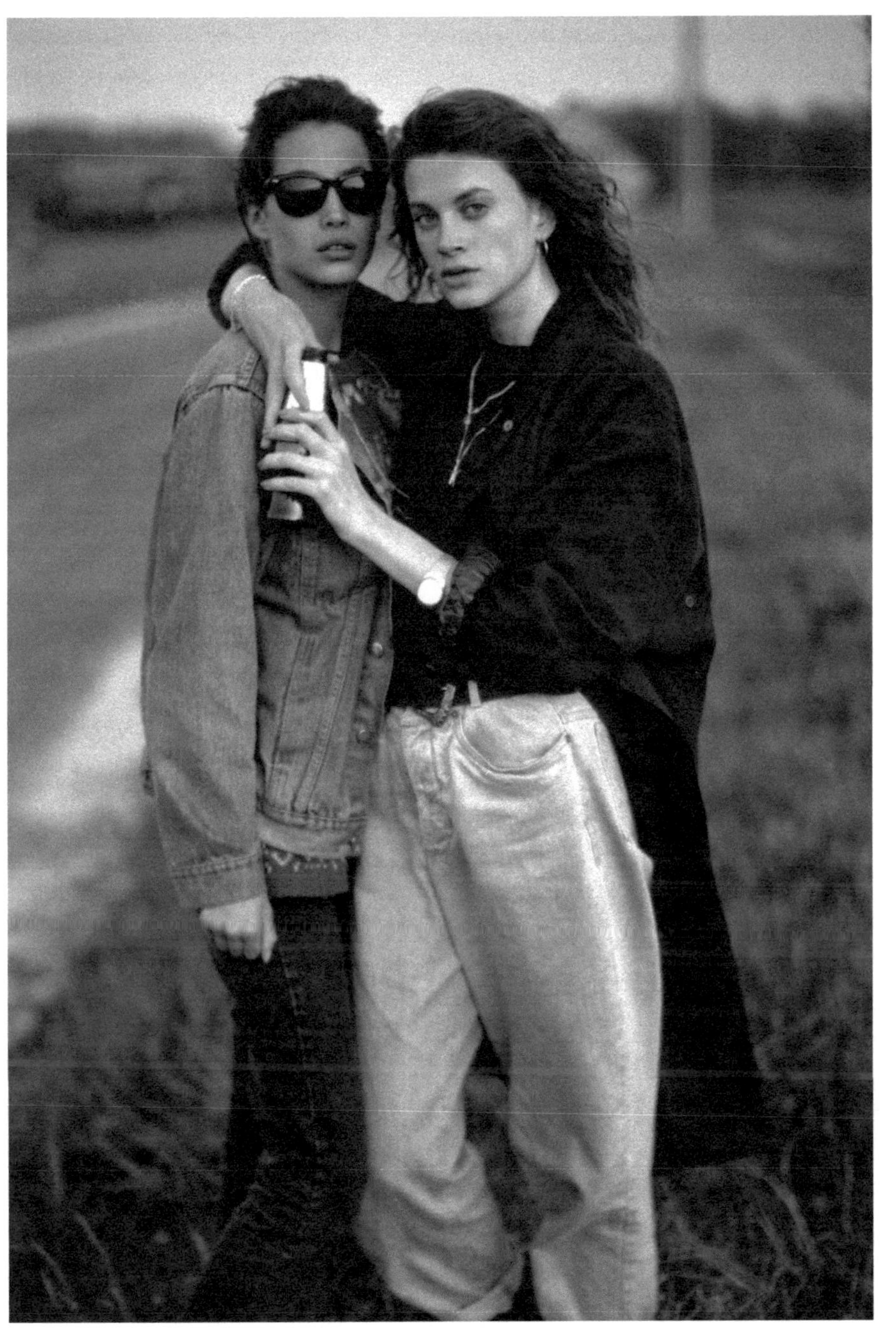

Christy Turlington and Kristen McMenamy, Old Montauk Highway, Montauk, New York

On the bus, Christy and I exchanged insults; I don't know how she kept a straight face with me in the green sequin dress. The fight continued back in the hotel room. While everyone was drunk, I remember pulling off my earrings and saying, "I've had enough of you!" Then, I couldn't get out of the dress because the zipper was in the back.

Did Christy push me? I may be wrong, but I fell over and tore the dress, which we hadn't shot yet. I managed to tear myself out of it all while fighting with her. I know she took pictures of me—maybe she will find them one day. I clearly remember how unattractive I looked in red lipstick and smokey eyes. Green sequins and red lips just didn't work with my skin tone.

32

Once I finally settled into business back home in New York City, I went through a few agents and tried to find a match. A good agent was always important to have. You need someone whom you could trust and who was well connected—or at least who was smart and disciplined enough to make connections. They would be representing you both personally and professionally. It's a relationship.

Not having a business sense and judging solely from their backgrounds and personalities, I, sometimes, made crazy choices based on, "Would I hang out with this individual?" The problem was I'd forget who I was hanging out with!

One such agent was Gaye. (We'll leave her last name out.) Gaye was a Texas girl with a great personality and was loads of fun; everyone liked her. She was a good party person too, which should have been a red flag. Gaye loved her drink. As far as repping me, she was able to book me jobs back-to-back for a couple of months at a time. Once she felt she had enough bookings to keep me busy, she'd then disappear for a couple of months at a time.

An agent was meant not only to book jobs but produce them, and even though I had a staff to help execute the production, the agent was also meant to oversee the staff and personally accommodate the client off or on set. They were to act like a buffer between me and the client, especially on set for big productions. This was so I could do my job without having to stop and field questions or, sometimes, hold the client's hand—which a photographer would have to do if their agent wasn't around to do that for them.

So whenever Gaye disappeared, it would make my job a little more stressful. As an example, I had a big advertising job with either Revlon or L'Oréal in the studio, along with major models. Such jobs tended to bring everyone and their mothers from the client's office to stand around, watch, be entertained, meet the models, and basically eat everything in sight like a swarm of locusts. This particular job brought about twenty people to crowd my space—I would have needed not only my agent but the NYPD for crowd control. I needed to direct my assistants and, most of all, the lighting, which was critical on a beauty shooting like this. The other thing was that I didn't know who most of these people were; even when introduced, I didn't know their position at their company.

So here I was, making all those subtle changes to my light, when some guy came over and said, "I think you should probably lower the light and put it more to the left." *Who the fuck is this guy?* So I asked him. He said, "I'm the fucking accounts manager." The fucking accountant was telling me how to light! I was sorry, but I had to tell him to fuck off in the nicest way possible, while still using "fuck off" in my sentence!

Now where's my agent? I wondered. Gaye had disappeared, and even though we bombarded her with messages, *nada*, nothing, no answer!

The following day, I had an early call to do a location shooting in Westbury, Long Island.

The next morning was a beautiful summer day. The cars and location van were parked in front of my office on Broadway. And my agent was nowhere to be seen, I sent out a search party, but before I knew it, I saw Gaye walking down Broadway. She was wearing a top that was so skimpy I could almost see her tits—with short denim shorts, and she was barefoot and strolling as if she's in the countryside in a field of daffodils. In one hand, she was holding her sandals, in the other, a beer!

I headed her off before the client saw her. She tried planting a kiss on my lips. She was drunk.

"Oh, my God," I told her, "get the fuck home and sleep it off. And do me a favor and go back the other way before anyone sees you!"

If she hadn't been bringing in big bucks, she would have been long gone! From that day forward, we referred to her as "Tra La La"!

Once, on my birthday, I had bought the apartment next door, and it was still empty, so I threw a big party. That, she showed up for! Gaye got so drunk she was begging me and my friend Pauly to handcuff her (she had her own cuffs) and do as we pleased. When we wouldn't, she got so obnoxiously loud and sloppy that Pauly and I had to take her to my other apartment next door to chill out. She was so drunk she cuffed herself to one of the cast-iron columns, so we went back to the party. I had to send my girlfriend back to go through Gaye's jeans to look for the keys (the last thing I wanted to do) and please put her in a cab home. That was my agent!

I don't recommend hiring someone you would hang out with as an agent, no matter how much they are able to bring in. With Gaye, it would always take another month of me not working so she could catch up and start all over again. But the girl had spunk, I gotta say.

33

It took several years for me to get personally intimate and deeply into the social fabric of the fashion business, and another couple of years to become a solid member of a group of friends, a kind of club that you couldn't apply for. Such clubs have existed for generations in all sectors of society, from Fashion to Hollywood to the Art World and Geopolitics. My club consisted of the most beautiful young women in the modeling world, which in turn, gave me entrée to every other club, especially those run by men. I learned, soon enough, that women ruled, even when they didn't know it.

I knew this from how I was raised at home. The saying was "Augustus ruled the Roman Empire, but Livia [his wife] ruled Augustus."

The group who hung out at my place graced most of the top fashion magazine covers worldwide and were featured in all the designer and beauty advertisements while making record amounts of money and wielding tremendous amounts of power in their industry from their high demand. They also happened to be the most fun, most daring, wickedest, seductive, exciting young women I ever came to know.

I had their trust, friendship, and respect so long as my girlfriend was around to keep an eye on me. That didn't always work. As I said, they were also very wicked—as was my girlfriend. They were used to being naked half of the time backstage or at shootings; that carried over in my kitchen and on my dining table. Naturally, we were always partying. In winter, they'd come over on Friday nights and leave on Monday morning for work—thank God we were young. Nothing readied me for that. I got to see shit I honestly thought only happened in the movies. I was no angel, but they made me blush half the time. They were wild and all in their twenties. I was only a few years older, and I was happy to take the ride. I quickly realized how sexually sheltered my own childhood and adolescence had been.

Compared with all these girls, I had been raised in a monastery. I didn't have older brothers growing up in the house to show me the ropes. There was no Internet, and no one ran around naked. Come to think of it, the last time my mom saw me naked was the last time she changed my diaper. That came from being raised by the Virgin Mary; I was really in need of breaking out, and soon enough, I got a crash course.

Once I got into fashion photography as an assistant, I slowly got a peek, but nothing prepared me for the things that went down when I started working as a photographer.

Though my popularity with the girls went from rags to riches, once I started shooting, I never took advantage—it was how I was raised. It had been taught to me by my mom, and my mentor Lou Bernstein reinforced it. I always tried to maintain a high level of respect for all the women in my studio. What interested me most was taking pictures. I was a voyeur, in a loose sense of the word, once I was behind that camera. My obsession was making images, taking in and recording everything around me. It enabled me to become this other person, free of everything, and outside of myself. With a camera in my hands, I was detached from the world; I was single-minded and very focused. All I wanted was a great picture. My girlfriends and the models understood that about me, and they felt safe.

The girls I knew in the fashion business were really no different from the girls I knew growing up, in the clubs or in my old neighborhood. All of us may have been damaged goods, but we were all good people and loads of fun. To the outside world, we were all misfits and part of a circus. As a teenager, I knew girls in the clubs who were turning tricks for extra cash, and there were guys selling drugs. We all knew someone hustling something, and that shit never leaves your system.

Not too many years later, I met models who worked on the side, escorting older men in Hollywood or the Middle East in exchange for "expensive" gifts—no difference. Some girls, before modeling, had lived with a john and laundered counterfeit money when they were teenagers; now they walked the shows for Yves Saint Laurent. Even when they made it big, they would still go on trips to Dubai or Africa and smuggle back diamonds and cash. Because they were beautiful and famous, it was easier for them to be given a pass.

The modeling agencies would occasionally get calls from the secretary of some Middle Eastern royal. "We would like to offer five hundred thousand to Susie So-and-So if she would escort the prince to a gala next Friday night." The agency would politely pass along the message, telling Susie, "Five hundred thousand for a gala event sounds okay." But then

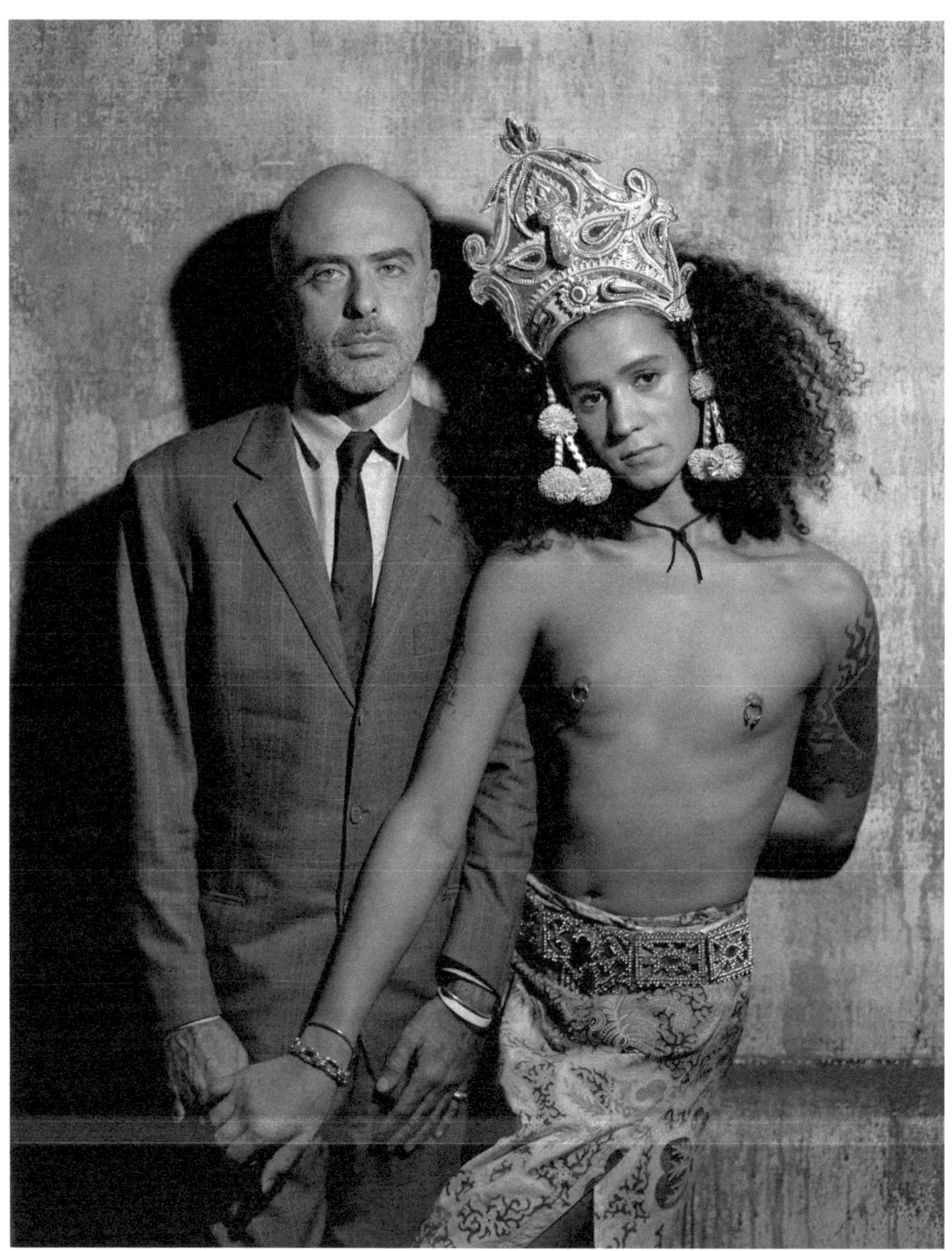

Francesco Clemente and Jaye Davidson for *Interview* magazine

the secretary might later call the agent back and say, "The prince would offer an additional one million dollars if Susie So-and-So would spend the weekend with the prince and sleep with him." The agent would get all indignant, "How dare you!" The royal secretary would respond, "Why? Carmen So-and-So (mentioning the name of an equally famous supermodel) accepted that fee just the week before."

I knew a girl who used to say, "A woman gets married three times in her life, the first for love, the second for money, and the third for companionship." My response was "What fucking bordello handbook did you read that in?" Years later, I learned it was a quote from Jacqueline Kennedy Onassis.

Everyone did what they had to do to get by and get out of where they came from. It's the nature of survival. Whether starting out as an eighteen-year-old escort in Hollywood, laundering money on the side, then walking the runway for Dior or Saint Laurent, eventually marrying an old rich dude, it's a story as old as the hills. Up until this past century, women had to survive by a different set of rules, and still, they came from a different sensibility with greater humanity for others than men. Empress Theodora of the Eastern Roman/Byzantine Empire was once a prostitute. As empress, she saved the throne of her husband, Emperor Justinian the Great, by commanding the troops to repel a revolt while her husband wanted to run. During his reign (her reign), she became a great feminist who enacted laws for women, including the death penalty for rapers. She created institutions to help destitute families and help women get out of prostitution. She created laws for women's rights to divorce and to own property. Only a woman who had her past could do something like that. Much of the time, it's exactly that kind of woman with street smarts who could help a man attain the power he aspired to. I wish I had a consigliere like her!

Like Theodora as an example, many of the models I knew who felt a need to marry for wealth or social standing eventually became cultured and influential women. Their own past made them more sensitive toward others; they used their wealth and position to generously help friends and people in need. Men with power are generally more selfish and greedier; they look to gain at all times, even at the expense of their friends, destroying or damaging others for sport and more power. It's ego-driven power-mongering. As Emperor Justinian did with his most loyal and successful general, Belisarius. Out of fear and jealousy, and an imagined threat to his popularity, Emperor Justinian stripped Belisarius of his rank and imprisoned him. It's also said he had him blinded and exiled. Either way, in general, it's something only a power-hungry man would do. Belisarius was later found innocent of charges of conspiring to overthrow the emperor. It was Empress Theodora who brought him and his wife back to Constantinople, back from exile. It's women who should rule!

There are exceptions to every rule. Another very famous young lady, a (very famous) model I knew, should have worked for the CIA; she knew everyone's personal business. She only dated the richest toads or the highest profile actors she could find. When the toad couldn't take it anymore and wanted out, she had her eyes and ears on everything of his and would threaten to call the IRS (and she would have done it) if he didn't fill her bank account or buy her a home in the Hollywood Hills or an apartment in Manhattan. Later, she made the mistake of trying that out on a well-connected Russian. He picked her up and physically threw her off his yacht while it was sailing, knowing that she couldn't swim. She somehow survived and prospered.

Me, I knew I was fucked up. When I did find a good girl, I'd get bored. I loved the nut jobs. I was hooked from an early age by the crazies. They were the most fun and caused the most trouble. They took drugs and loved other women; they had girlfriends like themselves and shared them. "Gypsies, tramps, and thieves"—the social register was filled with as many of them as there were forgeries hanging in major museums. I got to know half of Hollywood through my model girlfriends, but it all had a shelf life. It was all good, until it wasn't.

I've lived an irreverent life, but I've had a hell of a time. I've never physically hurt anybody. I've never stolen from anyone. I did a few things I regret, but haven't we all? Shit happens.

I'm an artist; I was always obsessed with creating images. All I wanted was a great picture. In between, I had dinner and shared drinks with royalty and with thieves. I belong to a group of traveling acrobats, trapeze artists, actors, painters, dancers, and more.

34

Human salvation lies in the hands of the creatively maladjusted.
—Martin Luther King Jr.

An intellectual is a man who says a simple thing in a difficult way.
An artist is a man who says a difficult thing in a simple way.
—Charles Bukowski

In the summer of 1990, I often spent weekends in Montauk with Julian Schnabel. He had rented the Warhol estate, which consisted of a group of fishermen cottages on twenty-five acres of raw and beautiful land with a large pond, facing the Atlantic Ocean. High reeds, stony beach, and surf. The main house was rustic, made of wood planks and idyllic; Julian had decorated it with some very tasteful art, including a Picasso, some Warhols, a Man Ray, a Picabia, and others. He built a studio in the center of the horseshoe drive in front of the house. Rough wide beams of wood, on short stilts with three tall open-air walls, like a three-sided handball court. There, he made the largest paintings I had ever seen.

Julian would find old used canvas tarps or army tents, tie them to the back of his jeep, and we would drive through the gravel terrain and puddles while I filmed with the tarp trailing behind. Eventually, his assistants would stretch those canvases as large as twenty feet tall. The markings, the scuffs and stains, from dragging the tarps through the grounds created abstract marks, in which we'd begin to see imaginary landscapes (like we do with clouds). Julian would then soak large rags or towels in black paint and throw them at the canvas, creating other forms on top of those marks, add colors, and glue a collage of old fabrics on top, hand-brushed name or a place. And there it was, magic: a finished painting. It was fantastic to witness.

At some point in the late '80s, I bought a 16mm Bolex moving film camera. It had three minutes' worth of film, and you had to handcrank it, but you could hand-hold it like a regular camera. It was a simple but incredible movie camera that I fell in love with. I started by shooting a roll here and there in between shots on fashion shoots, both black and white and color. During a British *Vogue* shoot in the desert with Stephanie Seymour, I shot enough to make a three-minute film and put it to music. It was a raw type of music video, mostly in black and white. I hired an editor, and we made the film, and things began to get super exciting for me. I would take my movie camera wherever I went. I knew this was where I belonged: making films.

With my Bolex in the summer of 1990, I began filming Julian every which way, from afar and up close on the beach, in the kitchen, at lunch, surfing—he loved to surf—and of course, while painting. With a tape recorder, I recorded us talking, the music being played, the sounds of his family swimming in the ocean. At the end of that summer, I returned to New York and back to work with a massive photography schedule, and that footage sat in my safe for the next thirty years.

No matter what anyone might say about Julian, I love him like an older brother. To me, the shit he used to pull was entertaining, though it could be annoying at times to many other people. At restaurants, for example, he would order what *he* wanted you to eat without asking you. Built like Pavarotti, and with an ego to match, he reminded me of my father, which included his humor and eccentricities. So I was able to put up with him a lot longer than most.

Like Vinny the Chin Gigante, godfather of the Genovese crime family, the notorious loungewear wearer, Julian would wear pajamas everywhere he went. If a jacket was required, he would just throw one on over his PJs. One sunny morning in Palm Beach, for example, while sporting his baby blue pajamas, he rolled up in a white Bentley convertible, picked me up, and we drove to the other side of the tracks, literally, to have breakfast. We pulled into the parking lot of a dive that resembled a greasy spoon out in the backwoods of Mississippi. The staff knew him, so they didn't blink an eye as he took a seat at the counter in his pajamas. They probably had one of his paintings hanging in a back room somewhere, which would be very typical of Julian . . . if there was a back room.

Once in LA, he said, "We're going to the track at Santa Anita." In all the years of our friendship, I had never known Julian to take a serious interest in racehorses, but somewhere out west, he had bought a racehorse. That day, he said we'd be meeting some friends of his at the track to watch his horse run in a race; he wouldn't tell me who the friends were.

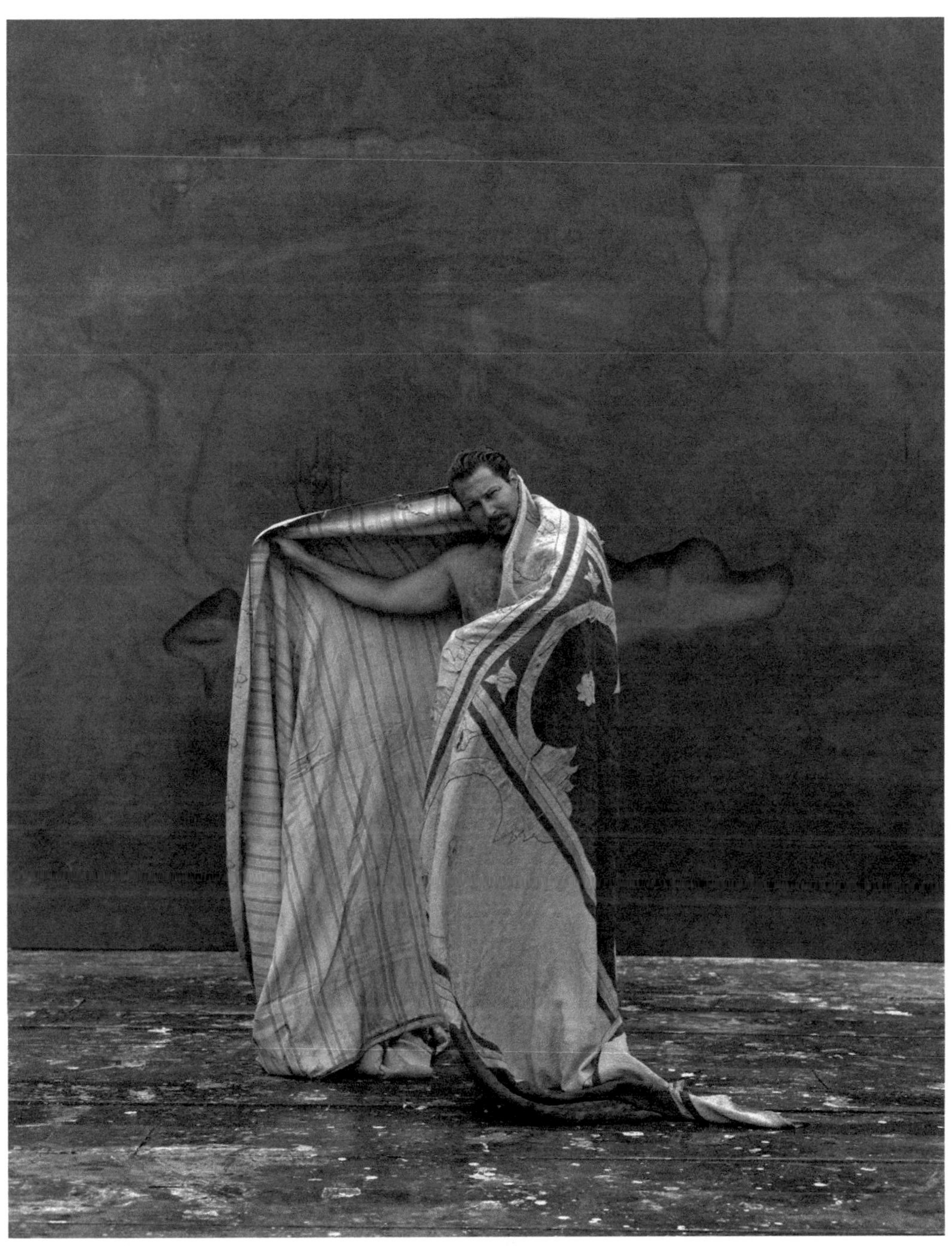

Julian Schnabel, Montauk studio, New York

When we met up with these friends, to my surprise, they were none other than Jack Nicholson, Sean Penn, and Charles Bukowski. All had come to cheer his horse to the finish line, and everyone placed a bet. Alas, it came in last. Jack, Sean, and I ripped up our tickets, but Bukowski disappeared. He showed up fifteen minutes later, seemingly counting some cash, maybe his winnings? I never did see him rip up any tickets. It's possible the old gambler knew better than to put money on Julian's nag. I could be wrong, but then again, Santa Anita was his home away from home. I think Julian sold the horse not too long after, never a dull moment—but I did get a photo of the horseplayers together at the track!

I took a lot of photographs of Julian over the years at his places in Montauk, Palm Beach, and New York City, mostly wearing his pajamas. We remain good friends to this day.

In 2020, I revisited the footage, and its magic was still there; time had made it even more special. With some help from Julian, I took that sound, and the footage, and made a thirty-minute short film. We debuted it during the 2022 Tribeca Film Festival at Vito Schnabel's gallery in Chelsea. Vito's also in the film, at five years old. Maybe now I can pick up where I left off, making films. Never too late, as they say!

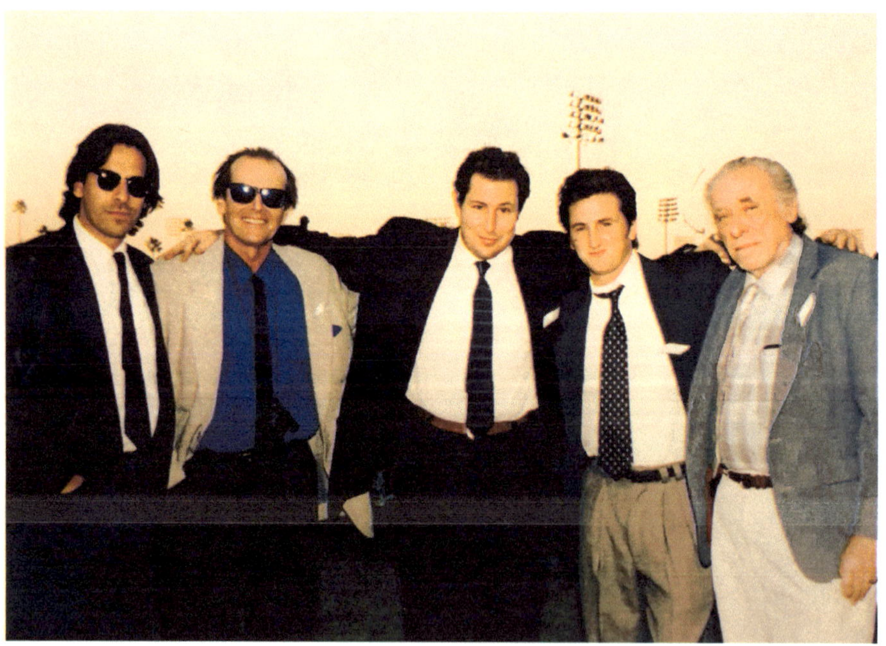

Sante, Jack Nicholson, Julian Schnabel, Sean Penn, and Charles Bukowski at Santa Anita Park

Through Julian, I met Peter Beard and his wife, Nejma, in Montauk, where they lived during the summers. Nejma seemed like a pillar of strength and a very sensitive woman, a person I'd put my trust in to hold down the fort. Peter was the adventurer in the wild, reckless and carefree. He was the great wildlife photographer with a philosophic point of view in his writings, whose pictures were both beautiful and critical of the endangered species being devastated in Africa.

Starting in the '60s, he split his time between Kenya and New York City. The difference between Peter's work and other photographers with a sense of conservation was that Peter was also an artist. His diaries are famous for their collages and contemporary mixture of nature and the social high life in which he lived and mixed partying with Warhol and Mick Jagger, while dating top fashion models and dining with Jacqueline Kennedy Onassis and her sister, Lee Radziwill. He incorporated that personal collage of his lifestyle into his large photographs later in his career to create works of art. They brought tremendous attention to his work, which became in demand and were collected by both institutions and great private collections.

As a nature photographer, he had a track record of going places and doing things in the wild that most people didn't have the balls to do. He was the guy who would lead you into the African bush and put you face-to-face with a charging rhino. He wouldn't get hurt, but you, on the other hand, might get gored. This actually happened to someone he was guiding in the wild while they were doing a documentary.

You never thought Peter's own luck would run out, until it did. He was attacked by an elephant and nearly killed. It shattered his pelvis, and the hospital was a two-hour drive away over very rough terrain, making every bump extremely painful. He survived, barely. I loved and admired Peter always, but I couldn't hang out with him for too long. He had a way, whether drugging or drinking, of outlasting everyone, on any night of the week. I just couldn't keep up!

One time, I called to let Nejma know I was coming to visit them while I was nearby in Montauk, and I was bringing my four-year-old son, Nick. Peter and Nejma lived in the caretaker's house on their property, on the cliff above the ocean beach, the last house before the lighthouse and national park. The main house, an Old Dutch–style home with a windmill, had burnt down to the ground. All that remained was the stone fireplace and chimney. Peter had had a darkroom in the place and, somehow, with all those chemicals and some vague mishap, the place went up in smoke, along with some important paintings, like a Picasso, so I was told—though, it may be all part of the myth, I don't know. What I do know is that the house was gone. All I ever saw were a few photographs of how beautiful it had been.

On the drive to their home, I started getting paranoid about my son's safety around Peter. *Suppose he takes Nick to the cliffside to see the ocean and . . . oh, my God. Suppose . . . suppose . . .*

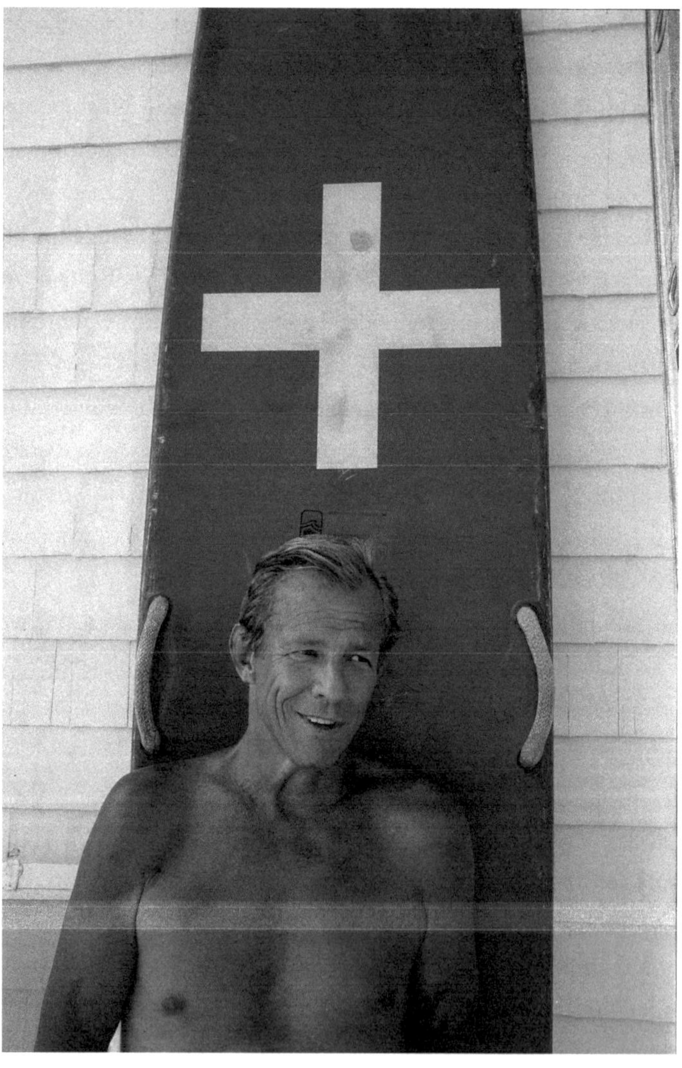

Peter Beard, Montauk, New York

I had to snap myself out of it. I was glad Nejma would be there. We walked into the backyard where Peter was working on his diaries, and Nejma came out to greet us. She got us drinks and handed Peter a beer with no opener. In his usual style, he cracked the top off the bottle by smashing it against the table, so the sharp glass edges were exposed, and he poured the beer in his mouth. He said he was about to take a walk to the cliff and absorb the negative ions off the ocean breeze. Holding his jagged beer bottle, he said, "Come on, Nick," and with the beer in his hand, put his arm around my son. The sharp end of the bottle cut my son right on the side of his eye, and the amount of blood that poured out made my legs weak. Nick, on the other hand, was laughing hysterically, blood all over him. In no time, Nejma appeared with a first aid kit and fixed up the gash on my kid's face. I was almost nauseous, and Peter felt terrible about it. Twenty-five years later, Nick still has a faint trace of that scar by his right eye.

After that incident, I visited Peter alone, just the two of us. As always, he was in his living room, cutting and pasting his endless diaries—this was before any of them were printed in book form. I offered to have my printer make prints of some of the great images of his. I told him I would need some negatives.

"I think they're in the shed," he said. "Come, you can help me find them."

It was a bright midsummer day, and when he opened the small side door to the shed, the interior was pitch black. Peter couldn't find the light. I felt and heard this crackling sound under my feet and couldn't imagine what the hell I was walking on. When he finally hit the light switch, I saw hundreds of negatives lying on the floor that we'd been crunching underfoot. I couldn't believe it. Peter was unfazed, said he was sure they were still printable. Completely unconcerned, not a care in the world. Was this a prime example of stoicism, of living only in the moment?

I managed to pick out ten negatives and brought them back to the city with me. I had my printer make ten silver gelatin prints of each as a gift for Peter. When I gave them to him the following week, he was so happy that he immediately gave one away to the mailman who happened to be passing by. "Oh, just put it in your mailsack," he said to him. "They look better with a little wear and tear." That was Peter!

The great thing Peter and Julian taught me was to let go of things: Nothing is precious and the more you try and hold onto things, the more you'll get stuck in the mud. I'm referring here mostly to the creative act, but the same principle can be applied to life.

In my short film on Julian Schnabel, he says at one point, “If an artist starts out by trying to save something within their painting, say a particular corner, they're fucked before they even get started.” I take this to mean that, if a painter finds an area in their painting that they feel is beautiful and right, they then try to hold onto that area and preserve it by painting around it. But in doing so, most of the time, the rest of the painting will not fall into place, especially if it's an abstraction. Only when you destroy that area you found so precious will the rest of the painting most likely come together. As Julian says, when the familiar appears, “I know this already; I want to do something that I don't know.” And if that means losing a part of the painting that he loves, he'd rather lose it. The same applies to photography and any of the arts. Sometimes you have to “kill your darlings” as they say, especially if they hamper your development. It's a bold move and usually worth it.

35

You have to have the mindset that anything can happen on a shoot, because it probably will. You have to stay open and go with whatever shows up.

I had an assignment to shoot Prince for *Gotham* magazine. I got to the studio early, as I sometimes like to do, to have a coffee and meditatively take everything in. My assistants had set up everything fast and easy. No one else was around.

Then, very quietly and with a calm demeanor, Prince walked in alone. He wore his purple suit with a fedora and was camera-ready. He introduced himself to me. I couldn't think of any star who had the courage or humility to arrive unaccompanied at a shooting. I was expecting an entourage, but there was no one else with him.

I told him the magazine people were supposed to arrive in about forty-five minutes, and he asked if I wanted to take pictures anyway before they showed up.

Since he was going to wear what he had on, it took me no time to cover many variations. The magazine only needed one shot for the cover and one variation for the accompanying story. I knew I had gotten them and told him so.

Prince very graciously said, "Okay, goodbye," tipped his hat, and left.

I turned to my assistants and said, "Did that just happen?"

What a sweetheart!

Ten minutes later, the magazine people came in, expecting Prince to arrive momentarily, and I had to break the news to them that we had already done the shooting, that Prince had been and gone! They were in shock and didn't believe me until I showed them the Polaroids.

I was still amazed at the sight of Prince arriving alone. I loved the guy for that!

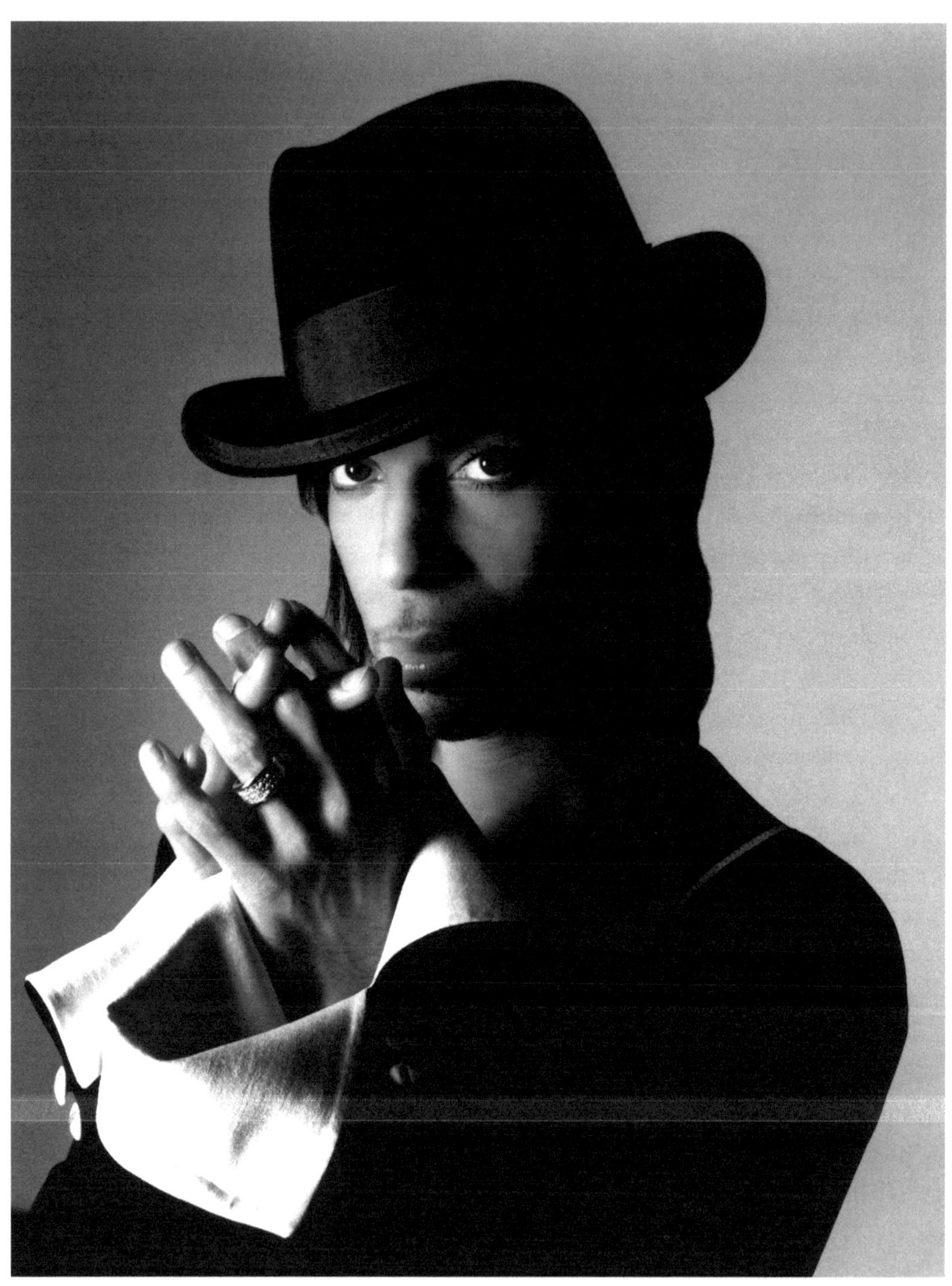

Prince, New York City, for *Gotham* magazine

36

I was never nervous about photographing any one person. I only got anxious about shooting because I wanted to do great work and was always in competition with myself, not because of my subject. Until I got to shoot Keith Richards for his *Talk is Cheap* album cover.

It was 1988, and I was in the Laight Street Studio with my crew, getting my shit together early. It was a 6:00 p.m. call time—late for me, early for Keith—which was rock 'n' roll time. While they were putting up the set, I was getting things cozy for Keith in another room. I had the Jack Daniels ready, a few joints rolled, and I prepared the room so Keith could have some privacy and comfort.

A few weeks earlier, Keith's wife, Patti—whom I had known for a couple years from her modeling days—had invited Kara and me over to their place for some drinks and introduced us to Keith for the first time. They were living in the building above Tower Records on Fourth Street and Broadway. Patti was a down-to-earth girl from Staten Island, who could rock with the best of them. Their place was a home, with their two little girls, Theodora and Alexandra, playing around in the kitchen with a friend, and a cousin of Patti's helping the girls finish up a meal. They made us feel right at home. Keith was chill, and in little time, I felt as if we had known each other forever, that he was one of the boys. I felt a sense of trust and let my guard down.

In the studio, my professional self-showed up, trying to play it cool. Keith wasn't there yet, which gave me more time to realize I was shooting Keith Richards from the Rolling Stones for his first solo album!

Once my friends knew I'd be shooting Keith, they all flipped and started making me feel more pressure and making me nervous, making me wish I hadn't told anyone. It would have gotten out anyway; my assistants alone were acting as if they were five-year-olds meeting Santa for the first time.

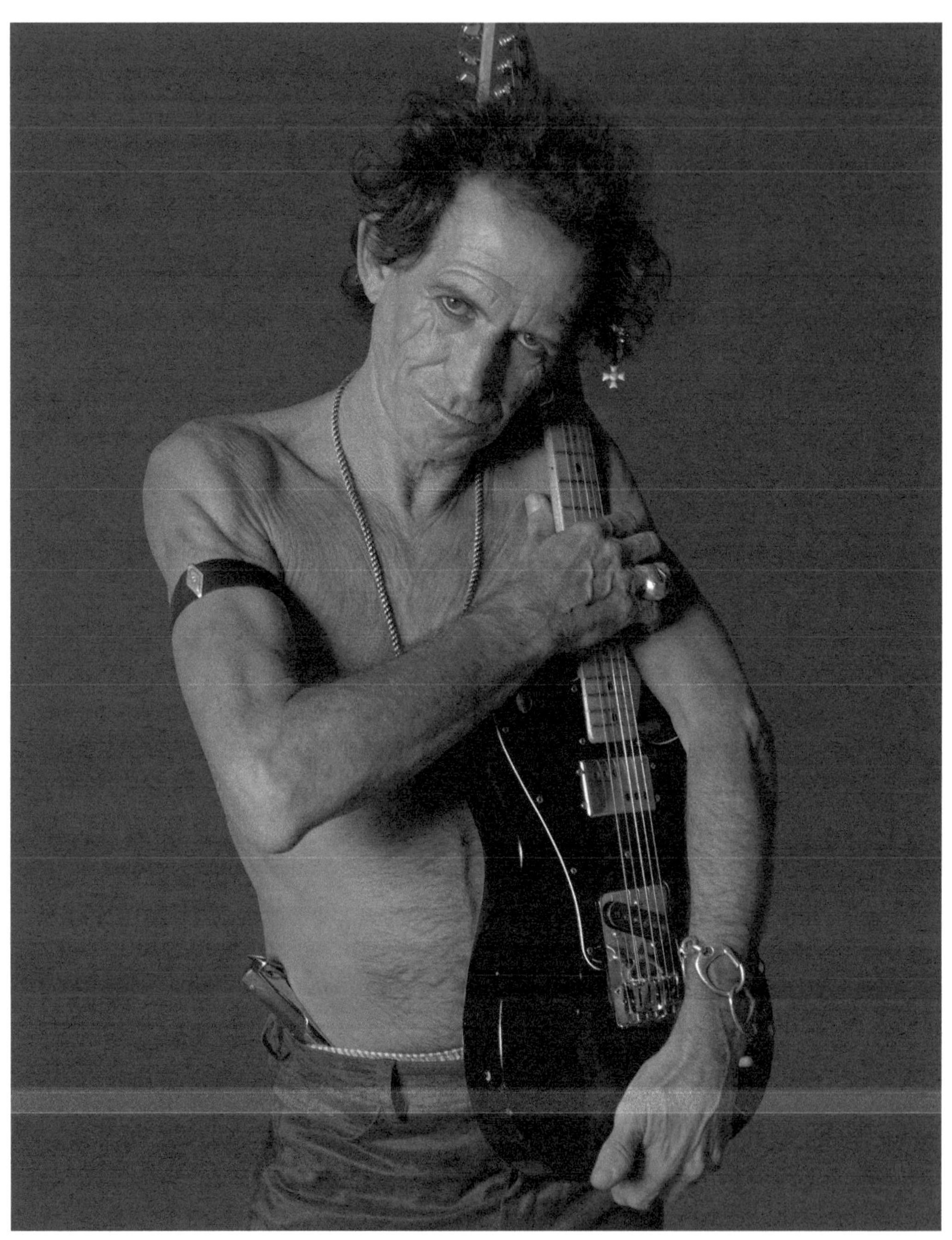

Keith Richards for *Rolling Stone* magazine

My hands were sweating now because I was being reminded that this was my chance to shoot Mr. Rock 'n' Roll. It's a first for me and that little evil voice in my head was saying, *Yaa better get some good fucking shots or else.*

Keith finally arrived. After I introduced him to everyone, I showed him to the private room, and he poured us some Jack Daniels. I decided to do whatever Keith was doing, so I drank mine down with him. Then another, then another. Good thing I was sitting down. He lit one of my joints and then had another Jack and another joint and another Jack. I was with him every step of the way—I wanted him to feel as comfortable as possible to shoot these pictures. Keith stood up, lifted his shirt, and pulled out a big fucking knife. *What the fuck?* He expertly flicked out the six-inch blade and produced a bag of coke from his pocket, then, using the knife, scooped some out and put it under my nose. I hoovered it up before I could say Jiminy Cricket! He did the same for himself. Now one of my eyes started to water, but then another scoop came up to my other nostril, and both eyes were tearing. He looked at me, started laughing, and poured me one more for the road, saying, "Okay, ready, let's do this!"

I tried to get up, but my legs didn't work. When I finally did get up, I was whacked! Out front on set, my assistant had to steady me. They looked at me and rolled their eyes as I gave them that goofy smile that read "I'm fucked up!" I don't know how I managed, but no one seemed to notice except my guys. Maybe I gave it away when I asked them to focus the camera for me? Nothing bothered Keith, of course. I managed to steady myself to get everything in focus, but I guess instinct took over. I did have to make a call for a delivery of my own supply. It was the '80s and I was shooting Keith!

I don't remember much else, but I heard everyone on set had a great time, and people were telling me what a fun guy I was; they said I had them in stitches! It took a day and a half for my head to clear and another half a day for the film and contacts to arrive. Everything looked great, and I couldn't wait to do it again!

37

On our way into Patti and Keith Richard's building, Kara and I ran into Russell Simmons, who had just moved into their building. He invited us over for a housewarming party he was having that coming weekend, which we happily went to.

Russell was just starting to make some money with his record label and bought an apartment that had previously belonged to Cher, fully furnished, which was funny because it was obviously a girl's apartment: pastel colors—pink, lavender, baby blue—everywhere, hollow columns posted around the bed in the bedroom, a large sphere or two just rolling around, and a ceiling in a pale blue with fluffy white clouds.

When I saw the place, I said, "Russell, what the fuck?"

He said, "It's Cher's, man. I got Cher's apartment and her furniture—this shit is dope!"

I had met Russell in the '80s around the time he, Lyor Cohen, and Rick Rubin created Def Jam Recordings. Rick was still going to NYU. They started out with Run DMC—Reverend Run was Russell's brother. Lyor Cohen went on the road managing them; this tall, skinny Jewish kid was managing all these gigs with shady promoters in some shady places. Lyor became the muscle for Run DMC on the road. Knowing Lyor now, I definitely wouldn't want to fuck with him or be on his bad side.

In the early '90s, my crew of guys and girlfriends (mostly models) would meet up at the Bowery Bar, and I would see Russell there on a regular basis. The Bowery Bar was on Fourth Street, just down the block from Russell's place. It was owned by our mutual friend, Eric Goode, who insisted I was responsible for his place taking off because I'd bring all the girls there: Kara, Naomi, Stephanie, and Christy, plus a whole assortment of actors and musicians. I also threw my first book party (for *A Private View*) at the

Bowery Bar. Joe Pesci, Robert De Niro, and a bunch of others in the movie and fashion business all came by.

At that time, Russell always had this one kid named Brett Ratner following him around. One drunken night, wasted on everything, my English friend Johnny Chappoulis and I were being outlandish and entertaining everyone in the bar, and Johnny got into a spat with the kid. Johnny called him a cunt—which coming from an Englishman doesn't have the same ugly weight it carries when used by an American; it's somehow funnier. Johnny was English, but his family's roots were Greek Cypriot. If provoked, he could become a street brawler. He was small but tough! I had to keep an eye on him now. Johnny grabbed a knife from a table and threatened to cut Brett's ears off. Luckily it was a butter knife, which broke the tension and had us cracking up.

Still, I had to intervene because the tussle was becoming a mess and everybody was staring at us, and Brett's not the fighting kind of guy. I took the butter knife away and pulled Johnny to the side to calm him down. "C'mon, you can't do that. You gotta go apologize. You just popped him in the head, and then you go and pull a butter knife on him!" We both started laughing again—a butter knife! I said, "Look, he's Russell's friend, and Russell's cool, so play nice, and let's just have a good time."

Johnny knew I was right. I walked him over to Brett. Everyone was still standing around because it had been loud and scary for a minute there. Johnny, soaked in adrenaline sweat, extended his hand and apologized.

Brett couldn't help himself and said, "All right, but ya didn't have to pull a knife on me!"

Johnny yelled, "It was a butter knife! Ya see, that's why you're a cunt! See, I told you he was a cunt!" And it started all over again. We broke it up, and I ordered drinks for the table.

Some years later, a shit series of events hit Johnny bad. It started with his wife leaving him for another guy, Johnny being the last to know, followed by a year of debilitating stress and terrible headaches where he could hardly even work. I sent him to my doctor, and I went with him for tests. They found he had a brain tumor the size of a baseball. He had a great group of mates come around and care for him, but nothing could be done, and he passed away, which was very sad for us all.

Johnny's family lived in England. They weren't rolling in dough, so I had to call some friends to chip in and help me raise money for his arrangements and transport home. Russell was the first to donate: five thousand dollars. And Brett, who was never close to Johnny for obvious reasons, gave me a thousand, unsolicited. No matter what, I'd never forget that. We organized a funeral for Johnny; then we sent him home to his family. God bless him.

We were a tight group of friends back then. We played basketball on the weekends all year long at Pier 59 and in the summers at Russell's place in the Hamptons. We worked together, too. With Def Jam and Russell, then later with Andre Harrell whom I loved, and his Uptown Records, where I shot Mary J. Blige and her first CD cover of *What's the 411?*; Jodeci, who wrecked the penthouse at the Four Seasons Hotel I'd rented for their album cover shoot; Heavy D; and more. As a result, I also shot Whitney Houston, Mariah Carey, Janet Jackson . . . the list goes on. The guys were really loyal to one another. I always respected that, and through them, I met a lot of great people, sometimes under unusual circumstances.

One time Andre Harrell invited me to a Knicks game. He said to meet him in front of Madison Square Garden just before game time; his intern was coming down from Uptown Records with the tickets. We stood around waiting for a while, and Dre said, "If this intern doesn't get here soon, I'm gonna have to fire his ass!" The kid showed up ten minutes later, out of breath—there was so much traffic he had to jump out of the cab and run the rest of the way down Seventh Avenue. Dre was so annoyed he didn't introduce me, so I introduced myself. He said his name was Sean Combs. After he left, I said to Dre he seemed like a nice kid.

He replied, "Yeah, he's all right . . ."

But apropos, in the words of Oscar Wilde (from *Lady Windermere's Fan*, published in 1892): "In this world there are only two tragedies. One is not getting what you want, and the other is getting it."

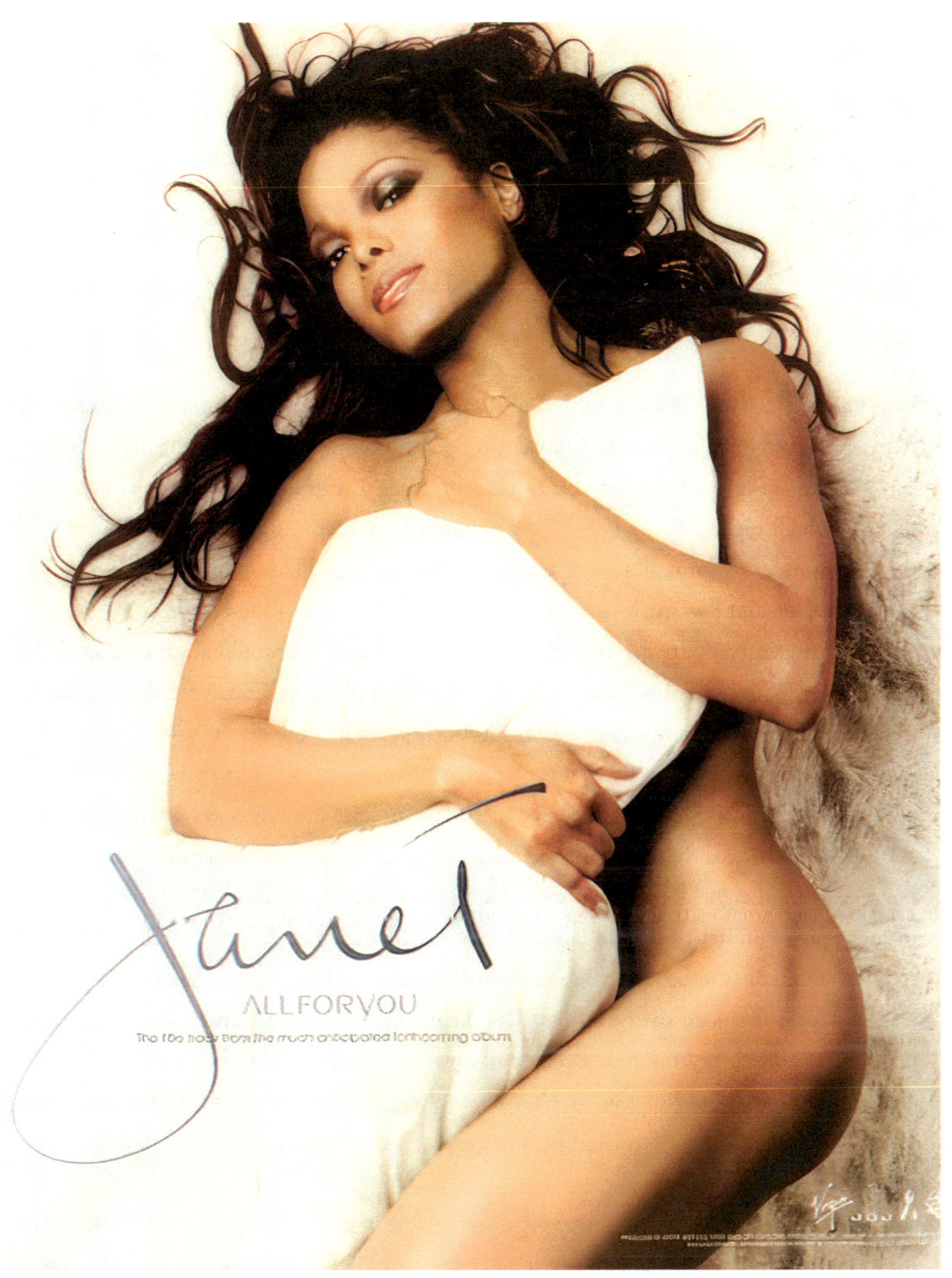

Janet Jackson on the cover for her single "All for You"

38

Late one night, I was in some subterranean club in London with a bunch of my British friends. Seemed like I knew everybody, lots of good-looking girls, lots of flirting going on. But you can crash quickly when you run out of drugs! I realized it was fun only because I was so high all night. I loved being a social butterfly, and this night, I hit every corner of the club, wandering from table to table, just like when I was a kid on my bike in Brooklyn. But it was late, and I wasn't into asking people for a hit here and there.

Over the years my friend, Nat, the future Lord Rothschild, would always invite me to stay at his place in London whenever I was over here, so this time, I accepted the invitation. I had the entire place to myself, along with his driver, chef, major domo, and the rest of his staff. I had total privacy, with five floors of fine furniture, modern art, and a well-stocked wine cellar, even if he was completely sober for years. I wasn't, and the manor was mine for a week!

He was overjoyed that someone was using the place! I don't remember the exact address, but it was about eight doors down from the home of the "Iron Lady," Margaret Thatcher, former prime minister of England. My room was extremely tasteful, in the refined English style. No fountains on the wall, no lamps with a peasant girl holding a basket of fake flowers, and no plastic covers on the furniture. I'd wake up and a talented French chef would cook anything I wanted for breakfast. Because of how I was raised, I always assumed a humble and respectful demeanor in anyone's house, let alone an English lord's crib. I would never take advantage, and always treated people the way I would expect to be treated, and that included the staff.

Back at the club, I went about saying my goodbyes to people. Every girl was flirting with me and asking me to stay and asking me where I was staying. I responded, at Nat's place, of course. I asked one of the girls I knew if she and her girlfriends wanted to come over to

Nat's place for drinks. They both looked at me, I thought, like I was out of my mind. I then gathered by their teeth grinding and jaw clenching that they were more coked out of their minds than I was. I thought, at first, their way of speaking was an aristocratic affectation; then, they asked me for coke, but I ran out, they could barely put two words together. They managed to blurt out, "Maybe later, darling," and then continued their drunken coke talk with one another. These girls were from aristocratic families with titles and money, some with titles and *no* money.

I just wanted to go home.

When I arrived at Nat's house, all the staff had left for the night, so the place was mine. I went down to the kitchen, which was full of all sorts of goodies to pick at and great bottles of wine. After I gorged myself à la Rothschild, I was ready for bed. I was halfway up the stairs when the doorbell rang. *Holy fuck, this has to be the girls!* I opened the door, and there was the beauty who couldn't speak her own language an hour earlier at the club. She walked right in and wanted a drink. She knew where the bar was, and of course, she knew Nat's townhouse and had been there many times before. So I followed her. Thirty seconds later, the doorbell rang again, and it was the other beauty; she too walked right in, gave me a big wet kiss, kicked off her heels, and headed for the bar. The zipper on the back of her dress was halfway down, exposing a very beautiful bare back. Maybe I'd hit the jackpot! Then I remembered all the coke I'd done, which rendered me useless and neutered.

As I was pouring myself a vodka tonic, the fuckin' doorbell rang again. *Now who?* One of the girls said, "Oh, I invited some people to join us for drinks." Before I knew it, there were about fifty people splayed out on every floor of Nat's place, including my bedroom. I knew most of the people, not all—some were good friends, but I was a houseguest here.

Downstairs in the kitchen, people were grabbing food from the fridge; there was coke all over the marble tabletop. I paused to do three hefty lines. Meanwhile, several people were drinking Nat's fine champagne, and half a dozen others were slurping Nat's vintage wines from the bottle.

More people kept showing up, and I started having a panic attack. I did a couple of more lines and then grabbed a friend and said, "Dude, there are people here I don't know. You have to help me host this thing."

"Nah, don't worry about it," my friend said, tapping out another bunch of lines. "Nat's happy someone is using the house."

Almost every flat surface looked like someone had spilled baby powder all over it. I gave up trying to maintain order and just joined in. I finished off a bottle of champagne I was carrying around, and I didn't even like champagne. I couldn't remember what day it was, nor did I care.

I don't know what time I woke up the next morning, but the place was spotless. When I made it to the kitchen, the coffee was ready, and the chef was preparing crepes. The major domo looked at me, and we both were smiling because I'd started speaking in tongues.

Halfway through my crepes, two attractive girls walked in, holding their shoes. I had no idea where they came from. "Oh, that coffee smells so good. Yes, I'd love a cup!" The night before they were great looking, but this morning, they looked kinda rough, makeup all over the place, wearing the same club outfits. One of the girls' hair was matted on her head like a flat hat. After drinking their coffee and a quick, "Darling, can you call us a car, please?", they were gone.

I looked at the major domo and shrugged my shoulders. "Nat's going to kill me. I am so, so sorry. I feel awful about this."

The major domo said, "No worries. It's been entertaining. You should have seen some of the characters we booted out earlier." Both he and the chef just laughed.

I knew it'd all been reported to Nat. Nothing was broken or stained, but there was a white carpet in one of the rooms, and I was sure, if you got out the Hoover, you'd come up with at least two kilos of coke!

Two days later, I called Nat and apologized for the party I threw in his house. Nat, in his gracious way, told me there was nothing to worry about. And a few days after that, he called me to say a friend had telephoned to thank him for the great party he had thrown. That partygoer was so whacked that he'd thought Nat was there! Nat was laughing about it, and then he said, "One day, I'll show you the security footage we have—it's insane!"

39

Interview gave me an assignment for a portrait of Thom Mount and his wife, Nikki. The press described Thom as a mini-mogul. At twenty-six years old, he had been made president of Universal Pictures, and he continued producing A-list Hollywood films when he left Universal to form his own production company, building a portfolio of big hits like *Bull Durham, Tequila Sunrise*, the Roman Polanski–directed *Death and the Maiden*, and many others.

I didn't find out about Thom's background till years later. I'd never paid much mind to people's careers. What mattered to me was that I liked the guy. I shot the *Interview* portrait of Thom and Nikki on my roof in SoHo. We became instant friends, and I developed an especially close rapport with Thom. He was a great, caring guy, and very humble, considering his position.

In 1988, Thom was in Paris producing the movie *Frantic*, with Roman Polanski directing. He called to ask if I would shoot some "special photography" for the film. The only other photographer he had hired for a couple of days was Helmut Newton. I jumped at the opportunity and got on a plane for Paris.

After being introduced around, I hung out, on and off set, shooting whatever I found interesting. I needed to focus on the two stars: Harrison Ford and Emmanuelle Seigner, Polanski's girlfriend, later his wife. As things rolled along, I would shoot the actors whenever they had down time. Polanski knew I was Thom Mount's friend and was very accommodating on set, but I spent more time with Harrison Ford, and after a week, we became very friendly.

One day, I heard the PAs calling for me on their walkie-talkies: Harrison wanted to see me in his trailer. I figured maybe he wanted to shoot some pictures. When I got inside, he

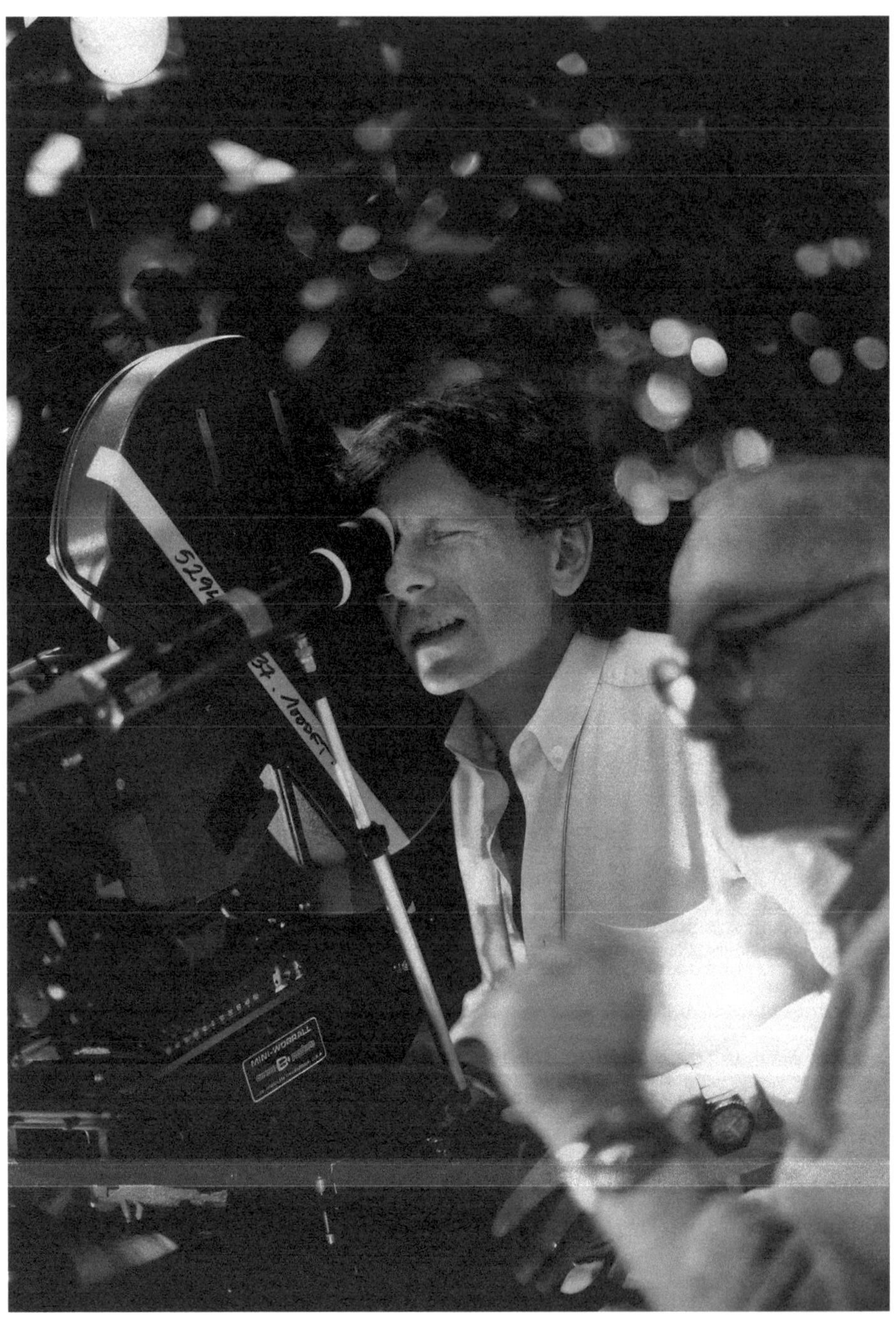

Roman Polanski directing *Frantic*

locked the door behind me, went to the back of the trailer, and returned with a very big Ziploc bag full of weed. "Humboldt County Gold, best weed you can find. Had it flown in, and it just arrived."

I was down for it; I had heard of Humboldt County Gold but had never tried any.

He rolled us a joint. I didn't know what hit me. Time went by, and there was a knock at his door, and someone called out, "Five minutes, Mr. Ford." Harrison had to be on set in five minutes. He got up, washed his hands, seemed perfectly fine. I tried to get up, but my legs weren't working. "What the fuck, Harrison? I can't move!" He got a big kick out of that; he was proud of his weed. He gave me his hand and yanked me up. I followed him into the studio where a club scene was to be shot. It was dark, lots of people, club lighting, spinning mirrored ball and all. I think because of that setting, the high felt more natural. Everything felt normal, and I got a grip on my senses. By the time they called "Cut," I even had some good portraits of Polanski.

Having been baptized in Humboldt County Gold, Harrison and I kind of buddied up for the rest of my stay. That first week was mostly indoor shots in the studio. I had mentioned to Emmanuelle Seigner that, whenever she felt comfortable and had the time, I would like to get some solo shots of her. I wanted to do a really great shooting for Thom, for Polanski, and the cast. It was my first time on a movie set. Polanski was an icon as a director, and Harrison Ford was Harrison Ford. I was really attracted to the environment.

As always, when it came to taking pictures, I'd let nothing get in the way of doing great work, especially with great subjects—and the fact that the only other photographer doing special photography was Helmut Newton meant I had to step up and really do something special.

After they took a break from filming (which meant getting really stoned with Harrison in his trailer), the next shot was with him alone in a tight interior that was meant to be a houseboat on the Seine. There was not enough room for me in there (thank God, because I had a major buzz coming on), so I stayed back, off set. Emmanuelle was there, too, and she came over and said, "Do you want to take some pictures? I know a good spot." She was a former model, so I figured she must have an eye for light and a good location.

Emmanuelle was an attractive young woman in her twenties with a naughty look in her eyes. I knew that look well (I began imagining all these great shots of her I could do). She seemed like a cool girl, and the cool girls always knew how to give you that look, checking you out with a sideways glance while discreetly letting you know they were checking you out. If you didn't respond quickly enough, they just might grab you by the hand, pull you into a bathroom, lock the door, then hand you a packet and say, "Here, chop us up a line."

I let my imagination run wild like I was being led into a secret club with her. Meanwhile, back to our imaginary bathroom, that cool girl would drop her panties and use the loo in front of you, making sure you got a flash (remember I was so stoned out of my head on Humboldt County Gold). Your job was to play it cool, as if this were normal behavior for you, and normal it became, and you would chop another line because you were that cool, too. It was up to you to make the next move, but would it be worth the grief if you got caught, because the temptress was often your girlfriend's best friend. It could be dangerous. The thought fucked up my high. I started sweating, I began to feel paranoid; this pot was like LSD.

Back to reality, we were in a huge sound stage with multiple sets built, and I needed to be out of the way and quiet. The set they were using was the nighttime interior of the houseboat, which took up a small section of the sound stage. Since it was still daytime outside, I was hoping for some natural light. Except for the set being artificially lit, the rest of the soundstage was completely dark. I needed a couple of portraits so I wouldn't have to think about them later. (Most art departments love taking single images of the cast members and cutting and pasting them together in postproduction like a collage to the point where you don't even recognize your original shot.)

We headed backstage, and Emmanuelle took my hand to guide me through this maze of scaffolding and props, my other hand holding two cameras and a shoulder bag with some lenses and film. We stopped by one of the large stage doors where a sliver of light was coming through from outside, not enough to shoot (but enough for Humboldt County Gold to whisper in my ear, "See, I told you, she wants you, look!"). She let go of my hand, leaned up against the door, and lifted the hem of her skirt, I think. It was too dark to see what else she was showing me, but her gesture was like a smack in the face.

Oh, fuck! My second day of a seven-day shoot—I would be gone in sixty seconds if word got out that I was back there alone with her. I began to sweat even more, I barely talked; I was tongue-tied! All I could produce was a goofy "uh-oh," so I played stupid.

Emmanuelle didn't say anything. She just rolled her eyes, snapped her bubble gum, and unwrapped another. I was just close enough to see her expression, which spelled out "What a dumb fuck."

I asked for a piece of gum, which she threw at me. I grabbed it in the dark off the floor. My mouth was so dry; it felt like I had licked the bottom of a birdcage. I took a few half-hearted pictures and got us the fuck out of there as fast as I could.

A couple of hours later, one of the PAs found me and told me Thom Mount wanted to see me in his office. I knocked on his door, and he let me in, sat down behind his desk. "Sante, I just want to tell you this. I love you, man, but if Roman has the slightest suspicion about you being around Emmanuelle, you're going to be on the next flight back to New York."

"Thom, you have to believe me, you know I'm not like that. I was gonna take some pictures of her and she takes me to some dark corner backstage and freaked me out. I got out of there as fast as I could!"

Thom said, "I know you're not like that, but Roman doesn't, so I'm just warning you. Be careful around her."

By the next day, I could feel something had changed between Roman and me. Nothing obvious, but my sixth sense said there was something (maybe I was paranoid), so I laid back and tried to be invisible.

That evening, we were waiting around for a light to be changed on set. Harrison and I had already smoked a giant spliff of Humboldt County Gold. Harrison was standing near me, and Emmanuelle and some crew members were there too. Roman had an audience and our attention. He's telling Harrison how he should be acting out this fight scene, and Harrison was rolling his eyes. Roman was showing off and was looking slightly ridiculous, acting all Kung Fu. Suddenly he delivered one of those Bruce Lee roundhouse kicks, right toward my face, a move that caused his pants to split.

Harrison turned toward me and said, "There is a God."

Roman stood there like a schmuck, checking his pants, torn from the bottom of his zipper to the back of his belt. Emmanuelle was laughing hysterically. Someone was sent to find him a new pair of pants, and Harrison and I went off to roll another spliff, cracking up.

The rest of the shoot went by without a hitch. Roman even gave me a signed book of all his films. All's well that ends well!

During that same time, I organized a shooting for French Vogue, a great magazine.

I had let them know I was in town and what I was doing, they arranged for me to do an editorial feature on Polanski and his muse, Emmanuelle Seigner. I arranged to shoot it in Les Bains Douches—at the time the hottest nightspot in Paris. The place used to be an old bathhouse; it even had a functioning pool. The shooting went well. Nothing out of the ordinary; everyone was happy.

I found out Joe Pesci and Bobby De Niro were in town. I gave their hotel a call. Bobby said to let Roman know they were around.

Paris was Roman's town and he wanted to show us a great night out, and most importantly, where the girls were. Where were all the great looking girls? At Les Bains Douches, of course. Les Bains had been redesigned by Philippe Starck and its DJ was David Guetta, before either of them had become famous. It was basically the Studio 54 of Paris, where every designer, from Jean Paul Gaultier to Claude Montana, threw after-parties following their runway shows. Everyone partied hard and it was a hangout for the fashion world. Polanski had even shot some scenes for *Frantic* in there.

The owner, Hubert Boukobza, made sure Roman and the rest of us had a prime table, anything we wanted to drink and more. De Niro, Pesci, and I did a walk around with Roman, checking the place out. At one point Roman stopped and we found ourselves in an odd spot, standing in the middle of pedestrian traffic. Joe asked me what we were doing standing here. Were we waiting for somebody? I had no idea. Bobby asked Roman what we were doing.

Roman turned to us and explained. "This is the ladies' room. Eventually they all have to go to the bathroom at some time!"

Joe said, "You got to be kidding me, let's get outta here, let's go sit down."

Bobby turned to me and said, "Fuckin' guy must be crazy."

I shrugged my shoulders till they touched my earlobes. It was a first for me!

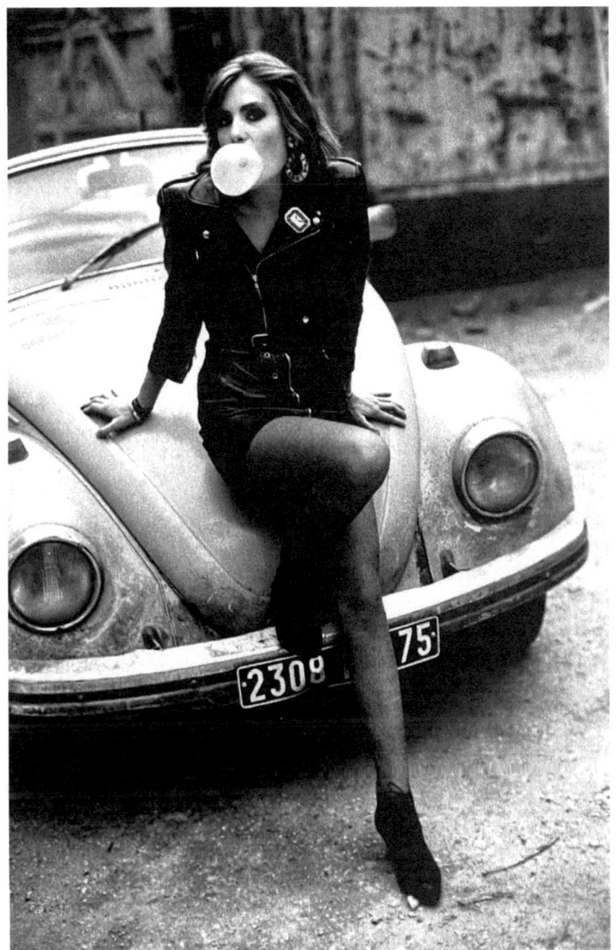

Emmanuelle Seigner off set on *Frantic*

40

Winter in New York City could be a motherfucker—cold, windy, slushy, and wet! It's when you wished for the tropics and, lucky for me, it was also when most clients shoot in warm weather locations.

I got the call to leave in January for a *Playboy* shoot with Rachel Hunter in Mexico! I was happy to go. I had known Rachel a long time, from the early days of her career. Fun-loving New Zealander that she was, I knew she'd make the trip entertaining, exciting, and memorable.

In pre-production, we found an eco-friendly place south of Puerto Vallarta. It was located on a lagoon that included a great beach. Horses, thatched roof bungalows, a beach bar, and terrific weather! My crew and I flew in from New York and Rachel came in from LA. We all met at the airport in Mexico City. We were picked up in two vans, and it was a two-hour drive to our location. Halfway there, we turned off the highway and got on a dirt road, and the smooth ride started to feel like a stagecoach. One hour felt like three. We were now in a lusher and more tropical environment, and it was getting dark. We could only see what the van's headlights illuminated. We then started passing through villages with all their lights out, which felt strange. It was winter; it wasn't late. It just got dark early, but it still felt weird. We finally arrived at the hotel, and it looked inviting in the dark, lit only by candles and torches.

It was around 8:00 p.m. and we were hungry. My assistants put all the cameras and equipment in the office, and we were shown to our rooms to drop off our bags. We'd then meet up at the outdoor dining room for dinner.

Our rooms were all singles and scattered around the property. They looked cozy—the beds had mosquito netting, and the candles made it really romantic. My own place had a

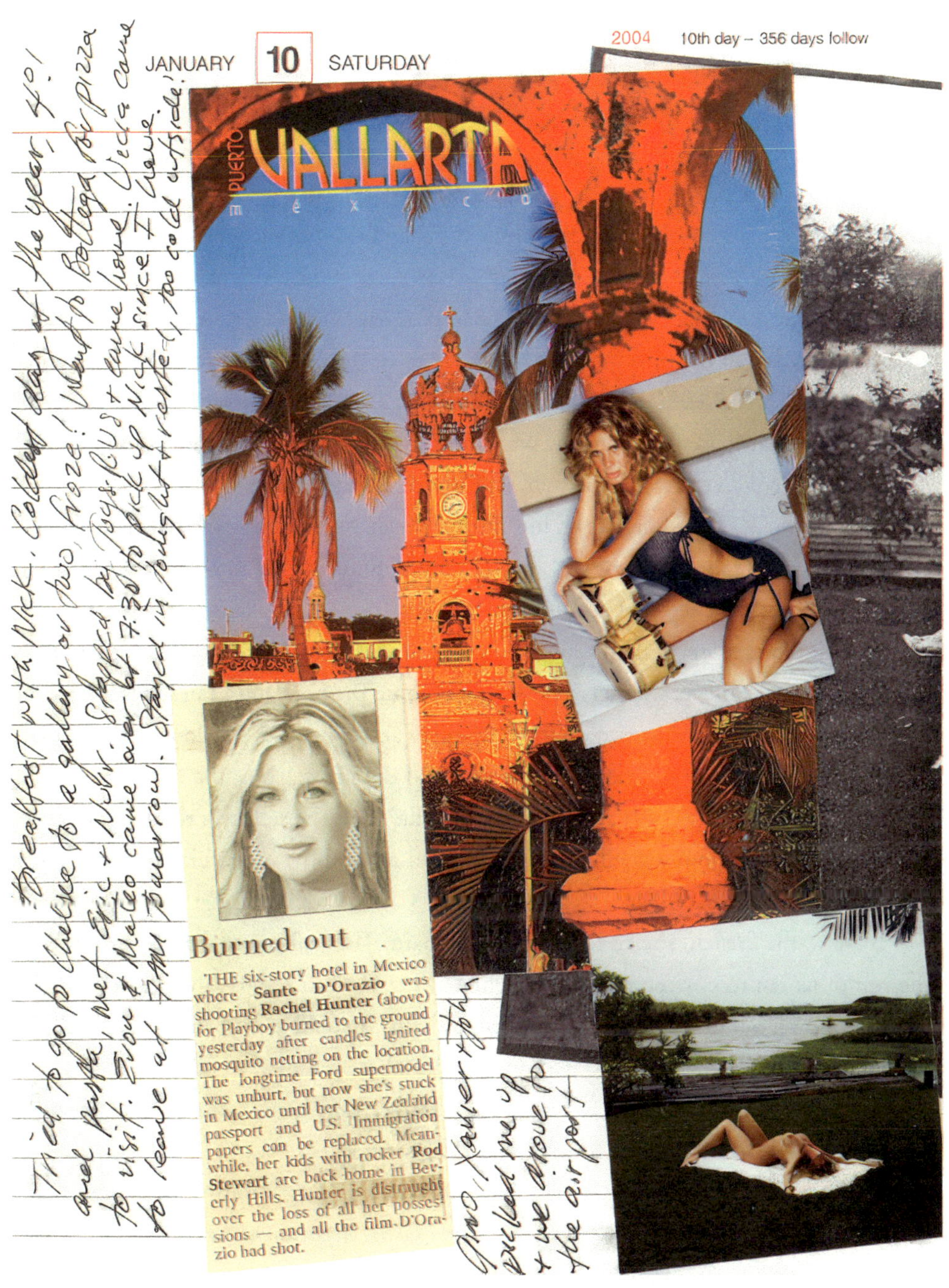

Burned out

THE six-story hotel in Mexico where **Sante D'Orazio** was shooting **Rachel Hunter** (above) for Playboy burned to the ground yesterday after candles ignited mosquito netting on the location. The longtime Ford supermodel was unhurt, but now she's stuck in Mexico until her New Zealand passport and U.S. Immigration papers can be replaced. Meanwhile, her kids with rocker **Rod Stewart** are back home in Beverly Hills. Hunter is distraught over the loss of all her possessions — and all the film D'Orazio had shot.

Sante's diary page, Rachel Hunter, Mexico, for *Playboy*

small porch that opened to the lagoon, and I could make out observation towers from which you could see the ocean.

I realized what eco-friendly meant when I went to the bathroom. There was no electricity anywhere, except in the office. Candles were everywhere, and you couldn't flush any toilet paper. That meant after you wiped, you had to put the paper in the basket next to the toilet! *Oh, man!* I got my shit together, cleaned up, and went to meet everyone at dinner.

By now we were really starving; we finally sat down and started with margaritas, chips, and guacamole. One drink later, we were feeling the buzz. A few of the waiters were hurrying about, and I wondered what the rush was—we happened to be the only guests, apart from another couple or two. I could see in the near distance a beautiful orange glow from over the trees, and then more of the help went running by. We wanted to order more drinks and, of course, food!

Suddenly, panic set in with the staff, and someone yelled, "Fire!"

Fuckin' Rachel! Her room was on fire. She had lit all the candles around her bed and left the windows open, and the wind had blown her mosquito netting into the candle flames. Her entire room, thatched roof and all, was ablaze!

The wind picked up, and now my assistant's roof next door was on fire. The room next door to his was the office, with all my equipment in it. The boys and I ran in with the roof burning above and started passing all the equipment and trunks out the door and windows, to the open lawn. There was nothing else we could do but watch as the flames reached a height of at least fifty feet. We couldn't fucking believe it. The staff was throwing buckets of water, which was no use at all. Someone handed me a bottle of tequila, and we all just proceeded to get shit-faced.

By now, the fire had spread to the trees and barn. The staff ran to free the horses, and the rest of us ran to our rooms and brought our luggage outside to salvage whatever we could! Running out of my room, I broke my little toe. I could see it flapping as I walked. Eventually, I found some tape and latched it to the adjacent toe.

One of the owners yelled, "Evacuate!" The flames were getting close to the propane tanks and could blow the whole fuckin' place to smithereens!

Since we were on a lagoon, we had to get on rowboats to get to the ocean side. *Every man for himself, grab whatever you can. There ain't no fire department coming to save us.* The place with its thatched roofs, towers, and lagoon started to look like a scene out of *Apocalypse Now.* All we needed was the smell of napalm and for the propane tanks to blow.

We all got into rowboats, laughing our asses off, drunk as fuck! Halfway across the lagoon we realized we were rowing in circles because it was so dark, and everyone was laughing and looking to see if the place was gonna blow. I took charge and got us heading to the other side. I asked my idiot assistants if they had grabbed any equipment. The morons looked at each other, all three holding bottles of tequila, and burst out laughing! Fuck it, I took a bottle and started swigging and passing it around. We got to the other side and gathered at the outdoor bar lounge and, from across the lagoon, watched the place go up in flames. This wasn't even day one of our shoot!

By then, we were beyond shit-faced, and fortunately for the owners (if I can say that), it started to rain. We walked along the beachside, and there were empty bungalows; a few of them were furnished, so we crashed, four to a bed.

When we got up the next day, we saw it had rained hard. One of my assistants was wrapped in a blanket, floating on a mat in the outdoor bar lounge, surrounded by vomit. We left him there and rowed back across the lagoon. All that was left of Rachel's room, my assistant's room, and the office were smoldering sticks. A couple of other rooms burned down as well. All the luggage we had left on the lawn was drenched, but thank God my cameras and equipment were in watertight trunks, safe and dry.

The management sent all the wet luggage to be laundered. My assistant found his brand-new Leica camera melted and useless. We thought that was funny; he didn't. My petty cash was all burnt up, as well as some passports and other documents. We ended up wearing clothes from the gift shop. Beige string pants and shirts, that farmer-look with leather sandals. In these outfits, in this environment, we looked like POWs out of a scene from *The Deer Hunter*.

Thank goodness the kitchen was intact, and they were serving food. Whatever other guests there were had left, and it was just us.

At lunch, someone said we should pack and go home. I said, "Go home? With what? We got no money. Our tickets got burned along with our passports. We ain't going anywhere—let's shoot! We don't need clothes 'cause it's *Playboy*! She's going to be naked anyway!"

So that's what we did. Our embassies in Mexico City needed days to have money wired in so they could get us out of the country. I didn't even bother telling *Playboy* until it was time to go. Even though the place was in ruins, there were still enough rooms for those of us who needed them. We spent the next three or four days shooting until we had everything we needed to go home, along with my film in the can!

I remember my assistant, Gino, unshaven and wearing his farmer gift-shop outfit, getting on the plane for New York in the middle of winter. His girlfriend met him at the airport with a coat. Half the gang had to go to Mexico City first to get new passports, including Gino. Why he hadn't changed outfits there? I'll never know. All he needed was a donkey to complete the look.

And Rachel didn't disappoint. She had been entertaining, exciting, and certainly memorable—just as I said she would be!

41

Man is not worried by real problems so much as by his imagined anxieties about real problems.
—Epictetus

I spent the last two weeks traveling on assignments for several magazines—Cabo San Lucas with Monica Bellucci, Acapulco with Rachel Hunter, St. Barths with Stephanie Seymour. I stayed away from phones or calling home as much as possible to keep a clear head in order to focus on my work. Then, it was time to go home and change hats to be what I'm not: a businessman.

The thought of it was depressing, and that night, my anxiety started as soon as I arrived and left JFK, hitting traffic on the Brooklyn-Queens Expressway. Making it home, I took a quick shower and hopped into bed, postponing messages with a pill for sound sleep. I woke up in the morning with an adrenaline rush from an erotic dream that I wished had been real, checked my shorts just in case, and was about to go back to sleep when my accountant called to tell me about some big payments that needed my attention.

That's when my nerves hit overdrive. The checks that had come in were still warm and already going out, along with what I didn't have to spare. Fuck! I started to feel that slight ache in my stomach. I tried to keep it cool, but my mind just went into fifth gear, and the brakes were not working. A panic attack was being delivered by DHL. The irrational became my consigliere, and I started to spin faster than a whirling dervish. I reached out to every guru I'd ever read about for help, but I had passed that Bodhi tree miles back. Then, I remembered the stash I'd put aside for moments just like this. I looked in the back of that drawer I'd thought was such a clever hiding hole, and there it was! I popped two pills for quick release and another for time release. Holding on and dodging every fear that had come to visit since I was in the womb. I waited till that first wave hit and the brakes began to slow me down. The second wave brought the color back to my knuckles, so I could take my hands off the wheel; now the car slowed to a stop, and I was sitting on the couch staring into space. Things began to be all right.

Afterward, I crushed some of the OxyContin I had and snorted 'em up the wazoo; my eyes began to piss water, so I closed them and leaned my head back to rest, knowing if I was lucky, I'd dream the dream that I'd wished was real, hoping that phone would never ring.

Later, my assistant picked me up for a shooting out on the busy streets of New York. My phone rings, and my assistant picked it up.

"It seems to be urgent," he said. "It's your mother . . ."

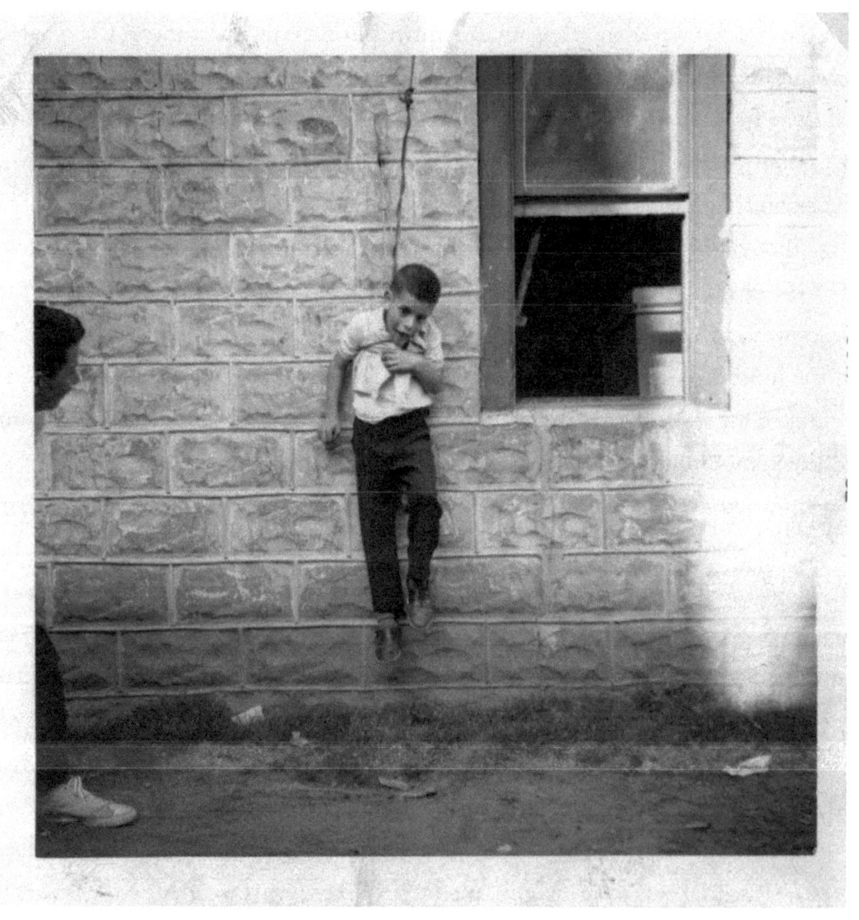

Sante, photographed by his brother Mike, directed by his cousin Mike

42

The Poet makes himself a seer by a long, gigantic,
and rational derangement of all the senses.
—Arthur Rimbaud

The pain is fading, the morphine working.

My night was a strange one. Very depressed, an apparition appeared who resembled Virgil, Dante's guide to the Inferno, now taking me through my Hell. Relatives long gone came to me; they told me it was over, and that I'd failed. I wanted to be no more, and the pain was like a deep gnaw to my side.

At home, in a feeble-painkiller state, I went downstairs. Unsettled, I changed bedrooms three-four times. I smoked, cursed God, ate junk, and smoked some more. Took another pill, desperate for relief. For what may have been an hour or a minute, I felt nothing more; I was gone. I only later realized that I was still present when I awoke where I last sat. Just darker, and in more pain, but with time, nothing mattered.

All things are borrowed, and nothing remains. All is now.

Darkness comes to us all at one time or another. For some of us, it's day to day, week to week, month to month, with varying degrees of intensity. Clinically, it's known as depression. Today, we're able to share about it and discover it's nothing to be ashamed of. More people suffer from it than we ever publicly knew before. Some say it's a chemical malfunction, and I personally agree, no different than your body not producing enough insulin and making you a diabetic. It has nothing to do with your character or intelligence. Dealing with it is hard on you and especially hard on the people around you. I know both sides because my mom had a rough time with it to the point of making her emotionally unstable at times, forcing me to care for her, which affected my own stability for the entirety of my life. So far, I've survived by teaching myself many ways of navigating it to stay alive—because the need for relief can come in the form of wanting to die.

Once this darkness comes over me and I fall into its pit, it's so hard to get out, let alone maintain my sanity. I have little control over its duration; I know it will pass, but I don't know when it will. But I've learned that, from that darkness, there are answers, insights that come with a sensitivity that others fail to see or feel.

Otherwise, I needed to dose myself into oblivion. I couldn't bear it at times and tried extreme means to stay alive, used whatever I could to get me past those times until I could find some light.

I would feel my strength diminishing and an abyss at my feet, as if I felt the cold air coming up from that infinite void below, calling me to lean forward. To avoid drowning in that darkness, I had to numb myself with substances, buying time to manage my sanity or what was left of it. Preferring to live in a drug-induced state, which to others resembled insanity. Or was it the other way around?

I've found that, within these deep, dark places, we can discover something of great value that unlocks forces and insights that laid dormant under better times. But first, you have to make it out alive by recognizing this unexpressed self. For me, the keys for this exorcism could come only through poetry and art. If you're able to tap into it and connect, then able to make it tangible, it will speak to you and invite you to be an artist. Art, at this point, is no longer decoration—it's a life-giving necessity to your existence. You can save yourself by going, as Joseph Campbell once stated, "where most dare not venture."

Like the myth of the hero, the journey involves "descending into hell to bring back what others never knew they needed." You may be thought of as crazy to even try, but the artist has no other choice. Within this madness is our salvation, our sanity. The risk is no risk, and fear is equal in the life or death of your spirit, so we go for it. It would be a greater folly not to try. Death awaits us either way.

43

I was home one evening when a friend called from London and asked if I'd mind watching over a girlfriend of his. "She's coming to New York City and doesn't know anyone there."

I said, "Sure, have her call me. We can maybe go and grab a bite together."

A few days later the girl, Natalia, called me, and I invited her over. I opened the door. *Holy shit! What a beauty!* She was stunning: taller than me, with pale green eyes and long dark hair. I was tongue-tied at first. But I was a gentleman. I invited her in and offered her something to drink. She had a witty sense of humor and spoke English perfectly well, with a slight accent. I asked where in Russia she was from, and she shot right back that she was not Russian; she was Ukrainian.

Natalia had never been to New York before and wanted to check it out. She told me she modeled occasionally, but it didn't really interest her; she was interested in art. She seemed quite cultured. She didn't know anyone in town and appreciated me inviting her over. She wasn't hungry and was happy just to hang out and watch American TV.

At one point, the news came on, standard local news fare—a fire in the Bronx and a rape in a park.

She yelled at the TV, "Rape, rape, rape! Americans are always going on about rape. What's the big deal? In Russia, everybody gets raped!"

I was shocked.

She said, "Americans . . . In my town, on your way to school, you cross the field, and you get raped. You go fetch some water, and you get raped. It is so common; it's no big deal."

My jaw was hanging, and I said, "Don't you call the police?"

"It usually *is* the police! Nobody cares. You get used to it."

Her phone rang.

She turned to ask me for my address and then told whomever she was talking to, "Okay, come pick me up. I'll come down in fifteen minutes."

"I thought you said you didn't know anyone in New York?"

"I don't," she said. "I met these ten Chinese men at the bar at the Plaza Athenée, that's where I'm staying. They want to take me to an art dealer's home for drinks, and it's near my hotel. They were having dinner downtown at Cipriani. It's not far from here?"

I was skeptical. "No, not at all, it's just five blocks or so."

She picked up her things and gave me a big hug and a kiss and said, "I'll call you tomorrow!"

I can be quite naïve at times, and I didn't want to draw any conclusions or be judgmental, but this really had me wondering. The next day, I called my friend in London, and he said, "Nah, nah, she's really cool. You'll like her."

The next evening, Natalia appeared with a bottle of vodka. The brand was unfamiliar to me. She soon had me laughing about her night out with the Chinese guys—nothing better than someone who can make you laugh and laugh at themselves too. She had a lot of spunk, as they used to say in the old black-and-white movies, and a lot of charm.

I asked her about the art dealer they had visited the night before. Even though she was interested in art, she wasn't too familiar with contemporary art. She found it comical. This art dealer had a beautiful home uptown in the East Sixties, with a swimming pool and these "stupid" paintings of soup cans they said were worth millions of dollars.

"These men went crazy for a big painting of Chairman Mao. Do you know who he is? I know because he was a communist leader. Why would anyone want a big painting of Chairman Mao with a green face that cost millions of dollars—these people are crazy!"

I asked her if the apartment was between Madison and Lexington.

"Maybe," she said, "it was near my hotel."

Okay, I had a fair idea who this mega dealer was and had myself a laugh.

I still know Natalia to this day, and I love her. Such fun and so funny, and even with many years behind us now, I still don't know what she does for a living, and I couldn't care less! I heard she had started painting . . .

44

It's an amazing experience to stand in front of a beautiful woman or model and be given license to look straight into their eyes. I have never taken that for granted; it's awesome. It's intimidating too, but it makes it easier for me to read my subject, to feel a vibe and vice versa, especially for a portrait; that's basically what a cover shooting is.

It's understandable that we are not permitted to do that freely, but in my profession, it's a must—for me at least. It's in the eyes that you can read someone; you almost feel you know them, even if it's only at a glance; we've all made eye contact, imagine it lasting for thirty seconds. Then, I can also see what reflections are in their eyes; too many or none at all can change the whole mood of a picture (It's why I always wear black). There is a moment, that point, where I'm stopped by my subject's gaze, and frozen by their eyes. From habit and experience, I usually turn away at a certain point. I'm in total awe but don't want to intimidate them. I make eye contact again through the camera and shoot, trying to recapture that first impression. If I feel the connection while shooting, then I'm almost certain they felt it too, and that's when I know I got my shot; that's when your sense perception must kick in. At its best, it's electrifying, thrilling, personal, intimate, and yet always respectful. It's a privilege few of us are afforded. It's magic, and when others see the image, they can experience the same magic. That's exactly what makes a good photograph for me. That's how I work. People need to see your cover in a window display from across the street. It's the eyes they'll connect with first.

It's only through this exchange with my subjects, eye-to-eye, via an invisible energy that's totally sensory that a connection is made (the eyes don't lie). I'm always awestruck by the women I shoot—great beauty has a way of doing that, no different than when in nature. I am usually more nervous to begin with than they are, especially when they are so vulnerable. I would never do anything to risk losing their trust. The process is a ritual and, if successful, can be experienced over and over again in a great image, that pure connection between photographer and subject.

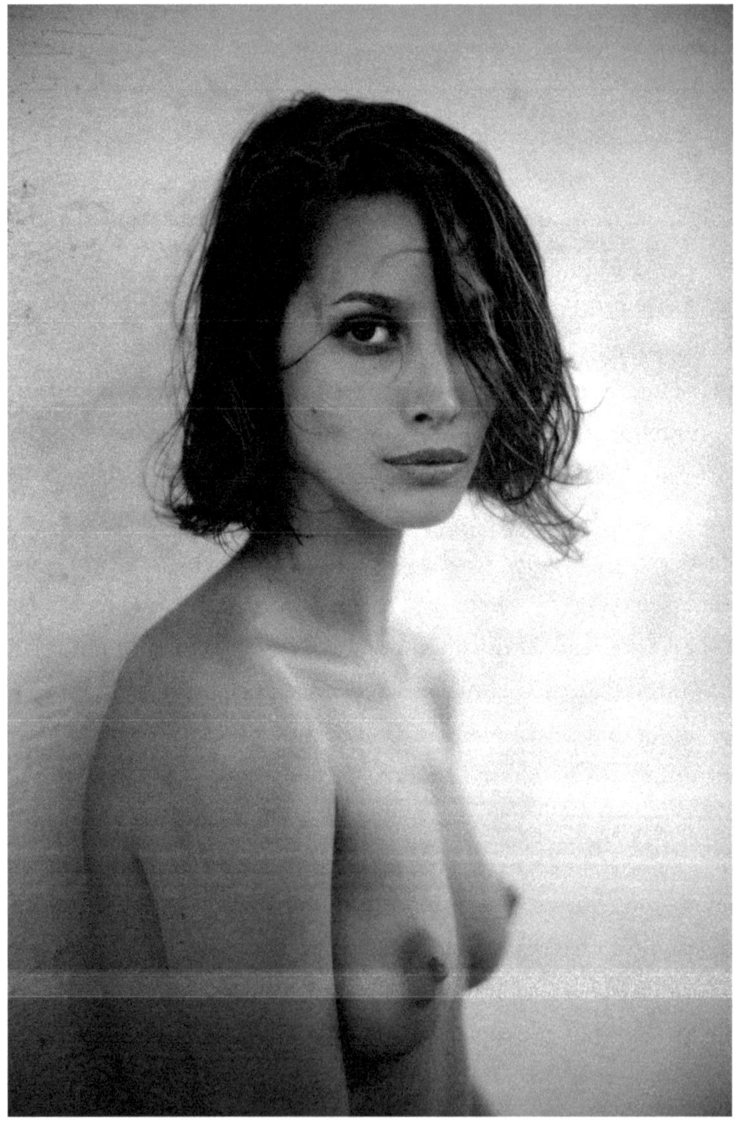

Christy Turlington, roof of the Mondrian Hotel, Hollywood, California

45

When things started taking off in my photography career, I left Brooklyn behind me and hoped not to go back. I used to say, if I ever had to go back, it could only mean I had failed miserably. It wasn't the Brooklyn of today and the city ain't what it used to be!

But I always went back to my mom's for Sunday lunch. I couldn't do without the tradition or the pasta. I would take my friends over for a treat, including some well-known people to surprise my mom. They all came—from Brooke Shields to Linda Evangelista, Mickey Rourke to Joe Pesci. It was the house I grew up in, a modest three-story house with a driveway and backyard. The top floor was a nice size attic that we rented out, like everyone else in the neighborhood, even though it wasn't legal to do so. My aunt and uncle lived on the second floor. Many families would split the ownership of large homes; it's an awful idea, take it from me.

When I set out traveling the world, I left the house in my mother's hands. A very capable woman, and fearless behind the wheel as well. She was then in her seventies, and she drove her car everywhere. She'd often drive into the city with the excuse of dropping off food for me. We saw each other a couple of times a week—sometimes to my annoyance, but she was very independent.

After my aunt and uncle died, their two older sons took over their ownership of half the house. My mom had the other half; later, I bought my cousins' half, and I owned the place, along with my mom. At first, I didn't want anything to do with the house, and the only time I put money into it was when something essential, like a boiler, broke down. I just couldn't be bothered. In truth, the whole neighborhood was kind of going to shit from when I grew up there, though it was still safe. But I had made it out. I was flying to Europe for the collections: London, Paris, and Rome. Back to New York, editing film, then to the

Caribbean for Victoria's Secret, and LA to shoot Janet Jackson for her new CD cover. I was getting spoiled with caviar, girls, and big money jobs. Fuck Brooklyn!

I told Mom to rent the second and top floors to whomever she felt good about. We figured out what the other homeowners on the block were asking and made ours the same price. She would rent both apartments above her "as is"—you paint and fix whatever you like. Mom was easygoing. She never gave anyone a lease; the tenants paid cash, and she left them alone.

Tenants would come and go. Some stayed a year, others five years, no problem. The only problem was that my mother loved everybody, and sometimes, she was gullible. If people liked her food, she trusted them.

I don't remember where in the world I was at the time, but she called to tell me she had rented the attic apartment to two beautiful Russian girls who didn't speak very much English "but they eatta my lasagna!" As long as they ate her lasagna, things would be fine.

This was before the wall came down in Berlin. Russia was still a communist country. The majority of Russians were in Brighton Beach, and they were mostly Jews. By the late '80s, more Russian immigrants were arriving, and new communities were popping up in my neighborhood. With all ethnic groups, you get the good and the bad. The good were the hardworking types with some kind of trade. The bad were the criminal element.

According to my mother, these girls were very nice and "so beautiful" with "*gambe lunghe*" (long legs). They told my mom they worked at a Russian restaurant up Coney Island Avenue. My mother was so happy with them that, once or twice a week, she would even drive them to work. It gave her something to do. This went on all winter long during my busiest travel season, so I didn't get to meet them. The few times I was at the house was in the evenings, and they were probably out, since they worked at night.

The second floor became vacant, and Mom rented it to two gay guys. One of them, named Nicky, was an Italian from Brooklyn; he was kind of butch and came off a little rough, very Brooklyn. He said he was a DJ, and years earlier had DJ'd at Studio 54. I had my doubts, but who cares? The other one was more delicate and fragile; his name was Pedro, and I never found out exactly where he was from. I met them when I went to Mom's for Sunday lunch. They seemed okay to me, and Mom had already made them some food, which they loved, and of course, that made her happy. I was happy they were gay. All my gay friends were clean freaks, so hopefully these two would help out with keeping the place looking clean and nice, take out the garbage, and things like that. They had a dog, and my mom didn't mind that. It didn't bother me either. I just asked that they clean up after Fido and not to let the dog loose on the front lawn or in the backyard.

Now Mom was collecting two rents, and I was back at work, shooting and traveling. Months later, I went to Brooklyn to visit my mom; I saw garbage piled up on the side, by the driveway, and it appeared that Nicky and Pedro had acquired a second dog. There was dogshit in the backyard, and I realized, once again, that human nature was, in general, selfish and equally full of shit!

My mom didn't seem to notice anything as long she collected the rent, so I needed to have a talk with these guys. My approach was always to be friendly and never put anyone on the defensive. I rang their doorbell and asked them to join me for a glass of wine. We sat on the porch, and I reminded them about our agreement concerning the backyard and the dog(s). I told them I didn't mind the second dog since both dogs were relatively small. However, they hadn't cleaned up, put out the garbage, or stayed out of the backyard.

In our chitchat, Nicky told me he was from Court Street in Brooklyn, which had always been mob country, both high and low level. All the Italians who worked as longshoremen settled around Court Street when they first came to this country, and anyone working the docks somehow knew or were somehow linked to the mob. Nicky in his braggadocio made sure to beef up that part of himself. I could not have cared less because anyone who talked about that shit usually didn't have any connection to it at all. At most, he may have had a friend whose cousin had a friend whose uncle was involved.

Nicky's big talk made me realize he was a jerkoff. Pedro, on the other hand, I liked. He was into arts and crafts. He made shirts, loose-fitting pants for the beach, leather and cloth shoulder bags, and so on. He would have been better off peddling his wares to tourists in Costa Rica, but here we were in Brooklyn. I felt like we'd resolved some issues, so I went back home with Mom's care package of food, and back to work.

Then I went off on another round of trips and was happily away from Mom and the house in Brooklyn. Sometimes I would be away for up to two months, and whenever I'd land home, starting at JFK, the ritual was always the same: I'd get into the car at the airport and call my mom to let her know I was safe. I was thirty-five years old by then!

This time was no different. I called, and she picked up. "Hey, Mom, I'm back."

"You home?" she asked, as always.

"No, I just landed, and I don't want you to worry."

"Oh, okay, thatsa niceh." I could hear the tone in her voice that I hated to hear—it's Debbie Downer.

"Ma, what's wrong now?"

"No, nothing, the guys uppa stairs no paya the rent."

"All right, it's only a week into the month; they'll pay it."

"No, they no paya fa two months."

"Ah, shit, you gotta tell me now when I haven't even stepped into my house yet! I bet you're happy to bring me bad news." Sometimes I think she should have been a funeral director. "Thanks, Mom, I'm so glad I called, and happy to be back! How about the Russian girls upstairs?"

"They no leavah the money. I no seeah long time."

Now I definitely didn't want to see my mom, but if I didn't fix this problem, it'd be in my face every day, twice a day, until I did.

On my first Sunday home, I went to Mom's house, called Nicky and Pedro, and fixed whatever problem there was. Seemed that they both were out of work, and since they knew I was coming over, they had borrowed cash to pay one month's rent, still owing us for the other. The Russian girls were upstairs. They both looked pretty haggard, but I settled things with them as well.

I headed into Monday having to tie up some loose ends on a big production, and also on four other jobs following that one. There were always problems to solve and decisions to be made. I needed a clear head.

Then late Monday afternoon, I got the phone call of all phone calls:

"This is Detective Ferrara from the Seventieth Precinct in Brooklyn speaking. We have your mom here at the station, and we need you to come in and pick her up. Don't worry, she's fine. We've been taking care of her, and she's been great entertainment. It was a matter of misidentification, but the real problem has to do with your mom's tenants. I can't explain over the phone, but we need you to take your mom home. She's worried you're going to be mad at her. She's a sweetheart, and she says she left the dough in the oven for your focaccia that she was planning to make. Don't worry. We made sure the door was locked and the oven was off. She wants to make sure you know."

Now I had to drop everything and get a car to drive me to the 70th Precinct in Brooklyn to pick up my mom. I could not imagine what the hell this could all be about. It was the last thing I needed. Plus, it was rush hour on the BQE.

When I got to the police station I found Detective Ferrara, a nice Italian guy, and he explained what happened: "Two of our agencies were conducting an operation. The two Russian girls in the attic were working at a strip club on Coney Island Avenue and were part of a Russian-run prostitution ring. Our team had observed your mom always driving them around and assumed she worked with them."

"What?"

"The other unit was working on a numbers racket downtown, and these two guys on the second floor of your mom's house were picking up and dropping off cash for a social club down by Court Street. We put our resources together and waited for all of them to be home at the same time to go in to make the bust. We thought your mom was in on it, and sorry, we had to cuff her."

"Oh, no, you're fuckin' kidding me!"

"Yeah, she got a little hysterical, but a lot of the guys here are Italian, and once we realized she wasn't involved, we started speaking Italian with her. Got about two dozen recipes. I apologize for the confusion. The guys in the back love her and don't want to let her go, oh, and she left her hearing aid at home. It was tough when she was hysterical. She was answering questions we weren't asking. One of the officers in the back, Mike Ferri, says he went to high school with you, knows you and your mom. He recognized your mom, says she made the best calzones. She told us you're a great photographer and that Julia Roberts and Oprah are friends of yours; she's really proud of you. Don't be too hard on her. She reminds us of our *nonnas*. She was worried you were going to yell at her."

When Mom popped her head out from the back room of the station, I couldn't keep a straight face—I just started laughing, gave her a big hug, and took her home.

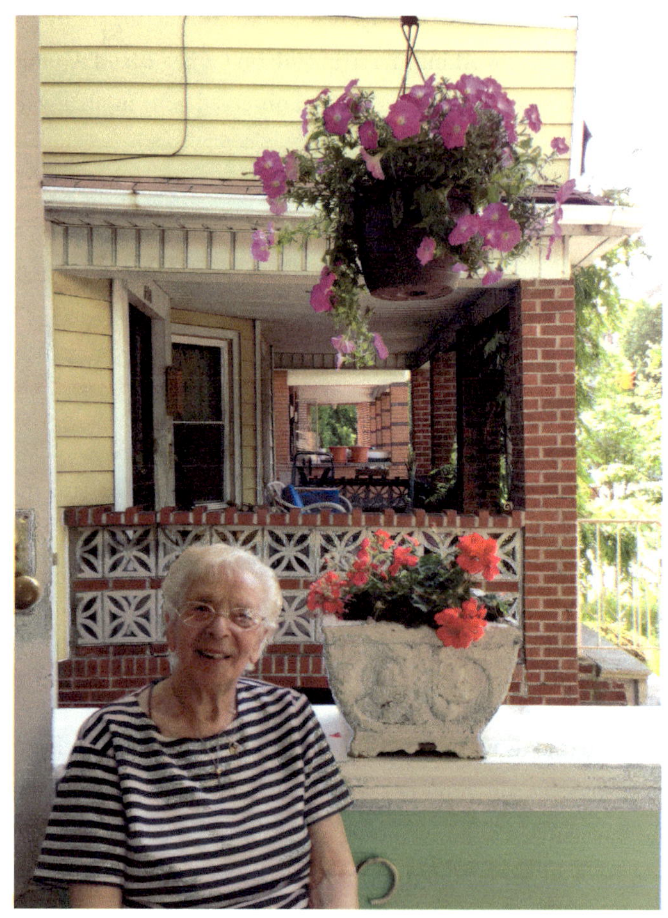

Maria D'Orazio, Brooklyn, New York

46

Poetry operates by hints and dark suggestions.
It is full of secrets and hidden formulae, like a witch's brew.
—Anthony Hecht

One summer day, I was walking across Spring Street when I glanced to one side and noticed someone panhandling. I didn't want to stare, but as I was walking, I heard the panhandler say, "Sante?"

I looked right at him. "Sammy? Oh, my God." I hadn't seen Sammy since we were teenagers more than fifteen years or so now.

Sammy grew up around the corner from me, three doors down from my father's barbershop. He'd occasionally hang out with my cousin Joey, who lived across the street. Sammy wasn't really able to hang out for long with anybody—there was something dysfunctional about him that no one understood.

At that time, in the '60s and '70s, autism hadn't been diagnosed. You couldn't let Sammy stay around for too long; he'd inevitably say or do something offensive or act out, and someone would tell him to leave. He couldn't hold down a job either, he got by doing mostly deliveries for local stores. He lived with his widowed mother who looked after him. After she died, he couldn't take care of himself; he was out on the street, sleeping in hallways and subways. He felt the shelters were too dangerous.

Sammy had a photographic memory. The first thing he said was, "The last time I saw you, it was October 16, 1973, on the corner of Cortelyou Road and East Fifth Street. You were wearing those funny plaid pants with a short leather jacket, and you had a shag haircut. You had platform shoes on, too. I always wondered how you could walk in those platform shoes."

We took a walk, and I bought him something to eat. He started telling me about everybody in the old neighborhood and had me laughing in stitches. I didn't want him to disappear, so I arranged to meet him again the next day. August was a few days away, a time when the fashion industry slowed down and everyone went on vacation, leaving me with time to work on my own projects if I decided to.

We met the following morning. Sammy told me things I didn't know about people we knew, and we laughed for hours. Everything he was saying was so close to home; I knew I wouldn't be able to remember it all, so I asked if I could record him. He agreed, and for the next five days, I recorded our conversations on my tape recorder. I even paid him for his time.

I thought it would be a great idea if we went back to our old neighborhood with my cassette recorder and my Bolex movie camera. We filmed and just went with the flow. I didn't want to stop. It was fun, but by September, I needed to get back to work. I tried to rent an apartment for him in Brooklyn, but he showed up drunk and sabotaged it—I should have known better.

Sammy mentioned he always wanted to be a writer, so I told him to write for me, and I would pay him by the page. Sometimes his stuff was funny, many times the same story, then the same story enlarged on the paper. I learned not to give him too much money at one time—he'd either get robbed or buy drugs.

That winter, I discovered he wrote poetry and decided to film him reading his poems. The previous summer, I had collaged sound to film, both recorded independently of one another, never in sync together, all with just one assistant. I hired a crew for a couple of days the following summer and put Sammy in front of a tarp reciting his poems in sync sound. Eventually, I married the collage of sound and footage with the sync sound of the poems against the tarp, and hired an editor, Jonathan Oppenheim.

My time with Sammy brought back many memories of growing up in Brooklyn. I made a lot of notes while working on my film with him. I wrote down my own stories, and along with the material I got from listening to Sammy, I was already on my way to writing a script. I got together with a great writer, a friend of mine named Frank Pugliese, who had a similar upbringing as me, growing up in Brooklyn. The characters I created were familiar to him, so it was easy for us to be in sync with the story I was developing. We spent a lot of time together and had a lot of laughs. I was having the creative time of my life. We put together a thirty-minute film, and it was accepted by the 49th Venice Film Festival of 1992.

Having that film in the festival, with Dennis Hopper as that year's president, was the culmination of a creative adventure I had never experienced before. It felt so natural to me and meant more to me than anything I had ever done in my creative life. I felt at home, at ease. This was what I wanted to be: a storyteller.

At that time, the Venice Festival did not include short films in the open competition; they were on exhibition only. After our screening, I got some positive reviews, a few handshakes, and before I went back to my day job, photography, I spent extra time on the Lido in Venice. I organized a shooting for Italian *Vogue* through Franca Sozzani, the editorial director, plus another shooting for *Interview* magazine.

Italian *Vogue* sent over an editor from Milan with clothing, hair, and makeup. Kara, my wife at the time, agreed to be the model. We shot along the Lido, basically the beach and old hotels where Visconti filmed *Death in Venice*, and where the film festival was held. We asked Dennis Hopper, who had been a friend for a number of years, to pop in for a shot or two for the Italian *Vogue* shoot.

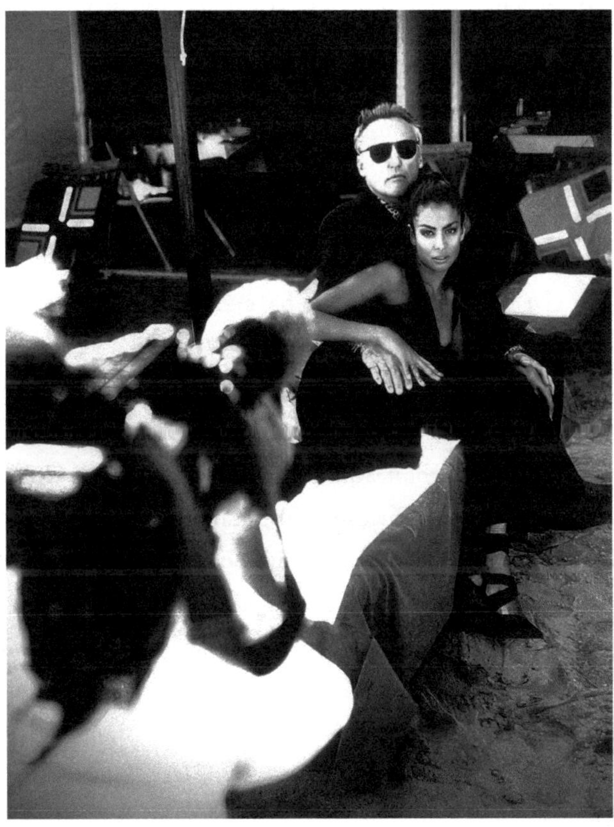

Kara Young and Dennis Hopper for Italian *Vogue*, Venice Film Festival

For *Interview*, I was to shoot Dennis, along with Joe Pesci, who was there for a film he had starred in about the photographer Weegee. Joe was also a friend of mine. I asked them if there was anywhere they wanted to go, anything they wanted to do. Joe suggested playing golf. "Joe, where the fuck am I going to find a golf course in Venice, Italy?" Joe found a golf course, of course, and off we went.

I'd nailed two assignments and had my film shown at the Venice Festival. I had been working for every magazine and had made a lot of friends. It was a great and very productive time.

Once you earn the trust of your subjects, models, actors, actresses, and do great pictures of them published internationally, your reputation grows, and you are granted access that allows you to freely call a magazine editor and say, "I'm going to Venice, I'm with a model, and some actor friends will be there as well. I'll give you all this talent for practically no effort on your part, and little to no expense either." They'd be crazy to turn you down. Access becomes very valuable for coming up with your own assignments. You're making enough money to cover some of the costs, and the return is that you're looking like a champ to every aficionado and fashion advertiser in the world. You're doing the hustle, and everybody is happy. A photographer, as with any profession, should never go to people and expect them to just give you something. You have to go to them and say, "This is what I can give and bring to you." *Basta!*

But I was also beginning to feel out of sync with the direction fashion was going, and since I was leaning toward film, I thought it would be smart to shoot more Hollywood celebrities.

Throughout the '80s and into the early '90s, fashion was where the real glamour was. Prior to that, for almost forty years, it was Hollywood that had cornered glamour. But by the mid-60s, with the war in Vietnam and our nation protesting, there was no interest in glamour films. Movies from that period onward did away with glamour with films like *Easy Rider* and *Midnight Cowboy* becoming the new wave in American Cinema. It was now more about realism and grit. There were icons like Janis Joplin and Jim Morrison in music, and movies like *Apocalypse Now*, *Mean Streets*, and *The Deer Hunter* portraying the real shit going down in our world.

If you wanted allure, romance, and the high life, it was in the fashion industry. Models like Christy, Linda, Naomi, Cindy, and Stephanie had become household names. Women aspired to be like them.

When fashion turned to "grunge" and "heroin chic," I no longer connected with that type of woman. It's why I turned to Hollywood. Movie stars wanted glamour back in their lives. Bruce Weber and Herb Ritts were the only ones shooting celebrities, and when I got in the game, I was able to apply my brand of a sensual modern woman to leading actresses who had never formerly been considered for a fashion shoot or a *Vogue* cover.

The fashion industry shot itself in the foot with grunge and heroin chic. They looked great on teens and twentysomethings, but they weren't buying at designer prices. Sales started going down; most women never wanted to be seen that way.

Then the experiment of putting a movie star in a fashion spread and on the cover of *Vogue* began. I really can't say who did it first, but it worked. Glamour was out of fashion with the new models and slowly they were replaced with movie stars. Sales started climbing with those Hollywood stars on covers and in fashion stories—women could relate to them. It snowballed into what we see today in magazines; the numbers proved it big time. The original supermodel monopoly had begun to slowly end and the transition to high-profile movie stars transformed sales for fashion magazines and advertising. I found a new home for the type of woman I loved to shoot. I was able to bring sex appeal and sensuality to high-profile celebrities in a way they had never been seen before in the world of fashion. The industry still hasn't looked back.

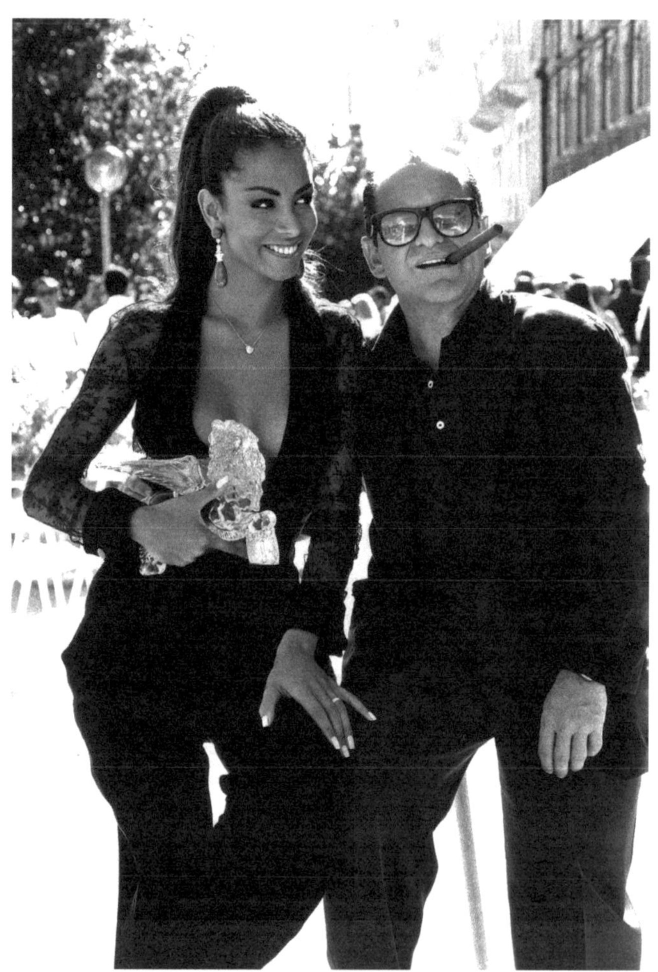

Kara Young and Joe Pesci for Italian *Vogue*, Venice Film Festival

47

Early in the year 2000, I had to have my first knee replacement, the result of a basketball injury combined with a menagerie of drugs, partying, and always going out (not good for circulation). After surgery, I was prescribed twelve OxyContin a day, for about three months. I'd be given vials of one hundred at a time; then I'd pass them around at my parties if things needed to loosen up. Everyone loved my parties. When I ran out, they gave me more.

My knee healed and lasted sixteen years, but now I was addicted to OxyContin. My dealer, I mean my doctor, gave me another supply with strict instructions on how to wean myself off, starting with halfing my usual dosage; six a day, then four a day the following week, then two, then one a day. One was never going to work, especially with the crowd I hung out with.

So I began to look for a substitute, any opiate of any kind, I'd try them like at a wine tasting. Whichever took the edge off and was easy to get ahold of would be the one. I came upon it one dreary fuck of a night when I had the jitters and nothing to take care of the dreadful feeling you get when you're addicted to opiates and don't have any to make you feel normal—forget about high, just normal. I called a friend who lived in the area, and he invited me over. He lit a joint and passed it to me. I took a few tokes. I was shaking and sweating, and he knew I was strung out.

Almost instantly, as if tapped on the shoulder by some magic wand, I was restored, at peace, whole. It was seductive and sensuous—and a relief. He rolled another joint and, with the paper still open, he took out a small glassine bag and tapped out small amounts of tiny white flakes onto the marijuana, then rolled it shut. I wanted to forget how good it felt, the opiate of opiates. I tried to stay away from it; the fashion industry had been doing it since the early nineties, most just snorted it—"heroin chic." It gave me a laid-back high, and my jitters went away. This kind of high was easy to get, cheaper than hundreds of OxyContin pills, and felt much better. I'd leapt from the frying pan into the fire.

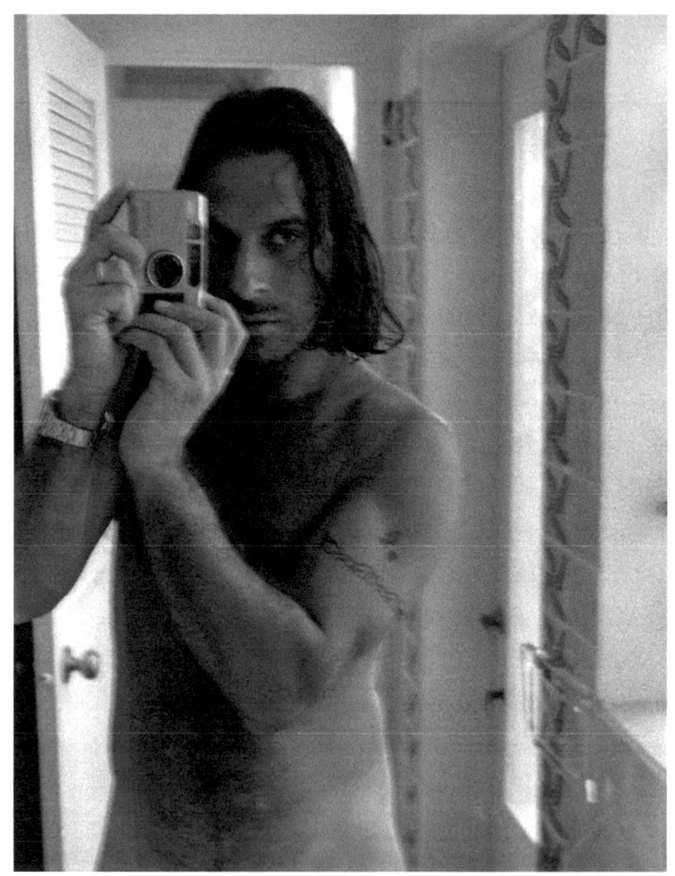

Sante, self-portrait, St. Barths

48

I realized that, despite all the jet-setting, high fashion models, and celebrities in my life, at heart, I was an old-fashioned Italian family man. My family meant everything to me, especially my son, Nick. When I got divorced, he was two years old, and it didn't take much for me to fall into a very dark depression not seeing him half the time. It broke my heart not to have him with me during Christmas and other holidays.

Even before Nick was born, before the divorce, the holidays had always been the hardest for me to bear, a trigger from loss during my adolescence. As soon as I started making good money in my career, I'd get past it all by going away during that time. I'd rent a house in the Caribbean or Hawaii and bypass all the negative triggers Christmas and New Year's unloaded on me, so I wouldn't get depressed. Palm trees, swimming in those blue waters, getting a tan. And if I was able to take my family and my mom with me, it didn't feel so bad.

But if I were alone and couldn't get out from under that rock, there were drugs to help me along the way. When the drugs didn't work, I'd turn and beg God for help, ask for a clue to be guided toward answers. When that failed, I'd resort to being an old-world Italian woman in spirit: having my cards read; consulting astrologers, soothsayers; dying for answers. I read a lot of Carl Jung on signs and symbols, and I became good at interpreting dreams—mine, as well as others. When you're desperate, any angle will do.

After making it alive through another holiday season alone in New York, after rendering myself numb and useless with whatever I could get my hands on, including some hard stuff, I got my first booking of the new year—an editorial shooting in Anguilla. I couldn't wait to get out of the cold, damp city!

Whenever I left the country, as a rule, I would never take drugs with me, but I had forgotten what one week without any narcotics could do to your system after you'd been using for a couple of weeks. The hard stuff was morphine based; it numbed the physical and emotional pain. Your body would get used to it in very little time, and once you stopped, your body would begin to feel every ache you didn't know you had. You couldn't even lie in bed because you could never get comfortable. Even the hairs on your skin would feel like they hurt, and you'd need painkillers to make it through the transition. I didn't have any, and I had to go back and dabble, a little here, a little there, to wean myself off, cutting back my usage in half. When I left for Anguilla, I brought nothing with me. I felt like a sad sack of shit.

I had packed every amulet I could find in my house: crystals, a rosary, prayer cards, a medallion of St. Christopher, the patron saint of travelers (who's since lost that title, according to a new church decree), a St. Anthony medal, patron saint of lost things. If I lost something when I was a kid, I was told to pray to St. Anthony and he would help me find it. Four out of five times, it worked, so I prayed to him to help me find me! I knew to keep my eyes and ears open for any sign of help.

I arrived in Anguilla with my editor and crew; the model was due to arrive the next day, and then we'd be location scouting. The magazine had rented a large villa with enough bedrooms for all of us. If I were healthier, I would have been thanking God for everything, but I wasn't healthy. My body was exhausted; I was shaky, physically, mentally, and spiritually. Coming off the drugs also compounded my depression and the demonic voices of fear within me. I named my demon "Chip," and he stood on my right shoulder, whispering deceitful things in my ear, taking joy in my pain.

I went to my room and closed the door. My whole demeanor made it obvious something was wrong, and everyone was sympathetic and kind about it. I got into bed and prayed for help to kill my demon, but there was no one home in my spiritually haunted house. I didn't emerge from my room till the next day.

The next morning, I had to put on my best face and go location scouting, still totally miserable. When we got back, the model had arrived, a sweet, young Brazilian girl. Everyone was planning to go out for dinner, but the mere smell of food made me nauseous. I went to my room and stayed there till the next morning. By then, breakfast was ready, and I grabbed a coffee, secretly adding a shot of whiskey to it. I needed anything I could get my hands on.

It had rained hard all night and was still overcast. The dirt roads were muddy with giant puddles everywhere, and more rain was forecast. I decided that we would just shoot around the villa; it was beautiful enough with a large pool and a walkway down to the water below.

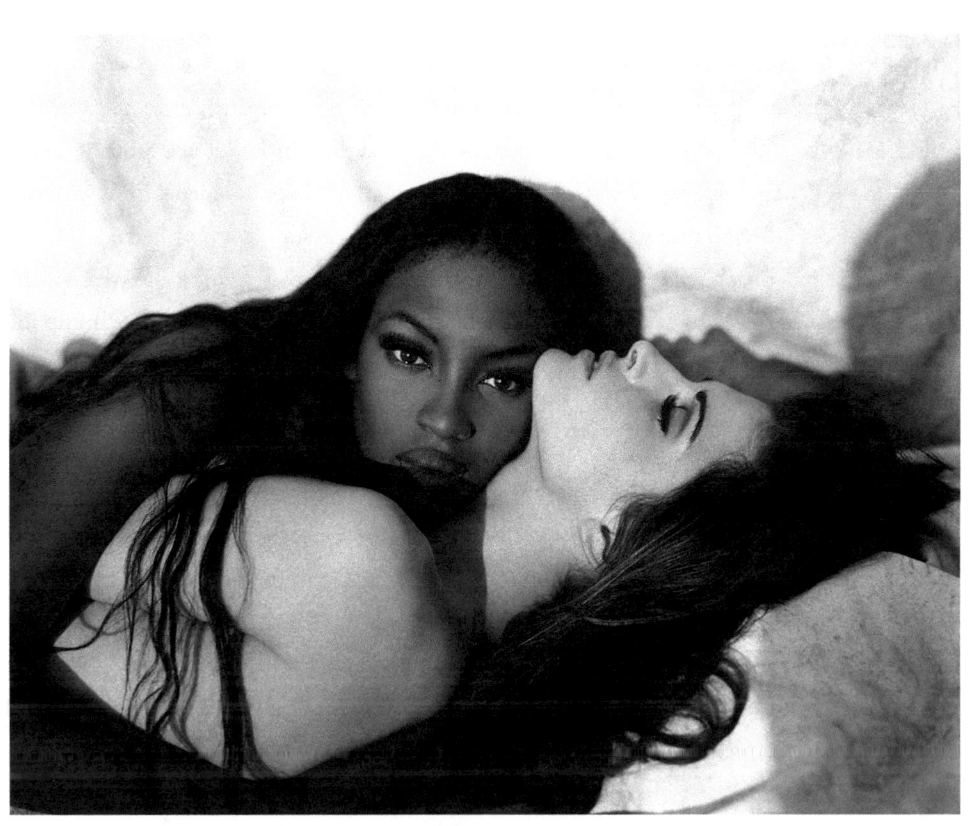

Naomi Campbell and Stephanie Seymour, Miami, Florida

Since the place was all white, it'd provide good reflections that would keep my model looking well-lit through the entire day. The best beauty light is an overcast day on a clean open beach—but this would be just as good, if not better. No matter what condition I found myself in, I was always capable of constructing a great picture. It came naturally to me, a blessing I took note of. I also thanked God I didn't have to go too far from my room. I took that as the first sign that someone was watching over me.

After breakfast, hair and makeup started in the living room. The editor put out the clothing nearby, and I poured another coffee and doubled the whiskey. It was 8:00 a.m. I sat down on the couch, holding on to my St. Anthony and St. Christopher medallions, with my prayer card of Padre Pio in my back pocket, and two small crystals from my bedside. While trying to make light chitchat with the crew, I poured another coffee and more whiskey. In between my mumbling to St. Anthony and the casual chitchat, there was a loud thump on the sliding door next to the makeup station. The model screamed and freaked us out, and when we went to look, a blackbird had flown directly into the glass panel of the sliding door! The fucking bird was twitching on the floor, and the model, being Brazilian, was making the sign of the cross and crying. Someone yelled, "It's alive! It's alive!"—but it had broken its neck and was dying. *What kind of fucked-up omen is this?* I went to my room, threw out my medallions and crystals, gave the model my rosary, and kept the Padre Pio Mass card in my back pocket. My assistant disposed of the dead bird.

My day hadn't even begun! What would Carl Jung have said about this?

All I could think was that St. Anthony and everyone else I prayed to had sent me a big *"Fuck you, you fuckin' moron . . . you wanted a sign . . . here's your fuckin' sign . . . stick it up your ass!"*

49

You have to die a few times before you can really live.
—Charles Bukowski

One cold, snowy winter evening in London, people were squatting near a phone booth outside a semi-abandoned building. The phone began ringing. One of the other squatters from the same building picked it up. The person calling was Bill Block, a well-known Hollywood agent, looking for the actor Jaye Davidson. The London end said, "Call back in twenty minutes. I'll let him know."

Jaye had been working as a hairdresser when, one night at a party, he met the film director Neil Jordan, who was in the process of casting his movie *The Crying Game*. Jaye went on to star in the movie, and the rest was cinema history. *The Crying Game* opened to great reviews. Jaye, a first-time actor, received a nomination for an Academy Award in the Best Supporting Actor category, and the film won an Oscar for Best Original Screenplay.

However, there had been no money in the budget for Jaye, the first-timer with no experience. The producers had barely enough for the production itself. And so, prior to the Oscars, with the film in the can and premiering at the Venice Film Festival that September, Jaye returned penniless to his flat in London where he was squatting—a situation familiar to artists of all kinds.

When Jaye walked out to the phone booth, in his bathrobe and slippers, he picked up the receiver and heard Bill Block say he had some exciting news. Jaye didn't give a shit. He had recently developed a major drug problem. When someone interrupted his buzz, it always made him somewhat belligerent. Plus, snow was falling.

Bill Block said, "Dino De Laurentiis is making a movie called *Stargate* and wants to cast you as one of the main characters! We can get you five hundred thousand dollars for four days' work!"

Jaye replied, "Fuck you! I want a million dollars or nothing."

Bill Block said, "I'll call you back in ten minutes."

The phone rang ten minutes later, and Bill Block said, "You got it! One million dollars plus first-class airfare for you and a friend. And they'll put you up wherever you want to stay!"

Life can change at the drop of a hat.

When Jaye arrived in New York, Naomi Campbell threw a party at her apartment, and everyone was there to meet Jaye. I was with my Kara, still my wife at the time. We met Jaye, and Kara discovered they had much in common. Jaye's mom was white, and his father was black; Kara's mom was black, and her father was white. It was a union of kindred spirits. I'm Italian, and we get along with everybody. From that night forward, a whole group of us, Kate, Naomi, Christy, Kara, and Jaye, went out almost every night of the week.

Two weeks later, I was shooting Jaye for *Interview*, and Kara was doing the interview. I called Francesco Clemente and asked if we could shoot in his studio on Broadway. Francesco said, "Yes, of course." I got some incredible shots, especially a nude of Jaye up against a gold leaf canvas that Francesco had not yet painted on. Jaye tucked his privates between his legs; he looked like an androgynous angel that had come to take you to Heaven or straight down to Hell—most probably the latter. The print resembled an Eastern icon painting. Those pictures still stand up today; they only get stronger with time. Francesco also had a Balinese headdress and sarong that Jaye put on, and I did a portrait of both of them holding hands—just beautiful.

Jaye was gay, but he was also the toughest motherfucker I knew. I was sure he could have kicked my ass. I asked him what kind of man he liked, and he said he preferred "blokes." He'd meet these straight tough guys in bars, usually married men of course, and have his way. He had a certain disdain for effeminate men, but he was very sensitive toward everyone . . . until they got on his nerves.

Jaye hated the paparazzi, and they were always running after him. One night, a paparazzo jumped out unexpectedly and gave us such a fright that Jaye socked him one by punching the camera the photographer was holding to his face. I think it must have left an imprint of the camera on the guy's forehead!

After a while, especially at the fashion shows, Jaye resorted to wearing ski goggles, hoping no one would want to take his picture, but that didn't work. Meanwhile, the more the two of us went out, the more fucked-up we would get. I started doing the hard stuff with him, the type of drug you took when you're troubled with the world and a great night out was staying in and drooling on the couch. It was a highly anti-social, anti-sexual drug that we referred to as "downtown." If we wanted to stay up for the party, we'd mix it with some "uptown," which is what we called cocaine. Then, we'd have a nice speedball.

Everyone in fashion was doing heroin at the time, but there wasn't much that was "chic" about it.

The time came for Jaye to go to LA to act in the new film. He brought along his friend Paul Rutherford, a member of the band Frankie Goes to Hollywood. That did not turn out too well, Jaye was too moody to handle, impossible to keep to a schedule, and he was strung out. No one wanted to be an assistant/friend and handler to a drug addict, I should know.

The Dino De Laurentiis film *Stargate* was a big production, one of those pre-digital extravaganzas with something like a thousand extras and a large crew. They built a set out in the California desert at the same location that was used for Charlton Heston's *The Ten Commandments*. The *Stargate* sets resembled pyramids from another dimension.

Jaye starred as Ra, an alien impersonating a god. He was getting paid one million dollars for four days of shooting, but when it was time for him to come out of his trailer and go on set, he wouldn't come out. Maybe he was whacked on something . . . or maybe the sight of this massive film crew and a thousand sweating extras waiting in the sand dunes made him nervous. He wouldn't come out. It was a producer's nightmare. A four-day booking turned into two weeks with huge cost overruns to pay the extras and the crew all that overtime.

Producers are covered by insurance, and an actor can't work on a film uninsured. It's called being bonded—you can't work unless you're bonded by the insurance company. After that movie, Jaye was never bonded again, and that was the end of his film career. The same had happened to Mickey Rourke, and his exile lasted fourteen years. Mickey only made it back because Coppola took the risk without bonding him.

Jaye returned to NYC, and we continued where we'd left off. His friendship meant a lot to me. But like all good things, it slowly came to an end. Jaye moved back to London. It didn't take him long to burn through his million-dollar paycheck. (Kara persuaded him to get his English teeth fixed, at least.) On each trip I made to London, I'd give him a call, and we'd go out and have fun—till it wasn't fun anymore. Jaye began to get more and more belligerent, even with fewer and fewer drinks in him.

The last time we were out together was when Tim Jeffries and Claudia Schiffer invited

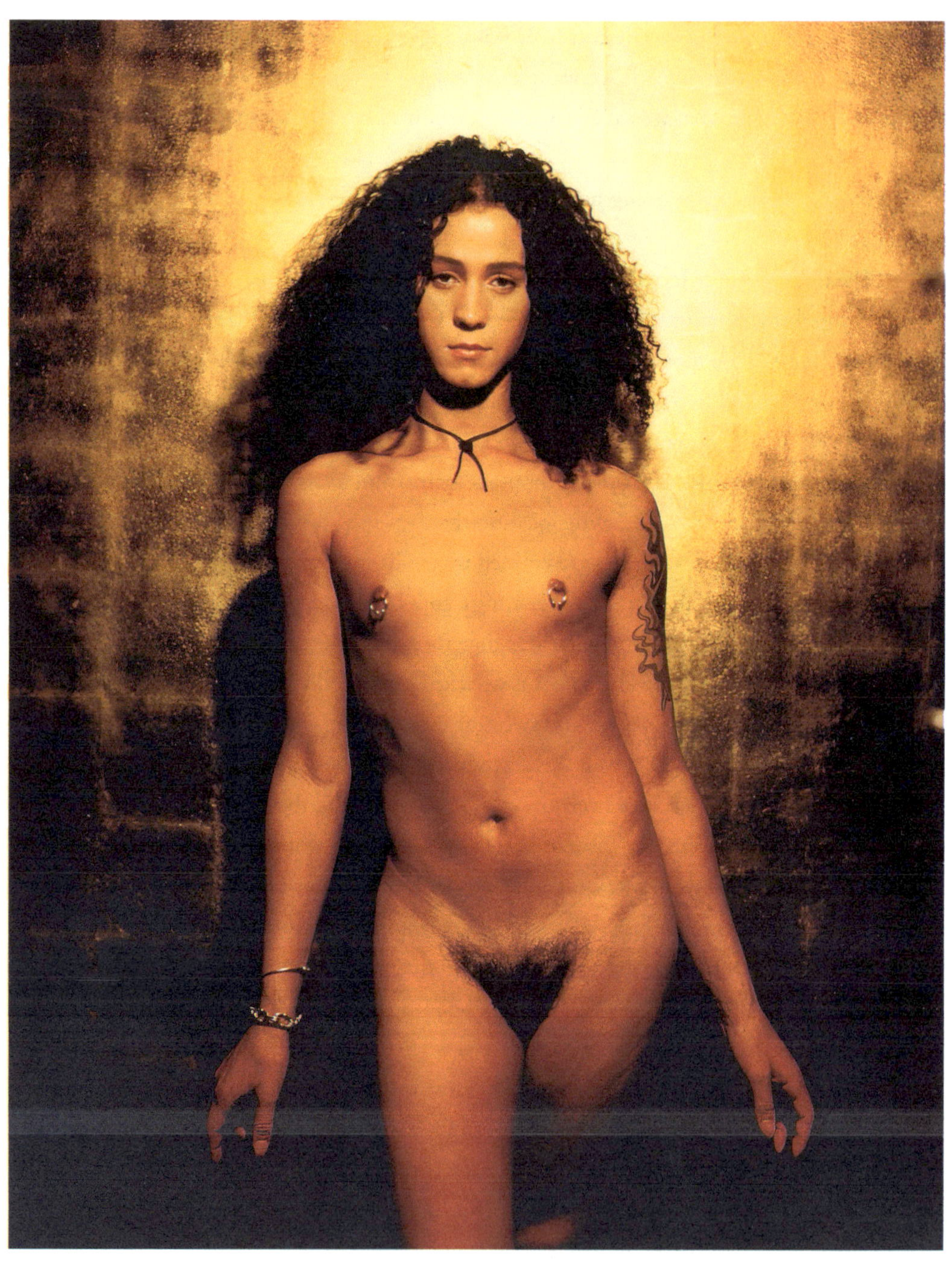

Jaye Davidson for *Interview* magazine

us to Nobu in Mayfair. Jaye had finished his second vodka tonic without having anything to eat. His rule since I'd known him was, "Either I drink, or I eat. I can't do both. That's how you gain weight!" His whole demeanor changed after he finished that second vodka tonic. I noticed him staring at Claudia with a devious look in his eyes. I was worried.

When Jaye got Claudia's attention, he said, "Claudia, you know I'm going to fuck your boyfriend, don't you?"

We all spit our food out and started laughing. Tim was an old friend of ours, tall and handsome, a real ladies' man. Jaye was gay but so open and butch about it—he did say he liked the blokes! He repeated it to Claudia again and again. I had to excuse us and take him out of there before he violated Tim right there at the table!

Jaye is sober these days but still can't get bonded in Hollywood. He's become a highly successful and probably the most (belligerent if you irritate him) loving florist in London. I've promised myself, if I got to make a film again, I'd find a part for Jaye. He's a natural. But I wouldn't be surprised if he told me to go fuck myself.

50

And if you arrive, do you know you are there?
—Rene Ricard

By the mid-1990s, I was making it big time, but I had little time to call my own. I had no time to see much of my family, no time to experiment, and no time to develop my first love—painting. The wheels were turning fast.

I didn't even have time to figure out if my pictures were any good. The only way I knew if clients were happy with my work was if they didn't call. If they did call, it was always to complain, demanding more choices—where's this, where's that? Clients only wanted what they were familiar with. They'd say they wanted original work, but really, they didn't. If an art director handed me a layout or drawing, to me, that meant they had already seen it somewhere else. I was interested in those found moments in between—before and after the familiar. I thought my idea of an original shot would thrill them, but it often didn't. Maybe I was in the wrong business.

If they saw a Polaroid and brought it back to their office, I'd be fucked. Polaroids served as a photographic guide for lighting, hair, and makeup, or it was simply a record of counting the shots done that day. The art director or client would sometimes get fixated on that one image, and even though I might have taken a far superior shot on film, they didn't wait to see it. They'd sit with that single Polaroid for a couple of days while my film was being developed. They would enlarge the image and use it in a layout to show their boss. That became the only image they wanted on film. That was the American market; it was too literal.

The late '90s were the beginning of the end of what I considered my golden years in fashion. Grunge. Heroin chic. Everything going digital. Designers and photographers in fashion were beginning to change the look of the girls into something less glamorous. My aesthetic of image-making—my type of model of the late '80s–early '90s, including the Kate Moss generation—was becoming less fashionable. Kate transitioned perfectly and became

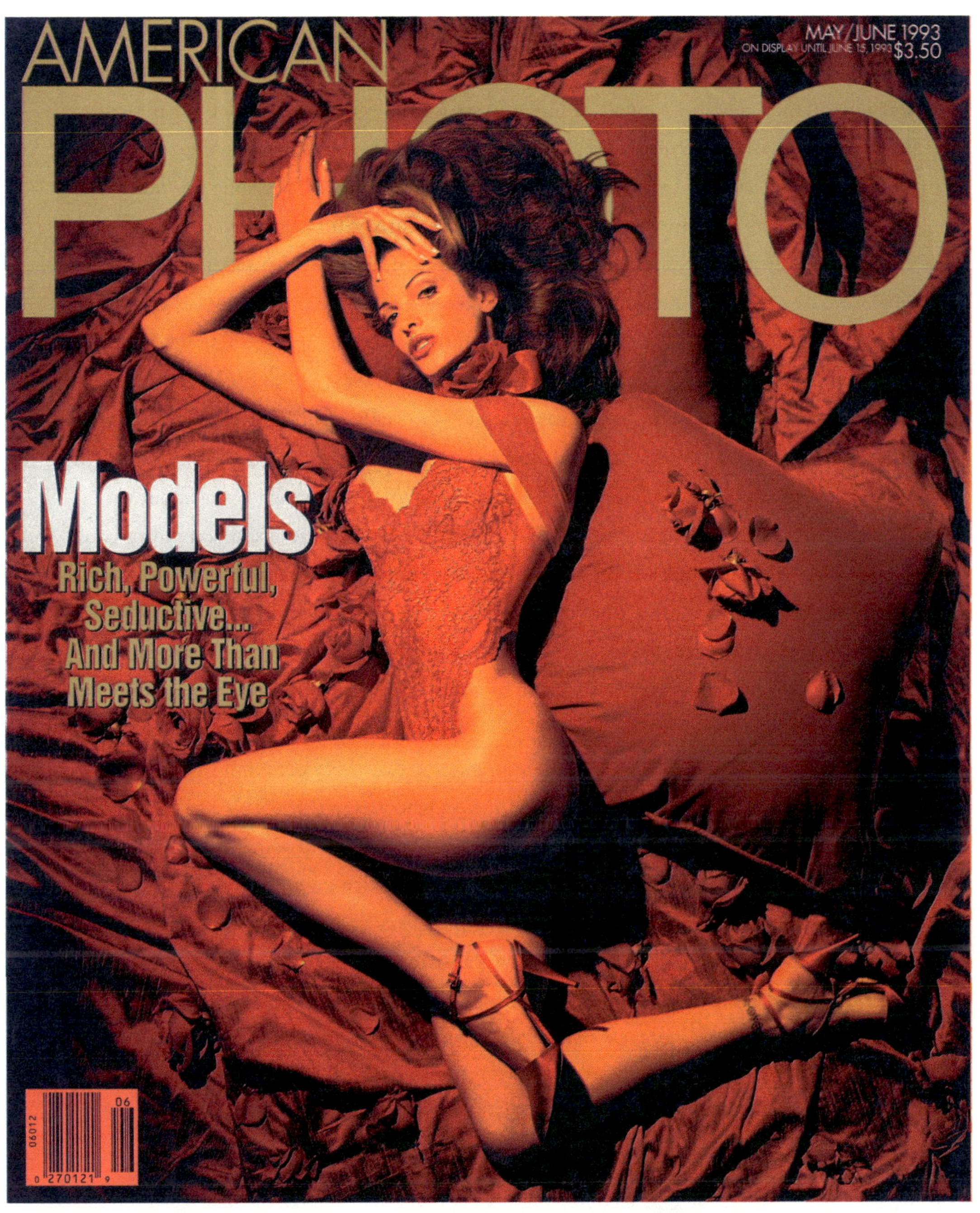

Stephanie Seymour

the face of the new generation. A lot of designers began featuring clothing that required a different look in models, inspired by the music and aesthetic coming from the Seattle scene like Nirvana. I made it through just fine, my goals photographically began to shift toward Hollywood because I began writing my own stories for my first script.

When I started out, I was in my mid-twenties, and the models coming up were in their mid-teens. Eileen Ford, for example, would only let Christy Turlington go out with me and my small group of friends. Christy was just seventeen, and I was responsible for getting her home by a certain hour (sometimes tough to do because she never wanted to leave the party). Naomi, Cindy, Stephanie, Linda, and Tatjana were all teenagers; Cindy Crawford and Stephanie Seymour I met shooting catalogs for Bonwit Teller and Bloomingdale's; all of us were young and beginning our careers, and editorially just budding. What I'm saying is, theirs was my generation, their look and style appealed to me most, and still does. They were feminine and sensual young women, and that's what my pictures were about.

They were the original supermodels. At the height of their careers, if you didn't feature one or all of them in your ads or your runway shows, no one would pay any attention to you. They literally controlled the market and, at times, overshadowed the designers who hired them. It was unprecedented in the fashion industry, and it didn't necessarily make everyone happy when they weren't available to you. It put a lot of power in theirs and their agencies' hands.

On the other side of the coin, I took it for granted that every night out I would be in the company of one or more of the girls, depending on who was in town. This also included our other model girlfriends like Yasmin Le Bon and Gail Elliott, and some of their boyfriends occasionally. I met half of Hollywood from hanging out with them. Every guy, not to mention the very famous, wanted to meet those girls. Every club and every restaurant owner invited me to their places. The PR was worth a fortune to them if "supermodels" showed up, but that never crossed my mind. I couldn't give a shit—those girls were my friends.

Besides, I thought everyone wanted me around for my charm, good looks, and personality!

51

By the late '80s, I had gotten to know many of the major players in the fashion world. The one designer I felt very close to was Gianni Versace and his family. I felt an unspoken kinship toward both him and, especially, his younger sister, Donatella, due in part to our shared Southern Italian roots. She was the precocious one, mischievous and playful. As head of the family and the company, Gianni, bless his heart, took things more seriously. It's public knowledge we all partied; we didn't consider it a problem—but we would never party around Gianni, never even mention it.

A small group of us would hang out together and bond over the ritual of sharing our drugs. It's not like it happened all the time, just when we were all together. Most of the top girls, some designers, and me, we were like a secret society, and we had other secret societies wherever we were. It was practically the social norm for a very long time, rarely while working, but always after work—our version of an evening cocktail. Staying at the Ritz, flying the Concorde, caviar, and cocaine. It was a glamorous life, a lifestyle I had never imagined that came into my life as a byproduct of success.

This is not to say there weren't other personal problems. There always were—sometimes because of the Ritz, the Concorde, cocaine, and caviar.

Then came July 15, 1997. Gianni was in Miami with Donatella and family. Gianni had purchased a mansion on Ocean Drive back when Miami was just beginning to happen. There were still vacant art deco hotels all over Ocean Drive and Collins Avenue. A great scene was developing, an atmosphere of the new. Gianni felt free to leave the house and walk alone to his favorite corner café. Nobody bothered him.

But on that particular July morning, he walked to the nearby News Café to sit and read his paper and buy some magazines. On his way back, a deranged wannabe party boy

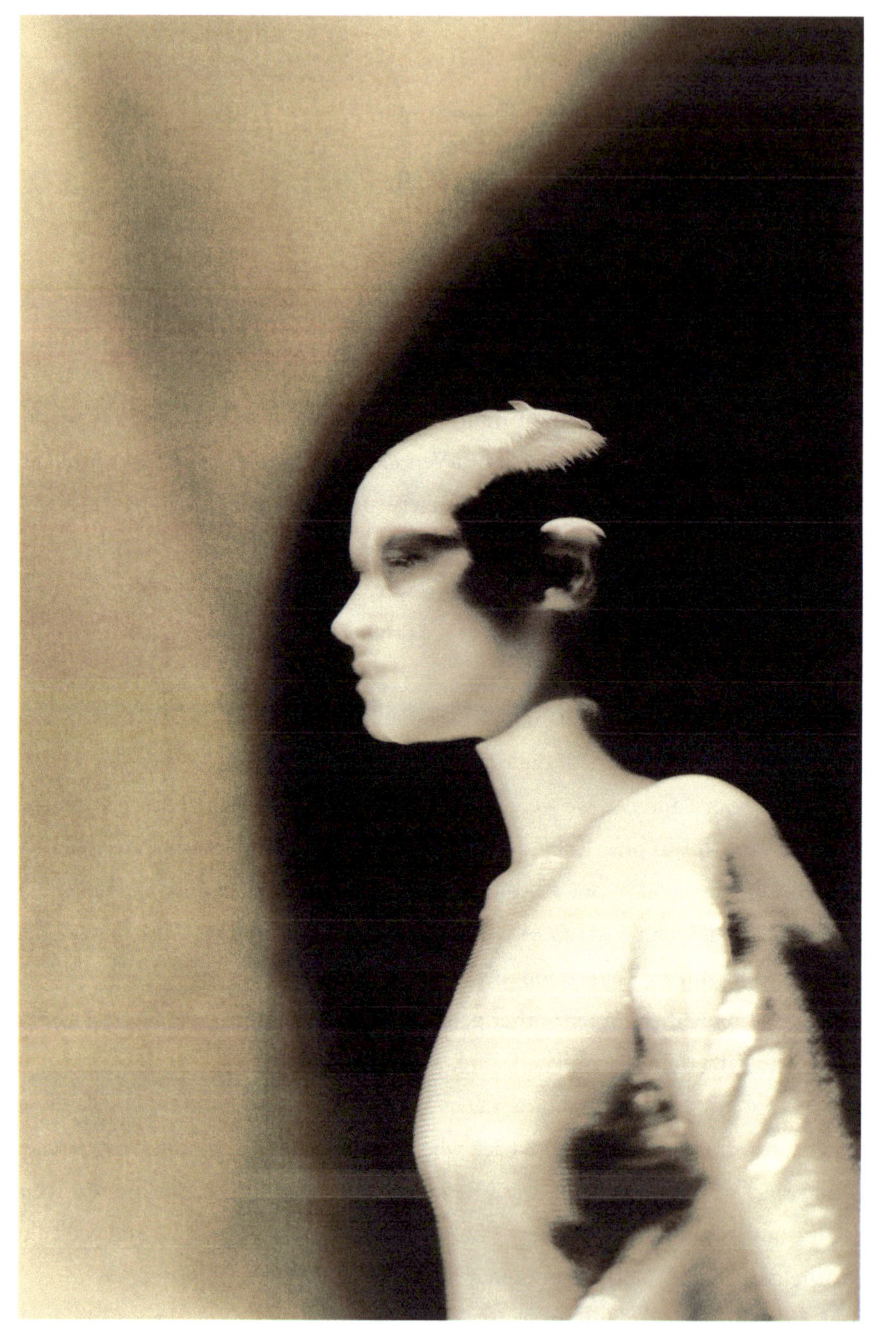

From *Gianni & Donatella* by Sante

ambushed Gianni on his front doorstep and shot him dead. The world turned upside down.

Back in Milan after the funeral, Donatella had to pick up the pieces for her family and for Gianni's sake. She was young and spirited, married to an American ex-model named Paul Beck. Always while Gianni was designing, Donatella would come in and give her opinion, "This is good. *This* isn't." They would fight a lot, as brothers and sisters do. At that time, Donatella wasn't designing, but she was Gianni's critic, muse, and greatest supporter. As he did every summer, Gianni had started designing for the spring/summer collections showing in October. But his work was far from complete when his life came to an end. Donatella got right into finishing his collection, and that October, I flew to Milan and made it my own personal assignment to cover the entire event photographically and make a visual diary in homage to Gianni, Donatella, and the Versace family.

There were two collections: Versus was the young adult line and Gianni Versace the premier, more sophisticated line. Both had a day of rehearsals the day before each show. I had four days to work with full access. Once acclimated, I can only say that I entered a trance-like state where I was no longer thinking. I was simply responding to my surroundings, and if instinct tapped me on the shoulder, I'd turn and shoot. Something was always there; I just had to sense it. If something inside told me to go to another room, then I would go. The action was wherever I found myself. I surrendered to the impulses of energy that were all around me and followed them.

Rehearsals started early and went late, very late. On the morning of the "Gianni Versace Collection" presentation, I was having coffee when I noticed a small white butterfly in the tented backstage dressing area. It was October in Milan. I asked several people later if it was normal to find butterflies at that time of year, and the answer was always no. I didn't say anything.

I believe in spirits, energy, vibe, intuition, and extrasensory perception. As a photographer, I learned early on how to be guided by these things . . . how to turn off the thinking part of my brain and allow the intuitive side to function. My motto was "If you have the time to think, you lost the shot." My senses inform me of everything in my environment.

I had a big day in front of me. All the top girls were in the show—Kate Moss, Naomi, Linda Evangelista, Carolyn Murphy, Shalom Harlow, and so on—and getting everyone ready for a dress rehearsal always was and still is a mega challenge. I made sure to keep an eye on Donatella. Everywhere Donatella went, the little white butterfly was hovering above and around her. I would turn to one of the girls, and without words, we knew not to mention it. The tragedy had happened only a few months before. We didn't want to risk Donatella getting all emotional over a butterfly; the atmosphere was already thick with the knowledge of Gianni's absence.

Donatella had so much on her hands, apart from all the intensive labor that went into making the clothing. It was like producing a big budget movie in four nights only; so many people pushing and pulling for answers to their endless questions, it made your head spin. We were all running on fumes by early evening, and we knew we'd be there at least another five or six hours.

Donatella would frequently light up a cigarette and survey the action in the room. Everyone knew to give her some space. She was putting together the pieces of a very large virtual puzzle.

I was close by, doing my own survey of the scene. Donatella lit another cigarette and, with the butterfly fluttering around her, turned my way. She noticed I was looking at the butterfly above her. I made eye contact with her, and she said, "I know you know that's Gianni watching over me," then smiled at me with a certain serenity, and looked away. A magical moment.

I never took for granted the beauty and majesty of a great show and performance, especially in Europe, but this one put me in another world. Only that survival mechanism—which we don't even know we have—enabled Donatella to pull this off. Someone was looking out for her, looking over her shoulder in spirit, as she might have said. It was a monumental event and a memorial all in one.

Every designer came in respect and homage. Armani, Lagerfeld, and many artists from the entertainment world. It seemed like the whole world of fashion was there to pay their respects. Taking these pictures and documenting this time was my own personal way of showing the love and respect I had for Gianni, Donatella, and their family. For me, the experience reaffirmed my beliefs in the unfolding of the many mysterious and invisible forces that surround us.

The following day was an incredible show; it drew a long-standing ovation, and it was a tremendous accomplishment by any standards; it was a masterful collection.

The next morning, I made preparations to leave, say goodbye to friends, and have a few delicious meals before flying home to NYC the following morning. The time I had spent shooting was both emotionally and physically exhausting. It took me a day just to compose myself before I could even think of the pictures.

Those were still in the days of film, so you couldn't look at the back of your camera and see the results immediately—as you can with digital. You couldn't see the results until your film was processed and you had the contact sheet in your hands! The anticipation was exciting but also anxiety-making. You wondered if anything had gone wrong with your camera, which was not unheard of. Was there enough light? (I didn't use a flash.) All your fears would whisper nonsense in your ear.

During the final and most important show, I didn't shoot from out front. Between the front and backstage, there was a long runway of black velour where the girls would appear, moving in and out of this void of space. Spotlights shifted, sometimes from behind, sometimes directly at the model walking to or from backstage. I hid within the velour curtains in the void of that passage, wearing black as I always do, and tried to remain invisible.

Being in that spot enabled me to also turn left, toward the front stage runway and the audience, or turn right, toward the exit where the girls turned to enter that dark space and disappear backstage. The pace of a show was faster than you might imagine. There was no time to change light readings, and the girls backstage had to change in very little time and get back out. Everyone's adrenaline was on max. Whatever happened in terms of light readings was left to the camera's auto setting. I was working without a net, which allowed me to see and not think—just how I liked it!

Between the end of that show and getting the contacts in my hands, I had to wait for six anxious days. When the contacts arrived, I wasn't sure what I was looking at. I didn't recognize anything. With thirty-six frames on one sheet, I had to look closely, as we usually did with a loupe. I was astonished—I had never seen images like this, ever, at least not in my body of work. The backstage shots where the light was brightest had some great moments with the girls that were more familiar to me, along with Donatella and all the preparations that went into it. These were shots I'd taken when I was hidden in the black velour passageway between front and backstage. I didn't recognize myself in those photos. They looked both magical and mystical.

My angle on the models was either full length when they were farther away or cropped off their heads when they were closer to me, so those magnificent dresses and materials became my subject. Because the light was moving and it was less concentrated—sometimes partially on the girls, sometimes closer or farther away from the light—it had caused my camera and lens to open longer and slower. The images looked like elegant apparitions moving in and out of the void. All the shots were in black and white, and Gianni's chain-link dresses appeared silver on the black background, like light hitting smoke in a dark room.

I still don't know how to explain those pictures to anyone, except that I had held the camera and something else took over. That's how magic happens.

I feel a need to further elaborate on the process of making pictures like these, extending to the physical properties that allow for other uncontrolled mysteries to help make their magic in print form. After editing the images, I sent them to my printer to make some silver gelatin prints. They were great, but something was missing. After some trial and error, he suggested trying some bleached silver gelatin prints. Sometimes a certain technique can be married with an image as though they were made for each other. In this case, it was not just technical; it was symbolic.

Bleaching is where you overexpose your negative to the paper and then overdevelop it in the developing bath or tray. After you wash it, you're left with a black rectangle with no real visible image. Then you place it into a tray of bleach that you keep moving. The bleach slowly reveals the whites, and the image gradually appears out of the black rectangle. Another magical process, and there's no real controlling the bleach, so no two prints are exactly alike, which I love. If left in a little longer, anything black in the picture develops a warm cream white tone. Tilt the tray a bit too long to the left and the black background has two mysterious tones of light and dark. The bleaching cannot be controlled or replicated by the printer. That lack of control of the bleach allows for nature to take over and paint the tones, like a person appearing through a fog.

The results could not have been better. I still consider this series to be masterworks for me. They do greater homage to my subject than anything I could have imagined.

Donatella became the principal designer of Versace, as she saved both the company and herself from going under and falling apart in the following years. I was back behind my camera again, shooting their collections in '98 and '99.

At the end of the '90s, I was about to enter a hell of my own, a hell whose existence I had denied for several years. My drug use had become more than a problem; it was now an addiction. It happened to many of us, designers and many models as well. A generation of the fashion business, at varying ages, needed to go into recovery. Speaking for myself, with the added struggle of depression, I slid down a steep and slippery slope. The romance was gone from my career. What began through my love of creativity had become a business that forced me to produce by lowering my standards.

Creating these magical Versace pictures was one of my visual highlights, but they didn't see the light of day for the next ten years. When I did get around to revisiting them for a book, I called Versace every year or so to ask for their blessings, and every year, they felt the time was not right. I understood, and over several years, I'd ask again with the same response.

Donatella finally gave me the go-ahead. I had a publisher lined up, and we got to work—laying out the book, designing it, with the best quality paper and printing available. It was titled *Gianni and Donatella* and published in October 2007, exactly ten years to the month of that show.

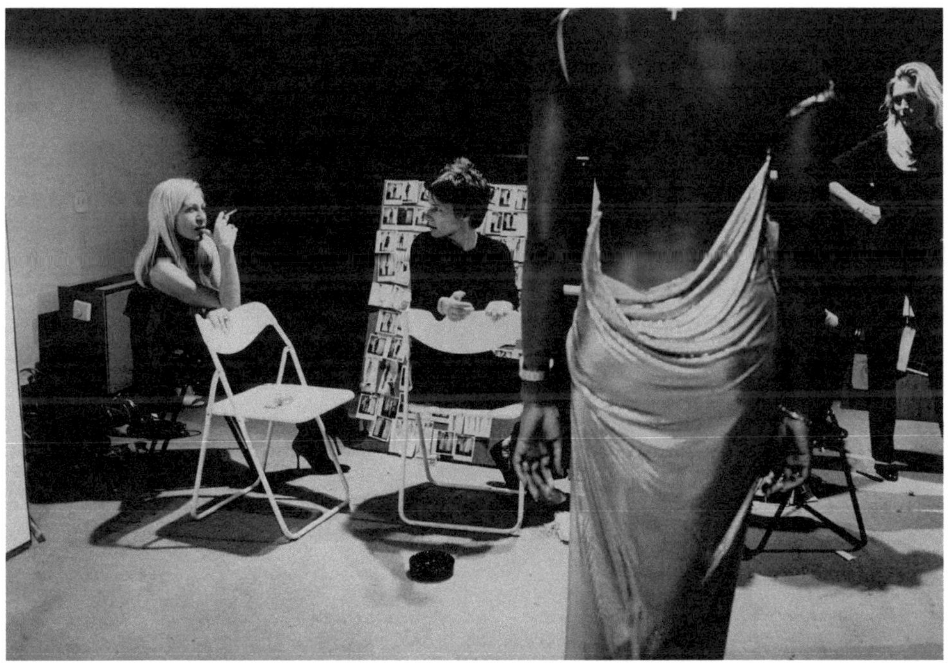

Donatella Versace from *Gianni & Donatella* by Sante

I had gone through ten tumultuous years of drugs, rehab, divorce, lawyers, and learning to be a single dad. When I got the first proof of the book in my hands after all those years, it captured the magic of that moment in 1997—magnificent, elegant, and richly printed. But with everything in my personal life needing my attention and the publisher not giving any PR support, the book was greeted by silence. Four months later, I got a call from a friend in London. He had seen my book in a bookstore on a table marked 50 percent off (and he didn't even buy it, the tightwad!)! I never did another book with that publisher. He subsequently reversed course in his business and went back to his roots, making calendars.

Things like this happen more often than people realize. Sometimes, it takes a generation or more for people to embrace a subject like this—after all, the book is a requiem. If this visual story were of Givenchy or Dior in the '50s, there's enough distance in time, and it would be viewed as a celebration of their greatness as designers and artists. Robert Frank once told me when the first printing of his pivotal book *The Americans* came out in France; it only sold four hundred copies. It was a total flop until later when it was republished here in the States.

As Andy Warhol said, "As soon as you stop wanting something, you get it."

But I still feel the same about the book and the images. They are special and historical. They document Gianni Versace's last show and Donatella's first with the most poetic grace ever channeled through me.

52

No great mind has ever existed without a touch of madness.
—Aristotle

One winter vacation, Kara (who was as tight with Naomi Campbell as I was) and I were invited to St. Moritz with Bobby De Niro and Naomi, plus our good friend Peter and his sweet ten-year-old son, Chris. Bobby was friends with Silvio Berlusconi (this was before he became prime minister of Italy), and Berlusconi had invited Bobby to stay at his extra-large villa anytime. The setting was magnificent—it had once belonged to the Shah of Iran.

On either the first or second night there, I fell into a deep sleep, yet I was conscious of my surroundings. I felt someone come into the room, but I couldn't move. I was paralyzed. As I remained in this quasi-dream state, a shadowy figure stood over me, then dropped down on me, and put a plastic bag over my face. I began to suffocate.

I managed to get up and out of my stupor, gasping for air. My heart was pounding; it was as real as it got. When I turned on the lights, the door to my room was closed.

During the years the Shah owned the house, maybe some fucked up things had gone down at that villa when he wasn't home, that's my guess, because there were restless spirits in the place, and I'd never say that lightly. I did some of my gris-gris chants and rituals, called upon my guardians with prayers, and never heard from that ghost again.

In spite of all the glitz and apparent glamour around, I was reminded to watch my back for the dark forces hiding in the shadows. I unfortunately discovered my best friend making a play for my girl on that trip. Maybe that dream was a premonition, a warning. He got what was coming to him later on . . .

After a week of skiing in the Alps, our next port of call was St. Barths. I had rented a house, and they had a rented one nearby. On the way to the airport, Naomi was starting to nag De Niro about wanting to get a boat and sail around the island, even though she couldn't swim. Naomi just kept going on and on about a boat to the point that Bobby had to start making in-flight calls to try and find a fucking boat. Shortly after takeoff, she was beginning to get on all our nerves, and she had already been twisting his balls before that. When we stopped in the Azores to refuel, Bobby had to get on a landline and try the agent in St. Barths for a third time. No luck. It was just before New Year's Eve, and there weren't any boats available, but Naomi wouldn't take no for an answer.

After we got to St. Barths, it took two more days for Bobby to finally get a boat. In the meantime, he asked me if I could do him a favor and pick up Chris Walken at the airport. I had never met Walken before, so Bobby let him know I would be picking him up and bringing him to the house. The weather was great: 90 degrees and not a cloud in the sky. I waited for Walken to clear the passport check. He came out wearing a black-on-black suit and holding a black attaché case, looking kind of pale and clammy.

"Where's your luggage?"

"This is it."

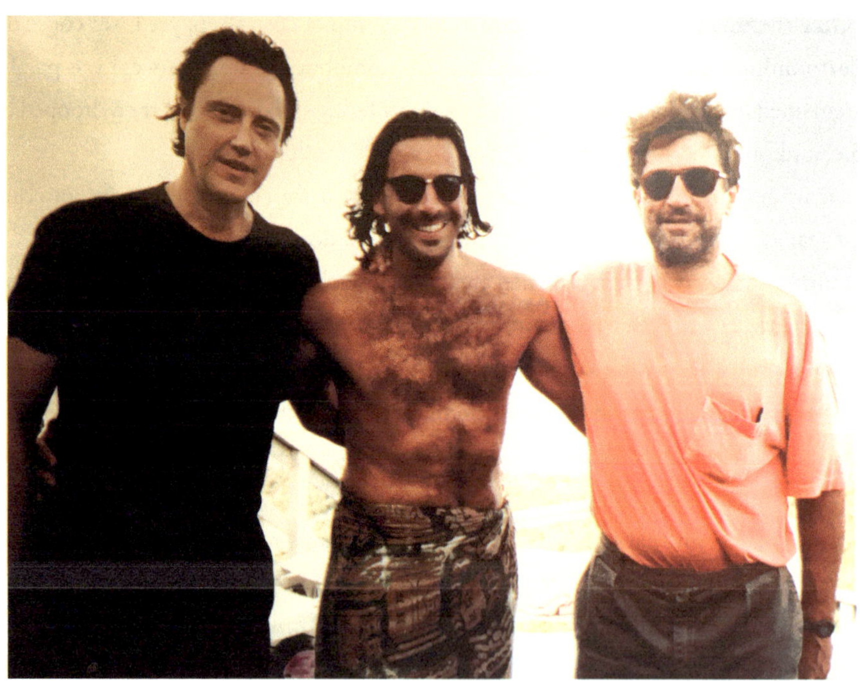

Sante with Christopher Walken and Robert De Niro, St. Barths

No luggage, looking like an undertaker. Later, Kara reminded me that Chris had been on the boat with Robert Wagner and Natalie Wood the night Natalie (allegedly) fell overboard and drowned. I wondered, and laughed out loud to myself, if Bobby had made a call to Walken to get rid of Naomi the same way. *Here's your fucking boat!*

The next morning, the three of them took off early together on their one-day boat trip. My rental was on top of a hill with views of the ocean on three sides. We organized a big late lunch with all our friends on the island over at the house. Bobby, Naomi, and Chris would come later in the day. Before lunch was ready, out of nowhere, it started to drizzle, so we moved everything under a roofed area of the terrace. Then it really started to rain; the wind picked up and then came the deluge. You could see the whitecaps on the sea. It didn't stop for about two and a half hours, which in itself was unusual in the Caribbean. Far out on the water, we could see one solitary boat, sails flapping this way and that, zigzagging the whole time, while the rain and wind only got worse. It was definitely theirs. We began laughing so hard we cried.

When they finally got back, we could hear the two of them yelling at each other as they drove up to the house in one of those half-golf cart/half-jeep type of cars with no side doors or windows, with rain blowing sideways from every angle. It was hard to keep a straight face. Naomi survived as she always did; she even thought it was funny. Bobby wanted to kill someone, and for the next couple of hours, he just kept mumbling, "Fuckin' boat."

Walken took it all in stride and said very little. He changed into some dry black clothes and sat with my friend's son, Chris. Little Chris was meant to do his part for the household by throwing out the garbage, but Walken was entertaining him, and he was captivated.

At one point, I yelled, "Hey, Chris! I thought we agreed you were throwing out the garbage. C'mon, man!"

Walken leapt to his feet, started apologizing, and asked where the garbage was.

"Not you, Chris! Little Chris!"

The next morning, on a sunny St. Barths beach, the boat episode was behind us. I was sitting on the sand with De Niro, the breaking waves at our feet, just the two of us, nice and quiet. It was early, and the beach was empty, except for a speck of a family much further down playing with an infant in the sand.

We went in for a refreshing swim, then lay back on the sand, chilling out. I noticed Bobby constantly looking down the beach. What the hell was he looking at? All I saw was that family with the infant, at what seemed like two football fields away. The father was taking pictures of his wife and baby. The wife and kid had their backs to us, which meant the father was facing us. Speaking as an expert, I could tell from how he was holding the camera that it was a point and shoot. He was certainly not pointing the camera at us.

"What's wrong?" I said.

"That guy has no respect. He's taking a picture of me."

Bobby had a real problem with people taking his picture. It could send him into a frenzy. He would freak out whenever someone would approach him in a restaurant, to shake his hand, or anything. Every time I went out to dinner with him, he was the only guy in New York who could find a totally empty restaurant on a weekend and still have to sit in a corner, hidden away, with his back to the empty tables.

"Bobby, come on. He'd need a three-hundred-millimeter lens to take a picture of you."

"Nah, I can tell. He's got no respect. But all right, I'll let it go."

I took another swim, and when I got back, Bobby was gone. I looked down the beach and could see him wagging his finger at the parents and the baby. The father was gesturing, palms up as if to say, "What the fuck? Are you out of your mind?" All I could do was sit and wait and shake my head. When Bobby got back, he said, "C'mon, let's get outta here. Baby picture, my ass!"

We headed back to the beach club to meet up with everyone for coffee and drinks. From the sand, there were steps leading to a short path up toward the pool with a beautiful view of the terrace and bar on the other side, and the mountains behind that. The opposite view, to our backs, was the path and the blue sea and sky, with small islands in the distance. Bobby was walking ahead of me up the steps onto the path, and I saw the back of a little old lady—I mean, ready-to-die old —wearing a flowery summer dress and an old-school straw hat with a white flower on the side. I realized she was doing a panorama shot of the place, with a video camera. Before I could say anything, she turned in our direction to get a shot of the ocean and the clear blue sky behind us.

Bobby walked right into her frame. "You got no respect!" he yelled at the little old lady.

She looked at him like he was a maniac. "Are you talking to me?" she asked of Travis Bickle from Scorsese's *Taxi Driver. (She had no clue who he was.)* "If you're talking to me, you're a very rude man! Who do you think you are?"

I kept walking as if I didn't know him. I wasn't about to get between him and the old lady having a fight.

53

Sports Illustrated gave me an assignment to shoot Niki Taylor and Naomi Campbell in South America for two editorial spreads. I knew both girls well. The location for the Niki Taylor shoot was a tiny island called Los Roques off the big island of Santa Margarita, Venezuela. For Naomi, we were to go to some remote hotel in the Venezuelan Amazon called Campamento Canaima; it wasn't so much a hotel as a group of straw huts, deep in the jungle,

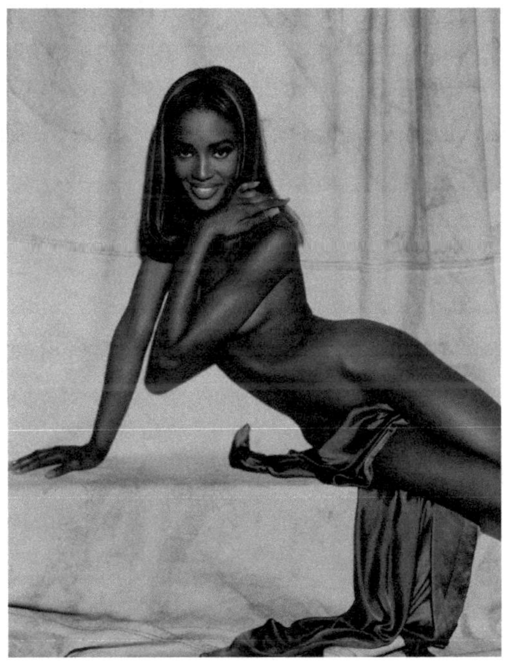

Naomi Campbell

surrounded by waterfalls. Clients used to splurge on exotic trips that made editorial shoots really special. Since I shot fast, we would have time to play wherever we were, and the girls loved me for it. We partied a lot, had tons of fun, and always came home with a winter tan.

I booked my crew, and I always tried to get my hairdresser friend, Bob Recine, to come with me. Bob and I would do a lot of partying together back home in New York. We'd have lots of laughs. He was like a brother to me. One of the first things we would do whenever we arrived somewhere would be to send out a search party to find drugs. We would never bring any with us, especially not to foreign countries.

In Venezuela, we started on the island of Los Roques in their Caribbean waters. We figured at the very least they'd have some good weed, and due to our proximity to Colombia, maybe even some primo cocaine. On the second day there, one of my assistants hit the jackpot. For twenty dollars, he came back with the equivalent of five hundred dollars' worth of the purest, cleanest cocaine I'd ever tasted in my life. No speedy rush, no nasal sting, no watery eyes—just an amazing, anxiety-free high with no stuffy nose or headaches to follow.

Five of us finished it off that night. Naturally, we wanted more, but my assistants couldn't find the guy. We sent the search party out again the next day to get a hundred dollars' worth this time. We couldn't wait to finish the shoot and party again that night.

But my assistant returned empty-handed. Apparently, the guy he got the coke from, a middle-aged fisherman, had come across a large blue plastic barrel filled with this top-grade shit floating in the sea while he was out fishing. We figured the transporters had thrown it overboard while being pursued by the authorities in a speedboat—we had seen that both on the news and in movies plenty of times. That's probably why we had gotten such a large amount for twenty bucks. The fisherman partied so much with his own merchandise that he had a heart attack and died. His family took the barrel before anyone could investigate and dumped it back out to sea. I'd never found coke like that ever again in my life. I guess the fisherman didn't either.

Once we were finished shooting Niki, we packed up for phase two. We went down to the Amazon, via Caracas, where the crew and I met up with Naomi at the airport and Nikki left for the States. The next morning, we location scouted, but we didn't need to go farther than the surroundings of our hotel. The place was beautiful with rivers and waterfalls and hardly anybody around. We joked about sending a search party out to look for some shit but figured whoever went might not be coming back. It was a real jungle out there.

Since we had time on our hands, after deciding to stay and shoot in the area, we went swimming. Then one of us discovered a souvenir shop where they sold crystals, T-shirts, mineral rocks, knickknacks, and postcards. I bought a postcard with an image of two local tribesmen with their hair in a bowl cut, their skin painted red, wearing feathered loincloths as they squatted facing each other and holding what looked like a bamboo shoot. One guy had the shoot in his mouth in the act of blowing; the other guy had his end of the bamboo shoot up his nose. "Hmm, Bob, take a look at this." He thought this might be worth investigating. I found a similar bamboo shoot and bought it.

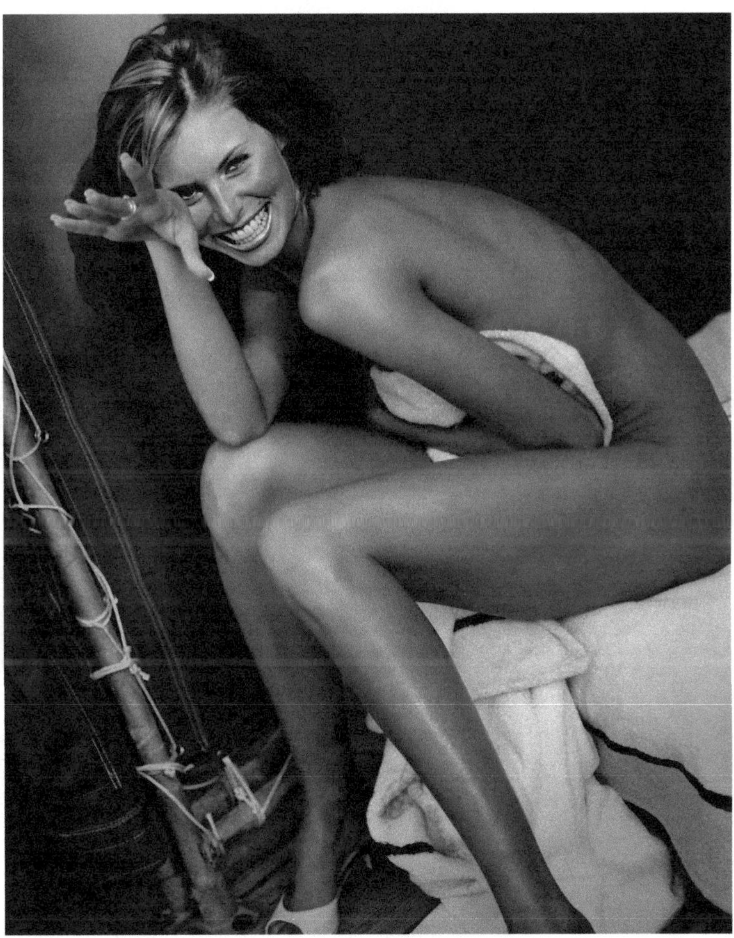

Niki Taylor

Outside, I ran into two guys in their late teens. They saw my bamboo shoot and had a chuckle. With a mix of Spanish, English, Italian, and hand signals, I showed them the postcard and asked what it was. They gave me some unpronounceable name and made a sign like sweeping across the sky. Ah, I got it—this must be some kind of hallucinogen.

"Can you get us any?"

He understood and nodded yes.

"*Cuánto*?" I asked. He said it would cost fifty dollars. Considering we were in the Amazon jungle, it seemed steep to me. The kid made a sign like walking and picking, grinding and shit like that, so I understood that they had to go pick the plant in the jungle. I gave him the fifty dollars, and he indicated that he'd come back the following night.

He came back the next night as promised and gave me an envelope containing what looked like crushed leaves and crushed seeds. I'd never smelled anything like it. He demonstrated how to put a little in the bamboo shoot and that one of us would blow it up the other's nose. Then, he made that sign again of a wave across the night sky.

Bob and I snuck off to his room and laid out equal portions like a ritual. With the sounds of the jungle and the waterfalls all around us, there was a feeling that something

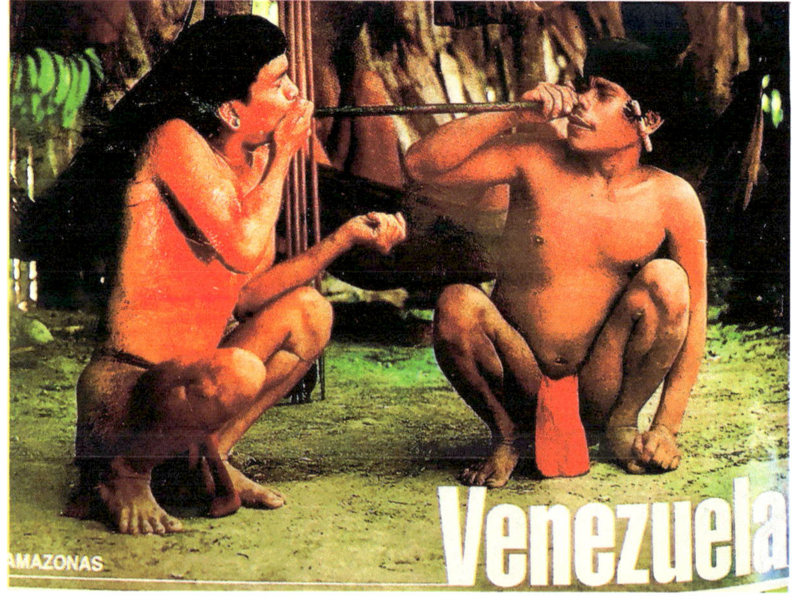

Postcard from the Venezuelan Amazon

sacred was about to take place. I volunteered to go first. Bob and I squatted opposite each other like in the postcard. Bob put the substance in his end of the bamboo, and I stuck my end up my nostril.

"Ready?"

"Yeah . . ."

Bob took a deep breath and blew that shit right up my nose, and I think it ricocheted off my brain. My eyeball on that side of the nostril almost popped out of my head, and it began to tear and was bloodshot in seconds. I needed a minute before I did the other nostril. Bob blew even harder and almost bowled me over with my other eyeball popping out, bloodshot and tearing, followed by a nasty headache.

Then, it was Bob's turn. I blew from my end, and Bob fell back as if someone had punched him in the face. We started laughing. I did his other nostril, so his eyes would look even, bulging out and red. Tears were coming down both our faces. Our noses got so inflamed we could hardly talk or understand each other.

I told Bob, "If I see those guys tomorrow, I'm going to kick their asses."

We went to our rooms and went to sleep.

In the morning, my eyes were still red and bulging, and my headache wouldn't go away. Then I saw one of the young guys from the hotel and asked if he could answer a question for me. I went and got the bamboo shoot, the crushed leaves, and the postcard of the two Indigenous South Americans. When I showed them to him, he burst out laughing and called his friend over, and he also started laughing.

One guy said, "Señor, these are dead leaves, tobacco, and dirt. How much did you pay?"

I told him fifty dollars, and they laughed even harder. I looked at Bob, who still looked like shit. We started laughing too. That guy who made the sign with his hand waving across the sky had probably been saying something like, "See you later, Sammy, see you in Miami!"

54

On one of those miserable nights when depression was kicking me in the teeth, I isolated myself at home and didn't want to see or be seen by anyone. The only way I could temporarily remedy the feeling of absolute dread was to get self-destructive by doing drugs. The most effective was "by chasing the dragon."

For those of you unfamiliar with the term, it means laying a small amount of heroin on aluminum foil and indirectly burning it from underneath that foil, causing the substance to go up in smoke, which resembles a fire-breathing dragon. You then chase that smoke with a straw you have in your mouth to inhale the smoke of the dragon. There are also the origin tales of opiates coming from the East, and this method coming from China, whose symbol is the dragon.

This evened me out so I could lie on the couch, watch something mindless, calm down. It temporarily stopped me from wanting to just break down and cry from a depression whose source was unknown to me at the time. It would come on out of left field and hit me like a brick. For some inexplicable reason, the Yankee game always seemed to be on TV at times like this, when something out the ordinary was about to happen.

The doorbell unexpectantly rang, and I mindlessly got up and answered it. It was the soon-to-be ex-wife of an aristocratic acquaintance of mine.

English aristocrats seemed to be the most perverse group of people I knew. Maybe it was their highbrow accent. The women always sounding superior and holier than thou. But the aristocratic women I met often gave me the impression that what they really wanted was a good spanking, at least that's what Jaye Davidson told me. They were so naughty . . . and frequently excelled in the sport of doing hard drugs. That was the cause of this Fair Lady's uncoupling with her husband, my aristocratic acquaintance. He was doing harder drugs than she was, and she made me look like a Cub Scout.

This was the last thing I needed. I unlocked the door and plopped myself back on the couch. She walked in, and before I could ask, she poured herself a drink, chopped a few lines of coke, and offered me some. I indulged since it was the middle of the seventh inning—my own version of the seventh-inning stretch.

Cocaine is a funny thing. Girls seem to lose their inhibitions, and it gets their libido going. For most guys, it also loosens inhibitions and churns the libido . . . but doesn't necessarily get the other parts to participate. I'm usually guaranteed to be left hanging like a rope. No matter how gorgeous the girl, no matter how desperately I'd try, it's like trying to put an oyster in a coin machine. I've always envied those two out of ten guys for whom it has the opposite effect. Another English friend would get so worked up after doing a lot of coke that he'd telephone a call girl at 3:00 a.m. and have her come over. She would arrive to find what he'd call his angry inch.

This particular English aristocrat was already juiced when she came up to my loft, really in the mood for a good shag, as they say. I was already wondering how I could *get rid of her so that I could watch the rest of the game.*

Before I knew it, she was in my bathroom running the water into my large Jacuzzi, which comfortably seated five. Bouncing in and out of the bathroom, she said, "C'mon, let's take a bath! Let's take a bath!"

I just said, "Go on in and start without me."

About twenty minutes after the water stopped running, I heard a scream from the bathroom. I ran in to see her standing there naked in the tub as the water was draining out, with her fingers splayed, screaming, "The ring! The stone! The emerald. Oh, my God! Oh, my God," over and over.

I told her to calm the fuck down. "What's going on? What happened?"

Apparently, she had been wearing a very large emerald ring, an heirloom passed down for generations, that had belonged to her soon-to-be ex-husband's grandmother, the matriarch of his aristo family. "Call a plumber! Call a plumber!" she yelled.

It was the bottom of the ninth! Man, she killed my high.

Where was I going to find a plumber on a Sunday night? They were hard enough to locate on a weekday. I made calls while she got dressed. I finally found a plumber, but he didn't take AmEx. I didn't have enough cash on hand and asked her if she had a Visa card. At the top her lungs, she called me a cheap fuck.

"Come on," I said, "he won't take my AmEx, but he takes Visa."

"No, you're just a cheap fuck!"

I made more calls and finally got someone who accepted American Express. He came over, snaked around, and found nothing. The girl was totally panicked and left in a hurry, as if it were all my fault. That was the last I saw of her for a long time.

About eight months later, I made it over to London. When I talked to people we both knew, the Jacuzzi story would inevitably come up. Turned out she was telling everybody her version—not the version where she was in the tub alone, probably playing with herself, but the one about what a cheap fuck I was. Fuckin' heirloom, my ass.

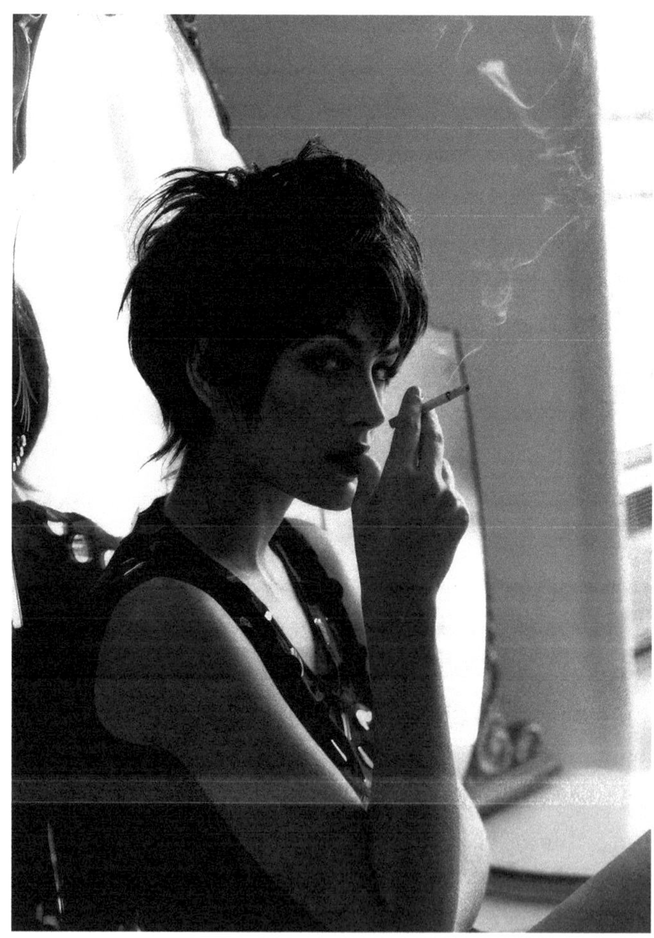

Georgina Grenville for Italian *Vogue*

55

After years of photographing and meeting people and making friends in the fashion world, art world, and entertainment fields, I could sometimes create my own shootings.

I had an excellent relationship with Italian *Vogue* and *L'Uomo Vogue*. Franca Sozzani, one of the great talents in the magazine industry, a visionary, was the editor-in-chief for both magazines, and I had known her since the '80s. Every so often, I would submit to Franca commissioned pictures that I'd shot on vacation with model friends who had given me time for a shoot. My focus for these images would be mainly on nudes—one, because I had always done nudes since my days in art school, and two, most importantly, I was a beauty photographer. That meant skin care or body care.

Commercially, a nude shot could fit a variety of clients' products for the magazine to feature: sunscreens, designer perfumes, lotions, an array of cosmetic products. Even those pictures of models and celebrities in the duty-free shops were considered beauty photographs. If I handed the magazine great nudes of a top model, they could credit any number of their clients—such as L'Oréal, Revlon, or a myriad of designer fragrances—to the picture for editorial purposes, and everyone would win. (You can't do that with fashion because it's seasonal, and the magazine and the designers have their own specific points of view to feature.) I could also give them last year's nudes, provided they had not already been published, and the magazine could then go ahead and apply them to their agenda. The images were timeless. It made things more flexible for me—no pressure and no editor getting in my way photographically.

You could say the same of celebrities. If they had a film coming out, or if there was anything newsworthy, I could hand in a great unpublished image of them. It didn't matter if I had taken it the year before. Otherwise, the magazine would have needed to make it a fashion story, along with the celebrity and designers featured together, and that could get tricky, especially with the men.

The guys I knew, like Mickey Rourke and Axl Rose, wouldn't have posed with clothing that was not visually part of their wardrobe. "I ain't no fashion model!" They wouldn't stand for the thought of being in any fashion editorials.

Working with these guys was like riding the wildest horse in the rodeo. They marched to the beat of their own tune. The only thing predictable about them was they were unpredictable. You had to be both a lion tamer and a magician to make things happen.

One summer, Axl invited me to join him and Guns N' Roses for part of their European tour. I looked up the schedule and found out they were basing themselves in London while touring England. Why not ask *L'Uomo Vogue* to let me do a series of pictures of Axl wearing his own clothes? They loved the idea but would need to send a journalist to do an interview. Knowing Axl, I knew that wouldn't work. As it was, he was already against having his pictures taken in general. The last person who photographed him was me, five years earlier in California.

I told *Vogue* that a journalist wasn't going to work and suggested I do the interview. Everyone was happy with that. I needed four days, but knowing Axl, I was worried. I paid my own airfare to avoid any dramas, and G N' R would put me up at their hotel in London. If I didn't manage to pull this off, at least the magazine wouldn't be out of pocket, and if it worked out, they'd reimburse my expenses. That took a lot of pressure off me.

In this field, the photographer is responsible for everything. If the model's a no-show, it's your fault; if an asteroid strikes, it's your fault. One time, I booked a girl for a client, and she showed up for the shooting with her long blond hair cut short. The client was upset and never worked with me again.

With Axl, I expected a high-wire act. In as much as he liked me, there were no guarantees as to what mood he'd be in during those four days.

I arrived in London early in the morning and ran into Axl's man, Fernando, in the hotel lobby. He said his mom, Beta, who was Axl's personal manager, was also in the hotel. I had known Beta before she met Axl and loved her dearly. Both she and Fernando were everything to Axl; they were family. They had arrived hours earlier, around 6:00 am, from whatever city Guns N' Roses had just played in.

Fernando explained that, on the night of a show, Axl would arrive by helicopter in the

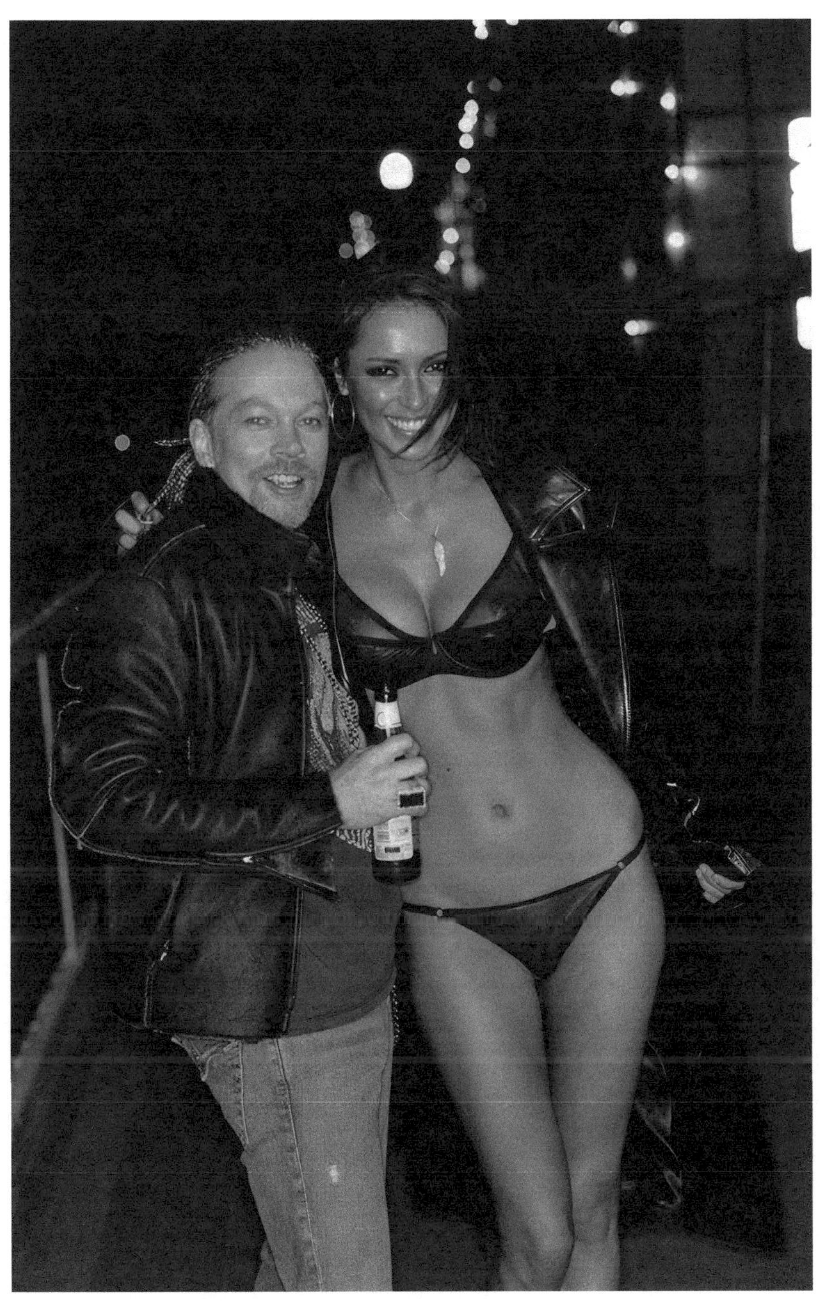

Axl Rose and Sasha, London, for Italian *Vogue*

early evening, perform, and fly back to London after the concert. He told me Axl was now asleep and "do not disturb," but they would be leaving that night for a concert in Birmingham.

Axl usually had a big breakfast first, around 5:00 or 6:00 p.m. So that evening, I had breakfast-dinner with Axl, Beta, and friends. Then we were driven to the heliport and flown to the concert, late as usual. I shot pictures on the helicopter, off the helicopter, backstage, front stage, forward, and backward. This went on for days.

My assignment included four or five shots of Axl in different outfits of his own and the interview. Somewhere in this routine of flying to and from the concerts, back to the hotel at dawn, grabbing something to eat, going to bed, and doing it all over again, I had to get him in the mood to sit with me, undistracted, to record the interview. I thought I'd get him on his two nights off during my four days there. But I had forgotten about the parties and all the other shit musicians on tour get up to on their nights off, and Axl was not in the mood to do anything else but party and let off steam.

By day nine, I had nothing. *Vogue* kept calling because I'd promised them they would have the pictures and the interview days ago. They were excited, so I had to keep dodging them. I needed to pull a jackrabbit out of my ass.

I remembered my friend Sasha Volkova, also known as "the Volcano," who lived in London. She was a tall brunette Ukrainian who turned heads everywhere she went. In heels, she had to be 6'2" at the very least. She was smart and could easily stand up to Axl—or anyone for that matter. I called her up. "Sasha, I need a favor. How would you like to do some pictures with Axl Rose?"

"Who?"

"Guns N' Roses, Axl Rose."

"I don't know who that is, but for you, I do anything. What do you need?"

"Wear a trench coat over your sexiest lingerie and the highest heels you can walk in and come to my hotel."

"What kind of coat? I have Prada, Gucci, every designer." I told her anything sexy would do.

She knocked at my door an hour later. She opened the coat and asked if I liked it. Does the Pope shit in the Vatican?

I walked her to Axl's room and told her, "Knock and say, 'Sante wants to know if you want to take pictures together,' and then open the coat and show him your outfit. Give me a minute to get back to my room."

I was on fucking day nine of a four-day shoot. This had to work. Back in my room, I got the call from Axl: "Where do you want to start?"

All I needed were four pictures minimum, some in his room and maybe one outdoors so that we'd photographically know we were in London. We shot till dawn. I didn't get four pictures; I got twelve. Afterward, I just let Axl talk into my digital recorder and got an hour's worth of conversation for the interview.

Those two hit it off big time. They stayed together for the next year, on and off, mostly on. And I scored big time with the Italians. Everybody said, "Wow, you're so lucky." Give me a fucking break.

56

One late fall day, that dreaded phone call came in. My mother had fallen, and there were complications. I rushed to the hospital. She was in the emergency room; it was serious, and by the second day, my family had flown in from Florida and around the New York area. All of us waited to hear any developments.

Ever since I was a kid, my mom had made me promise I would bury her in Greenwood Cemetery, not too far from our house. Greenwood is a monument to cemeteries. It's a national historical landmark on the original hilly landscape of Brooklyn, with lakes and specimen trees from all over the world that would bloom in different seasons. In April, the cherry trees are magnificent. It's where George Washington fought the British in the Battle of Brooklyn before he retreated to Brooklyn Heights. Both the Revolutionary War and Civil War dead are buried there. Four hundred acres, it's as big as Prospect Park, with huge mausoleums and Victorian sculptures erected by old New York families like Tiffany, Pierrepoint, Schermerhorn; artists like Basquiat and Leonard Bernstein; mobsters like Albert Anastasia and Joey Gallo. In the nineteenth century, people went there—and still today go there—to have picnics. It's the highest point in Brooklyn, overlooking the city and the bay. As kids we would sneak into the cemetery to explore, and eventually we would get chased out by some kind of ninja security officers; we thought these guys hid behind trees. They always came out of the blue and found us. Unless I'm lost at sea, it's where I want my sorry ass to be buried as well.

By the fourth day, my mom's condition was getting worse. She was in her eighties, and it was not looking good. My sister turned to me and said, "I think we should start calling family members and make arrangements. You bought the plot, right?"

The plot? Holy fuck! I never bought the plot that I had promised my mom I would. I drove straight to the administration office of Greenwood Cemetery. They told me they only had about a year's worth of plots left, but a few were still available. They gave me a map, and I drove around to look at the remaining areas. To my surprise, I found a bare area with flat stone markers indicating plots by number. I chose A12; it was close to a tree, and I liked it. I went back to the office.

The lady asked, "Where is the deceased presently?"

I said, "She's not dead yet."

"Oh, with so few plots left, we can only sell if the person is deceased."

"She's practically dead. She's going to die any minute. I promised her a plot."

"Sorry, sir, we'd be happy to assist you, but those are the rules. We're a national cemetery now."

I was devastated. I got in my car, panicking. What kind of son was I? My mind was scrambling; I was thinking I must know somebody who knows somebody who could fix me up here. I called my friend Connie, whose father was a longshoreman on the Brooklyn docks. It turned out he knew a guy from downtown South Brooklyn who owned a funeral home: Sal Russo, better known as Sally Bones.

I knew that neighborhood well—all the old-school Italians lived there; that's where Perry's father, Tom the Bomb, used to take us when he made his payoffs. It was mob country, and if anyone needed to get rid of a body, they'd call Sally Bones. Someone once told me how it was done. They would choose a good-sized casket, put the body in face down, then lay the padded fabric over it and put someone's recently deceased grandma on top. Nobody would know that Grandma Vitali was buried in the same casket with Jimmy Four Fingers. Pretty ingenious.

"Sal, is that you?"

"Yeah, who's this?"

"Sante, Frank Scalisi's friend."

"Oh, yeah, he told me you'd call."

"I'm driving to Brooklyn to visit my mom at the hospital soon."

"Okay, call me when you're on the Brooklyn Bridge."

"You want me to call you when I'm driving over the Brooklyn Bridge?"

"Yeah, that's what I just said. What are you, deaf?"

"Okay, got ya, thanks, Sal."

I got in the car to drive to see my mom. On the Brooklyn Bridge, I called and said, "Hey, Sal. It's me, Frank Scalisi's friend. You told me to call you when I'm on the Brooklyn Bridge. I'm on the Brooklyn Bridge."

"Okay, good. How long you planning on being by your mom's?"

"Just a couple of hours."

"Okay, call me when you're done."

Two hours later—

"Hey, Sal, I'm wrapping up at my mom's."

"Okay, meet me at Greenwood Cemetery in half an hour. Pull into the gate."

"Sal, excuse me for asking, but you want me to pull into the first gate or the second gate?"

"Pull into the fucking gate and wait for me in the funeral lane, and if anybody asks, tell them you're waiting for a funeral."

I didn't even want to ask. I drove to Greenwood, and when I pulled into the first gate, I saw a funeral lane to the right. At a funeral, the cars trailing the hearse had to stop there before the hearse passed through the second gate, a monumental Gothic structure that also housed the administrative offices. Nobody was around, thank God, so I pulled over to the funeral lane and waited for Sal. About twenty minutes later, a Cadillac pulled up next to me. The driver was a rotund guy who looked like Weegee. He wore a Borsalino hat and had two more Borsalino hats on his back dashboard, I guess in case his first hat blew off.

"Sal??"

"Sante?? All right, wait here. I have to go to the office and do my song and dance. I'll be right back."

I watched Sal pull up to the Gothic gate and saw him go into the trunk of his car and pull out three shopping bags. He went into the office on the right and came back out with two shopping bags. Then, he went into the office on the left and came out with no bags, got back in his car, and drove up to me.

"Okay, go up to the other gate and park the car on the left side. Do you know where the plot is?"

"Yeah, yeah, I'm pretty sure, I think I know."

"Oh, you think you know. This place is bigger than fuckin' Prospect Park. You think I want to get lost following you around? You said you know the number, right?"

"It's A12."

"Now I gotta pick up my guy inside and let him take us there. You follow but stay behind a bit; he don't need anybody knowing he's doing this for me. When you see us stop, you pull over, keep a little distance, and don't look at the guy. You get out of the car and wait for me but look the other way. Don't look at the guy!"

"Okay, okay, no problem."

The guy came out of the office and jumped in Sal's car, and I followed them at a distance. He took the same roads I would have taken. Past Revolutionary War Hill, past the cherry trees, to the other side. When they stopped and pulled over, I stayed back like Sal said. I got out of the car and looked the other way. After a short while, I heard Sal.

"Pssst, pssst, PSSSST!"

If I turned around, I was going to see the guy that I was not supposed to look at. Sal *psssted* so loud I knew he was pissed. So I turned around, and he started walking toward me, and I shrugged my shoulders like, what the fuck?

"I told you not to look at the guy."

"Sal, you were *pssssting* at me so loud you sounded pissed, so I turned around."

"You sure this is the plot you want?"

"Yeah, I came here twice before to make sure I favored this area and this plot, I decided. A12."

"Okay then, do me a favor: go walk over and go stand on the plot number and don't look at the fucking guy."

"Okay, but I ain't turning around if you start *pssssting* at me again." I walked over and stood on the plot, looking everywhere except toward them. To someone driving by, I must have looked lost, and that's kind of how I felt. But at this point, I'd have done anything to secure this plot I'd promised my mom since I was a kid.

I heard one car door close. *Fuck this, I'm turning around.* The guy I was not supposed to look at was in the car, and Sal was motioning to me to follow them. I got in my car; we headed back to the administrative building, and I kept my distance, and the guy went into the building. Sal waved to me and asked me for my credit card. I gave it to him.

"I'm going inside to do the paperwork, and I'll bring it out for you to sign. Wait for me on the other side of this gate."

After several minutes, Sal came out with my card and the deed to the plot. It cost me fifteen thousand dollars. Sal showed me the deed and the receipt; everything was settled except for one thing. Sal would be holding the deed until I came back with Sally Bones's payola, five thousand in cash. It was steep, but I was making big bucks at the time, and besides, I had an artist's sense for money—which meant no sense at all.

Sal said to call him later; he'd tell me what to do. All I knew was I had to go back to meet him at some point at the funeral home downtown with his share for the deed. In the meantime, he told me to wait a minute, and he ran to the trunk of his car and pulled out the same kind of shopping bag as the ones he had dropped off earlier at the administrative offices.

"Here, take this. It's a gift. And don't forget to call me later."

We said goodbye, and I didn't even look in the bag until I was about five blocks away. It was a loaf of brown bread, fresh and still warm.

I called Connie and told her we'd made the transaction. "But what's with the bread?" I asked.

Connie said, "Oh, he gave you the bread. He always does that. It's prosciutto bread. His sister makes it at the convent."

"You're kidding me!"

"I kid you not. She's the baker at the convent downtown. You know that church towards the highway? It's actually a funny story."

"Okay, I'm waiting."

"When Sal was young, he got hit by a car and was close to death. His sister was the black sheep of the family, and she was turning tricks on the street. Sal was in the hospital a long time, and his sister went to church and prayed every day and told God, if Sal should survive, she would stop everything and dedicate herself to Him and the church. Sal, as you see, survived, so that's exactly what she did. She entered the convent, turned her life around, and became a nun. She's been baking for them now for over thirty years. She makes the prosciutto bread."

I started picking at the bread. It was really good; I'd eaten half by the time I got home.

Around two hours later, I called Sal to set up a day and time for me to pay him his cash so I could take possession of the deed. He instructed me to meet him at the funeral home in two days and to put the cash in an envelope and wrap it in a *New York Post* with a rubber band around it. I figured he knew what he was doing.

The next day, I picked up my ten-year-old son, who would be staying with me for a couple of days. Nick loved movies like *Star Wars* and *Indiana Jones*. To share something I knew he'd never forget, I told him about Sally Bones and the mob and how I went to get the plot at the cemetery for Nonna. How they'd buried Jimmy Four Fingers in the same casket as Grandma Vitali. I had him going. When I told him about Sal's ex-prostitute sister becoming a nun and a baker at the convent, his face lit up. He had a great sense of humor.

Then the clincher. I said I needed him to come with me to make the payoff at the funeral home. I had already gotten the cash, and I showed him the money I had put in the envelope and wrapped in the *New York Post* with a rubber band. Nick was so excited; he almost couldn't sleep; this was an adventure straight out of a movie.

The next day, we got in my car and drove to South Brooklyn, to the funeral home downtown. One thing I told my kid: if Sally mentioned his sister, keep a straight face or we would end up in a casket with someone's grandmother. I pulled up to the funeral home and parked behind a hearse.

Before we even got out of the car, two goons in black suits came walking right at us.

My son said, "Uh-oh."

I rolled down my window, and one goon said, "What do you want around here?"

"I have a meeting with Sal."

"All right, wait a minute." He went to the hearse and came back with a ruler, a large white plastic ruler that said, "Funeral Home." "Put this on your dashboard. No one's going to bother you."

My son's face got really serious as we went inside. I had the *Post* rolled up under my arm. Sal came out and welcomed us like we were customers; he walked us around, showed us a room with a creepy, life-size Madonna in a black wig like the one my Cuban friend Noel's parents had in their living room when I was a teenager, the only other time I saw the Madonna in a wig.

Sal took us into a large room where they had caskets to purchase, some with the lids open, and while Sal was talking loudly about the different styles, he whispered to throw the package in the coffin here. I flung the rolled-up *New York Post* into the casket. Sal obviously didn't want to share the money with anyone else, so he closed the lid as if it were a demonstration. He then quickly escorted us out and stopped in front of a fireplace by the front door to show us pictures hanging on the wall. He pointed to one of them and said, "This one is my sister."

I gave my son the look, and he kept a straight face.

Sal then gave me the deed and said, "Wait here a minute." He ran to the back and came out with a round aluminum tray with a see-through cover. It was still hot. "Take these. My sister made them, fried mozzarella balls."

We said thank you and got in the car and left.

About a block away, my son said, "You think we should try one?" He opened up the tray, and there were a dozen of them, and of course, they were delicious. We finished them off before we even got to the Brooklyn Bridge.

So with everything we went through to get the plot, my relatives flying in, the family drama, what happened next? My mother pulled through and made a full recovery. She was fine. I wanted to kill her.

Whenever she pulled that shit on me again, "I'm dying, I'm dying," I'd turn to her and say, "Ma, you can die already. I bought the plot!"

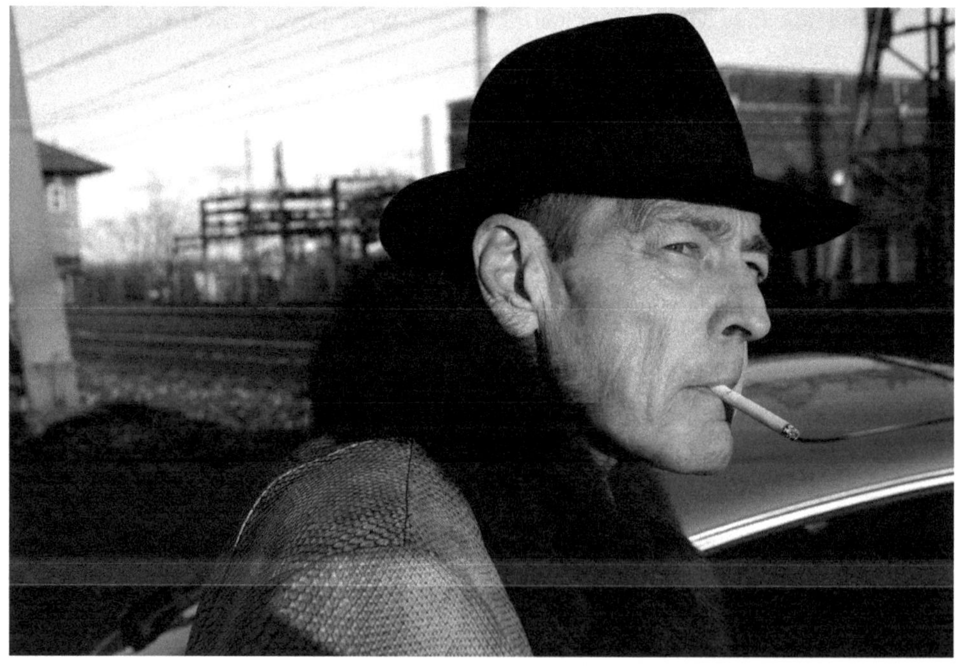

Nick Tosches, Jersey City, New Jersey

57

I fell in love with every girl I shot . . . for a minute, at least. I confused falling in love with their image with falling in love with the person. We artists would sometimes project all our ideals onto our muse and believe them for as long as we could. Some of us would get whacked immediately, while others would find themselves slowly bleeding out. It didn't matter how smart you were. We'd all lie to ourselves for the sake of being with a beautiful woman. The bigger the lie, the higher the price.

I was always fighting my own demons. I was serving a lifetime sentence of being a mook and further fucked up from being raised by an emotionally handicapped and depressed mother who drained me for attention and absolutely ruined all my relationships with women. I spent a lifetime trying to run away from her and could never get too attached to any woman for very long out of fear of another lifetime sentence chained to another dependent.

And if I started to see my mom in some of my own behavior, I began to run away from myself. How did I escape from me? Drugs, for sure, but I also started hanging out with all the "*puttanas*"; they were easier to get along with, and I could erase any image of my mom in them.

In my entire adult life, coincidently, I only dated one Italian girl. Her name was Monica. She was a model, of course. She couldn't speak English, so I spoke Italian with her. It lasted three weeks. She happened to be at my place in the city one day when my mom came over to visit. She somehow endeared herself so much to my mom that my mom invited her to our family Thanksgiving dinner without asking me. Monica had pulled the poor-me routine, how she was alone here in New York with no family around, etc.—very Southern Italian. She had my mom eating out of the palm of her hand, like taking candy from a baby. I hated that shit 'cause my mom taught me how to emotionally manipulate, and I hated myself whenever I recognized myself doing it.

At Thanksgiving dinner, Monica was talking to everyone and helping in the kitchen, and I could tell everyone was thinking, "Wow, this girl is just right for Sante!"—which only got me more pissed off. After that, I didn't call her for three days or answer her calls. I finally picked up on Sunday morning, and she gave me the "I don't know anyone in New York, can I come over?" routine. I had a million things to do, but I said, "All right, but I'm going to be out half the day." So she came over, and I went out to take care of a bunch of errands.

When I came back, not only had she cleaned my apartment and done my laundry, but she'd also made enough Italian food for twenty people and packed some up for the refrigerator, just like my mom would do. I threw her the fuck out and never called her again. I was too familiar with that whole routine, and I knew what was attached to that package—the guilt, the jealousy, the misery. I said *no way*.

Another thing that made all relationships tough for me in general was my being a fashion photographer who worked with the most beautiful women in the world. That's why I only went out with models because that's who I was surrounded by. At least they had an idea of how the business worked and they felt somewhat secure, having an ear to the ground in the same business.

I was also an artist fighting for my voice. Art always came before anything; it came first, and I always let that be known. Kara was only one girl in my life who understood that. My boy was the greatest gift I've ever received in my life, a channel of love I never knew existed before, and for that alone, I'll always be grateful to her. We were together for eight years, the first six were fantastic, fun, and inspiring. The last two years were the worst and took me years to recover from them . . . if I ever did.

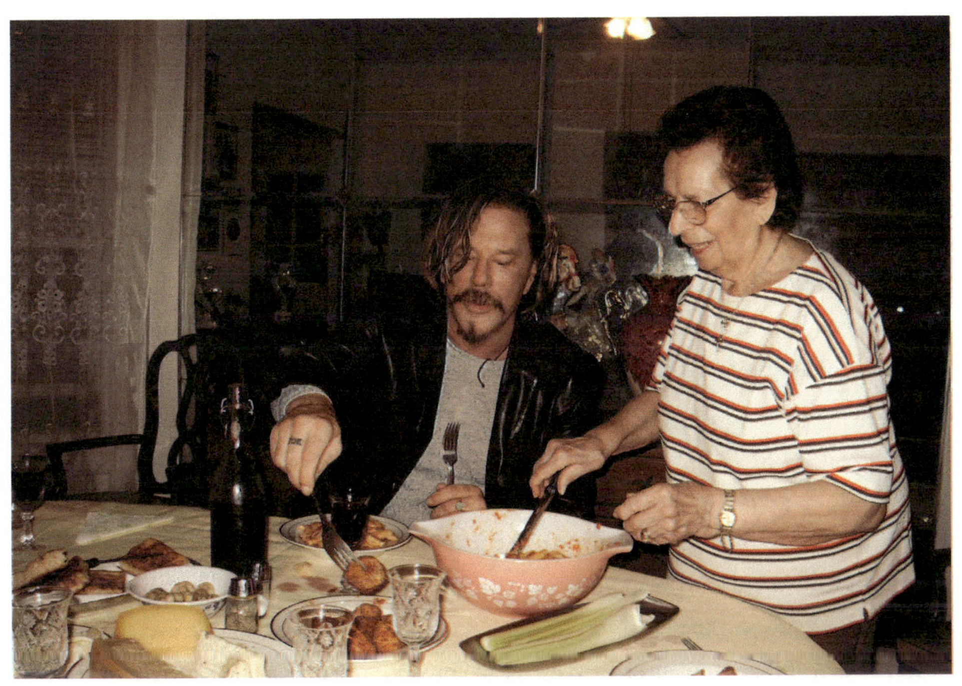

Mickey Rourke and Mom "Nonna" D'Orazio

58

Banshee (noun) Definition: A female spirit in Irish and Scottish stories who cries loudly to warn people that someone is going to die soon. Synonyms: demon, phantom, spirit.

The word *banshee* has become more popular in the last twenty years than it had been in the previous two hundred years, at least, here in the States. Every time I hear it spoken, it reminds me of an incident that happened some years ago.

Back in the '90s, Kara and I would often get together with Naomi and Bobby DeNiro for dinner in New York City, where we lived. I had known Naomi since she was around sixteen years old, and she was always a character and often could be quite tumultuous and outspoken. She could also perceive slights where no one else could see them. Sometimes I thought she was nuts—but God forbid you question her perceptions because she was usually right. She possessed a weird sixth sense; she knew if someone was talking about her in New York, even if she might be in London at that moment. I'd always try to convince her that she was imagining things.

De Niro, on the other hand, didn't appear to possess that particular gift. He was convinced *everyone* was talking about him. He sometimes seemed a volatile fusion of Jake LaMotta in *Raging Bull* and Travis Bickle in *Taxi Driver.*

The combination of Naomi and Bobby together was always unpredictable and combustible, comparable to, say, riding the Cyclone at Coney Island with a case of nitroglycerin and C4 explosive sitting on your lap.

We had arranged to have dinner together. As usual, he had made reservations at the only restaurant in Tribeca that was empty on a weekend night. Bobby was running late because he was location scouting for the movie *A Bronx Tale*, which he was scheduled to direct.

We didn't mind him being late; it would give us time to have drinks and hang out together. But a ninety-minute wait turned into too many cocktails. I was starving and had already eaten most of the bread. Naomi grew irritated and fidgety. Suddenly she burst out, "He's fucking someone! I know he's fucking someone!" Kara and I tried to calm her down, but that train had already left the station. By now, I was working on my third or fourth vodka tonic, maybe even my fifth. We tried to distract her by ordering some food.

Bobby finally arrived and sat down across from Kara and next to Naomi, who gave him the evil eye *and* the cold shoulder. Bobby rolled his eyes as if to say *Now what?*

I reached for more bread while Kara tried to start some light conversation, but Naomi went on the attack. "You're fucking someone! Who are you fucking? I know you're fucking someone! You're a cheating whore and such a liar! I hope your dick falls off!"

Then Travis Bickle turned to her and said, "You talkin' to me? I hope you're not talkin' to me?"

Kara stood up and took Naomi by the arm and escorted her off to a neutral corner, the bathroom. I ordered another vodka tonic and a double for Travis.

Our drinks arrived, and I downed one after the other. Soon after, the girls returned to the table and took their seats.

Bobby, seated opposite Kara, leaned forward and addressed her as if Naomi and I were not there, "Kara, sometimes your friend Naomi says things that are not so nice."

I couldn't control it—I gave such a guffaw that my vodka tonic flew out of my nostrils, and I almost choked.

Naomi delivered a swift hard kick to Bobby's shins under the table. Several drinks were knocked over. The waiter approached with our food just as Jake LaMotta upended the table, flung it over, sending everything crashing to the floor. Then, he got up and stormed out of the restaurant. Naomi picked up and ran after him, more likely to kick his ass than to apologize.

I was left sitting there with Kara, my napkin on my lap, still holding my knife and fork. I turned to Kara and said, "Shouldn't we eat since the food is here?"

She gave me a look and said, "Get your shit. We have to go save them."

I followed her out. We hurried out onto West Broadway, and we could hear Naomi screaming from a block away. You would have thought she was being murdered—but, in fact, *she* was throwing anything she could find at him.

He ducked and weaved as he screamed repeatedly, "Help! She's a fucking banshee! Help!"

We did intervene because two passing brothers were about to pounce on Bobby, assuming this white guy was bothering a sista! We quickly explained the situation and calmed Naomi down somewhat, while Bobby continued running in the opposite direction, screaming, "She's a fucking banshee! She needs help!"

We were going to put Naomi in a cab, but she was now talking calmly on the phone, and twenty minutes later, she announced that she was heading to Bobby's place around the corner to spend the night.

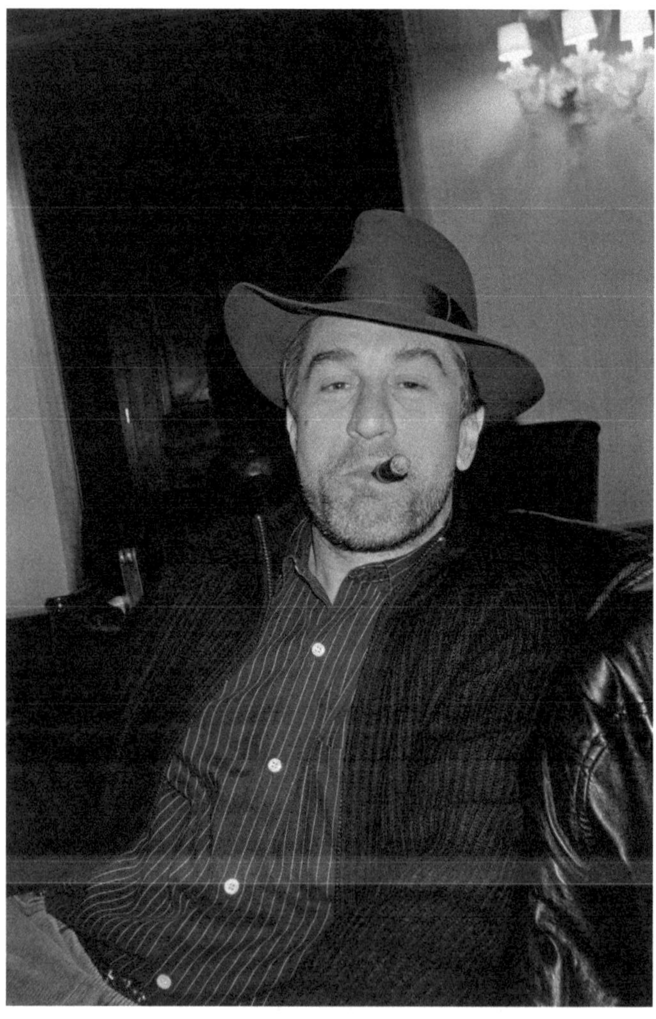

Robert De Niro, St. Moritz

59

I lay on my couch one night, coming down from a numbed-out high after another unfulfilling shoot I did just for the money. I couldn't seem to get past these jobs and move on. I took each one so personally, and this kind always let me down, even if I was getting a ton of money and my name wasn't on it. I sometimes had to take bad pictures to make a living, and it killed me. I had to get high just to numb the fact of doing shit work. I needed to sleep, so I swallowed a pill strong enough to knock a donkey out.

Soon after the pill went down, my doorbell rang. I only answered it because I thought it might be a friend with something more to get high on. A female voice said, "Hi, sexy, I'm coming up to get you!" *Oh, my God, I can't believe it. She was one of the hottest, sexiest actresses around.* I buzzed her in. I'd been working with her now for a short while, and we were always flirting, but I'd keep myself out of harm's way because she was the face for an internationally well-known cosmetic company, and it was a great client. I know where my bread is buttered. Plus, she was at the tail end of a high-profile breakup, and I didn't need to get in the middle of it with that kind of attention, especially from the press following her around.

As I unlocked the apartment door, I remembered the horse tranquilizer of a pill I had just popped, ran to the bathroom, and stuck my fingers down my throat to heave it out. No such luck. I heard her coming in and her slurry voice saying, "Come out, come out wherever you are." She was wearing a short plaid Catholic school skirt and dangling her panties on one finger, a smirk on her face. She had come from dinner just around the corner and had obviously imbibed a good number of drinks.

Meanwhile, I had spent the last three or four hours getting whacked on shit that gave me erotic dreams but left me hanging like a rope. I didn't have a chance! She threw me on the couch and rapidly disrobed herself and me. I was staring at every guy's (and many girls') wet dream, in the buff, and there was no way my johnson was going to show up! I knew I'd have to go down there for two or three hours to make up for it. I dove in headfirst and went at it like a champ. Her long, beautiful legs clamped me in a headlock. I had been down there for some time when I could feel myself getting sloppy, slowing down, and then the pill kicked in. When she heard me snoring, she pulled my head up and smacked me so hard that I woke up and continued as if nothing had happened. I came to the next morning, slumped over with my knees on the floor and my face glued to the couch. I looked a wreck, my hair flattened on one side with one eyelid glued shut, and my beard looking like a glazed doughnut. She was long gone . . . and she never answered my calls. That was our first and last date . . .

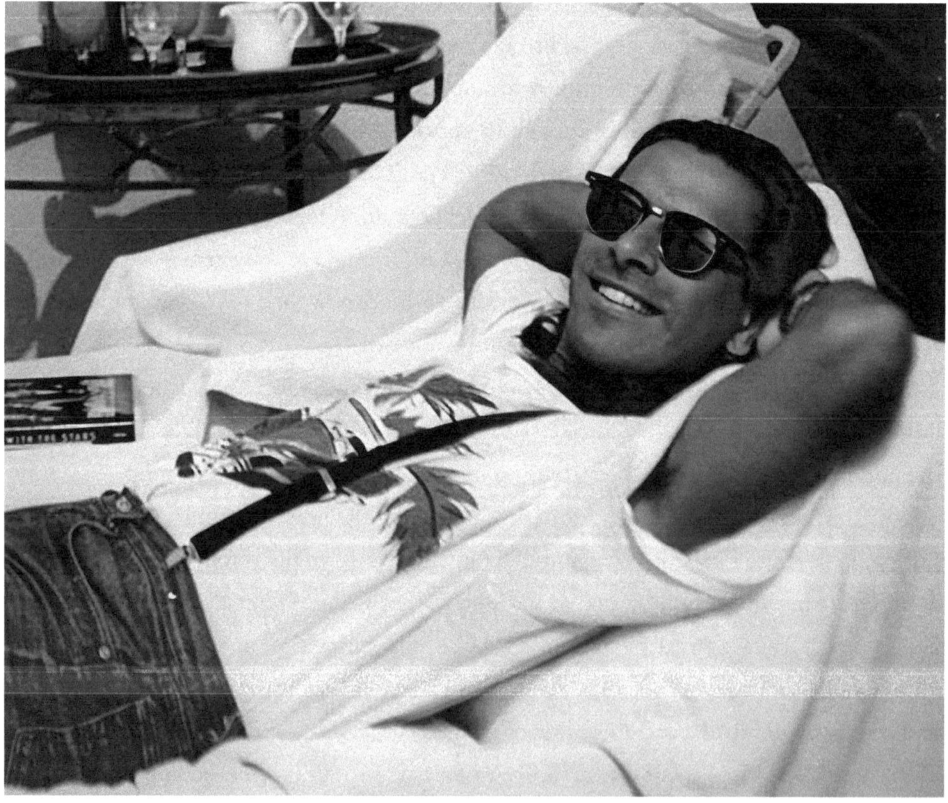

Sante, just kicking back

60

Society demands imitation.
—Carl Jung

If *everyone* likes your work, it may be because it's mediocre. To define anything for yourself, you need to challenge yourself and everyone around you. Choose to be different and run with it—that's what it means to be an artist. Say something, even if it's "Go shove it!" Just don't expect *everyone* to like it. When you appeal to the right and the left, it puts you in the middle, which, by the very definition, is "mediocre." Everyone likes what's familiar. If they all pat you on the back, take the attitude that they probably don't know what they're talking about.

When I started out in fashion, I went with a definition of beauty that my art-school training led me toward. I figured, if the model looked great, then whatever she was wearing would look great. People would want to feel like that; it was aspirational. If it were a perfume, then a sensual image of the nape of her neck or a hand to her breasts would be poetic enough to inspire a sense of what the fragrance evoked. You could feel that scent from the image. The key was to feel it when I searched for it with my camera. This made me a really good beauty photographer, and, in time, as I learned more about fashion, I was able to combine beauty and fashion in the same manner. But being inspired by others was quite different from copying them.

If I went in with reference images of other people's work, as many photographers do, I would be imitating someone else. If I stopped thinking about them and allowed the experience with my subject to be immediate, I could respond to the excitement of that immediacy. Once I'd feel a sensual connection, I knew I had something in the image.

You also have to know when you're responding to someone else's image while shooting. It's way too easy to get excited about an image that inadvertently replicates an iconic image by one of your heroes. You fool yourself into thinking it's yours, but it's not; it's a copy, and everyone else knows it when it's published. That's fashion, and different magazines have been shooting similar collections forever, and most likely copied that same photo you're referencing a zillion times. That's what I mean by "everyone likes the familiar." It just ends up hurting you in the long run. Helmut Newton once said to me, "I don't mind when a young photographer just starting out is copying me. I get annoyed when a forty-year-old is doing it!"

A themed collection could be photographed in as literal a manner as the designer showed it on the runway. I prefer to reinterpret it and find *my* vision in that collection. Maybe the model's hair is down as if she spent the night out, her makeup somewhat smudged. Then she appears through the styling, and I respond to what's beautiful for me. Maybe I lean her in the corner of a room where a sliver of light vertically touches part of her face and does the same for the fashion. In the shadows, you can still see the details of what she's wearing. The mystery of this kind of beauty is what I always look for. I like to work with the elements that are around and available to find *my* picture.

I need the surprise and excitement of a real experience—a realism that I discover for myself through shooting outside in my urban world. I respond to what excites me with light when I'm with or without my camera; the experience stays with me, and I can recall it when I see it again. That sensory perception is who I am; it's a self-portrait. It comes from my background and training in street photography.

Helmut Newton recognized himself in the expressionism of Germany between the two wars; it's where and when he grew up. Peter Lindbergh found it in the characters and their idiosyncrasies of his post-WWII Berlin, along with his compatriot Wim Wenders, with whom he shared the same aesthetic as in films like *Wings of Desire*. Robert Mapplethorpe, on the other hand, realized it in the homoeroticism of his lifestyle mixed, paradoxically, with the ideal forms of Hollywood glamour photography of the 1930s-40s that George Platt Lynes, George Hoyningen-Huene, and Horst P. Horst personified.

Everyone creates images based on how they see themselves through the filter of their own times and experiences. They recognize themselves in the images they create. All else is imitation.

Artistically speaking, my training didn't allow me to be that forgiving or compromising when handing in work I wasn't convinced of. Editors found me difficult or stubborn with the choices I handed in. One editor didn't understand why I took my images so personally. I put a lot of pressure on myself to do great work, to find that iconic image that stood out

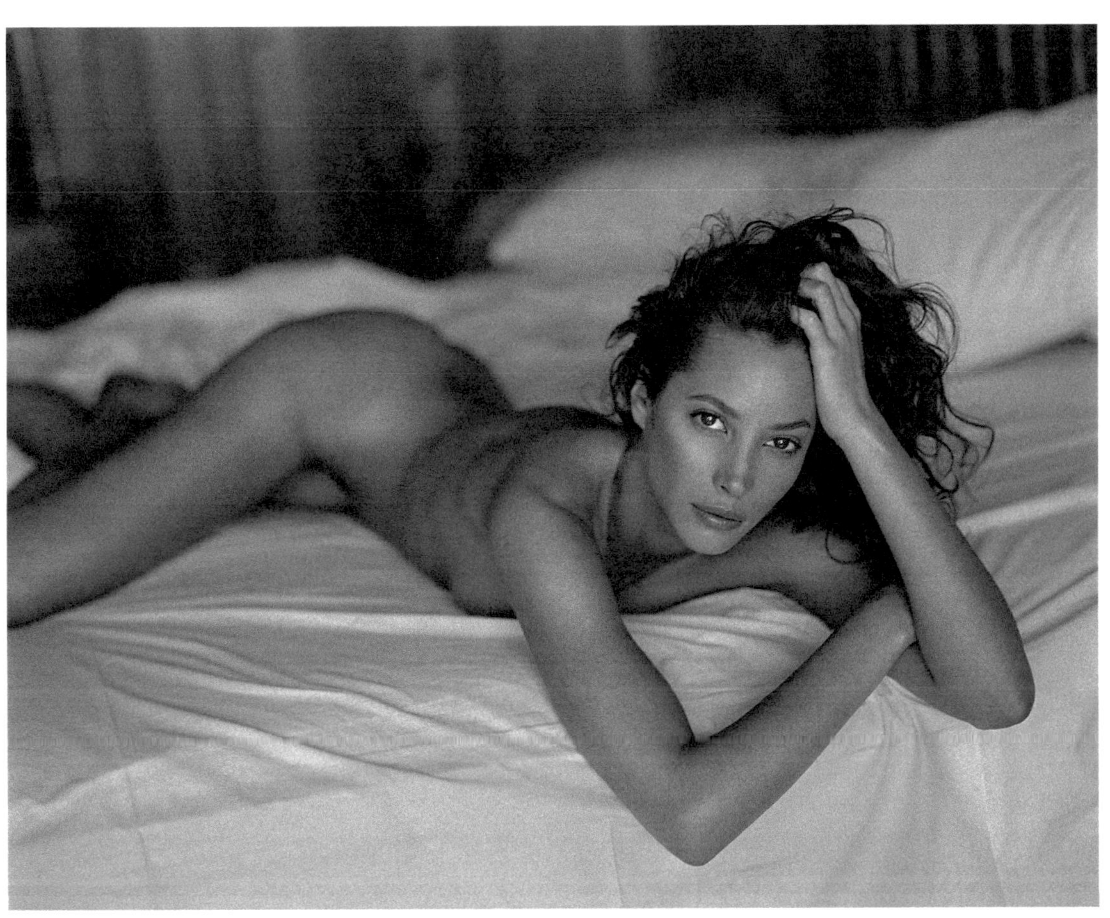

Christy Turlington, Panoramic View Hotel, Montauk, New York

from the rest. I stood out because I was doing sexy and sensual pictures with elegance, especially my type of beauty nudes of all the top girls. By the late '90s, that aesthetic had become well-known, but not back in 1980s when I started shooting. It was what I was drawn to from my fine art studies, my environment, and the people in my childhood growing up. My pictures of men are the best visual example of the guys I grew up around. It's why my work began to get noticed. It had an individual voice of its own.

It may not always be a conscious act at first, but in time, I learned to respond to my instincts and intuition, to a recognition of myself in my images. That doesn't happen overnight.

61

Shooting with Mike Tyson was a test in what it took to be a photographer in the celebrity and fashion field. First things first, I needed an idea of what tools or camera I should use, something that felt comfortable and gave me the flexibility and quality I demanded. By mid-career, I had been exhibiting internationally at galleries and museums, and I was making large 48" x 60" black-and-white prints. They required a larger negative, so I preferred a 6x7 Pentax. I consulted with my assistants on how much film I needed for that camera and this subject. Next, a backup for speed, that would be my 35mm camera, and I calculated how much film that too required, both black and white and color. I liked shooting in natural light whenever possible, but I needed lighting equipment in case I had to switch and shoot inside. I needed a shitload of equipment, especially for, say, going to shoot Mike Tyson at his home in Las Vegas. We always had to be on the ready for anything.

Esquire magazine had commissioned the assignment. They booked me not only for the quality of my work, but also because they knew that I was a pro and I'd produce worthwhile images no matter what, meaning I could handle any given situation and pull a rabbit out of my ass if necessary.

I try to keep things simple and not manipulate the image. Use whatever I see in the frame, only crop if I have to. This comes from my street photography training with Lou Bernstein.

My Brooklyn hustle always came in handy, plus the ability to stay cool and calm. I always managed to make people feel comfortable with or without my camera. After several years of shooting, something always seemed to surround me like a protective shield, my persona transformed once I had that camera in my hands. If I needed to direct a large crew with sizeable personalities, I was able to swiftly take over.

I flew to Las Vegas with two assistants from New York and another from LA. We had

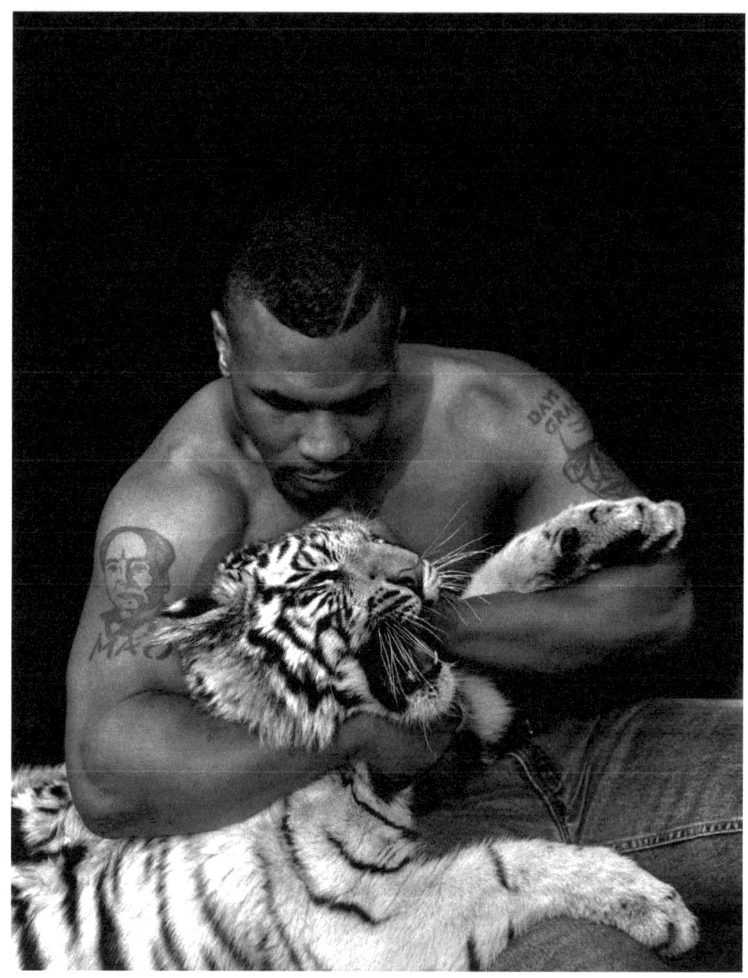

Mike Tyson, Las Vegas, for *Esquire* magazine

a van at our disposal, and my guys double-checked the equipment that night. In the morning, we drove out to Mike's house, pulled up to the gate, and rang the bell. I announced myself and there was a pause. The answer was, "Mike says he's not into shooting today. Come back tomorrow."

I was surprised but not surprised. The only problem was, we were supposed to be on a plane heading back to New York tomorrow. I asked the voice on intercom, "How about I park across the street and we let Mike chill a bit and think about it. We can always shoot later?" No answer. So we parked across the street and waited an hour or so, then rolled up to the gate and rang the bell again. I got the same answer: "Come back tomorrow."

I called *Esquire*, and they made some calls on their end and had no problem with us staying. They just needed to okay the costs and extend the hotel reservations. We went back to the hotel, ate, drank, and played at the tables.

We drove back to Mike's house the next morning. I rang the bell and announced myself, and the voice said, "Mike doesn't want to shoot right now. Come back later." So we took a spin around the neighborhood. My assistant pointed out Wayne Newton's house and Liberace's house. Then we drove back to Mike's. I had the number of Mike's assistant, so I called him. He was a nice, reasonable young guy. He told me he was doing his best and said I should just hang out. A little later, a car came out of the gate. It was the assistant running an errand. He pulled up next to me to introduce himself and again said he was doing his best.

Time for me to pull a rabbit out of my ass once again. I got on the phone and called Russell Simmons. By then, we'd known each other for twenty years. Russell knew my family—my mother had made pasta and calzones for him. Mom was also at Russell's wedding to Kimora Lee in St. Barth's, where she said something really funny. Kimora was very tall and towered over everyone in heels. Russell was in his sneakers. My mom was six rows back, and Reverend Run was presiding as, what else? The reverend. In her distinctive Italian accent, my mother turned and asked, "Why Russell no stand up? Why he on his knees?" My wife, Kara, said, "Maria, he is standing up."

Mom looked surprised, and she said, "I no believe."

On the phone call, I explained my predicament to Russell concerning my Mike Tyson situation. No sooner had I hung up with him than the gates opened, and Mike's assistant came out and waved us in. "That was a good move, calling Russell," he said.

While my assistants began to unload the equipment, I went inside and got introduced to Mike. He was just hanging out with two of his friends, doing nothing in particular. "Russell really pumped you up," Mike said. "He tells me you're from Brooklyn. What do you want to do?" I asked if I could look around, take a look outside. He told me to go ahead.

I was in the backyard looking for a few spots to shoot when I heard what sounded like a dog running toward me from behind. I turned around and saw a white fucking *tiger* on the loose and about to leap on me! I practically shitted myself. Mike came out laughing with his friends and grabbed the tiger. He said, "Oh, man, he wouldn't hurt you. He's a baby!" The baby beast was bigger than me, but at least I knew what my first shot was going to be.

My assistant threw a black velvet cloth over the tennis court fence. I asked Mike to take off his shirt and wrestle with the tiger for my first and best shot. Later, I took a picture of us together. I was a decent-sized guy, but I was half as wide as Mike. I couldn't imagine getting hit by him—it would be like getting hit by an 18-wheeler doing eighty miles per hour. He could definitely kill me. But he was a gentle, sweet guy. I liked him. What took three days to put together took me an hour to shoot! I liked Mike, and he loved me for how little time it took!

I managed to do some of my best work ad-libbing my way through life as a photographer. The one constant was always being ready, always having a camera within reach regardless of what kind.

Axl Rose and I had become friends, and he invited me to his house up in the Malibu hills. I went by myself just to hang out, but I had a camera and film with me. I also brought the same black velvet background I'd used during the Mike Tyson shoot. It was an 8' x 12' drop cloth. Coincidentally, I happened to also have a skull in my trunk. (Doesn't everyone have a skull in their trunk?) I usually packed according to whom I was visiting. With Axl, I packed a skull.

After hanging out a while, I suggested we do some pictures, and Axl was cool with that. I took my black velvet cloth and draped it over the tennis court fence and had Axl pose for some portraits. All shot in natural available light. I loved shooting people's tattoos, so I had him take off his shirt. Then a torso shot, another favorite image of mine. This time, I asked him to drop his pants, like a classical nude, and then hold the skull in front of his crotch. Simple and easy. After we were done, Axl paused a moment.

"Hey, wait a minute, how did you get me to drop my pants?"

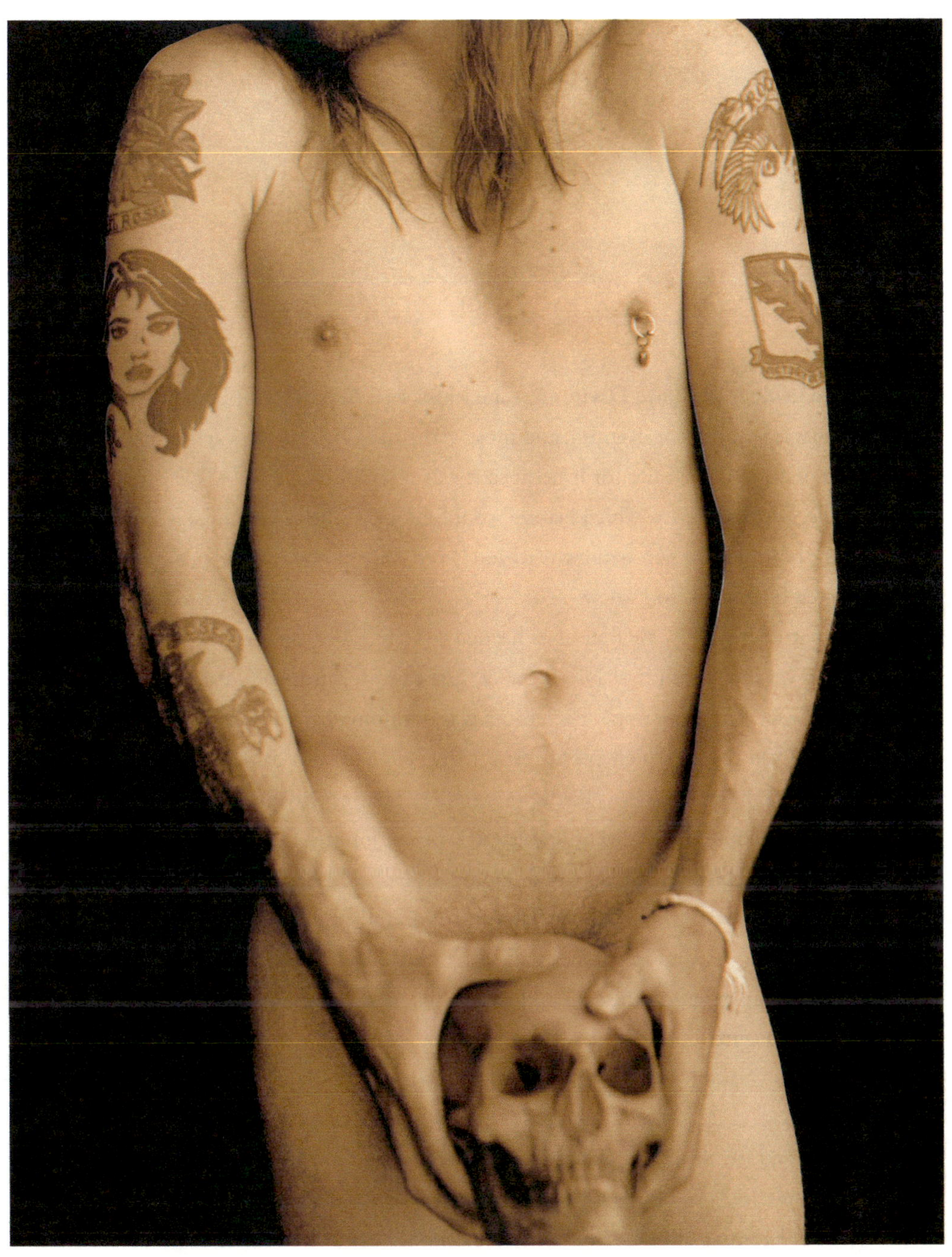

Axl Rose's torso with skull

62

I was out one night with Jaye Davidson, Kate Moss, and Naomi Campbell. Any night with these three was bound to be eventful, and most of the time Naomi was the instigator. Drama was in her nature! I loved her for it because it was often outrageous, hilarious, and always memorable. You never knew which Naomi would show up. She's a Gemini, and many times, it would be both sides of her—and woe to you if you were on the receiving end of the wrong side. I'd seen both sides, so I knew.

That particular night, the four of us headed to Café Tabac, our home away from home. Café Tabac was located on East Ninth Street, just east of Third Avenue and owned by our friend Roy Liebenthal. The upper back room was our domain. We always knew most of the crowd, and given the girls high-profile especially, people would come over to our table to chat, gossip, laugh, maybe have a drink. It was more of a very private club with a very tight membership and fewer than twenty tables. It's where Johnny Depp met Kate and where Bono would sing a birthday ballad while sipping his Irish whiskey. "Just another glamorous, wild, and fabulous night at Tabac," as famed author and columnist George Wayne would say. George would have us in stitches with his antics. I have a great photo of him holding steer horns he had taken off the wall and put on his head, with Naomi flashing the biggest of smiles for the entertainment he was providing.

One night, Naomi, looking fab as usual in a sheer silk dress by Ghost, had a sudden change of mood, as if a switch flipped. She could go cuckoo in a nanosecond!

George said, recalling the scene, "I think I called her a fake Jamaican, and she threw her drink in my face! So I dumped a jug of water on her weave!"

She ran screaming after George, and the rest of us scattered in the restaurant. The thin, wet Ghost dress clinging to that fantastic body made her look naked. After she grabbed someone's dessert and flung it at George, he ran into the poolroom and snatched up another pitcher of water. Naomi saw him with the pitcher and fled down the stairs with George in hot pursuit. They both ran out into the street where George doused her a second time, just as Tony Shafrazi was arriving in his car. Naomi jumped right into Tony's ride, and they took off into the night, leaving George behind with an empty water pitcher and someone's dessert all over his back.

That was how the night began, and afterward, we carried on as if nothing unusual had happened. Naomi went home to change and freshen up, and we met up at my place to continue the party! She was mad at George for a long time, but eventually, they agreed to let bygones be bygones. They had one of those love-hate relationships.

On another memorable night in Tabac, Valentino and his partner Giancarlo Giammetti showed up. I had met them in my early days shooting the collections in Rome. They were fashion royalty, and pre-Café Tabac, they wouldn't have given me the time of day. I had shot their couture for Italian *Vogue* multiple times, so they knew who I was, but if I had asked them the time they would've looked at their watches and kept on walking. To them, I was just some scrappy kid from Brooklyn. I didn't know what their problem was back then. To this day, even though we've become friendly, and after twenty-five years in the biz, I could still feel that haute couture air still exists, mostly from Giancarlo, whom I've come to love.

I saw them both recently. Valentino gave me a kiss on both cheeks, and Giancarlo, always unforgiving, gave me his left hand to shake. I'd always found that rude and arrogant, and in most countries around the world, it is—that's the hand you wipe your ass with! Giancarlo doubtlessly still remembered the time I got him good:

It was a birthday dinner for my then-girlfriend, Kara, at Café Tabac. Christy Turlington, Naomi Campbell, Stephanie Seymour, Dennis Hopper, and Robert De Niro graced my table, among others—a starry gathering for a siren's birthday.

Meanwhile Valentino, Giancarlo, and Bob Colacello and their group were seated at the table next to ours. Giancarlo waved to me like we were old friends—this was during the days they ignored me—so I waved and said hello, just to be polite. At this point, I'd had quite a few drinks in me, and I was having a jolly old time. Kara got up to go to the ladies' room. Giancarlo stopped her and introduced her to the others at his table and took a picture of her with Valentino. When she got back, Christy got up to go to powder her nose and got the same treatment. Hello, kiss-kiss, a picture with Valentino.

A while later, I had to go to the bathroom and as I was passing their table, Giancarlo summoned me with a formal command: "D'Orazio, *vieni qui*!" (Come here!) I paused at their table, but he didn't introduce me to anyone (awkward). Then he pulled out his Instamatic camera and told me to take pictures, for him, of everyone at *my* table! I paused for a minute and then said, "Uh . . . okay." I happened to have the same exact camera, not digital but film—which took a few days to get the images developed. I went to the bathroom, and on my way back to my table, I put his camera in my pocket. Then I took out mine and took all these pictures of the girls and guys at Kara's party. I could see Giammetti was really happy at the next table. What he didn't know when I gave him back his camera was that, in the bathroom, I had shot about six candid frames of my dick with his camera. And they weren't pretty, either; it looked more like a sad baby turtle in my hand.

A week later, Roy Liebenthal, my good friend and the owner of Tabac, told me that Giammetti had called to tell him what happened. "You know what that son of a bitch did? He took pictures of his small dick with my camera! Well, tell him I faxed them to everyone in Rome!" We laughed our asses off.

The next time I saw Valentino, he gave me a big hug like we were old buddies and told everyone the story, every time I later saw him, of how I gave it to Giancarlo "*alla Romana*" (the way Romans would)!

Kate, Jaye, Paul, and Sante at a party, New York City

63

Whenever I tried to save something for a special occasion, whether it was money or a favorite suit, I'd end up losing it somehow. How did this happen? One, I wasn't, and still am not, good with money and numbers. My brain doesn't work in any logical way. Two, as much as I tried to rid myself of old, off-the-boat family habits, I would unconsciously fall into them due to my upbringing.

Coming from an immigrant Italian family who lived through the war in Europe, I was told that everything had to be "saved for a rainy day." So, when I bought my mom a beautiful Hermès scarf on a trip to Paris, she would admire it, then put it away, and continued wearing the shitty one she had owned since who knows when. At home, the couch and lampshades were permanently housed in plastic. In the summertime, as a kid, I'd sit in my shorts with no T-shirt, watching TV with no AC, and my body would be glued to the couch as if with adhesive tape. I'd have to tear myself off the heavy plastic just to stand up to get a drink.

When my father bought one of the first color TVs, there wasn't much room for it in the house, so they put it in my room. I must have been ten or eleven years old at the time, sitting there watching the color TV, and my father came in and smacked me in the back of the head.

"What did I do?"

He said, "Why you watcha the new color TV? Go watcha the old one!"

"Why did you buy this one?" Then I'd get another smack. You're not supposed to use the good stuff; you're supposed to save it!

I thought of all the things I didn't buy in order to save. For what? I wasn't thinking of being a spendthrift and pissing money away, but unlike my parents, if I did purchase something, it was meant to be used. I wanted to treat myself to the things I earned. Once I was able to recognize my parents in myself, I'd pull back and stop that behavior.

"Use it or lose it" became my mantra. Great wine? Let's have it! Caviar with Crystal Vodka? Why not? Truffles? Absolutely!

I loved my friends and always had parties with them in my loft. It was like a giant den, warm and cozy, with velvet curtains and couches. There's a big Jacuzzi and steam room where I'd often find people lost in the bubbles.

I would invite my guests and make us some pasta and bring out more vino. I always had goodies to eat from Di Palo's or Dean and DeLuca, loved to treat myself and my friends to good food. *In abbondanza* (Eat in abundance), as they say in the old country! But the biggest hit with all my guests was my mother's home cooking. She would drive in from Brooklyn, loaded up with Tupperware, filled with various dishes she had prepared. The food would last for days, and I'd have a who's who of people eating it and asking for more. From Quincy Jones to Mick Jagger, from all the supermodels to my super! Mom never taught me how to cook (except for pasta, but not the sauce, a lot of good that did) so that I would always be dependent, hooked on her food. If she had been a drug dealer, we would have been rich!

The one other prized foodstuff every good Italian must have on hand is a nice dry hard salami—*salsiccia*, as it's called in Italy. You'd see it hanging on the racks above the cheese display in the Italian grocery stores, like Di Palo's on Grand Street. A few slices with bread, parmigiana cheese, and a glass of wine, and you'd have yourself a mini-meal.

Salsiccia! Italian-Americans always mispronounced Italian words by dropping the ending or vowels. To me, that's as bad as putting ketchup on pasta. In their newly formed Italian-American dialect, they would pronounce *salsiccia* as "salgeech." The salami would come in all sizes and in the shape of a cucumber. They were long and thin, short and fat, fat and long, so naturally it also had phallic connotations. As a term of affection, and manhood, guys would also address a friend as Big Salgeech, or his small son as Little Salgeech, or just plain old Salgeech. "Hey, Salgeech, how you doin'?" would bring a smile to everyone's face. "Hey, there's little Salgeech. He looks just like his father." It meant that you were close to each other, and if you were very close, you could just refer to your friend as Sal, even if his real name was Vinny.

Where the hell am I going with this?

Let me explain how I slipped, how I unconsciously regressed and lost my favorite imported Italian salgeech.

A friend of mine brought me a prized *salsiccia*, or salgeech, from Puglia, where my family was from. With just a taste of it, I could close my eyes and it would transport me back to another time and place, to fond memories of my childhood. I treasured that salgeech and decided to save it for a special day, so I hid it in the back of my refrigerator.

One night, a wild girlfriend of mine came over with her own bottle of tequila. She said hello, gave me a kiss, went straight for the music, and started dancing and throwing her clothes around while I tried to catch up. We always had a blast.

Later that night, we were famished, so I made us some pasta. I turned around and saw her drunk, naked ass leaning into the fridge, and then popping out holding my salgeech!

"No, not my salami!" I screamed, and after a brief struggle and plenty of laughs, I got my salgeech back and put it in the fridge.

After we ate some pasta, it was time to call it a night. She needed to get home, so I called a car. By the time I got dressed, she had left. I looked out the window and saw her wave goodbye and get into her car.

It was a good time to have some of my prized salami from Puglia. I went to the fridge . . . and it was gone! Thinking it was funny, she had stolen my salgeech. I couldn't believe it. I looked all over just in case. I called her, but she knew better than to answer her phone.

The next morning, when I left the apartment, I took the stairs. There, lying on the bottom step, was my salgeech. I examined it closely, and I could see she had nibbled off the tip and then discarded it. I took a picture of it that I later put on my fridge as a sad reminder to never save anything for a rainy day. I should have known better than to let my salgeech get away, instead of enjoying it while I had it. Maybe I should have cut off the nibbled tip and feasted on the rest—I mean it was still perfectly wrapped. But I wasn't thinking straight; I was too depressed. I never got to taste it. Sometimes you just never fucking learn. Rainy day, my ass!

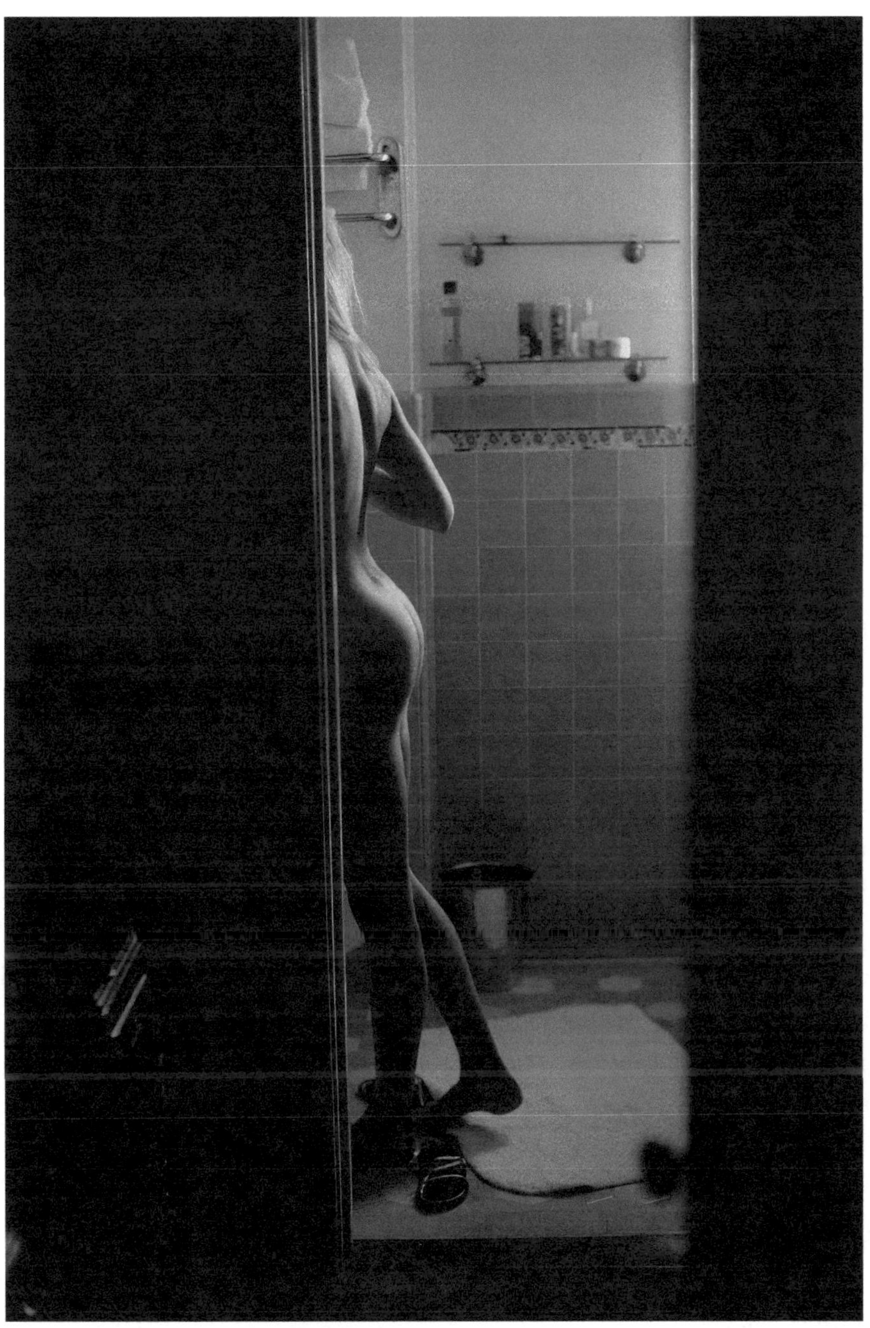

Natalia Vodianova, Chateau Marmont

64

In our constant quest for drugs, everyone had done some crazy, funny shit. On one of those nights at the Bowery Bar, we ran out of coke. My friend Victor said he knew a place a couple of blocks away, so I took a walk with him to a bodega. He told me to follow him to the counter and he'd introduce me to the guy behind the counter and give him the password, which was "Gerber," like the baby food. After he introduced me, we went in the back to the baby food section.

There, behind the shelves was this Puerto Rican guy halfway out of a floor panel that accessed the basement. He stood at knee height and looked like a midget. Victor said, "Gerber," and we told him how many—the coke came in tiny Ziploc bags at about forty dollars each. He went down the stairs and got them for us, and we went back to the front counter, paid the guy, and left. As always, part of the fun was in the process. We had a good laugh and went back to the party.

Two weeks later, I was at the Bowery Bar once again, but Victor wasn't around. I was with a couple of girls who wanted coke, so I thought of the bodega. One of them walked with me to Second Avenue, and I found the place. I went to the counter and asked the Puerto Rican guy for "Gerber," and he pointed to the back. I went to the back and saw the other Puerto Rican guy, who was now sitting on a stool, and I said, "Gerber."

He looked at me. "No, only Beech-Nut."

I didn't know what that meant. I could only assume it was the hardcore stuff. I don't do that shit. I said thanks and left.

The next week I ran into Victor, and I was curious about the password and told him what happened.

He said, "Beech-Nut? What the fuck is that?"

I said, "I don't know. That's why I'm asking you."

"Where did you go?"

"The bodega you took me to on Second Avenue and Fourth Street."

"Second Avenue? My bodega is on Third Avenue! You went to the wrong place, motherfucker!" and he laughed his ass off. "You're lucky you didn't get your ass kicked! They probably thought you were a cop!"

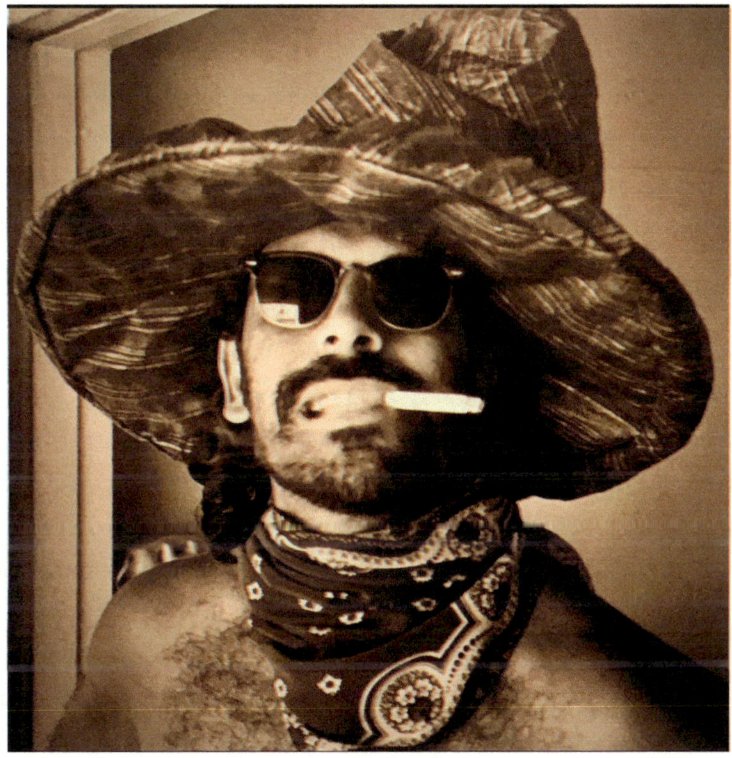

Sante, Palm Beach

65

Only the guy who isn't rowing has time to rock the boat.
—Jean-Paul Sartre

My girlfriend left her diary open next to the bed, practically an invitation. I glanced at the open page, and in capital letters, it read: *I HOPE HE DIES!*

It's safe to say we weren't getting along. We had been together for eight years and had passed the point of no return. Spite was our only means of communication. My girl's partner in crime was a true Salome, a temptress who lured men away from salvation. She was sexy beyond belief and gave of herself gladly. My girlfriend was of the same mold. Together, men would leave their families and sell their kids for them.

Let's call this temptress by her nickname, "Cookie," and tag my girlfriend "Vanessa." Vanessa and I were on the East Coast, Cookie on the West Coast; we'd see each other often, and when we did, it was always very sexy and promiscuous.

Words are hard to find to describe the sexual energy they possessed. They were sorcerers—people would do whatever these two desired, and they had a magical ability to seduce anyone, man, woman, or beast! It was like black magic, mesmerizing!

Generally speaking, great beauty in women has that kind of power over others, whether those women know it or not.

From my experience, I've met many young women, models, with these qualities, and they usually have one thing in common, they usually come from troubled homes of some kind, and they use their sex appeal as a means of communication and approval. It's the syndrome of "she's an angel with a broken wing." And men respond with, "I can help. I can fix and save her." Marilyn Monroe is the best example. The seduction manifests itself in the way they talk to you and the way they touch your arm or shoulder when they speak to you, and especially how they look at you in "the eyes." The girls I knew started practicing when they were very young as a need to be wanted, which most times came from a lack of that at home. They knew how to make you feel like you were the only one that mattered. It's an art, like casting spells.

As young women, they didn't necessarily know how to control those powers. They could sometimes attract dark forces as well—and many of these girls had attracted the sexually abusive kind, coming themselves from those homes or environments. I say this not as some kind of analyst, but from direct knowledge and experience. Their spell over men became their modus operandi for steering through their adolescence and young adulthood. It became their means of defense and survival. That bewitching power didn't ever leave them; as they matured they just learned to use it more sparingly or when useful. They were always drawn to the dark—it was a sexual thing. Just as they were attracted to witchcraft, "just for fun," and referred to themselves as witches. They lit up a room wherever they went and left behind them a trail of bodies and broken hearts, of both men and women.

Like the mythical sirens, they were half bird, half beautiful maidens, singing enchantresses luring passing sailors to their doom. If you have met one, even just in passing, consider yourself lucky to have gotten away. I didn't. I was told I possessed that certain kind of energy myself, but I was able to apply it to my art and get it out of my subjects photographically. The girls sensed it too—that's what made my images so appealing and alluring.

Cookie, Vanessa, and I first met on the set of various shootings (they were models), and we were seduced by one another. Over time, we started always being together, but those two were inseparable. We weren't always together because of the nature of our jobs. One would be away while the other two were together, or the three of us might all be on separate projects. But wherever we went, there was always something sexual going on, and everyone wanted a part of it—and a piece of us, but especially the girls!

Along the way, I befriended a guy through an artist friend of mine. Because of the trust I had for my friend, who was like a brother to me, I allowed myself to trust this new guy. He was an older man—or appeared to be, buttoned up, very unlike me. I had long hair and wore cutoff T-shirts and leather vests. He parted his hair on the side, wore suits, and occasionally wore an ascot. What drew us together was our passion for art. He had entrée to many artist studios, museum back rooms, and various private collections. I felt privileged to have this access—it fed my passion.

Occasionally, the girls and I would take him with us to dinner. Cookie didn't get why we'd bring him along. It took a year for her to even remember his name; she referred to him

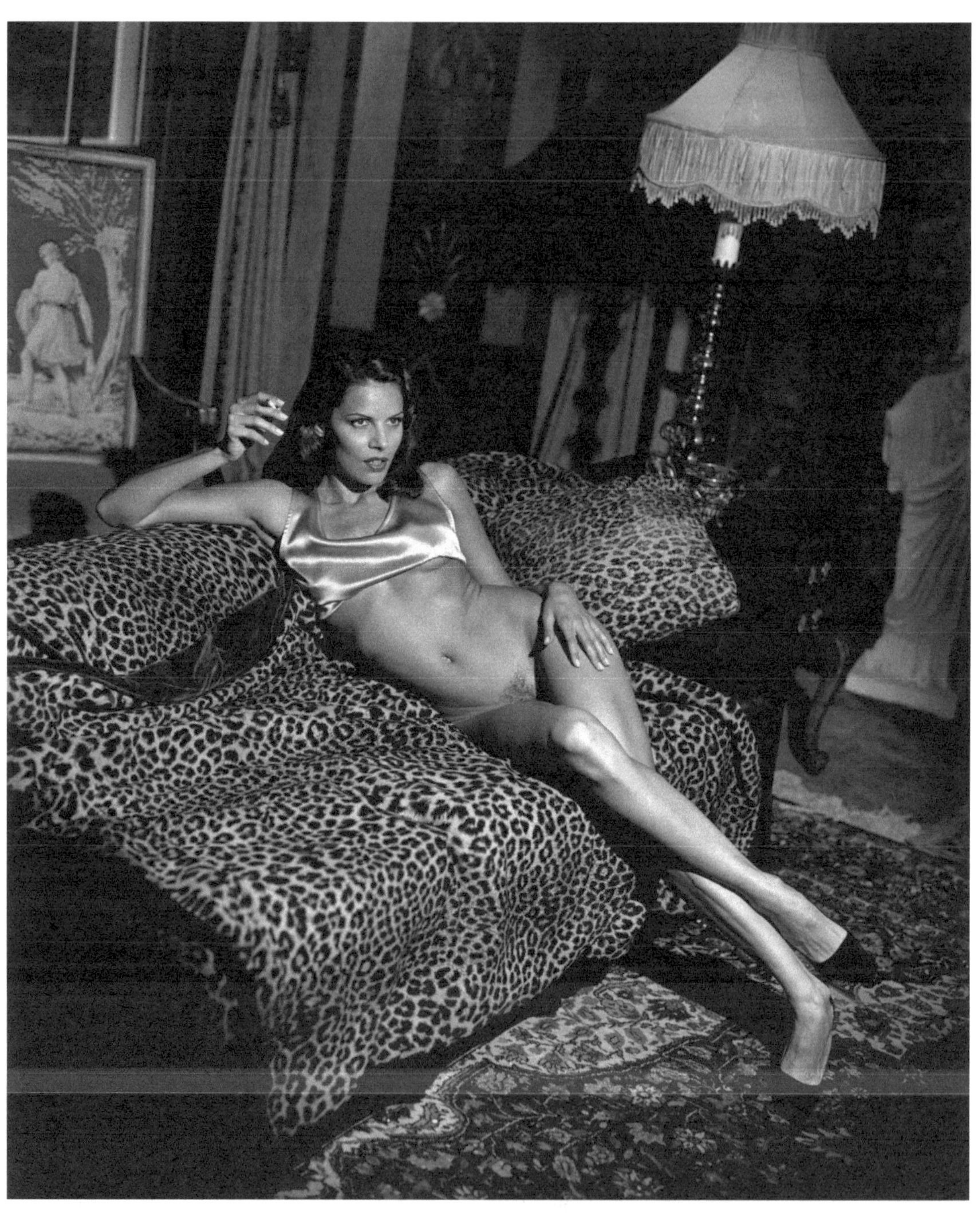

Tahnee Welch for *Playboy*, Old Westbury, New York

as "the rich Jew," and I'd be mortified yet couldn't help laughing from her delivery. We knew him as Ziggy, short for Ziegfried. Although he was Jewish through and through, he wore his Savile Row tweeds and ascot, hoping to make people think his ancestors had landed at Plymouth Rock, rather than at Ellis Island, like mine had. "A dashing Buddy Hackett" was how *Vanity Fair* once described him.

He had his own past, I later discovered, and by then, his dirty laundry was everywhere, including spending time in federal lockup. He had cheated through most of his life at everything including Monopoly but got caught once and was sent to jail for taxes. He had inherited a fortune and now ran his family business. His art collection made museums jealous.

Meanwhile, the sirens and I were out of control and misbehaving madly. Whenever the two girls left town together, some kind of trouble was bound to go down. They were a tag team, and lovers to boot. I would eventually get in the same kind of trouble, sometimes with Cookie, too. The whole thing got out of hand, and we all eventually paid a price, one way or another, especially for Vanessa and me. These kinds of sexual things never last long, and after much damage had already been done, I tried to call a truce and salvage things. But Vanessa didn't want to hear it, and things escalated beyond repair.

However, my friendship with Ziggy got stronger and more consistent over time. He started coming around more often to hang out, sometimes too often. He'd even give me advice about my girlfriend problems. Sometimes we'd get on his private plane to go to an art fair, or sometimes even vacation together.

One day, Vanessa couldn't get in touch with Cookie, which was very unusual. They were always in contact. Cookie always wanted what Vanessa had, and Vanessa always gave Cookie advice about what to say, what to do. A bunch of girls relied on Vanessa for that; she had street smarts and was quick-witted. Now I didn't hear from Ziggy, as a matter of coincidence. One night, I'd just got home late from being out with some friends, and I was at my door, getting out my keys, when I could hear Vanessa yelling at someone over the phone, at the top of her lungs. She didn't even stop when I walked in. I had never heard her scream like that at anyone. It was scary.

I found out Vanessa (my girlfriend) had been having an affair with Ziggy for who knows how long. That was a knockout blow! Now Cookie had started her own affair with her best friend's secret lover, my "friend" Ziggy, and taken off with him to Acapulco.

Vanessa stopped speaking to both of them for the next fifteen years. Ziggy tried his best to lay blame on me somehow, saying that I was neglectful of Vanessa and that she seduced him. Can you believe this asshole? He had the hots for Cookie the entire time and got her away from Vanessa where he could divide and conquer. I had some big decisions to make because Vanessa was living with me. I was no angel; we went overboard with our promiscuities. I had slept with all her girlfriends by then, and she with my friends, men and women. It was an awful tit for tat. Once bitten, I became a vampire myself.

Ziggy, "the dashing Buddy Hackett" with the tweed suits and hair parted on the side, was a friend no longer. I was too old to do anything old school; besides, he had teams of lawyers. I called him out on it, told him he was a scumbag and plenty more. I couldn't help talking shit about him. Instead of an apology of any kind, Ziggy went around town telling people he was going to destroy me and fuck me up and that I'd regret the day I was born. The nerve of this guy. I later realized his animosity ran deeper than just this. Jealousy was a factor in his betrayal. An artist's wife I knew even called me to warn me; she was frightened for me. People like Ziggy liked to ruin people's lives, especially when they were the ones who were guilty. It was some kind of reverse pathology.

During this time, I had written a script with my friend Frank that I was planning to direct. Along with a great casting agent, we were shopping for a producer. One guy we met was kind of comical in a sweet kind of way. He was small in stature and a fast talker with lots of stories. He was also a partner with a well-known action movie star in a production company. They had already made three or four big budget movies at forty to fifty million dollars each. No joke. He invited me, Frank, and two other friends to his house on Staten Island for a barbecue, so off we went.

It was a big, beautiful house with a backyard facing the water with views of the Verrazzano Bridge. In one room, he had what must have been a hundred framed pictures of himself with every famous person he'd met in Hollywood. The house looked like an Italian American museum of the guy from the neighborhood who had made it big and moved to Staten Island. We went into the backyard to get something to eat, and the producer—let's call him Tony—introduced us to Abe Hirschfeld, who was then the parking lot king of New York City.

Abe sat on a beach chair eating something with mustard—it was all over his fingers and on his shirt. His wife was there too, looking like a cadaver in a wig. They would have looked perfect on the boardwalk at Brighton Beach with Abe eating a knish.

Tony told me that he had Abe over because they were looking for investors. That made sense. I liked Tony—he seemed like a family guy from the old neighborhood. We had a good laugh together. We promised to stay in touch because he was seriously interested in our project. I left him the script.

Back home, I was still dealing with this fucked-up shit with Ziggy, who now wanted to bury me for something he did. A guy with that kind of wealth could accuse me of causing a pimple on his ass. He could keep me in court long enough that my lawyer fees would wipe me out. Guys like Ziggy weren't used to anyone calling them out, and they were in constant denial of any fault of their own.

But I still followed the rules I grew up with in Brooklyn. You never fuck around with a friend's girlfriend or wife. If you did, everyone would hate you and go up against you. You would no longer be trusted. If you did that to a friend, what's to stop you from doing that to anyone else? So, how could Ziggy ruin me?

Meanwhile, a friend of mine called to ask if I wanted some info on the Staten Island producer. "Of course, I do. You kidding me?"

"Okay, check this out: He is a producer for big budget movies, but his silent partner is one of the biggest old school mob families in the country. These guys found a way to launder their money through the movie business. They also get other investors involved from outside the family to make it seem more legit. Your friend in Staten Island is a beard for the mob!"

My first reaction was "Oh, shit!"

"Don't worry. They do produce legitimate films," my friend said. "To give a guy like you a couple of million to invest in is a good thing. Look, even if the film doesn't make any money, it's still a win for them in the laundering of their cash."

Thank God they took a real liking to me! They saw a cash cow and wanted to invest in my name and reputation as a photographer. I was going to have to find a way out and get my script back.

The very next phone call I got was from a woman-friend who worked for Condé Nast, my employer, a company that owned every *Vogue* and numerous other fashion magazines around the world. She'd overheard part of a conversation the publisher was having with Ziggy. Apparently, they had some business interests together, and she knew nothing of our falling out. But what she heard was nasty. Ziggy was trying to convince the publisher to blacklist me.

What a motherfucker! Now it's my livelihood, and it affected not only me but also my family that I supported. This was really bad news. I also knew I couldn't do much about it. I couldn't fight him in court—that was his turf, and I would be ruined. It really fucked me up. I had seen Ziggy behave that way but never thought he would turn on me. He was incredibly adolescent in wanting to get me back somehow. He once named one of his race-horses after me. After this blowout, he had it castrated! Now I think it's really funny!

The next day, Tony called from Staten Island asking if I could come out there on the following Saturday. Some of his partners wanted to meet me; they liked the script.

Here I was juggling all this shit, and I had to stay calm. So I took Frank, my writing partner, and went there for lunch. Everything went smoothly. The boys really liked me and Frank. We were all from similar backgrounds and were neighborhood people. What they didn't know was I'd been trying to get far away from this element my entire life.

After lunch, Tony took me aside for a minute and asked, "Are you all right? I mean, I'm sure I'm the only one who noticed but you didn't seem yourself. I could see something was on your mind. What's goin' on?"

I was surprised at how perceptive he was, considering how short of a time we had known each other. I don't know why, but I told him about Ziggy, my girlfriend, the threats I was getting, everything.

He asked me, "Who's this Ziggy? Seems like a real scumbag. What's his full name?"

I told him, and he said, "Did he ever invest in some movie project last year, about an artist?" He named the film.

I recognized it. I said, "Yeah, that's him."

Tony was incensed. "What a scumbag prick! And now he's threatening you! Jesus! I'll tell you what, I have an idea. I can kill two birds with one stone."

That next Monday morning, Tony from Staten Island called Ziggy's office to get an appointment with him concerning a movie project. A week later, he went up to pay him a visit, along with a couple of guys in suits. They gave him their legitimate proposal, chit-chatted about mutual people they knew, and halfway through, apparently, it had dawned on Ziggy who they were and who they represented. At the end of the meeting, they shook hands, and Tony said, "Oh, by the way, Sante D'Orazio is a good friend of the family. We think you should be nice and do the right thing."

I got an apology letter from Ziggy two days later. I still have it in my diary. He blamed the girls, of course. I wasn't interested in his excuses, but it did put a smile on my face. I never made the movie with the Staten Island crew, but I managed to retrieve the script. They ran into delays with their other projects. I didn't hear from them after that, until one day I read in the *New York Post* that they had all got busted and went to federal prison. Shit happens!

Vanessa moved out and started dating Donald Trump. Go figure.

The following year was a disaster for me. I went to see a psychic, and she said someone had put a curse on me. "A woman, someone very close to me, she's a witch." I knew who she was talking about—it was a double whammy from both of those fine young ladies!

Ziggy eventually married Cookie. He left his wife for her. Like the movie *My Fair Lady*, he tried to transform Cookie into a society dame. She went from rock 'n' roll to Mary Poppins, but that kind of lie couldn't last. It was a soap opera. She started eating pills like M&Ms. "Page Six" should have given them their own column. Ziggy was cuckolded so many times that we lost count. He continued to take her out in public to social events and make believe nothing had happened. The poor girl would be sitting at a dinner, stoned on pills, and sobbing her eyes out, while Ziggy continued his conversation with whomever and ignored her. Mr. Sensitive, he never was.

At the end of the day, I think she put the hex on him too. With all his smarts in business, and all his wheeling and dealing, he never had her sign a prenup. She had him by the balls.

Like my mom used to say, "You wanted a bike. Now you have to pedal."

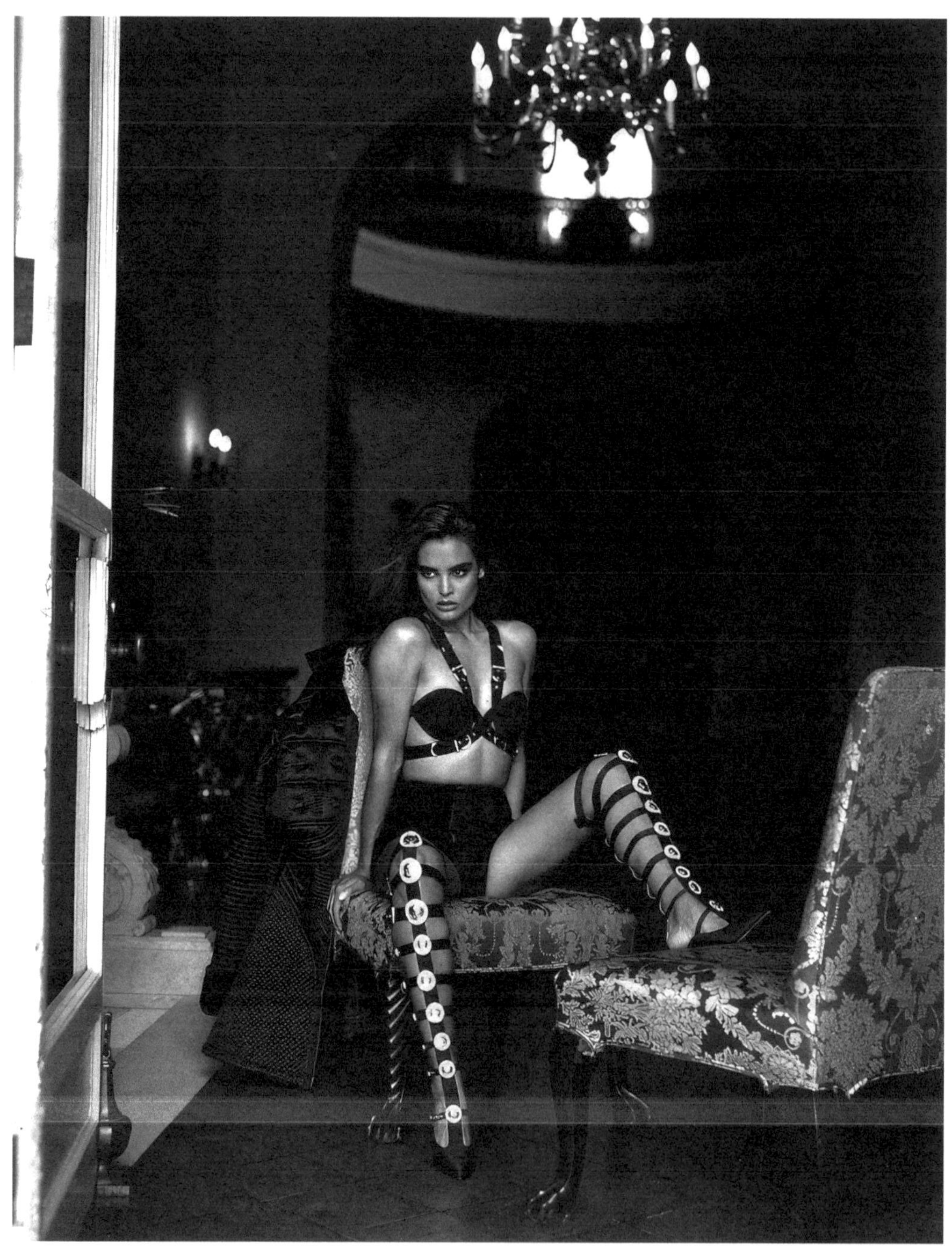

Talisa Soto in Versace for Italian *Vogue*

66

We mature with the damage, not the years.
—Mateus Williams

After fifteen years in the business, I had reached a plateau as a fashion photographer that people only dream of. Yet I was still unsatisfied as an artist. My need to explore other less commercial mediums was becoming a pipe dream, and the quality of my photography assignments was increasingly less inspiring. In my frustration, I became more reckless in my personal life. I became a thrill seeker and daredevil, willing to burn down the house and jump through flames in the process. But before I could light a match, something else made a direct hit on my house, with everything I owned inside it. Divorce.

Everyone handles things differently. Some people can just deal with it and somehow keep moving. In my case, metaphorically, my lawyer handed me a wooden bit along with the paperwork, saying, "Put this between your teeth before you start reading. You're about to be fucked, and it's gonna hurt!"

This had nothing to do with my ex-wife's faults or my faults. We were both irresponsible and stupid; maybe I was the more stupid—I didn't have a prenup either. I was in love, but in any case, it takes two to tango. The effect on my psyche, along with my chemical imbalance, could have been the final cocktail, even for a healthy mind. All I could do was resort to my old remedies, and so I doubled the dosage, which only made the mixture more volatile and fragile.

In a divorce, the finances are supposed to be evenly divided, fifty-fifty, but that's for what you already own. With all the other yearly expenses I had to pay for, my share came out to about 30 percent take-home. With fees for both lawyers, private school for my boy, health insurance, ex-wife's rent (a triplex, of course, the first check I wrote her was for a cool million dollars!), throw in child support, nannies, housekeeper, and even birthday parties (nothing but the best!), the list went on and on. And I won't get into how broken up I was about not seeing my son every day.

The capper was having to pay half the market value of my art collection. Those paintings were sacred objects to me, and many I had acquired before I even met her. I never bought art as an investment. I bought it because it added value to my daily life. It also enabled me to live with my heroes. The church has always drawn pilgrims to its sacred shrines because they claimed to have a skull or fingertip, the relics of some saint. I had a Warhol Electric Chair, and unlike the church's fingertip, mine was authenticated. After all the appraisals, I paid her half the market value of my entire collection. I kept the paintings, and thank God, that turned out to be the smartest thing I did. Still, I doubled the dosage again of whatever drugs I could get my hands on. Half the value of the loft was justifiable; she had paid for it. It didn't matter that she earned more than half a million dollars a year as a model; the appraisal of my income was based on three of my best financial years. Now I was forced to take on jobs and work with magazines that I would never have worked for, but they paid me big bucks because my covers made them money. But those earnings were never mine to keep; they went directly to the lawyers, then to my ex. I never fully recovered.

The quality of my work began to decline, and as it did so, my disappointment turned to anguish. Things were not supposed to go this way. I wanted to die from the depression alone. I slowly moved on to harder drugs. When the shit first hit the fan, I was just six months away from directing my first feature film. The money I had saved would have helped me through the lean times I anticipated while getting my feet wet as a first-time director.

I became impatient and miserable at work. No one wants to work with a miserable bastard. My dream was dying. I was too broken to think I could climb that mountain again in my forties. I challenged God to dispense with me.

Money had always meant so little to me . . . until I didn't have any. When a bill arrived one day, demanding $15,000 for my son's tuition, I had $17,000 to my name. I paid the school fees, and with the $2,000 remaining, I bought a suit at Prada for $1,800 (I was on a budget), then went to Raoul's for dinner with a friend, to dispose of whatever was left. If I was going down, at least I was going to look good. I had the matches and was ready to burn down the rest of the house; I hated myself and hated life. Then a few days later, out of the blue, a royalty check for $25,000 arrived. Somebody up there still wanted me around.

In time, I learned how to forgive myself and all involved and build from the wreckage of the past. I picked myself up, and maybe because I got kicked so hard in the nuts, my voice sounded like I was a castrato in a Haydn opera. On Holy Days or anniversaries, certain saints are said to bleed from their wounds. Each year, on my wedding anniversary to be exact, I too bled, but from where the sun don't shine! Every year henceforth, I symbolically bit down hard on that same wooden bit my lawyer handed me on that dark and fateful day of my divorce, and it hurt for many years to come. Things were never the same again.

67

The depth of darkness to which you can descend and still live is an exact measure of the height to which you can aspire to reach.
—Pliny the Elder

My mind would race. I'd forget to breathe. Panic would set in, my chest aching and my heart pounding. I wouldn't know where to turn, except to my medicine cabinet or my hidden stash. It was so bad, and sometimes it was too late to call or wait for someone, anyone, to come over with whatever drugs they were holding.

A real desperation would set in whenever I'd have a panic attack with no one around to help me through it and with nothing available to settle my nerves to neutralize this inner fiend. Everything hurt. Once I hammered through a wall behind my kitchen cabinet and the adjacent plaster wall, where a friend had dropped a bag of dope through a gap in the wall. (That sneaky cocksucker would buy drugs and hide them in my home without me knowing, but that drop I happened to know about.) I found its location and hammered through the plaster, leaving a big hole there until I fixed it two weeks later.

The demons, more terrifying than anything you can imagine, lodged in my mind . It might take only one spark from the outside to trigger them. Many times, it was something as simple as the sound of my mother's voice gifting me her pain. My chemistry would change immediately; I could feel it start in my head and enter my nervous system like a poisonous serum shot into my veins. I could even taste it in my mouth. Anxiety, depression . . . it was evil.

I tried meditation, yoga, the gym, holistic medicine, acupuncture, antidepressants, but nothing brought me the immediate calm I urgently needed more than chasing the old dragon, or a line or ten of coke. A pill would take too long. My emotional state would go from 0 to 90 in five seconds flat. If possible, I would retreat and hide with a stash under my pillow. If friends didn't hear from me for a long while, it was because I was in a dark dialogue with myself. If I had to work, then I'd bring my stash with me to the job.

There were only two other things that could keep me calm: The first was being behind a camera. It's where I learned to stop spinning. I'd communicate with the gods through images. There was a psychic communication between me and my subject that brought on a certain inner peace. The second method of relief was being in the flow of painting. To have a brush loaded with paint I could stroke across a surface—there, I could lose myself in a meditative place. I could feel the quiet voice of nature.

Not having that was so destructive. I'd hear a demon's voice instead, and once that demon within me had bitten, only that billowing smoke of the dragon could kill what was gathering up deep inside me.

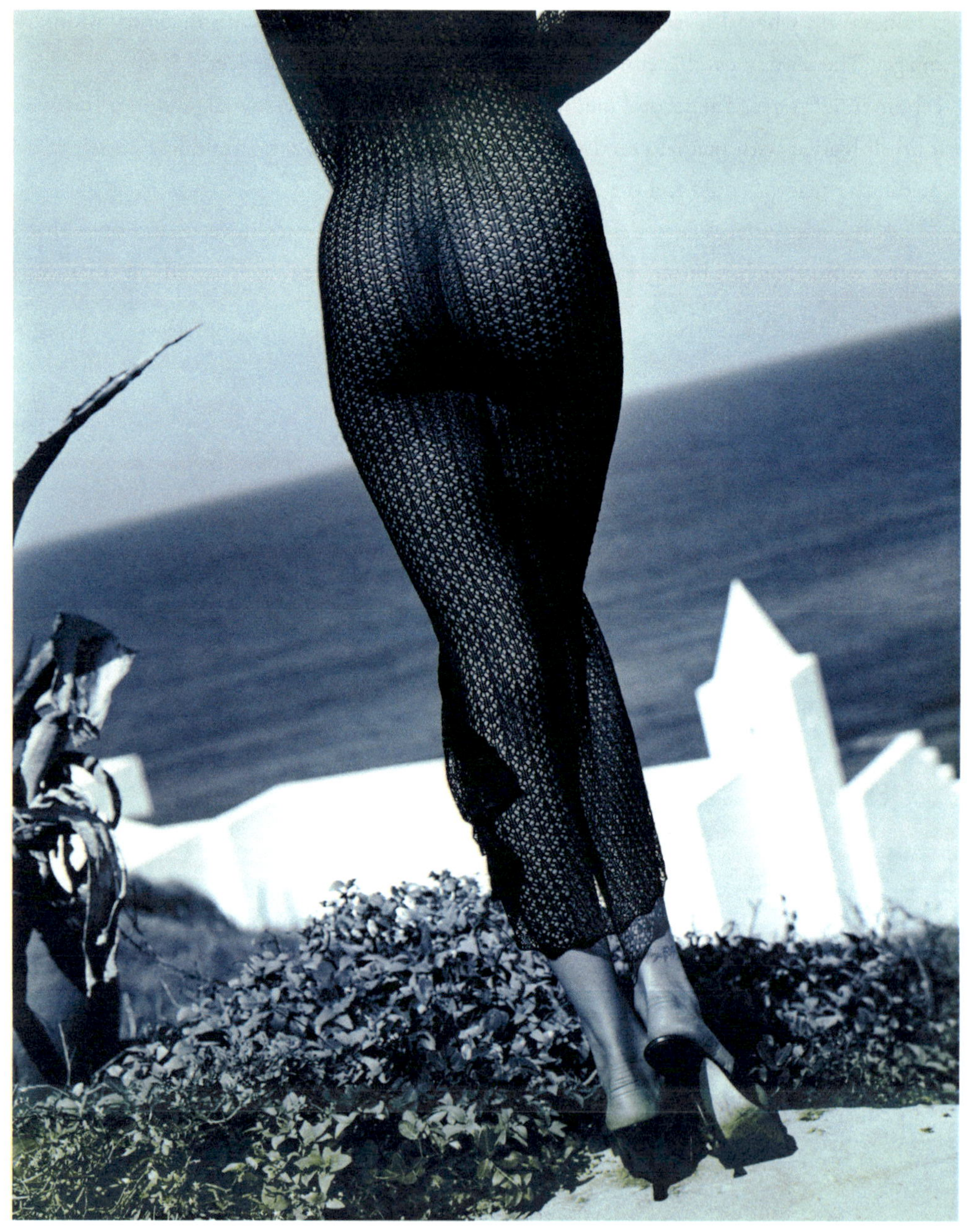

Torso, St. Barths

68

It was the end of July, and I was sick and tired of being sick and tired.

I checked into Hazelden, a no-nonsense in-patient addiction treatment facility in Minnesota, booked for a twenty-eight-day stay and some long overdue rehab.

Once admitted, I wasn't allowed to leave the property, a sensible rule because otherwise most patients would simply go and cop when the craving kicked in. Another house rule was men lived separately from women and were not allowed to mingle because many addicts would simply give up one habit for the next most accessible one, sex. A couple of my fellow patients got kicked out when they crossed that line.

The first of August was my father's birthday, and the day found me jonesing in the hospital ward while carefully monitored by nurses helping to wean me off my drugs of choice. They gave me some pills to mellow me out, and I prayed hard to my dad, asking him to help me through this. He had died in '72, and I'd kept him in my thoughts every day since. It may have been the combination of pills, the rehab, or just everything that was happening to me, but in the silence of the ward, I felt my father's presence. It comforted me, reassured me that things would be taken care of. I surrendered, and a sense of peace came over me.

After three days in the hospital ward, three patients from my assigned unit introduced me to the others I'd be rooming with for the next twenty-eight days. One of them, a man with white hair and a matching mustache, became my unofficial sponsor while here in rehab. His name was Henry, and his room was next to mine. I spent the first week staring at the floor, nodding out from the meds. On the fifth day, just as I was beginning to come out of my stupor, Henry took me for a walk in the late-summer sunshine. He told me he'd been married for a long time, and he had a grown daughter, also married. Like most of the residents in long-term relationships, this was his last stop. "Either you get help, or we're through!" he told me. I liked how honest Henry was. Most of the guys at Hazelden were like that. Some were funny about their addictions, others tragic.

By the second week, I had started to get a handle on the routine: wake up, make my bed, morning prayer, individual or group therapy, line up for medications—but I wanted to get the hell out of there. I wanted the comfort of my misery. And then one morning, I was making my bed when I heard a rumbling through the wall. Some kind of commotion followed, then rapid footsteps and voices getting louder. I stepped out and found a small crowd gathering outside Henry's room. Looking inside, I could see him in his bed under the covers. "What's going on?" Someone told me Henry had died in his sleep—passed away with that loud rumble that sometimes accompanies your last breath here on earth. All the worries, plans, regrets, and heartaches, over. He had told me how much he loved his wife and daughter, and I hoped that love would live on in their hearts.

Activities were suspended and counselors were sent out to talk through the shock many of us were feeling. I went and sat by the lake. With everything going on, I'd forgotten I had a letter in my pocket; someone had handed it to me that morning. I opened it and pulled out a single sheet of paper.

Dear Daddy,

We spent the whole day here in Montauk. Nonna bought me a butterfly net, and I ate all the fish she made for me. We walked around, and I threw rocks in the water. Come home soon, I miss you!

—Nick

Dear Sante,

Your mom is here with us. Nick loves her so much, and he's so sweet to her. He looks so much like you! He loved the watercolor you made for him and wants me to frame it ASAP. I'll send you some photos. It seems you're rediscovering your light; it's where your creativity flows from.

Protect this valuable gift so you can pass it on to your son.

Take care of yourself.

love, Kara

I sat there and thought about how much I loved my son and how kind my ex-wife was to keep the lines open while I got better. I thought about Henry and everything that had brought me to this moment, and I remembered the old joke: If you want to make God laugh, tell him all your plans.

By the third week, I had a routine down. On Sundays, I went to church, which was the only way to get out to "civilization." I'd sneak out of the service after thirty minutes and go to the 7-Eleven to buy Tylenol or Excedrin, the only thing I could get my hands on. Even that was prohibited, but the joy of contraband was a cheap thrill.

Week four, I got a call from Diane—my partner, my studio manager, my sista from another mista. She'd heard from *Playboy* magazine's photo editor, asking if I'd want to shoot a

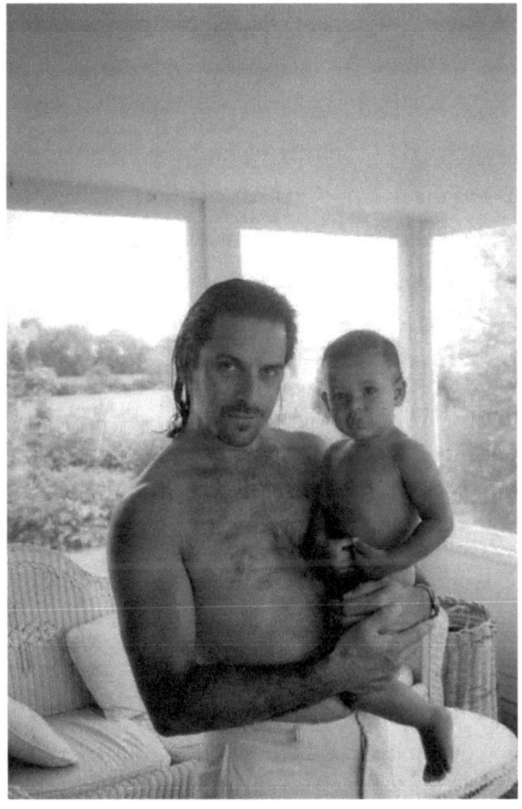

Sante and Nick D'Orazio

Pamela Anderson cover and a ten-page story. "Wow!" was my first reaction. "Yes, yes, yes!" was my second. I had shot four covers for the magazine, and Pam had been on the cover eleven times, but we'd never worked together. Within minutes, we'd confirmed for late September.

I had surrendered and gotten a big result. I was going to shoot Pam, a Super Babe, for the cover of *Playboy*! I could already envision the pictures I would take, and I knew they would be great.

That week, I felt I owned the joint. I started loving the place and was feeling healthy and more alive and alert than ever. Not a care in the world. I became my ward's team leader, which was like being class president for about twenty-five guys, from politicians to musicians to car thieves.

Then came Day 28—rehab over!

I flew out of Minneapolis and back to NYC, feeling strong, clean, and healthy. I had forgotten what it was like to be whole. I checked into the Hazelden halfway house for outpatient group therapy, read some AA literature, searched out different meetings, and hated most of them. But I finally found a good meeting on Sullivan Street in SoHo in the basement of St. Anthony's Church—Vinny the Chin's old parish.

Vinny the Chin was the onetime godfather of the Genovese crime family who used to walk around the neighborhood in his pajamas and bathrobe, acting deranged. It was method acting to avoid being indicted. I saw him doing his act quite a few times. Always with the bathrobe. His brother Louis was a parish priest up in the Bronx, but the family still lived in the neighborhood of St. Anthony's. As a matter of fact, many years earlier, someone mugged Vinny the Chin's mother and stole her purse. It made the cover of the *Post*. The following day, the purse was left intact on the steps of St. Anthony's with a written apology. I would have left a hundred-dollar bill with it for his mother!

I got myself a sponsor at St. Anthony's, went to the AA meetings in the church basement, and about six weeks after leaving rehab, I flew out to LA with my crew to do the *Playboy* shoot.

We checked into the Chateau Marmont, my home away from home. After a good sober night's sleep, we drove up into the Hollywood Hills to a John Lautner home known as the Goldstein House. After we got settled in, everyone was nervous in anticipation of meeting the talent.

Pamela showed up with no makeup and slightly wet hair. She was still the most gorgeous thing I had ever laid eyes on, and with a personality to match. What a thrill. My first shoot, fresh out of rehab. They say good things begin to happen when you get sober, that the gods will smile on you, and that day I felt like the poster boy for Sobriety and Clean Living!

She had an exquisite body, perfectly proportioned, aside from the obvious. Great legs and waist, beautiful blue eyes and a gorgeous smile. She started flirting with me immediately; she had charm to burn, and seductive, sky-blue eyes.

I knew from experience I couldn't and wouldn't cross any lines. Rehab and AA emphasized strongly how important it was in early sobriety not to get into any relationships straight out of the gate, and that included random sexual encounters. And I knew these pictures might make pop history.

Throughout the workday, Pam kept coming on strong. Her allure was enhanced by her minimal outfit, six-inch heels, and diamond studded earrings, that was it! The pictures were getting better and better as the day went on. She got closer to me after each shot, leaning on me to look at the Polaroids. She made me blush at times. My pictures are incredibly important to me, more important than anything, especially when I'm hitting the mark, and I was hitting it on every shot. I kept working through all the heavy flirting. I'd been doing this for almost twenty years; it happens often while shooting and usually ends when the last shot was done.

As we began to get down to the last shot, Pam was insisting we should go out later for margaritas. I wasn't drinking, so I just blew it off. But she had tequila on her mind, and she wasn't going to take no for an answer. As she persisted, I started to sweat. I walked outside and called my new sponsor, Jerry, in New York. He wasn't answering the phone. What kind of sponsor was he? I needed answers. This was one of the hottest women on the planet, and she was definitely into me. My sober voice was whispering, How many weeks out of Hazelden? Keep it together, you can't go back!

Another call to Jerry with no fucking luck. None of my friends would understand. Pam Anderson was flirting with me and wanted us to go out tonight and have margaritas! What? I didn't have any other numbers to call from the program. After the last shot, I was having heart palpitations, and I agreed to go on one condition. The crew could come with us. She had no problem with that.

An hour later, we were seated in a Mexican restaurant, and Pam, in a super friendly very sexy way, was on me. My crew was having a great time, and I was feeling like a eunuch. As they were ordering drinks, I took a bathroom break and went back outside, and I called my sponsor

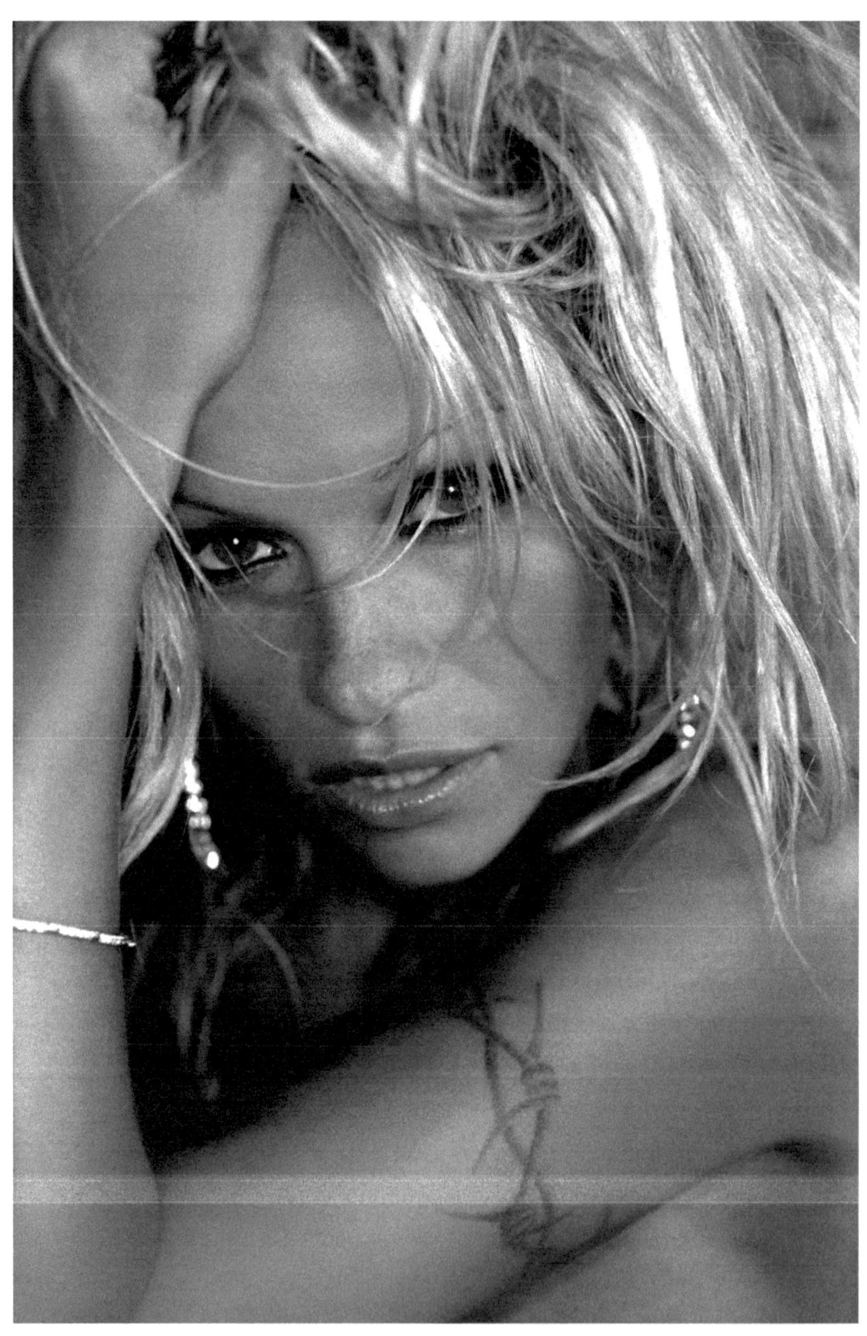

Pamela Anderson, for Sante's book cover *Pam: American Icon*

again—still no fucking answer. *Maybe he started drinking again?* My mouth was dry, and I was having a panic attack. I started chain-smoking in the parking lot and pacing, hoping for a miracle.

Back at the table, two large pitchers of margaritas and multiple ice-cold cervezas had arrived. I ordered the mandatory Diet Coke. Pamela already had a drink down, and when my Diet Coke arrived, she looked at me and called me a party pooper. In all my degenerate wild days, no one, I mean *no one*, ever called me a party pooper! I couldn't believe this was happening. Beads of sweat rolled down my chest and back, staining my shirt. Everyone at the table was bombed, and after three more pitchers of margaritas and some food, Pammy yelled out, "Let's go to the Chateau and order more drinks!"

Two more secret calls to my sponsor had gone unanswered. I had to get through this and exert my inner will to maintain my sobriety. I thought it would be over once we got back to the hotel, but no. Pammy was sloshed, and every one of my shithead assistants and crew was in a similar state. Off we went to the stylist's bungalow by the pool. More pitchers of margaritas, another futile call to my sponsor, and now Pam was flinging the pitchers of margaritas around the room. She's drenched in tequila, rolling all over me on the couch. For her next trick, she got stark naked and ran out to the pool! I heard her screaming my name, and a voice from my crew yelled out, "You better go get your girlfriend or she's gonna drown!" As I ran out the door, someone threw me a towel—a kitchen towel.

She was in the pool, breasts gleaming, bare-assed, ordering me to take off my clothes and get in the pool. It was close to midnight, and we had a second shoot day the next morning.

"Pam, come on, let's be good and get out, please?"

"No! No! No!" she yelled. "I'm gonna get you!"

Miss *Baywatch* babe minus her bathing suit began to drunkenly chase me around the pool. After three laps, I figured I'd run back to the room, and she'd run after me. It worked.

The party was over, and the place was wrecked. Everyone was splayed all over the place as if they had been gunned down. Not even Pam's jumping all around naked stirred anyone out of their stupor.

She talked me into getting her some dry sweatpants and a shirt from my room. But off came her clothes again. She was jumping on the couch, and I couldn't get rid of this femme fatale.

I was ready for a relapse. A naked Pam tackled me on the couch, looked me in the eye . . . and then a look came over her and she seemed to realize something. She got up, grabbed her clothes, and ran out the door. She went down in the elevator; I took the other one down just to make sure she was all right and managed to get into her car. When I got downstairs, her car had already disappeared. She was gone. Back in my room, I called her phone, no answer. Gone girl. Phew, that was close. I was proud of myself—I had stayed sober!

Tomorrow's another day, I thought. *Let her sleep it off, and hopefully we'll start an hour or two later.*

The second day of the shoot was at the same location, the Lautner House. The previous day's pictures were great, really great. Today would be a lot looser, a cherry-on-the-cake kind of thing, and maybe I would see how far I could push the images.

I was shooting a bona fide pop icon. No matter how high or low, she represented everything pop culture worshipped. In 1962, no one would have said Marilyn was an icon, even after her death. It took time and an artist like Warhol to recognize it and make her image into a work of art. Pam, like Marilyn, had a way of tapping into our subconscious. They both represented, in pop terms, the eternal feminine, the screen goddess, the sex goddess, the female goddess, the procreator of life, Mother Earth.

For me, the female form has always been sacred. That divine form is represented and embraced by the psyche of every culture throughout time. This goddess has the power of life. Her image, in any way, shape, or form, is symbolic of that divine feminine. Worship her! Women should rule the world!

At the shoot, I went into our various setting up routines with the crew; they all looked like shit from the night before, but everyone was on. I did my usual pacing around—"Let's be ready for this here and that there." Then I began my inward meditation.

Usually, I had to find a spot where no one but my first assistant could find me. I needed to clear my head. I had to direct the crew, to inspire them, get them to envision what I was doing but never show them exactly what to do. I worked with talented people, and I had to trust them. I liked the chance happenings, surprised by both good and bad. I fed off them, and I never took full control. To me that would feel contrived. I didn't want to create a picture so much as discover it.

I never know what I'm going to do until my subject shows up. I walk in and follow the light. Light changes constantly, never remains the same unless it's artificial light, and even then, my instincts change when on set. I have no problem arranging a complicated setup in one spot but then abandoning to capture a ray of light somewhere else. My clients would always freak out. "Where's the next shot, Sante? What do you want to do?" My answer is always the same: "I have no fucking idea. When she shows up, I'll know."

Pam, of course, was late. I expected it. She'd drunk enough to kill a horse. Two hours, three went by. She never showed up. Calls to her phone, her assistants, went unanswered. It was Sunday. I had another job lined up the following day in New York, so I'd better call *Playboy* first thing, LA time.

On Monday, I called Marilyn Grabowski, the long-time veteran of all *Playboy*'s shoots. She was a great woman, Hugh Hefner's trusted right-hand person, and a friend of mine. I told Marilyn we had a problem and explained the situation. I told Marilyn I'd come back any time to finish the job at my own expense. I really wanted to do this. The first day had been great. Marilyn promised to get back to me and said this wasn't the first time.

Tuesday, I got a call; it's Marilyn.

"Sante, we have a problem."

"I know, so let's take care of it."

"No, we have a problem."

"Okay, what?"

"She doesn't want to shoot with you. She says you made her uncomfortable. Maybe some other time, but not now."

"What?" I said. "Marilyn, when have you ever heard of me being rude, or not being a gentleman? Doing shit like that? Never in all my fucking years! And I've been sober almost two months now."

"Sante, I know, I know."

"And what the fuck does she mean some other time? Who's going to work with someone 'some other time' who's tried to take advantage?" An accusation like that could ruin a person's career, their life! I was shaking.

Marilyn said, "Don't worry. Don't do anything. I'll get to the bottom of this."

The film was being processed in the meantime. The next day, I saw the contacts, and they were kickass amazing, but I couldn't look at them objectively. But I was getting paid a lot of money, so I had to edit something for it.

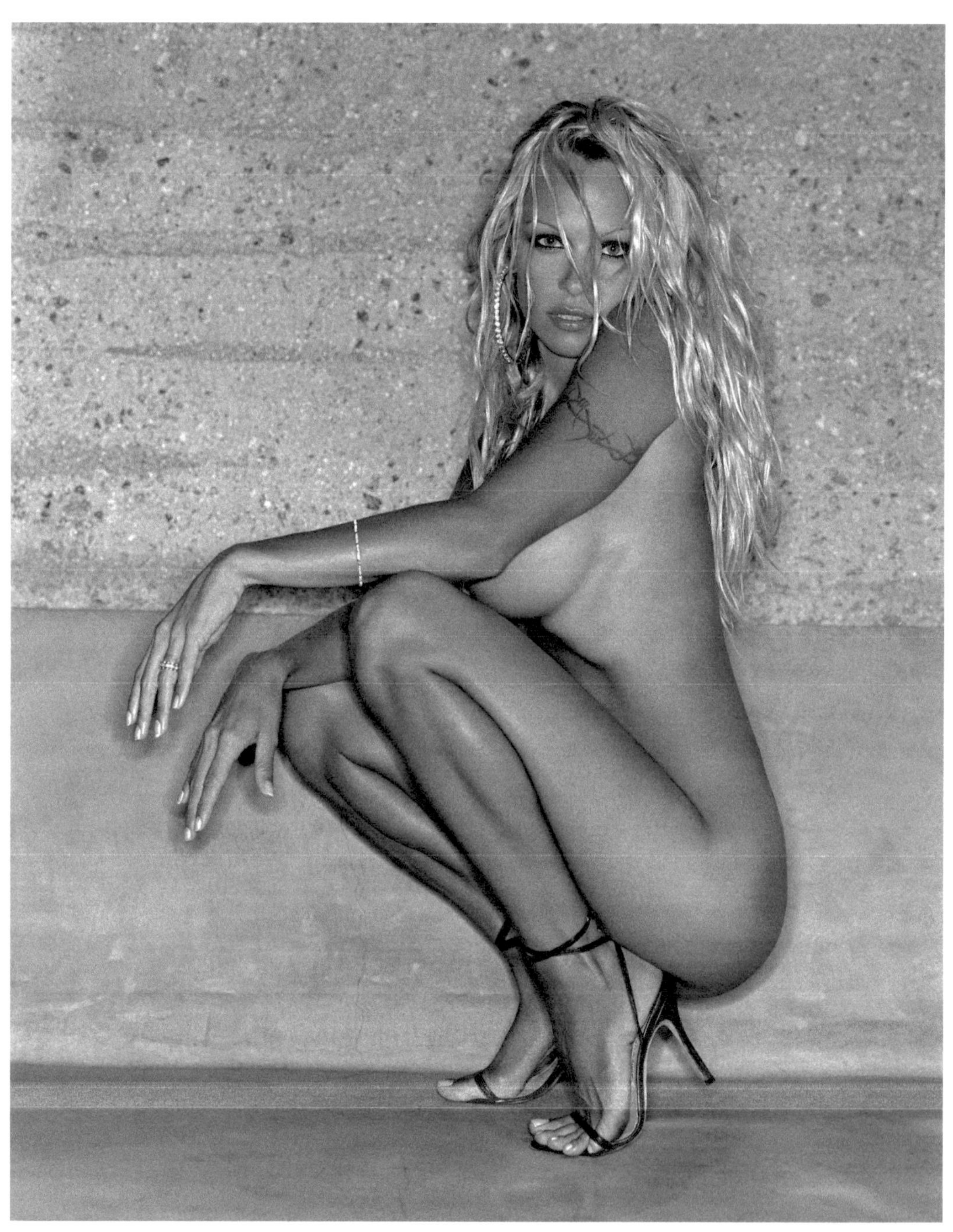

Pamela Anderson for *Playboy*

Two days later when Marilyn called, I told her I had plenty of material for the magazine. She told me to forget it, keep it. Now Pam wanted to shoot with David LaChapelle. Fine, fuck it! I just didn't want any trouble, and I was glad to stay the fuck away. I just didn't want to hear that story of hers from anyone. Marilyn reassured me.

Two nights later, a close girlfriend of mine called me from LA and said she had been at a large dinner table with David who announced he was re-shooting Pam's *Playboy* shoot and why. My name came up. I had my lawyer call Pam's lawyer, and he came down hard. Pam called me personally and apologized, saying it was a misunderstanding. I let it go, and never heard any more about it. So, I was canned; my pictures were canned. I got paid in full, but that was the last shoot I did for *Playboy* for a very long time.

Five years later, the gallerist Stellan Holm, a friend, approached me about doing a show. (I have to state this: Stellan is one of the most honest men I've ever met in the art world.) I took his invitation seriously, and he didn't disappoint me.

Pam's pictures had always been on my mind; they had grown on me with time, and no one had ever seen them. They were still in the can, and when I told Stellan about them, he thought they would make a fantastic show. I got up the nerve to ask Pam for permission and got a release with the help of Diane, my business partner. To my surprise, Pam was receptive and offered her support. She even flew in for the show. I couldn't believe how generous she was with her time and her person.

The night before the opening, I threw a cocktail party in my loft that Pam hosted. Stellan had designed a great catalog, *Pam: American Icon*, which has since become a classic. Jeff Koons, Richard Prince, and Glenn O'Brien had all contributed writings and reproductions of their own work referencing Pam. Stellan had also managed to get usage of a Warhol "Marilyn" image to connect the two blond goddesses in our pop iconography. The party was filled with artists and friends, and Pam, of course, was a hit. Her personality lit up the room.

The next day, I gave her a tour of the show at Stellan's gallery in Chelsea. The opening was at 6:00 p.m., and to my surprise, she said she didn't want to be there for it. She wanted it to be my night. It was incredibly thoughtful of her, and I knew she was right.

The opening was a big success, as was the catalog. The gallery was packed, with a crowd of people milling around outside in the street trying to get in. It's funny how things turned out. Letting things go can sometimes be a blessing! We both gained a lasting friendship.

69

One summer, in the middle of August, I was on vacation in Amalfi on the Southern Italian coast with my eight-year-old son, Nicola ("Nick"), whom we named after my father. When it was time to leave, Nick and I would go to Rome to meet his mom, and she would take him with her to Greece for the rest of the summer break.

In the meantime, I wanted to go to the Venice Film Festival, which was starting the first week of September, but I hadn't made any arrangements. I put in a call to my friend G, who owned a hotel and restaurants in Venice. He happened to be in Sardinia, vacationing on his yacht. G said, "Come and stay here with me, and we'll go together to Venice, stay in my hotel. Then my boat will meet us there."

After handing my son over to his mother at the airport in Rome, off to Sardinia I went for some sun and fun. On the second or third day on his yacht, G said, "C'mon, we're taking a ride to visit a friend." Four or five of us got on his dinghy and rode the waves for twenty minutes. My friend pointed and said, "There's his boat." I didn't see any boat, only a vessel that looked like the *Queen Mary*. "Yeah, that's it," he said.

As we got closer, I noticed a couple of guys on deck dressed in black. Closer still, I could see they were holding what looked like M16 machine guns—a private ship with armed guards, shit like this I never saw before, except in a James Bond movie.

"Where the fuck are you taking us?"

"Don't worry. He's a Russian friend of mine. You'll like him."

After we climbed aboard the *Queen Mary* lookalike, we were greeted by our host, a diminutive guy with a tan, wearing a floral shirt. His name was Karim, and he seemed genuinely happy to meet us. After a few drinks, we had a grand lunch, then more drinks, and Karim asked if we were going to Venice because he'd never been. I said that we were, and that I was very familiar with the place. He suggested I could give him a tour; plus he wanted to buy a hat. My friend had been very vague about Karim's background, and I knew not to ask too many questions.

Three days later, we were having lunch on board G's yacht, which was now in Venice, when Karim joined us. After lunch, he and I spent the afternoon walking the streets of Venice. I gave him the brief history tour that I had promised, and we even bought hats. He gifted me mine, a furry white Kangol cap, and he bought himself a similar style in black leather. We got back to the yacht in time for dinner. Karim was leaving the next day.

One morning, I was wearing my white furry Kangol, sunning myself on the back of the yacht, reading the papers. G came over and said, "That's a nice hat. Where did you get it?"

"Your friend Karim bought it for me. He told me to look him up if I ever get to Moscow."

G started laughing.

"Why are you laughing?"

"You know who he is?"

"No, because you wouldn't tell me."

"He's one of the biggest mobsters in Russia, with direct ties to the Kremlin. His brother was president of one of the breakaway republics. He was assassinated last year. Karim's a stone-cold killer. One phone call from him and you're gone, no matter who you are. He's on a list of international terrorists! He's not allowed in the United States even."

"What the fuck!"

"They probably have pictures of you walking around with him and buying hats. Yeah, and on the boat too!"

"Fuck you," I said.

The bastard started laughing again.

"I still like the hat and I'm wearing it, so fuck you."

"Yeah, go ahead, very easy to spot you in your white furry hat. They're probably running your pictures through the Interpol files to see who you are."

He was laughing it up as he walked away. I took off the hat and never wore it again. It didn't look the same back home walking around in New York City.

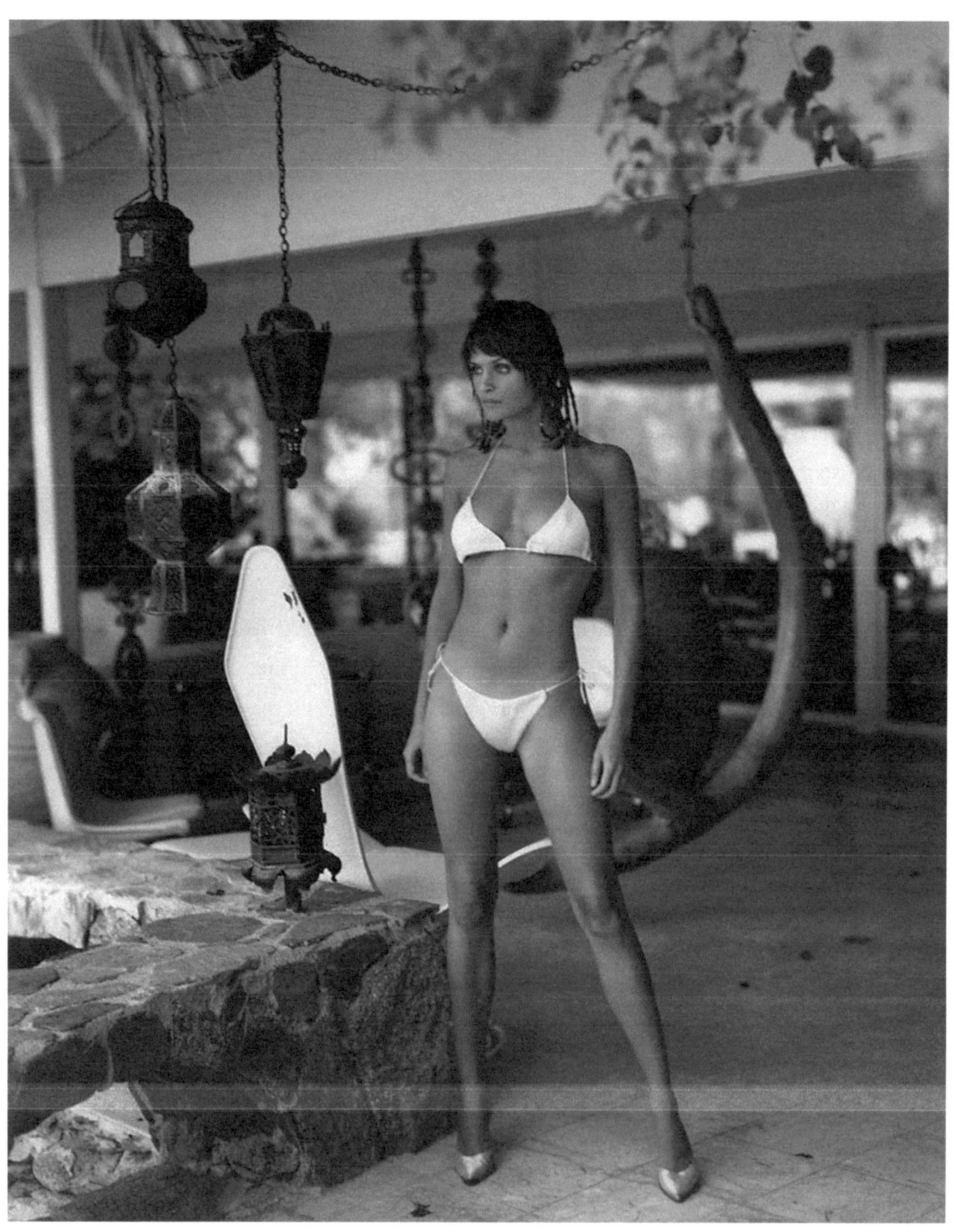

Helena Christensen for *Allure*, Palm Springs, California

70

Oh, God, make me be good, but not just yet.
—Saint Augustine

On certain weekends in rehab, the place had "family day," when family members would visit. As in school, you gravitated toward some people. This one guy I knew and liked was very sweet and good-natured. His name was Ralph, and he was vulnerable like a lot of us were. His wife, Alison, would come to see him, and she seemed very self-assured, like a no-nonsense kind of person. She didn't seem to give a shit about Ralph, but I minded my own business. After she left, Ralph opened up to me about their marriage being on the rocks due to his drinking and drugging. He came into rehab to straighten out and hopefully save the marriage. He had lost his job, while she was working in sales at a major pharmaceutical company. She was the head of her division, making great money.

Because I didn't have any visitors—most of my friends didn't even know I was in rehab, plus everyone I knew was in New York—I was assigned to be a consultant to any visitors who might have questions about rehab and its benefits or advice on a loved one and the meaning of their addiction, etc. I tried to be as kind and understanding as I could to all family members that visited, especially to the teens whose fathers I knew. I wanted them to understand that alcoholism was a disease, how it affected the chemical system, how anxiety and depression affected behavior. It was very rewarding to me when I felt I got through to these kids, and they seemed grateful to me for helping shed some light.

By my third weekend, I was temporarily promoted to lead the group of twenty-five guys, and I looked forward to another family weekend coming up. Ralph came over and was very excited that his wife, Alison, had decided to make another unscheduled visit; he felt it was a good sign for them as a couple. I had spoken to her briefly without Ralph during one of her visits, and he mentioned that whatever I'd said to her was a real plus and asked, "Would you be kind enough to help some more?" I was more than happy to oblige.

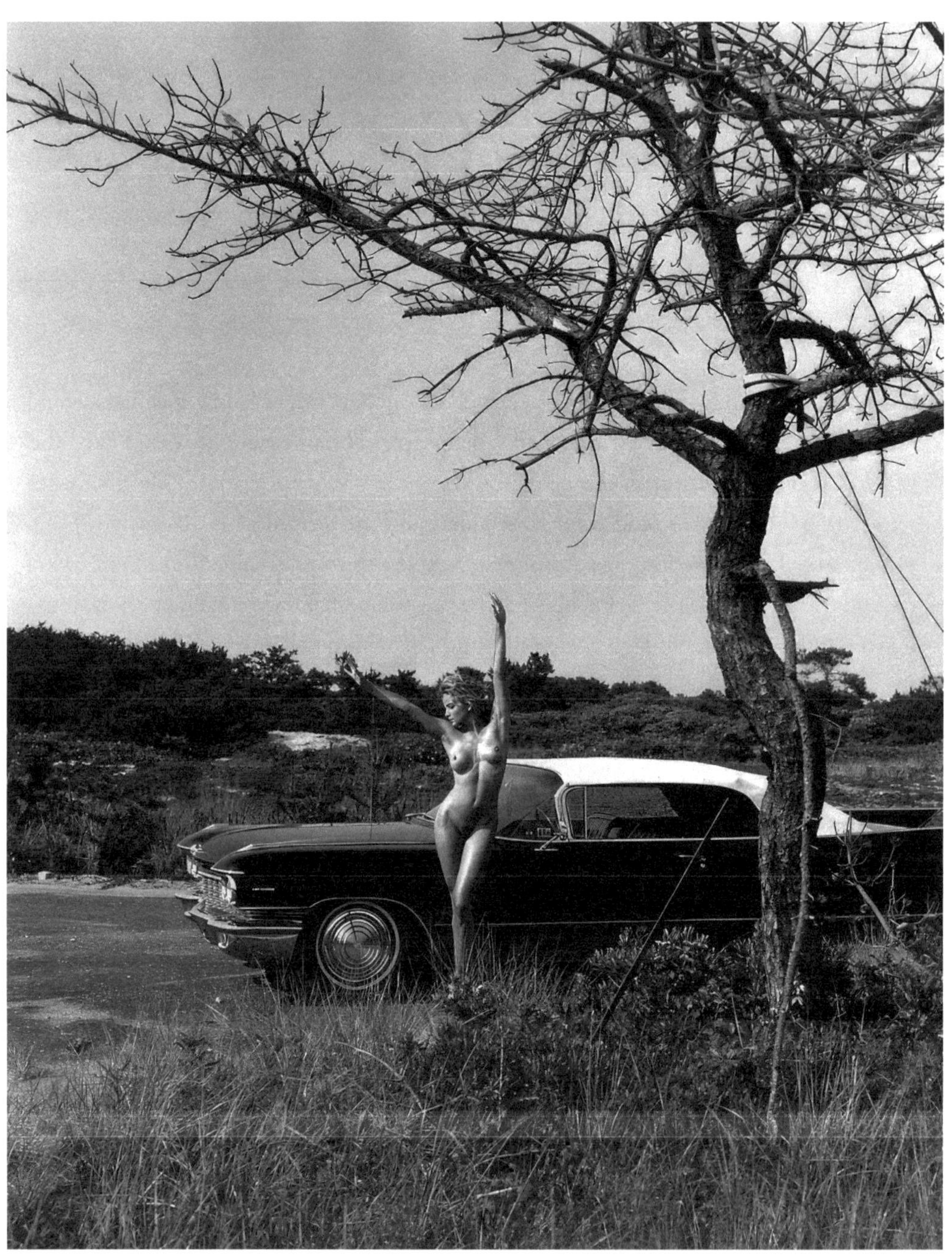

Rachel Williams for *Playboy*, Montauk, New York

Ralph was beaming when she arrived. After he and Alison spent time together and had lunch, they came over to where I was sitting. Ralph said he needed to run a few errands and asked if I would mind hanging out with Alison until he got back—a ruse so that I could talk with her on his behalf.

I said, "Sure. We can walk the grounds."

It was August. We were located by a lake surrounded by woods with short trails and grassy lawns; it was very pleasant. Alison liked that idea because she said she had a lot of questions for me. Her appearance was different than at our previous meeting. She had on makeup and wore contact lenses and looked very pretty—an attractive brunette with an athletic figure in a light floral summer dress. Alison asked a lot of intelligent questions, and because of her work, she very much understood the nature of chemical imbalance and dependency.

We were walking through a woodsy part of the property, and she suggested we sit down on the grass. The weather was perfect, not too hot and a nice breeze, the trees moving gently with that soothing sound of rustling leaves. Looking up, I saw how beautiful the sky was, crisp blue with soft clouds slowly moving across the treescape. When I looked down, Alison had laid back on the grass, and her skirt was hiked up to where I could just about see her panties, which were the same blue and white color of the sky and clouds. *Here comes trouble.*

She locked eyes with me as I turned her way, and as good as her legs looked from my angle, I knew I had to get the fuck out of there. I started having heart palpitations. I had to draw the line somewhere. I didn't need any more bad karma! I considered Ralph a friend! There were people in the world who stick to a certain code of honor. I hadn't met any so far, but they're around somewhere.

I was saved by voices coming closer in the distance and managed to get out of the situation gracefully. Once we found Ralph, I said my goodbyes and made my escape.

Two months later, I was back in NYC doing my thing, in my loft, when the apartment buzzer rang—to my surprise, it was Alison. Ralph had given her my number and address. She was in town for a few days for some pharmaceutical conference. She said she had something for me, "a thank you for being so kind" type of thing. I felt like I had to let her come up.

She told me she and Ralph had split up soon after he got out, and now they were getting divorced. He was drinking again. She handed me the gift she had brought. I opened the package; it was a box of two thousand blue Viagra pills, all in packets of ten. Alison said she had a trunkful at home to give out to pharmacies as samples. *Was she trying to tell me something?*

I went back to playing stupid. I just wasn't into it. I reminded myself about the rule back home in Brooklyn; "Never fuck your friend's girlfriend, let alone his wife, even if years go by."

Just then the doorbell rang—it was FedEx, thank God—and then I got a phone call from my office that put me in the clear, my assistant needed to come by to drop off a package. Saved by the bells. Alison left.

Ralph called me two days later to ask if there was any hope for him. He had gotten out of rehab before me, and we hadn't spoken since that time in the woods with Alison. He knew it didn't help things that he'd started drinking again, but once he felt he was losing her, he had gone straight to the bar, then to the liquor store. He was beating himself up.

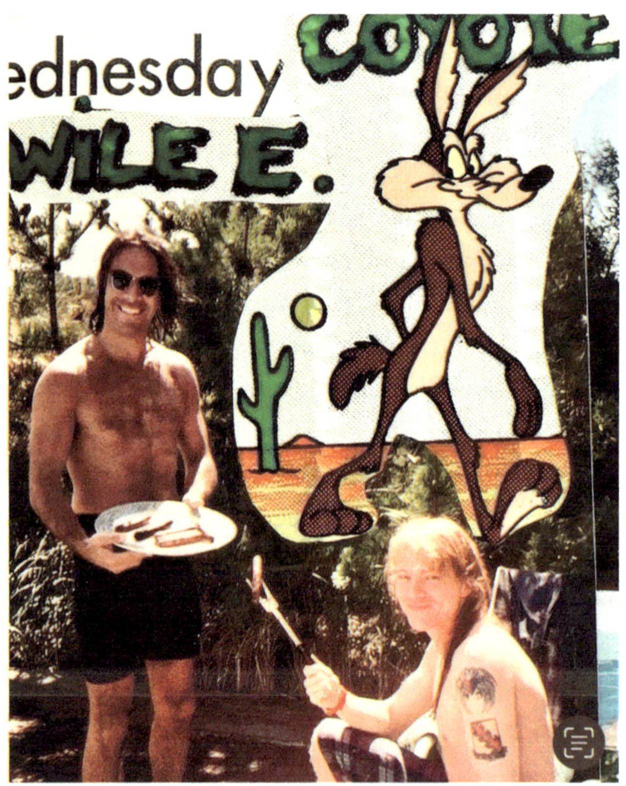

Sante and Axl Rose, Sagaponack barbecue, New York

I felt bad for the guy. What could I say while I was staring at two thousand Viagra pills still sitting on my kitchen table as I was listening to him? I told him to stop being so hard on himself, that things were hard for everyone. "Ralph, you know it's hardest on our loved ones. You might have to pull out and take a softer approach for both your sakes." I didn't know what else to tell him except to then recite some AA slogans.

A year and half later, I still had hundreds of those Viagra pills left. I'd given most of them away and even left some as tips for the waiters I knew, and everyone was happy.

I never heard from Alison again. When my stash finally ran out, the drug addict in me immediately thought, *Should I give her a call?*

71

I was about to have a big photo exhibition at Hilario Galguera Gallery in Mexico City. Years earlier, my old friend Damien Hirst had introduced me to Hilario, a great and really down-to-earth guy.

I flew down with my buddy Nur Khan and Mandy. She was lovely but crazy, full of trouble, fun, and more trouble. Mandy was a sexy wild child with a heart of gold. She was kind and generous . . . and she wouldn't think twice about working a dude for his drugs. We loved Mandy and thought she'd be great fun to have with us.

She helped the show take off; there was a big photo of her in the show. Hilario had put together a lot of press, and everything went well. The gallery threw an after-party at an abandoned church in the center of Mexico City. We hosted a couple of dinners, and then, the real fun began.

Damien and his assistants flew in to lend some support. At the time, he had a place on the beach south of Mexico City in Zihuatanejo, where he was currently working.

Hilario organized a visit to the home of a big collector of Damien's, a villa with lots of security and bodyguards all around. Mexico, at that time, was notorious for its kidnappings of wealthy people and their families. It was not unusual for rich people to have high security, at home, at work, and at play.

That night, the collector took us to a *lucha libre* wrestling match. The wrestlers wear colorfully designed masks meant to evoke the spirit of certain animals, heroes, or gods, a tradition that goes back to the Aztecs. The wrestler assumes that identity and almost never reveals himself. Several *luchadors* were known to have been buried wearing their masks. There's something sacred in it for them.

The collector had naturally brought along all his bodyguards; we had six of them constantly around us. Nur, Damien, and I bought wrestling masks and enjoyed the fun. It was an indoor stadium, and going to take a leak was like hiking to the other side of Madison Square Garden. When Mandy needed to go, Hilario, of course, volunteered to escort her. About twenty minutes after she got back, I noticed her turning around and looking at something or someone.

"What's up? What's going on?"

She confessed that she had ditched an ex-boyfriend in Utah and now he was stalking her. "He's here. I ran into him while going to the bathroom. He's by the exit up on the fourth row."

"Oh, fuck, what a drag this is going to be."

I told Nur, and we all turned to look, and the fucker waved at us.

Something had to be done. I went into Brooklyn mode. Nur was a world-class black belt at jiujitsu; he'd won gold medals at international competitions. And I was good at flinging garbage cans and body slamming.

"Nur, you go up to the exit on the right. I'll give you five minutes so he doesn't get suspicious, and I'll go up to the exit on the left. We are going to have a talk with this nut job!"

But as we made for the exits, Hilario stopped us and said, "Stay here. I saw what was going on, and I took care of it."

We found out later that two of Hilario's bodyguard friends had apparently grabbed the guy, thrown him in the trunk of their car, and dropped him off who knows where.

The next afternoon, we flew down to Damien's house on the beach in Zihuatanejo. He had rented us a house on the beach for our stay, a five-minute walk from his place. The beach itself was vast and curved, maybe a mile or so long with only about five homes on it, and otherwise empty.

I loved trips like this because I was usually able to get great shots and portraits of my friends and the people I was hanging out with. The environment always added something for me photographically. Damien was making these unusual paintings in a makeshift outdoor studio adjacent to his house—dark blue canvases with outlined drawings of shark jaws and skulls in white paint partially surrounded by white dots. They were beautiful. With my camera, I was always prepared for the unexpected. I shot the color of the paintings and black-and-white nudes of Mandy wearing only heels and the two pistols tattooed on her pelvis, aiming toward her private property. They are some of my favorite images.

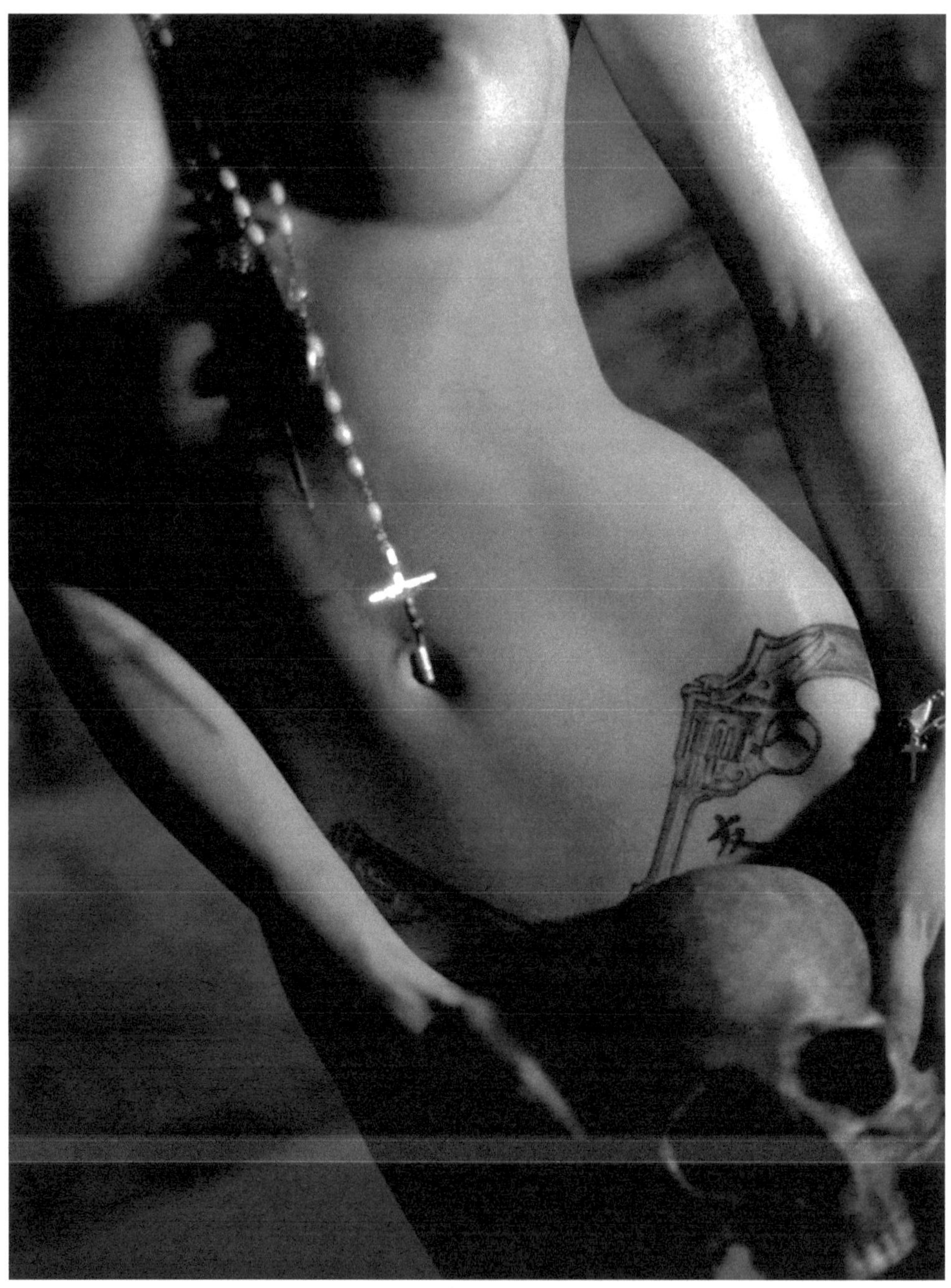

Mandy, torso with skull and pistols

One night, everyone wanted to go to another *lucha libre* wrestling match, but Damien thought it best we keep our profile low right now. The area was beginning to attract a criminal element, and we didn't have security. There had already been a few kidnappings nearby, and drugs were starting to appear on the streets. (Sometime later, when the cartels moved in, they announced their ownership of the town by throwing three severed heads onto the dance floor of a local club! By that time, none of us gringos were going there anymore.)

Mandy perked up when she heard about the drugs. I shot her a look that said, "*Don't even think about it!*"

I had first met Mandy through a girlfriend of mine named Charlice; they both had been models. They were beautiful and very sexy. To be young, beautiful, going out, and into drugs, you had better know how to hustle in a discreet manner if you didn't have the money. Things could get expensive when you liked to party. Charlice and Mandy were out one night with some wealthy young guy Charlice knew. He had a lot of cocaine, and what he lacked in looks and cool, he gained with the 'caine, so to speak. Back at his place, once they had finished his drugs, the girls decided to pack up and leave. He didn't much like that, and as wired as they were, he and Charlice got into a scuffle, and he beat her to a pulp. At 2:30 a.m., I got a call from Mandy, whom I didn't know at the time, and she told me they were at the hospital where doctors were tending to Charlice. She had told Mandy to call me; she didn't know anyone else whom she could trust and had no family around.

I had never seen anyone's face so badly beaten before, not in person, at least. I was truly shocked. I took her back to my home and called my lawyer. In the morning, we went to the precinct together, and the culprit was arrested that day. His wealthy family tried to hardball Charlice, but my lawyer was a harder baller. Through all this, Mandy stayed around and helped in any way she could. Eventually, after many more dramas, my lawyer got Charlice a settlement, but her modeling career was over, and the jerk who beat her up got out of jail. Charlice went her own way, and Mandy and I bonded as friends.

At the beach in Zihuatanejo, we would walk back and forth between the two houses. One night, I walked alone with a flashlight over to Damien's, and when I got there, someone said, "That was brave of you!"

"Why?" I asked.

I was told the beach was a stone's throw from an inland lagoon infested with saltwater crocodiles. They all started laughing and later showed me why. We went outside, and when we turned our flashlights toward the lagoon, all the crocs' eyes lit up. That was too much for me. Walking on the road at night presented similar hazards: rattlesnakes and, worse yet, coral snakes, not to mention the sea snakes, which are ten times more venomous than rattlesnakes. And, of course, there were sharks in the ocean. *What are we doing here?*

Then, the night before we were due to leave for home, Mandy disappeared. We went back to the other house; we walked the road, the beach, no Mandy. Had she taken a walk and run into one of these crocodiles or snakes? Had she gone night swimming and been attacked by a shark? Anything was possible with her.

We sat down for dinner, and about two hours later, Mandy showed up like nothing happened.

"Where the fuck were you? We were worried sick."

She said, "I took a walk to town."

"Alone? Here in Mexico? You don't even speak Spanish!"

"It's fine. I'm here in one piece."

Nur and I exchanged looks—there's something off about her story. Mandy didn't say anything else about it. We eventually went back to our house and packed for our morning departure.

We headed to the airport the next day. Nur and I were flying back to New York, and Mandy was flying to Dallas and then on to Utah, where she was from. We arrived early to the airport, so we grabbed something to eat. Mandy's flight was earlier than ours, and right before she left to catch her plane, she said, "By the way, I did go to town last night and bought some heroin to bring home, I've got it stuffed in my snatch—you can't get this stuff in Utah!" And she kissed us goodbye.

I almost choked on my food. Nur and I were in shock as she walked away laughing. I got so nervous I couldn't eat anymore. We both thanked God she wasn't traveling with us!

We worried about her the entire trip home. But we made it home, and she made it home. It was one of the last times we'd see Mandy for a long while. She got married twice, had kids, and went to nursing school.

Not long ago, I texted her out of the blue. She was still working at the hospital full time and missed us dearly.

"When you taking a trip to visit us in New York?" I asked.

"I'm dying to visit. I miss New York so much, and I miss the fuck out of you!"

"So why don't you come?"

"I can't," she said.

"Why? Work? The kids?"

"No"—a pause—"I'm on parole!"

"Oh, Mandy . . . that's why I love you!"

72

I got a call from *Interview* magazine asking if I would shoot a cover story of Raquel Welch and her daughter, Tahnee. They knew Tahnee was a close friend of mine at the time, and I had wanted to shoot her and her mom together for a long time. Once mom and daughter agreed, I called *Interview* and handed them the shoot on a silver platter. I was already going to be working in LA, and I had time to shoot Raquel and Tahnee in between jobs.

It was a terrific scoop for *Interview*. Tahnee, then twenty-six years old, hadn't been photographed with her mom since she was twelve. They had a very difficult relationship, and certain things in Tahnee's past had never been resolved. Raquel just wanted her daughter to love her and didn't have a clue as to what was bugging Tahnee about their past. Their problems were common knowledge at the time.

Ron Howard's *Cocoon* was Tahnee's breakout film. She played the alien beauty that Steve Guttenberg, the male lead, fell for. When I first saw the movie, I didn't know Tahnee. When I set eyes on her, it was love at first sight: Kara and I were on vacation in Rome and ran into her by chance in our hotel. She was in Rome making an Italian movie that wasn't going anywhere for her, and she seemed relieved to meet and befriend two Americans who had nothing to do with her project. That was the beginning of our friendship, and we became very close. She was beautiful and quirky in an adorable way, and like most artists I knew, she was prone to occasional flip-outs.

As time went on, I became more familiar with her upbringing. So when I put this shoot together, I knew things might get tricky. Tahnee knew she could lean on me for support, but I also had to make Raquel feel good and know I'd be there to make her look beautiful. I would need my kid gloves for this. Raquel, like all divas, was known to be difficult. I had a makeup artist with us—Paul Starr, one of the best in the business—but Raquel insisted on doing her own makeup. Later, when I worked with Sophia Loren, I discovered that all the movie stars of that generation preferred to do their own makeup.

Mother and daughter were getting ready on opposite sides of the same room. I had things I needed to do with my assistants, with the stylists, etc., but Tahnee would call me over and I would need to hold her hand and chat. When Raquel saw that, she wanted the same attention, and I had to bounce over to her and hold her hand and chitchat. Then, at one point, both women started flirting with me while making sure the other was aware of it.

I saw where this was going. I had one of my assistants call me and say there was a phone call from New York, and I'd disappear for a while. When makeup was done, Tahnee tried on a tiny pair of hot pants with heels. She looked gorgeous. Next, Raquel put on a bodysuit. She stood up and looked at herself in the mirror and did a little spin for me and, damn, this shit was getting crazy! It continued like this on the set—mother and daughter in fierce competition. I navigated between the two the best I could, hoping a fistfight wouldn't break out and they wouldn't start yanking out each other's hair. I had to get the shot by any means necessary, and I did. But by the end of the shoot, I was exhausted.

Mother and daughter changed into their own clothes and stepped out of their dressing rooms into the parking lot. Tahnee put her arm tightly in mine and, to her mom, she said, "Sante and I are going back to his hotel to have dinner, and you can't come." I stood there with a dumb look on my face. Raquel said fine. She told me how much she loved working with me, planted a kiss on my face, then headed to a car that was waiting for her. Tahnee and I went back to the Sunset Marquis to hang out and have drinks and a bite to eat.

Early the next day, the film came back from the lab, and I started editing. *Interview* needed the work ASAP to make the deadline for their next issue. It was a lot of film, and I didn't want to give them anything but *my* choices, which meant a tedious search through more than a thousand frames to select ten or fifteen at the most. The magazine planned to put the two women on the cover, and the number of inside pages would be determined by how many images I gave them to choose from. It was going to be a long day and night.

Sometime around noon, Raquel called and said, "Hi, I just wanted to know how the pictures look. I'm so excited!"

I told her I was just beginning to go through them, and of course, they looked great, but this was going to take me all night. The magazine needed the final edits first thing in the morning.

Raquel started grilling me: "How's my makeup look? Make sure you choose the ones where my legs look long . . . How about my hair?" It's not unusual for an actress to point out her best features to a photographer. I was no stranger to those directions. I'd say OK and then go look for *my* picture and surprise everyone with some magic, show them what they'd never seen before about themselves, their other side.

I assured her that she was looking great that day, that she could do no wrong, and not to worry, I was a pretty good editor of my own work. I assured her she was never going to look bad in a photo of mine.

About 10:30 p.m., there was a knock at the door. I opened it, and there stood Raquel Welch. I thought of my old friends—who would have believed that one day Raquel Welch would be knocking at my hotel room door? And all I was thinking was, *What a pain in the ass! I still had a ton of work to do.*

The guy at the front desk had probably recognized Raquel Welch, started stuttering, and immediately gave her my room number. He was probably on the phone to someone, saying, "You know who Sante D'Orazio is fucking? And I think he's fucking the daughter too!" I'd get that shit all the time from the gossip rags, and if I denied it, they wouldn't believe me and would print it anyway, true or false.

Not wanting to be rude, I let her in. All my transparencies lay in piles all around the room. In those days, color film came in transparency form, positives, slides, not negatives like black and white. I'd get them back by the roll so I could quickly scroll on the lightbox and cut out my picks. The lightbox was on the desk with some choices, plus a short pile of my first-round picks from other shots. I sat down to show her a few and gave her a magnifier loupe to look at the transparencies. She didn't even sit down; all she wanted to do was look at the picks.

I sat in front of the lightbox and Raquel's arm was around me. She bent over, looking through the loupe at the transparencies. She wore a loose thin silk blouse, and her tit was on my shoulder. I wasn't sure if she was wearing a bra. *Good God Almighty. What if she makes a move? I can't fuck my friend's mother . . . but then again, it's Raquel Welch.* I began to get nervous, started stuttering like the guy at the front desk probably was. She wanted to see more and more and more. I sat there, laying out slides like a blackjack dealer, with Raquel Welch's tit resting warmly on my shoulder.

She loved mostly everything, thank God, and when she was done, she left in a hurry.

I felt like a cheap date. I needed to take a break, so I went down to the bar. Passing the front desk, I winked, smiled, nodded to the desk clerk, and thanked him for letting her up. He gave me that wide-eyed look and said, "Sha-sha-sure, anytime." I figured, why disappoint him?

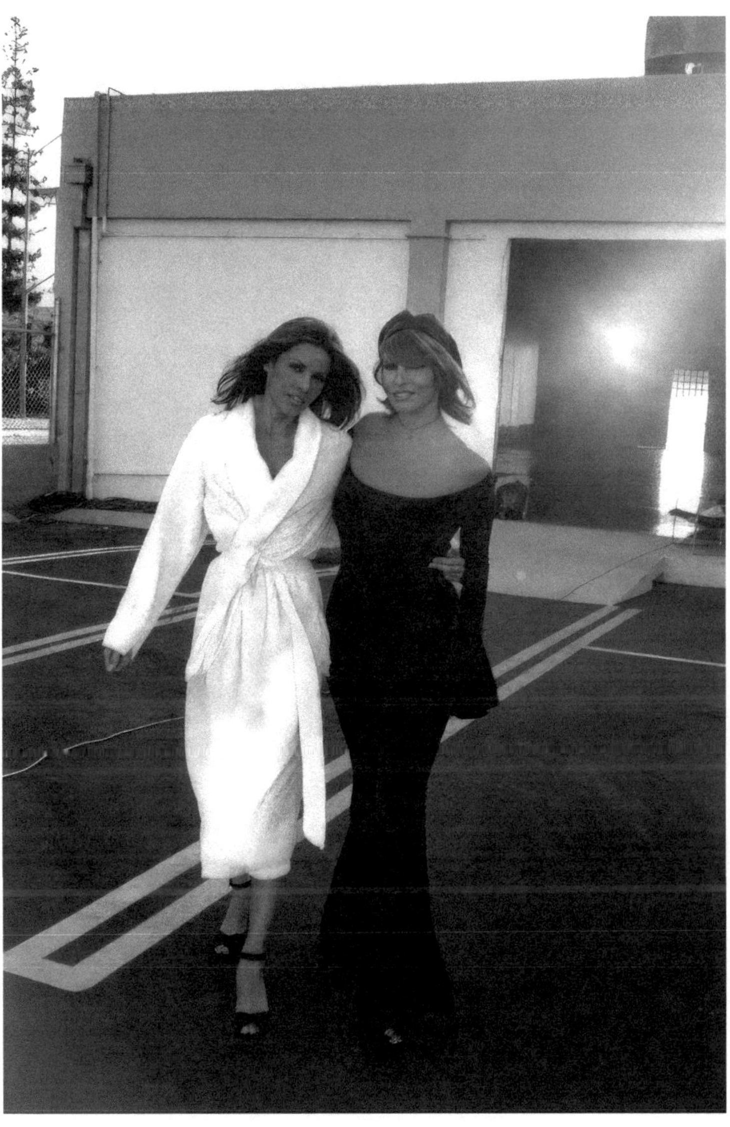

Tahnee Welch and Raquel Welch for *Interview* magazine, Hollywood, California

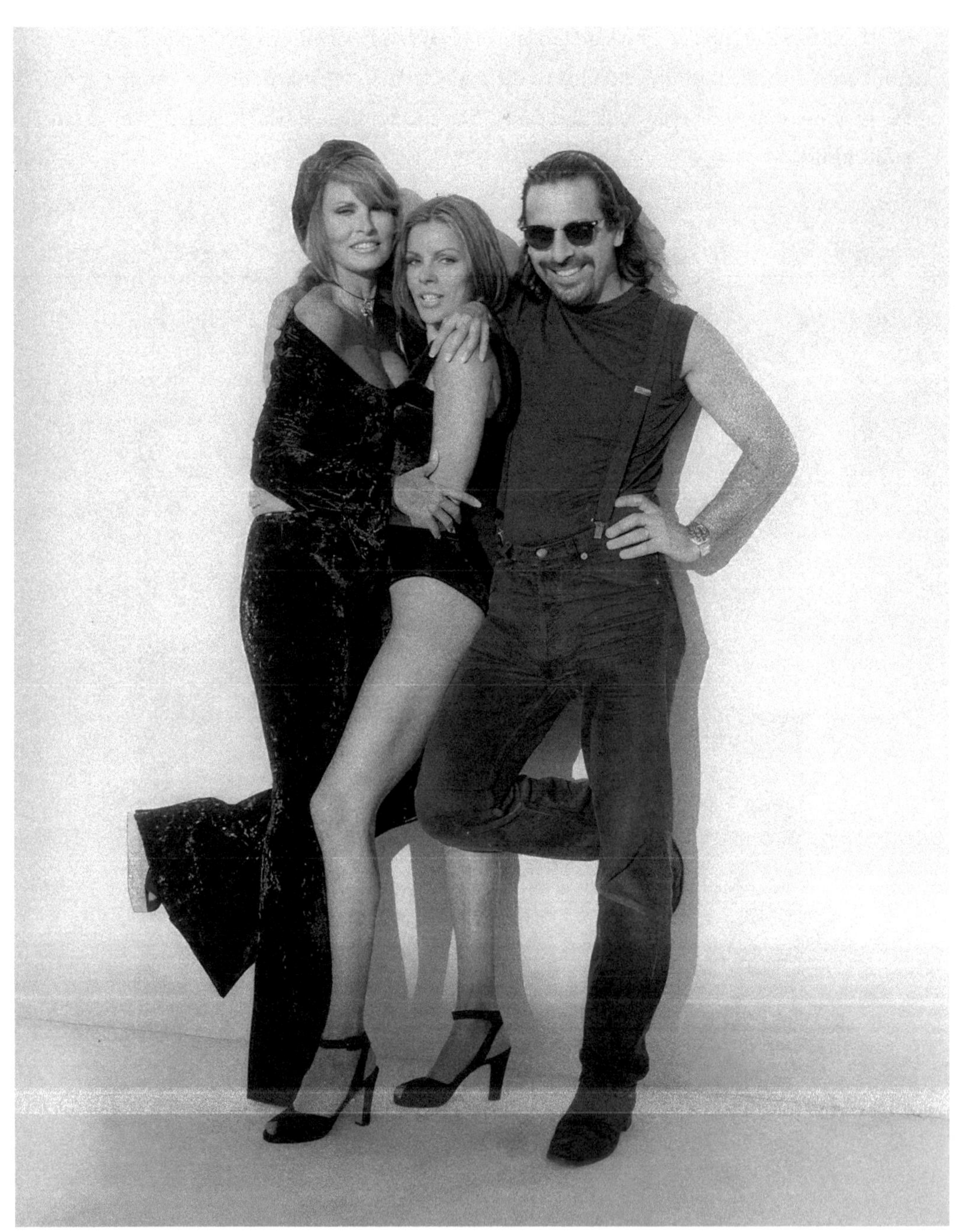

Raquel Welch, Tahnee Welch, and Sante

73

What we look for does not happen. What we least
expect is fashioned by the gods.
—Euripides

I chose to be an artist, which means living life in a circus—a high-wire act with no net. I grew up watching people close to me give up their dreams and living every day after with regrets. I wasn't going to do that. As a kid, I prayed every day that I would take this on as my mission in life and paint. I was sure of it, but God had other plans. He put a camera in my hands instead of a brush. I went along with it but didn't understand why. I followed the order, believing His grand plan would lead me to paint . . . but it didn't.

My camera brought money, and fame came in. My mom was secure, and my work was in greater demand. Still, I complained, "I'm a painter, and I want to paint!" The more I fought for it within myself, the more I paid a price and suffered for not being able to make room to paint.

Even the great Michelangelo complained when the Pope assigned him to paint the ceiling of that fucking chapel. I can imagine him saying, "Are you fucking kidding me? I'm a sculptor, not a painter!" He ran away and hid in the marble quarries of Carrara, where his friends, the stone masons, would keep his identity safe. The Pope sent the papal guards after him and dragged his ass back to Rome. Four years later, we got the Sistine Chapel. He hated every minute of its creation, of not sculpting.

That's what it felt like for me throughout most of my career as a commercial fashion photographer. I hated most assignments, and it was punishing not to paint and explore the unknowns. To distract myself, I did drugs and got laid a lot. To my chagrin, I somehow managed to do some great work in between.

I was very grateful for my fame and fortune, but I saw myself drifting further and further away from my inner self. I needed to search for the sacred and to manifest it through my art—the God force, the invisible, the spirits I knew were there. But all those concepts began to seem like the ideals of youth, out of touch with the real world.

That separation is what began to pain me, but I needed to ignore it in the face of this God-given opportunity handed to me. "For the time being, use what's opened to you and follow it; it will lead you to where you want to go. That search for the sacred will never go away; you will never lose it." That became my mantra. These words resonated in the echo chamber of my heart. The summation of everything my mom and my mentor Lou Bernstein taught me, including my readings of Carl Jung. Follow the road and the obstacles, they will lead you to where you need to go.

With time, the voice within me began to grow dimmer in the chaos that ensued once my growing success as a fashion photographer evolved. The type of photography that was now expected of me would not allow me to explore my vision with any depth. I made feeble attempts to paint, but being a Sunday painter made me want to slit my wrists. Artistically, I applied myself wherever possible with what was available to me, portraiture for one, and what had been my focus throughout all my student years, the Nude. I put everything else on the shelf and counted myself lucky to be in my own shoes, until the years of chaos overwhelmed me. I was lost.

74

In her old age, my mom started becoming more difficult, less active, more needy for attention.

She had been driving her own car since the early '60s, but at eighty years old, she was driving like Mr. Magoo. She'd pull out of her parking spot after visiting us in SoHo and head toward traffic while looking and waving at me and my son, Nick, the two of us grabbing each other cringing, not wanting to look. In the supermarket, her driving skills would step up a notch, taking the cart along at full throttle and crashing into everyone else's as if she were driving a bumper car at Coney Island. She wouldn't even notice and would just go on her way. Her car began looking more and more banged up with each visit.

I began to fear not only for her life but maybe someone else's too. It got so bad I had to make her stop driving. I turned in the car and found her a car service she could use regularly. But once she lost her wheels, she lost her independence. She could no longer come over to visit us whenever she felt like it.

It had to be done, but in time, she began to feel lonelier and more isolated to the point of not wanting to participate anymore in weddings, dinners with family, or even having her favorite oysters at Balthazar. She stopped caring. Only when other family members and I pushed hard enough could we get her out. When we did manage to convince her to go out, she'd soon enough want to go home in the middle of our dinner. "I no feela good!" she'd say. When we resisted, she'd make a scene, and she was very good at faking a fainting fit or giving the impression she was about to throw up. She would fake burp, force it, then gag. We'd all have to circle around, sometimes even carry her to the car, and she'd keep going and make sure to ruin the occasion. She was only happy at home in her nightgown, watching *Wheel of Fortune*.

Back in the day, when I'd be multitasking—shooting a cover for a magazine while busy with bookings and editing back-to-back shootings—Mom would decide she wanted attention and needed to see her baby son (I was probably forty years old at the time.). I'd get a call that Mom was in an ambulance again, on the way to the hospital, and I better come quick. I'd have to interrupt another cover session, jump in a car during rush hour traffic to Brooklyn, only to find out it was another false alarm.

She'd cry wolf whenever she got the chance; she was guaranteed a result that way, even if it was just to piss me off. When my son was born, it took the pressure and attention off of me. She was in heaven! She'd say things like "I never knew you could love someone more than your own son!" Then she would look my way, so satisfied. I'd roll my eyes.

When my son graduated from high school, my cousin Palma closed her restaurant and set up a celebration with tables in her garden area—a family occasion, Italian style! Nick's mom, stepdad, and my ex-in-laws from San Francisco came. My sister, Marie, even flew in from Florida.

When I went to Mom's house to pick up her, my sister, and my brother-in-law, Mom started up with her "I no feela good" routine." Marie was beside herself—living in Florida, she never had to deal with Mom. Marie was supposed to ride with me; instead, she had to try to get my mom ready and in shape for the lunch. I went by myself to the ceremony. When I got back, Marie was upset. My mom wouldn't budge or cooperate, and she couldn't be left alone. She was playing sick, and these guys had flown in just for this occasion. I wanted to kill her! Living far away in Florida, my sister had imagined I was exaggerating about Mom. I turned to her and said, "I told ya!"

I turned back to Mom and said, "You're not going to ruin my son's graduation day, your grandson who you love more than your own son!"

My sister started lamenting, "What'll we do . . . what'll we do?"

I didn't care anymore; I was so tired of these games. I had twenty milligrams of Adderall in my pocket. I cut it in half, crushed it, and put it in her orange juice. I told Mom it was vitamin C. She listened to me and drank the whole thing. I didn't tell my sister because she was a bad liar, and if Mom croaked, I didn't want to go to jail!

Soon, my mom's attitude changed. She got dressed and acted like she was feeling good. She wouldn't shut the fuck up on the car ride to the city. She even had us laughing at her dirty stories from the old country that we had heard a thousand times. She just kept yapping all the way.

When we got to the restaurant, my mom walked ahead of us to go in first, ready to party. It was as if my mom was suddenly thirty years younger! She went from table to table, saying hello, hugging people, laughing, smiling. I just couldn't believe it. At dinner, Mom, who never had an appetite, ate two portions of food! At the end, she didn't want to leave; she was having such a good time. Everyone was astounded and happy for her—and for us!

It was such a good result that I told my sister about the Adderall before we went in. She laughed so hard she cried.

At the end of the night, I put my mom, sister, and brother-in-law in a car that took them back to Brooklyn.

The next morning, the phone rang at 6:30 a.m., which to me was usually a bad sign. It was my mom's next-door neighbor. He knew Mom and her condition and all. He said, "I'm sorry to call so early but your mom is sweeping the driveway in her nightgown. She already did the porch and the sidewalk too!"

I called and woke my sister to go fetch her before she started cleaning windshields on Ocean Parkway. The Adderall was a great experiment, and we had my mom back to when she was fifty years old—a one-day fountain of youth.

I only had to resort to dosing her again one other time. I used the same method of crushing the pill and putting it in orange juice. She saw the concoction and asked if that was the same vitamin C; she couldn't wait to drink it down.

This time, when it hit, it freaked us all out. She literally started speaking in tongues! She looked at us at the dinner table and had no idea why we couldn't understand her. I could tell from her gestures she was saying, "What the fuck is wrong with you? You deaf or something?"

It scared the shit out of us. I thought maybe she was possessed. I was worried she might start crawling on the ceiling.

I gave her one of her own prescription anti-anxiety pills, and it calmed things down. It worked like an exorcism, and she stopped talking like Beelzebub. After that, she kept asking for that "vitamin C," but I never repeated that experiment again.

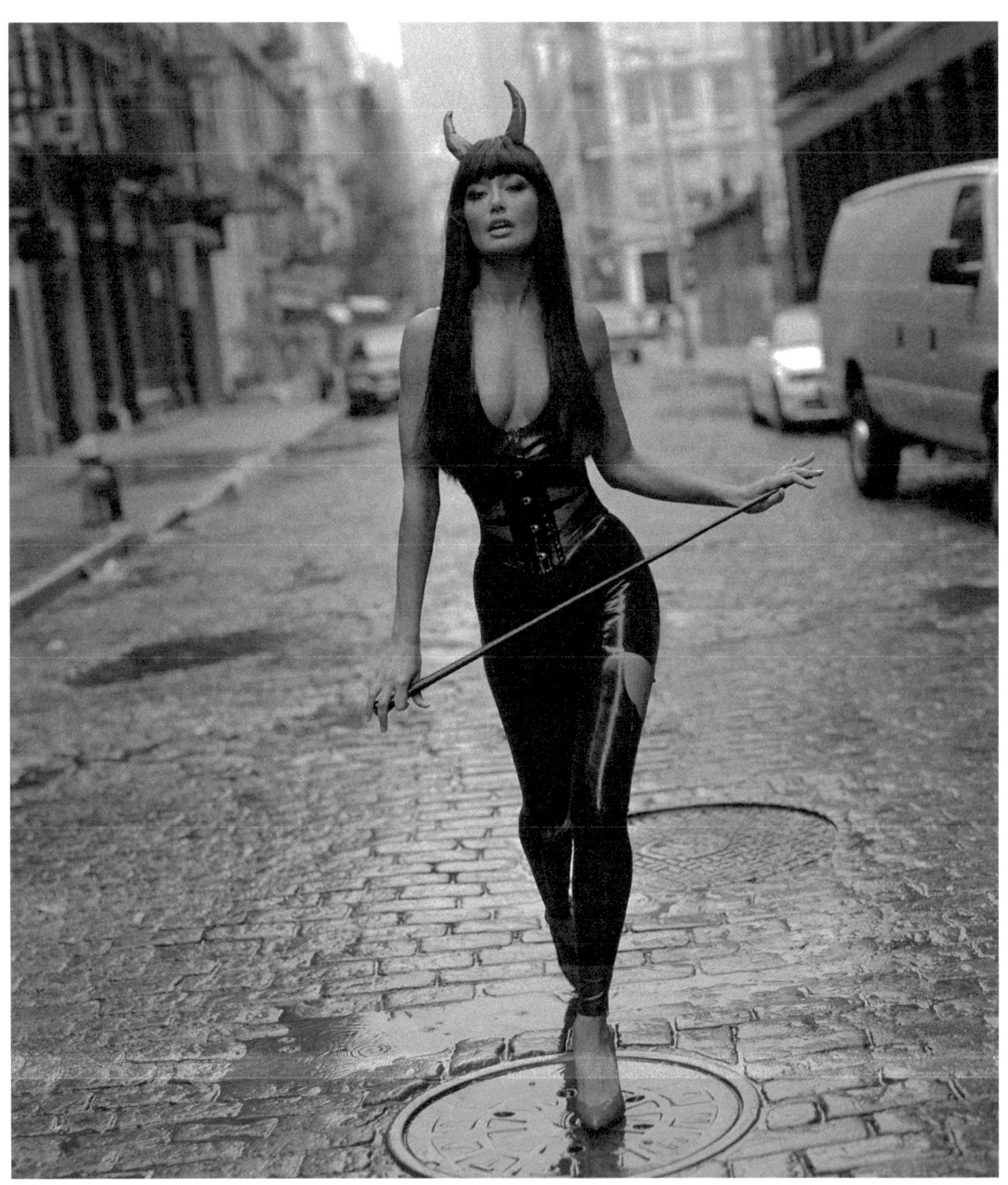

Sky Nellor, Crosby Street, New York City

75

Galina Kamolova came from an oil-rich part of the Soviet Empire, the northernmost part of the old Silk Road, where caravans on their way to the Middle East from China made that land rich in trade and culture. Galina was unusually tall and slender with a beautiful, model-like physique and long black hair and olive skin. She was a stunning woman with that exotic mix of Turkic, Mongol, and Kazakh blood. She was also an Oxford graduate and a classical pianist, very cultured in that Russian way, and could hold her own with anyone, from presidents to philosophers to playboys. She also was a whip and could drink me under the table anytime, with that gleam in the eye that hinted at a wild side.

Above all, she was a Russian oligarch. Raised in Moscow, where her father was once on the Central Committee of the Communist Party, she was used to being around powerful men, and she projected the confidence that power conferred. As was customary with many women of her high profile and social class, she'd had some beauty work performed. This went unnoticed by most men—unless they'd been in the beauty business for as long as I had. The women, on the other hand, they could even identify the expert hands involved. But most men were far too gullible in the presence of a beautiful woman, and besides, their eyes were always elsewhere.

I'd be lying if I said there wasn't any other kind of interest on my part, but I was already involved with another girlfriend, whose last name literally was Kill. (I'll leave it at that.) Galina seemed to have a spark of interest in me as well, but I didn't want to start juggling; I'd been scorched too many times in the past.

We had met through another friend of mine, whose wife was Russian. Galina was staying with this couple in New York. I had shot some gorgeous nudes of my friend's wife as a commission, and they had hung the work somewhere private in their home. At dinner,

Galina told me how much she admired those nudes and wanted to commission me for a similar shoot. I could fly to London and photograph her in her home. I accepted at once.

I knew that, as long as we didn't hook up, we could be great friends. Otherwise, I could see myself wearing a diamond dog collar attached to a very short leash. With my temperament, that was never going to work.

A month later, having booked a crew of hair and makeup from London, I flew over with my photo assistant, two cameras, three lenses, and a light meter. We all met at Galina's house and, after introductions, got started on hair and makeup. She had a great figure, high cheekbones, elegant breasts, and dark almond eyes. We had discussed doing the nudes in a similar style to those of our friend in New York. I always liked using articles of clothing from someone's own wardrobe to start. Their choices would become part of the portrait, even if it was only bits and pieces or just jewelry and heels. I loved heels. This would align with my strengths as a beauty photographer and set the direction right away for the rest of the shoot.

Time to start. I cleared the set, put up Styrofoam boards and reflectors for her privacy, so she didn't feel like she was being gawked at by my crew, being she'd be nude, and I described what we were going to do. She would lie face down on her velvet couch so her body wouldn't be exposed, and she could wear anything she liked from what we had chosen. I left the room to let her find her comfort zone.

And then, out of nowhere, she sat up in her robe and decided she didn't want to do it. This was the whole reason she flew me over—to shoot the nudes. But she explained that one day she might run for political office back in Russia and didn't want anything floating around that could damage her chances.

I knew that was bullshit, but nothing I could say or do could change her mind. In thirty years, this had never happened. We had discussed the details of the shooting just the previous day. She basically just chickened out.

What to do? With the magic gone, my excitement drained away. This was the kind of shooting the average fashion client would love, but it was not good enough for me, except for a payday. I loved making magic; I was expecting to make magic. Galina wasn't a model, though she had the figure for it. A nude would have compensated for certain things; it would have made her more vulnerable, more sensual, and brought out her strengths. But it wasn't meant to be.

A month later, I guess when she saw the framed prints of our salvaged photo shoot, she put them away somewhere, never to be seen again, unless I came over to visit, maybe. The only compensation for my disappointment was the shitload of money she paid me.

I decided to stay on in London for a couple of days. Galina invited me to dinner one night with some mutual friends. We met at Cipriani. As I sat down, I couldn't help noticing two tables over, a group of at least ten young girls, all nicely dressed, sitting with one guy who looked like a gypsy sword swallower from the circus. It was an odd scene, but the girls seemed to be having a good time. The sword swallower looked kind of somber with his thick black curly hair, four-day growth, white denim jacket, and wraparound shades. A pimp maybe? Nah, not in Cipriani. Then who walked in—English royalty! It was Prince Andrew.

He made a beeline to our table. He seemed to be in a jolly mood, greeting our Russian hostess like they were old friends. He sat next to Galina, and she introduced everybody. When it came to me, he said, "Ha, so you must be on the menu tonight." He had a stupid grin on his face. A real wanker, as my English friends would say. I made believe his remark went over my head, but I wanted to smack him one. Then he went off to sit with the giggly gaggle of girls and the gypsy sword swallower. What a schmuck.

During dinner, Galina casually asked if I would like to go with her and some friends to St. Petersburg for a gala dinner at the Hermitage. The Hermitage! What an incredible collection of art—it would take six months to a year, if not longer, to go through that museum. The only time I had been to Russia was when I was shooting Helena Christensen for British *Vogue* in 1990, when St. Petersburg was still called Leningrad. I said yes right away. All I could think of were the masterpieces I would get to see in the flesh. The British couple sitting with us would be coming along, and three other British friends of hers. We were to leave on her private jet the next day.

At the airport the following morning, Galina introduced me to her other friends: one was in the jewelry business, one in PR, and another in hedge funds. For the entire flight to St. Petersburg, all they talked about was money. That surprised me because they were British—the Brits were usually more reserved when it came to discussing money. These guys were probably transplants, but I didn't give a shit what they were; it was tacky. And the jewelry guy got on my nerves; he was trying to sell stuff to Galina non-stop. Otherwise, the trip in her private jet was primo. We arrived in the early afternoon, rooms awaited us at the Grand Hotel, plenty of time to get ready for the gala and have drinks before leaving.

Everyone was in evening dress: the men in tuxedos, the women in Dior, Valentino,

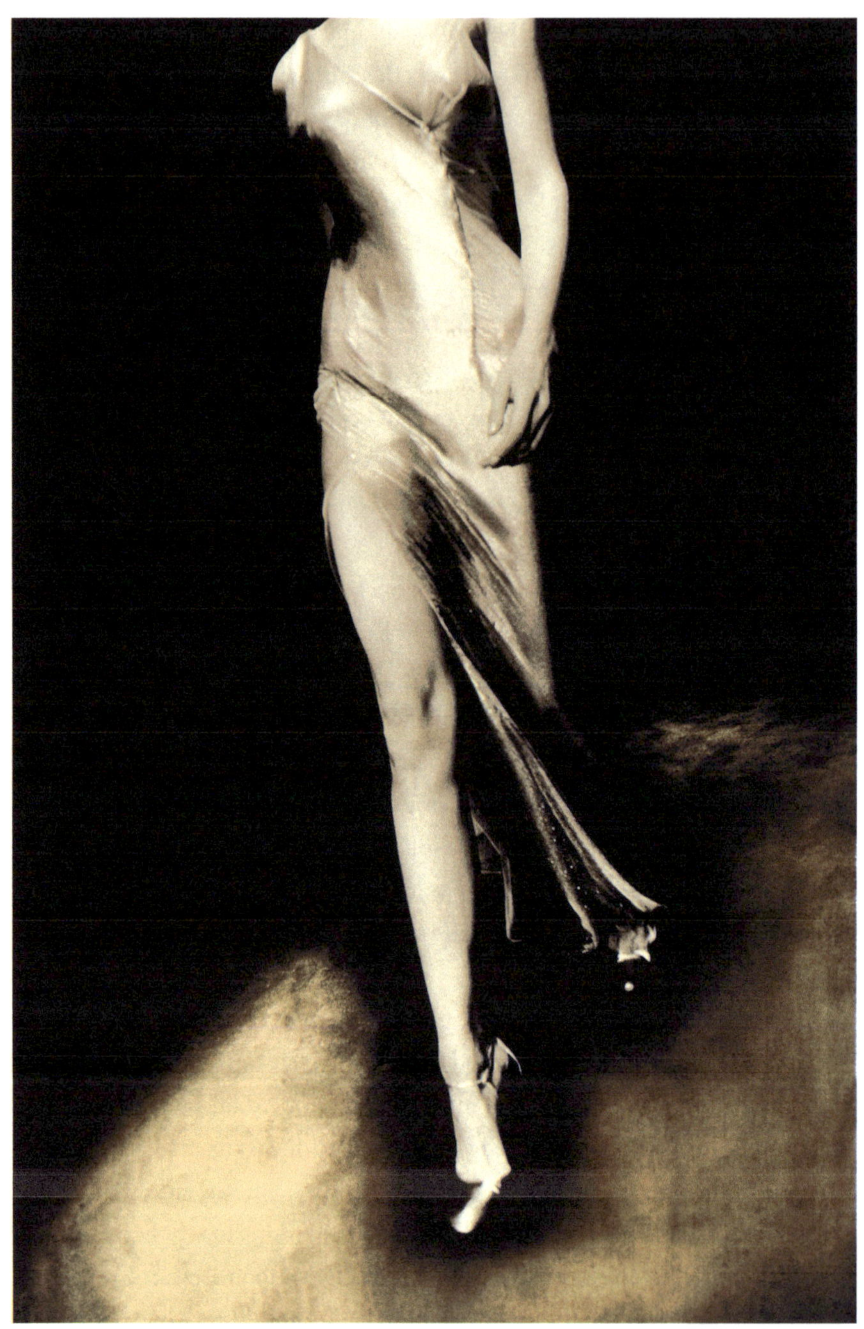

From *Gianni & Donatella* by Sante

Givenchy, etc. We piled into a white stretch limo. I had a small camera and was taking pictures; the ladies were all excited, showing lots of leg and slamming down shots of vodka. At the Hermitage, we were escorted through elegant halls filled with Greek and Roman art, to an outdoor area that was partially under a tent. Speeches were being made, more drinks, a toast here and there, and then dinner was served.

Three quarters of the way through, it started to rain cats and dogs. It became torrential; everyone ran for cover. I made my way inside, close to where the waiters were coming and going. I needed to use the bathroom. Someone gave me directions, but I found myself in a cellar with arched and vaulted ceilings. It was like a basement maze. Someone told me to go up the stairs and through the door to the right. I went upstairs and opened the first door I saw. I found myself alone in the Hermitage galleries, first in a roomful of Rembrandts and other Dutch masters; then turning a corner, from one room to another. There was a Van Gogh, one that I remembered hanging in my public-school auditorium at P.S. 179 in Brooklyn (a reproduction, of course). I remember staring at that painting from kindergarten to sixth grade while the class was watching some school play. *Fishing Boats on the Beach at Saint-Maries-de-la-Mer,* this one was a watercolor. I never saw the real oil painting in the flesh. What a coincidence. It was like seeing an old family member from yesteryear. I was astonished, and not a soul around. I was completely alone with all this incredible art. What a gift. As I was wandering among the masterpieces, my phone started ringing. It was Galina. I didn't answer and kept walking, as if in a dream. All the lights were on, and there was nobody but me and art history.

I wanted to find out if this one Kazimir Malevich painting, *Black Square,* was here. I should have done my homework. Malevich was a Russian (from Kiev) avant-garde pioneer of abstract art at the very beginning of the twentieth century. In 1915, he went straight to the core of our abstract language by simply painting a black square on a white background. He saw the black square as a holy image, a new way of visually entering the spiritual through the void and finding God. It became an icon of transcendence that could substitute for the traditional Russian Orthodox icons. The black square was about feeling the space through your sense perception as opposed to any kind of literal descriptions. It's a direction I'd been interested in since my school days.

The phone rang again. "Where are you? We're all in the limo waiting for you! We're going to karaoke!"

I was here in the fucking Hermitage, and these yo-yos wanted to go to karaoke. "Kari-fucking-okey! I can't believe it! You're telling me we have to leave the Hermitage for karaoke?"

"Yes, unless you want to sleep there tonight?"

I told her where I was and that it would take me a minute to get to them. I looked around and realized I was completely lost. That door I'd come through was the kind of hidden door that, from this side, looked like part of the wall. I couldn't find those Rembrandts I had seen . . . I knew I had taken a few steps up, a few steps down . . . I was getting deeper in, distracted by all the great paintings.

My phone rang again. I knew Galina wouldn't stop calling, but there was no one around. I yelled "Hello!" hoping someone would appear and direct me out. Nobody answered. It was beginning to feel like an episode of *The Twilight Zone*.

I spotted another hidden door and managed to pull it open. A staircase led me down to the cellar. I could hear voices, so I followed them and encountered some kitchen staff and waiters who directed me to the exit.

The limo was rocking from side to side with disco lights and music. Everyone was slammed from drinking straight vodka. My hostess was making out with her girlfriend. I was hating on all of them.

We got back late to the hotel, and I heard we were flying to Moscow in the morning. I realized that was my one visit to the Hermitage. At the airport, I bought a postcard of the Malevich painting as my consolation prize. I found out the *Black Square* was no longer exhibited at the Hermitage; it was somewhere in Moscow, but I would miss that chance too. I was at the mercy of these philistines. In Moscow, we got a private tour of the Kremlin, including areas closed to the public. The biggest thrill the Brits got was seeing the crown jewels, diamonds and gold owned by the Russian State. They all got wet at the sight of that bling, including the guys.

When we had dinner together, I didn't do much talking. After dinner, we went to a club. I was still pissed off. If I had known anyone in Moscow at the time, I would have bailed on those guys. We were due to leave for London the next day. I called some friends there and made plans in advance for a night out.

On our last day in Moscow, we were to have lunch together at some hotel with an outdoor patio, then leave for the airport. I couldn't wait. We took a minibus to this hotel midway to the airport. That wanker jeweler was still trying to sell Galina more bling. I was going to open my mouth, but I'm glad I didn't. I gave them all dirty looks. During lunch on the patio, these English cocksuckers realized the World Cup of soccer was starting in an hour; it was England versus Germany. "We have to stay! We have to stay!" they shouted. I wanted to slit my wrists, theirs first. We all went outside for coffee and sat around a garden table waiting for the match to start.

I paced around and began chain-smoking in a nearby gravel driveway. Suddenly, three SUVs pulled up and a SWAT team jumped out with machine guns drawn. I thought that the oligarchs had stopped doing that kind of shit, but apparently not. You could see everyone got a fright from this incident. A small guy dressed in white and wearing a hat got out of one of the SUVs and started walking toward me on this narrow gravel path. With his head down, he walked right up to me. I couldn't see his face because of the hat. Belligerent me thought I was back in Brooklyn and thought to myself, *Fuck him. Let him walk around me.* He lifted his head, and we looked at each other for a split second, and I screamed out, "Karim!" He screamed out, "Sante!"

It was Karim from Sardinia and Venice, my new Russian mob boss friend. "I like your hat," I said. He had bought it with me. We both started laughing and gave each other the biggest of hugs, and he invited me to join him for a drink. I shot a quick glance over at the Brits, sitting there with their jaws in their laps, and went inside with Karim.

There were six young girls, all dressed up, sitting at his table. He invited me to stay and said, "You know who I'm meeting here?" (I'm not going to mention him by name, but he's a very famous Hollywood producer from New York, known to be a bully, who I've known for a long time.) This scene was right up this producer's alley. I imagine he was somehow involved in raising money with the boys in Moscow. When he arrived, we chitchatted for about ten minutes. It's good the producer saw I was there with Karim. If he ever got any ideas in New York that he could push me around, at least he knew that I was tight with the Moscow crew. I gave Karim another big hug, said my goodbyes, and got out of there.

I went back to chain-smoking and sat at the empty table next to the Brits. They were staring at me in silence, their jaws still hanging open. I looked at them and shrugged my shoulders, "What?" I said as I lit up another cigarette.

76

It's a strange thing when you think you're sane, but others know you're batshit crazy.
—Sante D'Orazio

I was fifty-one at the time. My girlfriend, Natalie, and I were at Miami Art Basel. On our last night in Miami, we were at Joe's Stone Crab with a packed house and a packed table with some art collectors, some I knew, others I didn't, including friends from NY who came down to party. Talking, drinking, eating, telling stories. Then I ate a stone crab, a specialty of the House, but it just didn't taste right. I should have spit it out. But we were shoulder to shoulder, so not to be rude, I swallowed it. And the dinner party continued.

Later, at another party, I broke out in a sweat and began to feel weak. I returned to the hotel and broke out with a high fever. I took three Advil and fell asleep.

The fever returned the next day. Three more Advil got me through the airport. We boarded our flight to New York, and once I got home, I was relieved to get into my own bed. My fever got worse, and I became disorientated. In the middle of the night, I went to the bathroom and peed dark red blood. As I left the bathroom, my legs gave out, and I fell to the floor. I crawled back to bed and called my doctor at dawn.

He examined me in his office and told me to go home, pack a bag, and go to Beth Israel Hospital, where he'd have doctors waiting for me. While packing, I began to shiver uncontrollably; I couldn't even handle my cell phone to call an ambulance. I felt cold, so cold. Natalie called my doctor, and he told her to take me in a cab, not to wait for an ambulance. I was shivering like never before—even the driver was concerned. When we arrived at the emergency room, doctors were waiting there to take me in. The last thing I remember was collapsing on the floor and nurses rushing over with heating pads.

I was diagnosed with E-coli. I was put on life support, then an induced coma. My blood, toxic from sepsis, had begun to shut down my organs: liver, kidneys, everything. At some point, my heart stopped. I had flatlined, and I was clinically dead for more than the critical time necessary to revive me. With enormous effort and some intensive resuscitation, the doctors and nurses brought me back to life.

A week later, I awoke from the coma in a white room with no windows and with my wrists and feet bound to the bed. My tongue and throat felt like I had swallowed sand. I had no idea what was going on or if it was day or night.

"Water, please!" I yelled to no one. "Untie me please! Help me! Let me go!" I pulled on my restraints, yelled again for help, and the nurses just passed me by. I went in and out of time. I was dying of thirst, and no one seemed to give a shit.

"I just want a drink, and where the fuck am I?"

Somebody said, "Please lower your voice, Mr. D'Orazio!"

"Answer me, please! Why am I tied up?"

Then, my two saving graces appeared: my cousin Pam and my business partner of the last twenty-two years, Diane—both were like sisters to me. Now they seemed like angels!

"We're here, so just relax and be quiet!"

But I kept it up.

Diane leaned close to my ear and said, "Just shut the fuck up!"

Pam said, "If you don't behave, I'll bring your mother in. She's in the other room."

"No, please! Fuck no! All right, all right, *please* don't bring her here. I'll behave!" The last thing I needed was a hysterical Mediterranean mourner carrying the cross with her saints in procession behind her. I'd rather be back in a coma.

Finally, a nurse gave me ice cubes for my dying thirst, but they still wouldn't untie me. Slowly, I came to understand that I was in intensive care, and I had been—and still was—acting like a raving lunatic. My doctor told me later he hadn't expected me to make it once I flatlined.

The doctor also told me that, when I had come out of the coma, I was in such a rage that it took eight men to hold me down. I was ripping out the tubes from down my throat, up my nose, and in my veins. I was told by my doctor that it was that same rage that helped me pull through, a will to survive. That's why they had to tie me down in my bed, but my mind was somewhere in surreality.

In its late stage, E-coli is most often fatal. Family members started coming around that same day I gained consciousness. My brother, Mike, put his phone by my ear to say hello to his son. I was okay with that but thought it was odd. Then my cousin Nicky from New Jersey appeared. I *never* saw him. He's the cousin every family has that you never see, and when you do, they continue in the middle of a conversation you were having ten years ago. I asked him what he was doing here.

"Oh, I came to say goodbye."

"Goodbye? Why, where you going? You movin' or something?"

Then someone took his arm and gently pulled him away.

I turned and asked my brother, "Where the fuck is he moving to?"

They finally unbound my hands and feet and gave me a small plastic cup of apple juice. It was heaven to my senses. I was still in intensive care, but with the apple juice and morphine, I didn't care.

Eventually, when everyone left, they moved me to my own room—in fact, a suite with concierge service. It was Beth Israel Hospital, but it seemed like the Four Seasons of hospitals. Ring the bell and a guy would come in, dressed in a white shirt, black tie, and black vest, with anything I wanted to eat, anytime of the day or night. I couldn't believe it! If I wanted Chinese food from Chinatown or a steak from Raoul's, they'd get it for me. But I was still on a morphine and apple juice diet. There was a big couch in my suite, and if I wanted a visitor to sleep over, they'd convert the couch into a bed. What kind of place was this?

(Much later, when I was off the morphine, I saw I had signed the hospital bill, which totaled $20,000. Another piece of paper had my signature agreeing to the terms for concierge service, which wasn't covered by my insurance. I must have been whacked out of my mind when I signed that one. On the other hand, I got two weeks of first-class service! What's money for?)

My suite was on the second floor, and I had a view of that small park between the hospital and Second Avenue. It was winter and the trees were bare. Snow was falling. It looked like a Hallmark card.

The bed was super comfortable, with a large TV on the wall in front of the bed. I'd watch movies; every one of them was a great movie from the '40s and '50s I'd never seen before.

I was wired up with tubes and needles in my arms and a three-pronged IV in my neck, maintaining hydration, antibiotics, and my morphine drip. I held on to that control button 24/7 and was constantly trying to get more morphine out of it, but the feed was timed and controlled. The old drug addict in me needed as much as I could get; I was feeling so nice and high! I'd tell the nurses I needed more, and they would sweetly refuse, but every

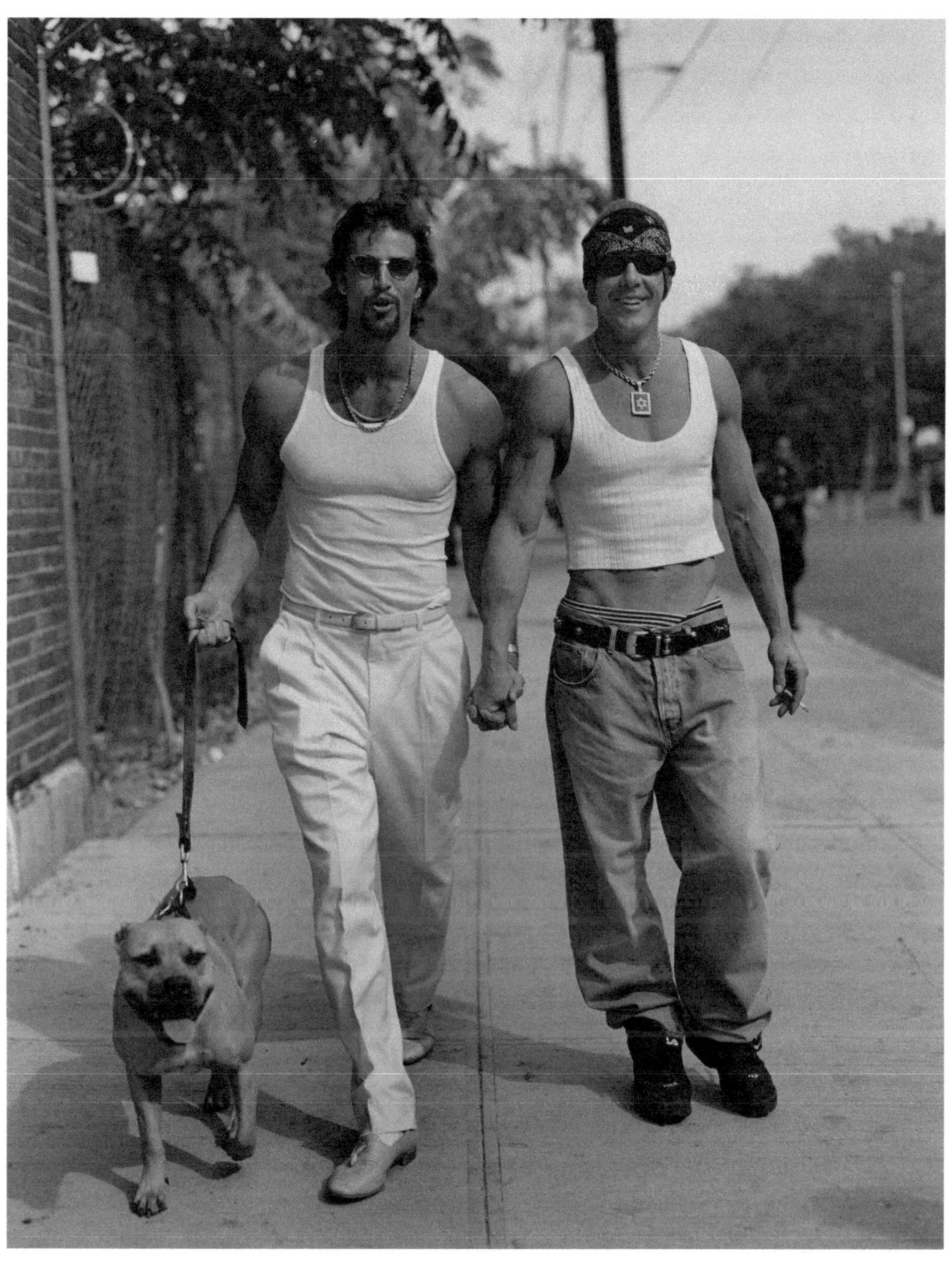

John Enos and Mickey Rourke on the set of *Bullet*, Brooklyn, New York

six hours, they did give me two OxyContin on top of the morphine drip. And every three hours, a nurse would come in to take my blood pressure and my temperature to make sure I didn't have a fever. They also would inject something into my belly—to this day, I don't know what it was.

After I had settled in, flowers and friends started arriving. I hadn't shaved, so I looked pretty rough. I had lost thirty pounds in less than ten days, and I had an extra-large scab on my forehead from having ripped some tape off when they were trying to hold me down (I think). It looked like my third eye. My hair was crazy—it stood up and out sideways. When I looked in the mirror, I almost didn't recognize myself. I looked like Charles Manson.

My friend Nur came almost every day, God bless him. Nur and I had been partners in crime for ten years or so. He ran some of the best downtown clubs and after-hours joints in the city. He always claimed me as his best friend and consigliere, which I was. Once, after hours, he was on his way home from the club with a group of girls, and the driver was rude to one of them. They all got into a fistfight, and Nur came to the rescue; then he got arrested at three o'clock in the morning. He woke me up, and I had to go to the club and get him bail money, five thousand dollars of crumpled up bills—singles, fives, tens, and twenties—in a brown paper bag. I admit it looked pretty suspicious, but I didn't have a checkbook, and they weren't taking credit cards. This is what brothers do for one another. Back in the hospital, we always had a laugh together, but I was usually high as a kite.

One evening, Nur was with me in my room when Mickey Rourke walked in. I'd known Mickey for years, but it was a total surprise. I had met Mickey in the early '90s—I can't remember exactly where. We reminded each other of people we grew up around, I guess, and I could easily see through his facade, as he could see through mine. It was obvious to me that he had a good heart and needed to have a cover to protect himself from being hurt. I knew because I was wearing the same overcoat, so to speak. Over the years, we'd done a lot of great shootings together as well. Though we didn't see each other often, we'd become lifelong friends.

"Mickey, holy shit, what are you doing here?"

"I don't know. I got a call, and they said you wanted to see me, so here I am."

It was Nur who had called him, of course. Apparently when I was coming out of the coma, while the eight men were trying to hold me down, I was screaming for Mickey Rourke and Joe Pesci. I guess I thought they could come to my aid! Nur also told me that when they calmed me down, I turned to him and recited "Mary Had a Little Lamb."

But how cool was it that Mickey showed up? He was shooting *The Wrestler* on Long Island, so he got a car and came over. He brought me different kinds of T-shirts, long underwear, and chicken soup. During my two-week stay, he showed up two or three more times and always brought me chicken soup. I'll never forget his visits. He could be such a sweetheart.

As for Joe Pesci, Nur said he couldn't find his number. Joe had lived somewhere on the Jersey Shore; then he moved to LA. He was another person I once felt very close to, like family. Our relationship grew apart through distance and time—but I have great, fun memories and pictures that still make me smile. He didn't know how much I loved him.

One night, it was snowing hard outside. I got out of bed and just sat looking out the window to watch the snow falling on the trees in the park. There was no one in the park, no footprints—it looked so quiet.

Then I noticed a guy standing very still between a tree and the park bench. I had noticed him the day before too. It was eerie how still he was; the snow was piling up on his hat and shoulders. I was thinking this fucker had been there for two nights now and looked like he wanted to jump out and mug someone. I shut off my lights so he wouldn't see me. Nur walked in, and I called him over.

"Nur, take a look at this fuckin' guy. He's been standing there for two nights, and the freakin' snow is even piling up on him." I pointed him out.

Nur looked out the window and said, "That's a fucking statue, you moron."

Really? I wasn't so sure, but I was the one flying high on Oxy and morphine. Then it dawned on me—it was a statue. Funny thing what OxyContin and morphine could do to your eyesight.

After a week, with the 3:00 a.m. shots to my belly and the constant checking of my blood pressure, I was getting no sleep and feeling irritable and even more out of my mind. There was an old lady in the room next door, and every night, she moaned so loudly, forget about sleeping. I couldn't even nap.

One night, I was so beside myself that I yelled out, "Hey, lady, would you shut the fuck up?"

The nurse came to my room and turned the bright light on—I thought I was in a Korean deli all of a sudden—and said, "Mr. D'Orazio, how could you?"

"She sounds like she's dying over there. Why don't you give her some morphine?"

"She's on morphine, and she *is* dying."

"Well, give her some more. She's going to die anyway." The shitty things you say when you're whacked.

The staff was starting to hate me. I had been there now for almost ten days, plus the time in intensive care, and with no sleep, I looked and felt like a zombie.

This moaning went on another couple of days and nights, and even with the morphine, I was losing my mind; she was really loud. You would have thought she was on the couch in my room. I threatened to go over there and smother her with a pillow.

Then, around the third night, about three in the morning, it got quiet, and I was falling asleep when the nurse came in to take my temperature, check for fever, blood pressure, along with the shot to my belly, the usual routine. I asked her, "How much longer do I need to be here, I haven't slept in a week? By the way, what's with the lady next door, what, did she die or something?"

"She died."

"Finally! Now I can get some sleep!"

I wanted out. I came up with a few schemes. I was able to walk about in the unit as long as I wheeled my IV stand with me. There was a large living room with lamps and big soft couches—it looked more like a lounge than a hospital. With my gown and my drips on wheels, I was able to scan the place. I was serious about busting out.

Nur came to visit that evening. I told him my plan and that I'd need his help later. I'd need him to be the lookout. When the lights were low and the front-desk nurse went to someone's room, he could signal me, and we could get in the elevator and out of there. As out of my mind as I was, I remembered both the look on Nur's face and what he said: "You're a sick fuck. I'm not helping you escape."

"Nur, I can't believe it. You're one of them, Judas!"

Nur was shocked and hurt that I called him Judas. (He reminds me to this day—he really took it to heart—and I have to remind him how insane I was and the amount of morphine I was on, not counting the eight OxyContin I had already taken that day.)

Twice I tried to make it to the elevator, only to be grabbed by a nurse who said, "Where do you think you are going?" Another time, Nur, my cousin Pam, and a nurse were chasing me around the couches until they finally nabbed me. They should have put me on a leash.

Both the daytime and nighttime nurses wanted to kill me; they couldn't wait for me to leave. Then, one night, Naomi Campbell came to visit me. I have to give it up to her; she

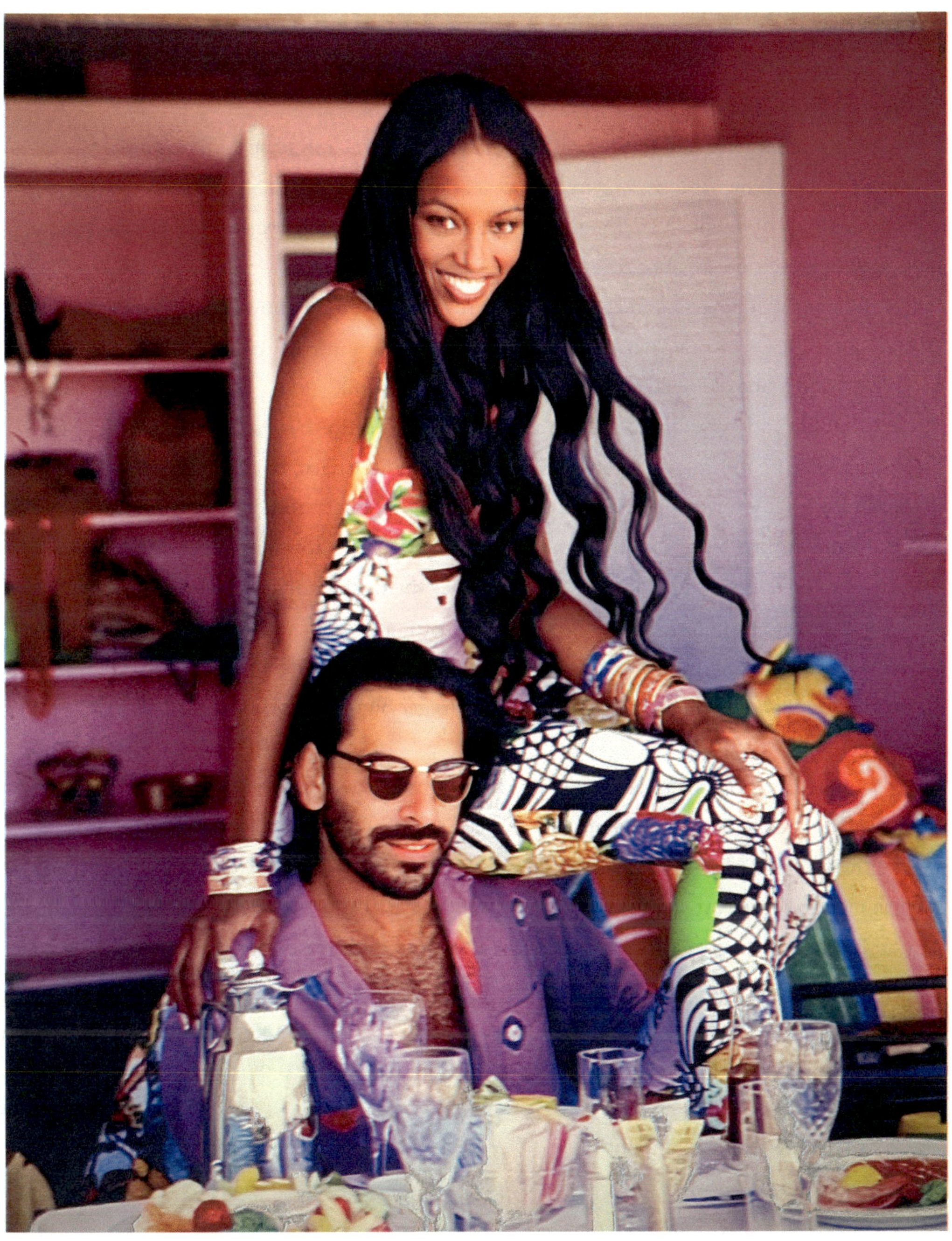

Naomi Campbell and Sante in Palm Beach, Florida, for *Allure*

was always there when it counted! We had been through many adventures and misadventures together over the years, some funny, others funnier. First, Mickey had come to visit, then, Naomi Campbell. That changed the attitude of the staff.

Naomi brought a large basket with fruit and chocolates and stayed quite a while. She sat on the bed with me, and we watched a movie. I loved her for that. She even came a second time during a different shift. The nurses went nuts—some of those fine ladies were Jamaican, as Naomi is on her mother's side.

Naomi has a big heart and a generous spirit. People should know that all that crap they read about her is mostly nonsense. From time to time, someone may get hit in the head with a phone, but the good she does far outweighs the bad.

Thankfully, I was able to shower as long as I held onto the drip stand. I had a rough beard and still had the scab on my forehead. I wanted to shave, but the nurses didn't want me handling anything sharp just yet. I was still looking like a nut job.

One morning around six, when it was time once again for the fever check, I told the nurse I wanted to shower. She put white tape over the three-pronged IV in my neck so that it wouldn't get wet. She removed the other IVs from my hand and arm, just for the shower. When she left the room I put on my pants, tucked in my hospital gown, put on my boots, my coat, grabbed my Prada bag, and managed to get out of the hospital.

As soon as I was on the street, I was on a mission: I was going to Paragon Sports. I had always loved collecting pocketknives. Every country I visited, I'd buy a local type of pocketknife, a folk-art knife, made by some well-known artisan. In the hospital, while I was hallucinating from my cocktail of drugs, I watched this show where these guys made big classic knives over a fire with raw materials. It got me thinking of this one knife I had seen at Paragon that I really loved. I got to the store at 8:30 a.m., and it was still closed, but I could see employees inside.

I knocked at the door and got somebody's attention. I yelled out to him, "Open up! I want to buy a knife!"

The guy waved me off and yelled, "Get the hell out of here before I call the cops!"

I yelled back, "I want to see the manager!"

He yelled back, "I am the manager! Now get the hell out of here!"

I went to buy a coffee. That's when I saw my reflection in a shop window. No wonder he told me to fuck off. My hair was nuts; I had dark rings under my eyes, twelve days of stubble, and the scab on my forehead. To top things off, I had my hospital gown tucked into my jeans, with hospital bracelets and an IV prong sticking out of my neck, all while clutching a large leather Prada bag to my chest! If I saw someone looking like me, I'd cross the street to avoid them.

At 9:00 a.m. sharp, I returned to Paragon and peeked inside to make sure the manager wasn't standing around. I walked in and up to the second floor where the knives were located. I found the knife and asked the salesman to show it to me. He got the knife from the cabinet and proceeded to tell me who made it and where in the US it came from. It had a beautiful Damascus three-and-a-half-inch blade with all its wavy patterns and a pearl handle. The salesman rang me up for eighteen hundred bucks. I handed over my credit card. I think they would have sold me a loaded gun for the right price! I didn't care how much it cost; I was still flying from my hospital cocktail! (And I still have that knife.)

I jumped in another cab and went home. Suite or no suite, I didn't want to go back to Beth Israel. Somewhere in all this business, I had called a masseuse to meet me at the house. When I got home, I was greeted at the front door by my cousin Pam and her husband, Pierre, who looked totally freaked out—all they needed was a butterfly net! The masseuse showed up, and we all went upstairs to my loft, and all I remember is Pam on the phone with my doctor and an eleven-foot-tall Julian Schnabel painting falling on me. Good thing I caught the crossbar of the painting's stretcher, or else I would have gone through it!

My cousin sent the masseuse away and eventually persuaded me to go back to the hospital. By the time I checked in again, my old room was ready. A welcome home party, I did not get.

77

After my trauma of having E. coli and being in a coma, I was no longer the same for a long while. I thought I was the same, but no one else did.

My nervous system felt like a ticking time bomb. Loud sounds physically hurt me, like pressure from a sonic boom, or a punch to the chest. No one seemed to feel it but me. Sitting in a restaurant, I could hear every individual voice separately and yet all at once. Then everything would speed up, and I'd break out in a sweat. I'd hold on as best as I could till I got out of the place, which was never soon enough. It was "post-traumatic stress."

In the early stages of my recovery, I couldn't handle the phone and the doorbell ringing at the same time. I'd burst into tears and curl up on the floor. Ten years later, when I thought it was behind me, if things got super stressful, I would feel it boiling up again. I couldn't handle even a long conversation with a friend. The TV would freak me out with its loud sounds and violence. Watching *National Geographic* and the animals on the Serengeti during a beautiful sunset, I would begin to calm down. Then, a fucking cheetah would run out and grab a baby gazelle by the throat. I'd freak out all over again. I'd turn to PBS and watch the artist Bob Ross, with his gentle, peaceful voice, paint a soothing landscape with his fucking #3 fan brush until even he got on my fucking nerves. Then I'd go pop a pill.

I could only make one decision at a time, wait, stare into space, and then make another decision. It was just like painting, and that's what I did. I returned to my spiritual home and started painting, a wish of mine for many years. Alone, meditatively, I slowly began doing some good work with no distractions, no longer being pulled in every direction and having to make constant decisions about yesterday, today, tomorrow, and as far ahead as next month. That's what the photography business was and is like. I couldn't stand it, and I couldn't take it anymore. Painting began to heal me. With time, I painstakingly progressed both personally and artistically.

There were plenty of naysayers, including artist friends, who couldn't understand where I was going or why. I didn't want to give up photography, but I couldn't work with all the chaos involved. My nervous system needed calm. On a shooting, I always had to be the glue that held everything together. I just couldn't divide myself into the many people it took to direct a shoot. First, I had to put all the pieces of myself back together again.

When I thought I was whole, I let everyone know I was back in business . . . but my old colleagues were on to the next new thing. I don't blame them. Too much time had gone by. You can't get off the spinning wheel and expect to get back on five years later. Fashion is about what is new—even if it's regenerated and regurgitated, at least it's new; it's "in fashion." I was somewhere in limbo. Luck had turned its back on me.

My titanium knee of fifteen years earlier started acting up and got worse; MRIs and other tests showed I needed to have the replacement replaced. It's called a revision. After a year of limping and not being able to function without pain, I had the surgery. After, I went through four months of physical therapy and never fully recovered. I limped through another year in constant pain. I couldn't shoot; I wasn't mobile. More pain led to pain meds. I also discovered you never fully recover from post-traumatic stress. Given cause, it's easy for symptoms to return, as they would during the next coming years.

Two years later, my back started acting up. I went for pain management, epidurals, another MRI. They told me my back problems stemmed from my knee; the titanium implant was microscopically loose. I had to get the surgery for a third time, this time to revise the revision.

Months of rehab and limping followed, and the pain shifted to my spine: three slipped discs, a problem with the vertebrae, and then sciatica. My body shrank an inch from the curvature that developed. The injuries and meds caused me to put on weight, which complicated my knee problem and exacerbated my pinched nerves and spinal issues. I constantly felt like someone was kicking me in the knee and shins with a metal-tipped boot. I couldn't walk more than two blocks without turning around for home.

I felt cursed. I began to see the end of the road for me and almost lost all hope, even if artistically, I was still confident that I could get in the ring with anybody. I needed Lady Luck, but I felt that she just wasn't there anymore and that my career as a photographer was over.

The pain continued. I needed spinal fusion surgery, the most painful post-surgery ever! Soon after, the Hospital for Special Surgery called to tell me there was a recall from the manufacturer of the prosthesis in my knee. It was defective and chipping apart within my tibia. On to my fourth knee replacement and revision, on the same knee, unbelievable!

My body needed healing in a bad way, and my nervous system was fucking with my mind. Meanwhile, I was making the best paintings of my life, and no one could give a shit because I was a famous fashion photographer.

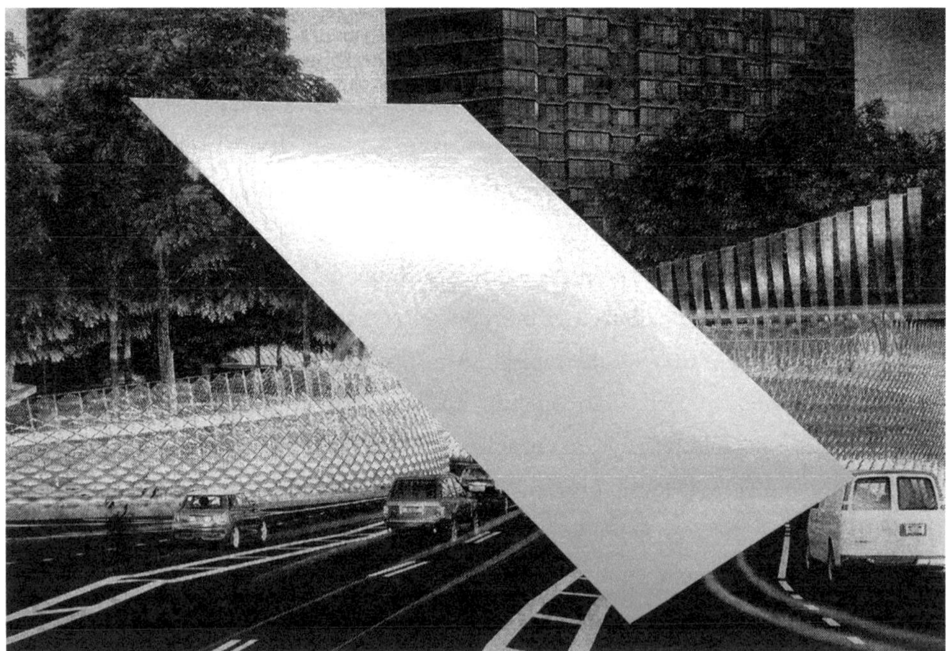

Portal painting by Sante D'Orazio

78

All cruelty stems from weakness.
—Seneca

> Hey, fuck you, you fucking fuck! You still owe me an apology you piece of shit for insulting me and my family at dinner! A text is no apology you twat! You're a fucking pussy for not calling me! You insulted your own family too by the way! You drunken fuck-face piece of shit. Fuck you!

This is a text I sent to a Japanese art dealer whom I exhibited with a couple of times in NYC, and with whom we shared a number of mutual friends. On this occasion, he had behaved very badly toward me and my family members, both personally and professionally.

Now, after sending something like this, would you ever work with this guy again?

I did.

Let's call him Mr. K. We had known each other for years and always enjoyed a respectful relationship. I appreciated his deep interest in art and especially Japanese photography. I even bought some photographs from him by one or two Japanese photographers he represented for my personal collection, and I recommended his work to my friends. Occasionally, I would attend the small exhibitions he installed in his gallery, and over time, I got to meet his family. One time, I extended an invitation for them to join me and my family at my cousin's Italian restaurant for dinner. His sons, like my son, were in college. They were smart, well-educated, and well-mannered Americanized boys, in sharp contrast to Mr. K's distinctively Japanese accent and demeanor.

He and I, along with our mutual friends, would meet up at different shows, dinners, and art fairs, in different cities like Miami or London and, throughout the year, in New

York City. Mr. K had an exhibition space in a gallery building uptown, tiny in comparison to the others in his building.

His father, I understood, was one of the first Japanese dealers to bring modern Western art to Japan after the war and made a name for himself out of Tokyo. Mr. K grew up as a highly cultivated man and retained his elegant Japanese manners, all while transplanting himself and his family to NYC and breaking out on his own, away from what I was told to be a domineering family patriarchy.

I've seen where children from cultures based on constant male parental domination can negatively affect the psyche of children, especially when this domination is not reinforced with love. The same holds true for the opposite, as in my Italian upbringing, where the expression of love becomes a dominant maternal tool of oppression to control and manipulate you into being a mamma's boy. Either way, you're damned.

Mr. K was very traditional; I liked that about him. He always seemed an honorable man, but I slowly discovered he turned out to have a very distorted interpretation of the relationship between friendship and business. Sometimes I felt he looked down at my manner and sense of humor. But I attributed this to our different cultural backgrounds and gave him the benefit of the doubt.

Mr. K liked my work and, in the years that we knew each other, we assembled several beautifully organized shows in his gallery. He was a perfectionist, sometimes a bit too much so—like the time he threw a shit fit over the frames I ordered because they were off by less than one-sixteenth of an inch. It didn't matter that the thirty-five framed pictures looked beautiful and that I got him a $5,000 discount—they had to be sent back! That's when I knew there'd be problems on the horizon if I got too involved with him, so I treaded lightly, cautiously in words and deeds, and began to walk on eggshells around him.

He took me up on my promise to treat him and his family to dinner at my cousin Palma's Italian restaurant on Cornelia Street in the Village. He brought his wife and sons, plus the director of photography from the Grand Palais in Paris. I brought along my son and my girlfriend, and my cousin set us up in our own private room.

Mr. K wanted to represent me and seduce me by suggesting the possibility of organizing a major show of my work at the Grand Palais, and at the scale of a recent exhibition of Helmut Newton's work they recently had with a catalog and all. That kind of show would be a turning point in anyone's career. We poured the wine, made some toasts, and sat down, ready to enjoy the food and the company.

My cousin served us a four-course dinner with appetizers, and as much wine and grappa as we desired. To my surprise, I discovered that night that Mr. K couldn't hold his liquor. We hadn't even had our main course yet. When we stepped out for a cigarette, Mr. K began to stagger. The rest of us didn't even have a buzz yet. We went back in and didn't think much of it and indulged in a feast of great dishes that had been prepared for us. I was proud of my cousin Palma's culinary taste and happy to be treating Mr. K and family as my guests.

At the end of dinner, I went to use the men's room. Meanwhile, my drunken friend, Mr. K, had asked for the check—even though I had distinctly told him this dinner was on me and my family. By now he was inebriated, or better put, stoned drunk! On my return from the men's room, I saw him trying to decipher the check, and before I knew it, he stormed out to the main room of the restaurant, cursing and shouting that he was being ripped off because he's Japanese and that this place is a shithole!

I ran to grab his arm and the check and to pull him back into our private room. My cousin was mortified. Other customers were still eating dinner. She ran over to us, along with some alarmed staff, and tried to explain to me all the things she gave us gratis.

"Don't even bother mentioning it," I told her. "Of course, I know that. This guy is just totally shit-faced! Look at him. He can't even stand straight! I'm so sorry and embarrassed."

When I turned around, Mr. K had both his fists raised. He was trying to pick a fight with the transgender waitress! I dragged him inside the private dining room again. He yelled to his family, "Let's get out of this shithole!"

My cousin was still trying to explain the check and probably needed a Valium at this point. Everyone in our room was startled and got up from the table. Mr. K began to literally march out like a little boy at the head of a parade, wielding his invisible baton! His poor wife and two sons were aghast, apologizing as they chased after him. The director of photography from the Grand Palais had also bolted after him. I was sure I would never see him again.

Two days later, the drunkard sent his wife, a very sweet woman, down to my loft to apologize with a bottle of champagne. He didn't even have the respect to apologize himself, to me or to my cousin; he sent his wife. I waited a month, never got a call, so I called him and repeated verbatim the contents of my original text, which exclaimed some choice words in my native Brooklyn dialect and accent, which began with "You Fucking Fuckhead . . ."

After that phone call and incident, would you ever work with a guy like this again?

Like a moron, I did!

I try not to hold grudges, and with so many mutual friends, I maintained a facade of friendliness. I had a lot of personal and professional issues at stake. He had asked multiple times to represent me exclusively, but each time, I politely turned him down. I let bygones be bygones, but I reminded myself of the numerous misunderstandings that made working with him so problematic. Worst of all, I noticed how he talked shit about all our friends and about artist friends of mine too—basically, whoever was not in the room. Don't work with Mr. K again, our mutual friends said, he has anger issues. As I would later discover, he was a professional backstabber to boot.

During my slow and difficult recovery from all the surgeries, I couldn't work or earn a living. Mr. K was aware of it all and acted sympathetic. Thankfully, my photographs had become collectible, and I managed to earn an occasional income through sales; it was my saving grace. But as an artist, I also had to develop new projects, which required investment money, and production was costly.

A year had gone by since my dinner with Mr. K when he came once again into the picture. We had maintained our amicable facade throughout that year but didn't socialize much anymore. I was uptown, visiting some galleries in his building, so I stopped by to check out a show he had up. He invited me into his office for coffee. At the time, I was selling an Irving Penn platinum print to help raise cash for my project, so I asked if he was interested in buying it. He said, "Why sell Penn when you can sell Sante D'Orazio?"

I said, "Fine. You know anyone interested?"

He said *he* was. "Why don't we do a show with big prints, and I'll buy four or five large ones from you?"

Those prints were going for a good price. That would put me where I needed to be. It was my only motive for this show. I talked it over with my studio manager who wanted a signed agreement, but I agreed with a handshake, which was common at the time. What could go wrong? After all, much of the art world had always dealt in handshakes, or at least used to. And no matter how anal the guy was, Mr. K had always been honest in the past.

In the meantime, I could start up my project with my lab: Twenty large prints, mounted on aluminum, custom frames to my specifications. I put up what money I had, knowing the sale of just four or five of the framed images he agreed to buy would cover it. I had assets hanging on my walls at home in the form of valued paintings from my collection that I wasn't going to sell, but I was short on liquidity. You should never financially commit to a big project until the money is in the bank, but I just didn't want to delay production. Sometimes, you just have to take a chance, I thought, especially when you trust someone you considered honest.

But almost as soon as my pictures were hung on his gallery walls, Mr. K reneged on our deal and told me he no longer wished to buy the four or five framed images we had agreed on.

I had to restrain myself, even though I wanted to kill the dishonest, lying, backstabbing crook. I was up shit's creek without a paddle, and my hands were tied. But there was nothing I could do but have patience and hope he'd make some sales. By now, my lab was going into its third week of production, and my pictures were on this lying bastard's walls.

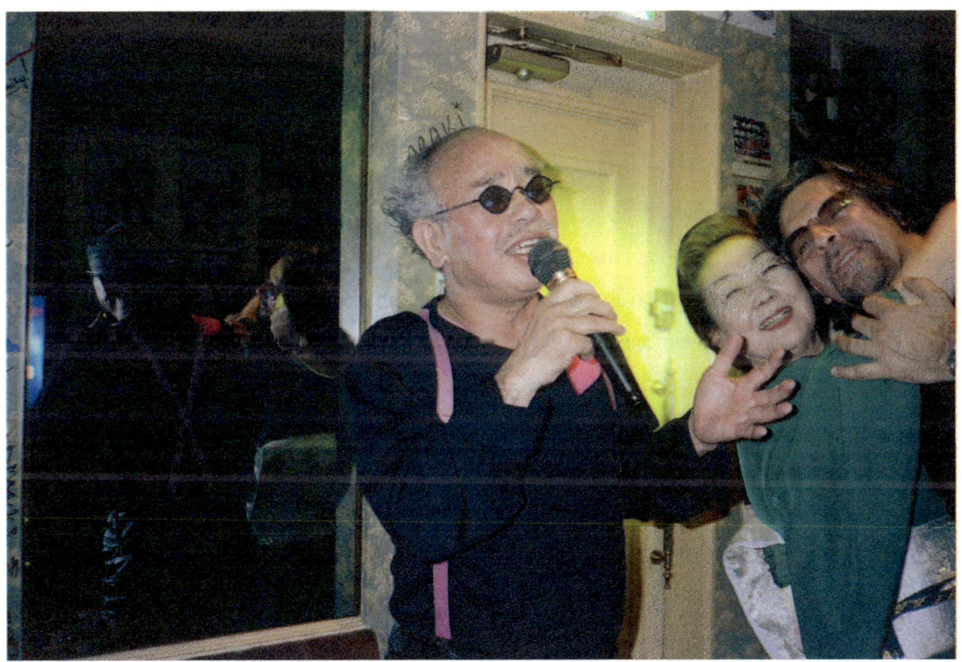

Nobuyoshi Araki and Sante singing karaoke, Tokyo, Japan

I called some mutual friends, but they were no help. It seemed everyone but I knew Mr. K was a sick individual. Meanwhile, he was telling me not to worry, that the pictures in the show would sell. But I *was* worried because someone I trusted was giving me the shaft! I, however, couldn't cut myself loose at this point; I needed those sales.

The show opened, and it looked beautiful. A few days later, I went by the gallery and again brought up the handshake deal about him purchasing the four to five prints. He said, "Oh, I can't be responsible to pay you. I was just talking." It dawned on me—this was payback. This was the power play of a petty and weak man. I was sure he took great satisfaction in it, especially since he knew I was handicapped, physically and financially. It was a cruel gesture by a dishonorable man.

"No, we had a deal," I said. To which he ignored and didn't reply.

The show had been up a month, and unless you were notified of the exhibition through his gallery, you wouldn't know to come in. The gallery was small, one thousand square feet, and located in a building of mega galleries. He made no sales and sent back my frames damaged—intentionally, I surmised.

I was in and out of the hospital at the time and unable to check and prove it was him in court. My studio was closed during my convalescence, and I didn't have any staff. Through his own invented paranoia, Mr. K decided, out of pure spite, to renege on another agreement, saying I still owed him money for frames from an earlier exhibition a year back. He knew I was strapped for cash, so he sued me in small claims court, knowing full well my lawyers' fees would sting. I was hoping he'd get run over by a truck and die a violent death so I could be clear to deal with my pressing health concerns.

By now, I had had enough of this petty thief. Two years had gone by, and I had gone to court six or seven times, which was located a short walk from where I lived. I wanted to see what it was like to represent myself. (I did much crazier shit when my PTSD affected my decision-making). His lawyer was a putz who looked like he came out of central casting, playing a down-and-out Perry Mason. He made believe he was on my side and that his client Mr. K was emotionally challenged. I agreed. I had made some of my own print sales, so when I got tired of it all, I negotiated to make him two large prints and call it a day, basically paying him to get the fuck out of my life for good. This had all become too petty with all my pressing needs; plus, my mom's health was beginning to fail. So for the low cost of the printing, which I didn't have to spare two years back, I bought him off for a measly sum, regardless of whatever he could sell them for. From my perspective, I paid him to fuck off, and he was happy to do so. Life is how you see it.

Months later, Mr. K. left a message for me. He wanted a birthday gift returned, something he had given me seven years earlier. I re-addressed my original text to him:

To Mr. K, Fuck you, you fucking fuck . . .!

With a P.S.:

This goes for your lying fuckface lawyer too!

Then I blocked all his calls and went back to work.

I haven't seen or heard from Mr. K's sorry ass since. *Sayonara, you fuckface piece of shit. Karma is going to be a bitch!*

In the meantime, I heard he has since alienated all of his friends, and his wife caught him cheating on her. He now sleeps alone.

79

Many years ago, I got a call out of the blue from German *Vogue*, asking me to shoot a cover for them. This was later in my career, and it had been a long time since I'd worked with them. They wanted me to shoot an iconic European actress for their special anniversary issue, and they had thought of Sophia Loren.

I thought, *Great, I would love to shoot Sophia again*. I had photographed her a number of times before, and we had become friends. The Germans thought the two of us would be perfect together.

"Okay, well, when, where, what's her availability?"

Then they confessed, "We don't know. We were hoping you could reach out and present this idea of a cover story to her."

"Oh, I see: you're asking me to shoot because you can't get her. Okay, tell you what: send me a signed fax on the Condé Nast letterhead confirming the cover and a ten-page story, and I'll see what I can do."

Twenty minutes later, the fax came through. I called Sophia at her home in Geneva. She said she would love to shoot with me, and maybe we could go to Milan, to Giorgio's (Armani), and use his clothing. "I love him," she said. "He's like a brother to me." Terrific.

I called German *Vogue* back literally fifteen minutes later and said okay, and I told them the dates, the location, and that it would be Giorgio Armani and his collection, in his house and his studio.

I ended up with great shots of Sophia, as well as of Giorgio Armani, a beautiful cover, and ten gorgeous pages inside. Access!

The first time I worked with Sophia Loren, it was also in Milan, also at Armani's residence.

I'd arrived from NYC the day before the shoot. That evening, I'd had a bad night, tossing and turning in bed with a 103-degree fever, sweating and soaked. But no way I was canceling. We arrived at Armani's for a 9:00 a.m. call time. After we waited around doing light tests, Sophia arrived in hair and makeup. (She did her own makeup.) I shot my first pictures, and she could see I wasn't feeling well.

"Sante, *tu hai bisogno della mamma.*" (You need your mom to mother you.)"

"*Lo so, ma è a casa a Brooklyn.*" (I know, but she's at home in Brooklyn.).

"*Allora ti faccio io da mama.*" (Okay, then I'll take the place of your mother.)

She went to the kitchen and proceeded to make me a bowl of broth and pastina. I was told later that she was famous on movie sets for making pasta for her crew. Along with some aspirin, which she also provided, I began to feel better, and we made some beautiful images.

A month after the pictures came out, I was home in New York with some friends, and my mom was there, cooking for us. The phone rang. It was Sophia Loren to say how much she loved the pictures. She then asked if I could please do her a favor and make a print or two for her.

I said, "Absolutely, it would be my pleasure, but you have to do me one favor."

She said, "Of course, what's that?"

"You have to say hello to my mother."

"Of course, I'd love to."

"Hey, Ma, telephone for you; it's Sophia Loren."

My mother said, "Get out of here. Can't you see I'm cooking?"

"No, really, Mom, it's Sophia Loren."

She grabbed the phone. When she heard Sofia's voice, my mother was speechless at first, and then she started talking in English.

I said, "Ma, she's Italian, remember?" We laughed our asses off, and my mom was in the clouds jumping up and down for joy.

"I justa talka to Sofia Loren! Waita till I tella the ladies at the school!" Mom worked at a public-school kitchen with ten other Italian women.

I loved doing that for my mom. I did the same with Brooke Shields; I brought her to my mom's house in Brooklyn for calzones.

"Hey, Mom, I'm bringing Brooke Shields over to have calzones with us."

"Get outta here!"

Brooke's another sweetheart, and her mom, Terry, loved me too. She said I reminded her of her first boyfriend, Frankie, from Newark. Both Brooke and my mom would always ask how the other was doing for the next twenty years.

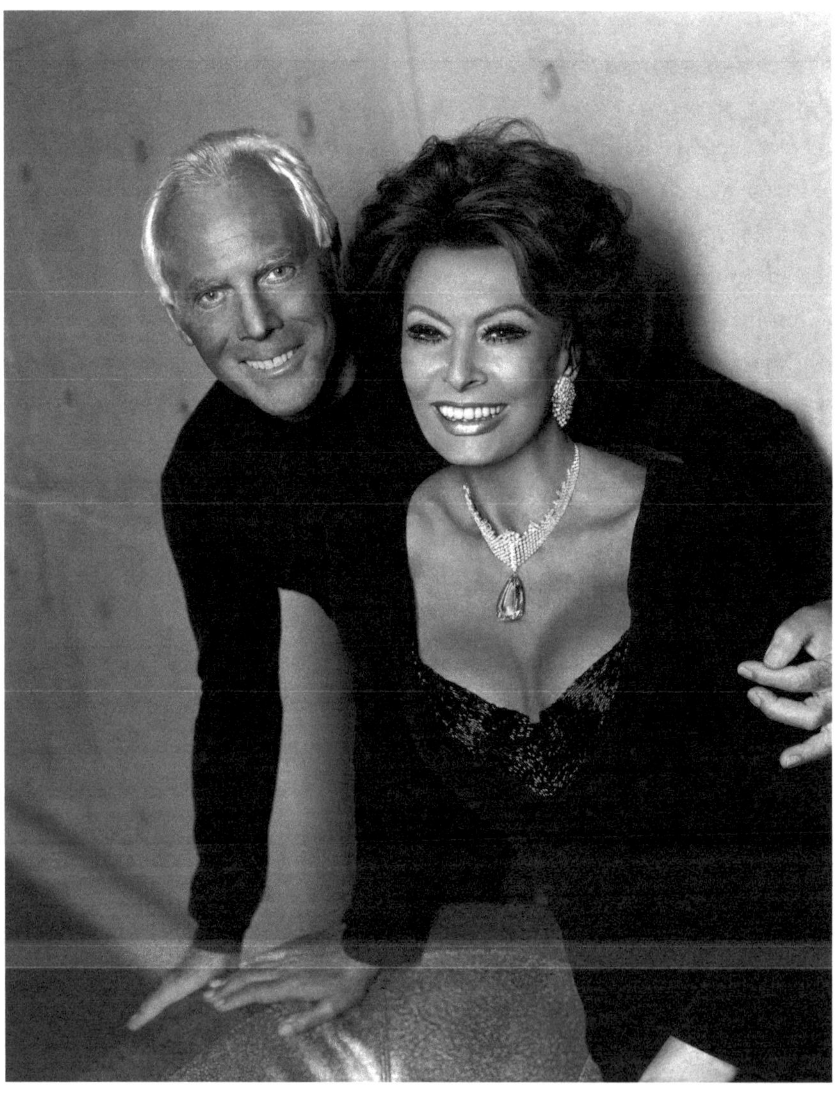

Giorgio Armani and Sofia Loren for German *Vogue,* Milan, Italy

80

"Eat your food! You know one day I'm not going be here anymore, and then you will miss my cooking, so eat! Everything I do, I do for you! If something happens to you, I will die!"

This routine started soon after my mom stopped breastfeeding me. I lived in perpetual fear of my mom's death; she would remind me of that impending event each time I didn't finish eating her meals. The thought of her dying was traumatic for me. I carried that fear into late adulthood. I came to realize that living every day with the fear of her death was to experience her death every day. I recognized much too late that she had a fear of life itself. Fear of loss, fear of losing me, fear of poverty, fear of fear.

She was gifted with an incredible operatic voice, but the idea of her going out alone into the world had paralyzed her small-town family. It was dangerous out there. When the fear of danger prevents you from doing things, you're not living at all. So she lived vicariously through me, and that was a burden I carried until the day she died. With her and her family as an example, I gravitated toward my fears.

Fearlessness is not the absence of fear but the willingness to walk into it. What we most fear doing is often exactly what we need to do. It's what you don't do in life that will kill you, or at least prevent you from living a fuller life. It's worth taking the risks and betting on yourself. There's risk in crossing the street, so why not go for it?

I'd spent my life running away from my mom's fears and living as an emotional captive. I wasn't going to replace my dad, and I didn't plan on finding myself at fifty living with my mom. I had seen my cousins do that.

When Mom passed away at the age of ninety-six, she had been in failing health for a few years. I was prepared but still scared of the day I had dreaded since childhood. I was afraid of what it would do to my psyche, afraid it would destroy me. That day finally came, and in her dying moments in her hospital bed, I saw her look past me, waving for someone to come to her. She called out to her mom to come and take her.

Death was here—it was no longer a false alarm. I sat holding her hand, her eyes were closed, and I whispered in her ear, "I love you, I love you, I love you." She took one last breath, and then she passed on to that other world. Still holding her hand, I whispered again, "I love you."

Like those who thought the world would end in 1984 or 2000, who watched with fear as time moved on, and then the sun rose again the following day, and all was well. She was free of her fears, and so, at last, was I.

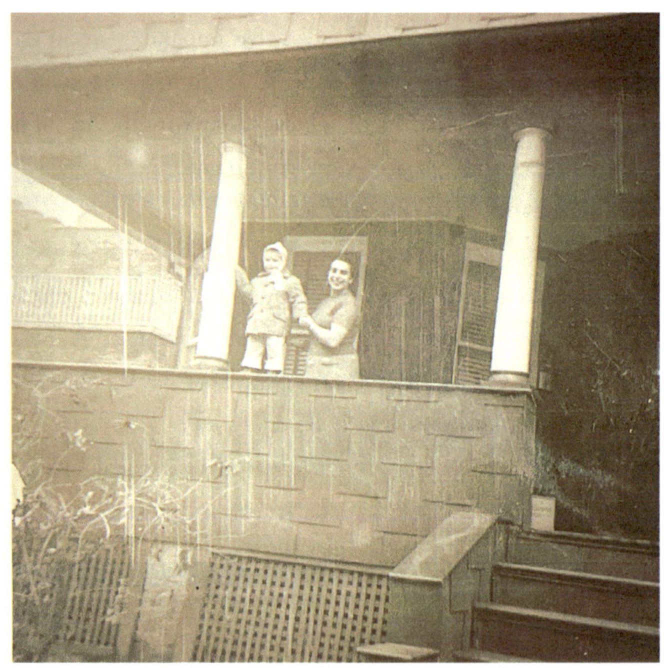

Sante and Maria D'Orazio

81

You must be ready to burn yourself in your own flame; how could you rise anew if you have not first become ashes?
—Friedrich Nietzsche

It took three years for the post-traumatic stress to settle. It didn't go away, but at least it settled. During this time, I was fragile, and I could only be still and quiet. I remained at home, away from the noise and chaos outside.

During my first year of convalescence, I began to remember and recognize what I was seeing in the dark space of that coma and my brief time spent in death. There were dust-like particles floating as if in a ray of light in a dark room. That apparent empty space that exists between here and there, or just between any two things, was filled with life-forms that I couldn't recognize before this trauma.

Those particles were no different in form than all the invisible waves of sound and energy that make our world what it is. The exception is that I was one of those particles, and I recognized others in that same form familiar to me. It was blissful. I now believe all empty space is full of life that is imperceptible to most of our limited human nature. On a greater scale, it most probably belongs to that side of nature we call God. This could never be described in terms of its metaphysical form as such in the past. It only made sense through myth, metaphor, poetry, and Art.

I began to paint in the quiet of my home where I felt protected. I could connect once again with myself as I did as a child, unmolested by the outside world. By painting, I began the healing process. Eventually, I asked myself how I could paint that space between here and there. It was a fundamental question of making the invisible visible; it was an abstract space that would challenge my perception. So, I began a slow road from one set of images to another, never knowing where it would take me.

It was all trial and error and staying away from the familiar. Allowing the errors to guide me as I searched for what I didn't know.

I thought to myself, *You won't lose your mind attempting this because you would have lost it already before you even tried*. In the end, it's the process of healing and transformation that counts and one through which you search for a discourse, without answers, to open-ended questions about the nature of our inner universe.

I couldn't unsee what I'd seen. There was no turning back.

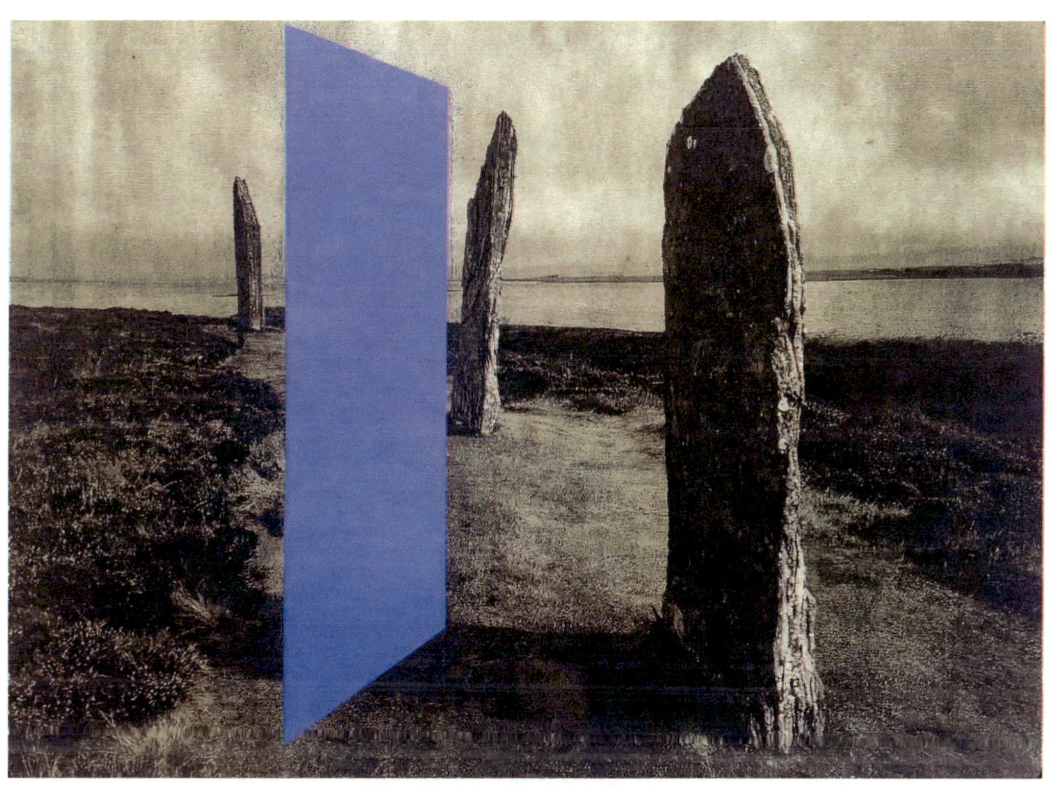

Portal painting by Sante D'Orazio

When you're in the shit up to your neck, there's nothing left to do but sing.
—Samuel Beckett

ACKNOWLEDGMENTS

There would be a long list if I wanted to acknowledge all the people in my life who helped encourage me along the way.

First and foremost would be my mom; though later in life, she became a real pain in the ass, I now only remember her with great love and comedy. No matter the circumstances, she always pointed to the positive and pointed me towards the open doors I didn't know existed. She always pointed me towards the light and led me to open those doors when they presented themselves.

I can only tell you here of those few who immediately come to mind who lifted me in my youth and taught me their wisdom and spiritual self-defense necessary, along with the means to combat the forces of self-doubt through knowledge, study, and a pedestrian self-aware guidance.

On top of that list would be Lou Bernstein, who not only taught me philosophy, but taught me "how to see." A philosophy of art and life being one and the same. He said, "The way you see the world is the way you see yourself. Never make less of others to make more of yourself; that's the meaning of 'contempt.' The way you photograph others is the way you see yourself; everything is a self-portrait."

I took emotional beatings from him through his criticisms of my youthful work, therefore myself. At the time, I took it all personally, but I welcomed it and returned for more; it made me a better photographer and, most of all, a better person. I remember him saying, "You may hate me right now, but one day, you'll love me for this." Fifty years later, his teachings still guide me, and I love him for it.

Then I have to acknowledge our neighborhood bookie and oddsmaker, who took a young kid aside and gave me his Brooklynese words of encouragement that I never forgot, along with a smile and a laugh whenever I think of it. Sally "TickTock," also known as "the Wizard of Odds," who saw me walking home holding a framed portrait drawing I did of my father who had recently passed away. The frame, which I could never afford at that time, had been made for me for free by a kind Arab man who I barely knew. He was relatively new to the neighborhood and now rented what was once my father's barbershop since before I could remember. What are the odds of having a portrait of my father framed there?

Sally "TickTock" called me over and asked, "Hey, kid, what you got there?" I showed him the portrait, and he held it in his hands. Looking at it, he asked, "You did this? With a pencil?" He paused and looked me over, then said, "Kid, your father would be really proud of you, and I'll say this much for ya; if you was a horse, I'd put all my money on ya!"

I laugh now; I never forgot him saying that. It strangely meant a lot to me. Words of encouragement that I need to acknowledge from such an unlikely source. I thanked him, and then had to ask, "Sally, why do they call you 'TickTock'?"

"Because when they place a bet, it's like an oath to me, yooz only, only have a certain amount of time to pay up! The clock is ticking and tocking, and you better do the right thing. Your best bet is on yourself, my friend. Dat's what I say, 'TickTock,'" said the Wizard of Odds.

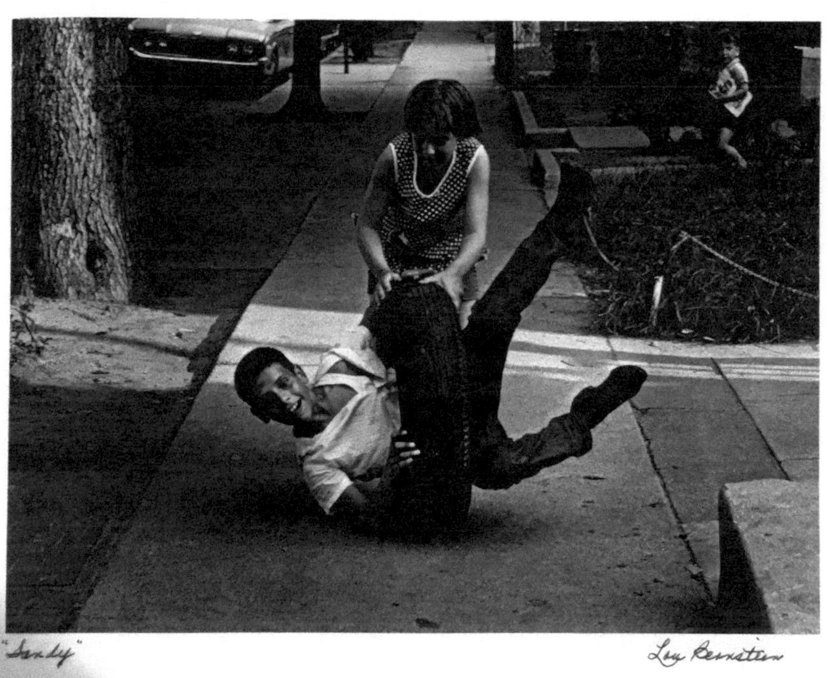

Sante and neighbor photographed by Lou Bernstein, Brooklyn, New York

BIBLIOGRAPHY

Chapter 2

Jung, Carl. *The Red Book: A Reader's Edition*. Translated by John Peck, Mark Kyburz, Sonu Shamdasani. W. W. Norton, 2012.

Chapter 11

Schopenhauer, Arthur. *Parerga and Paralipomena: A Collection of Philosophical Essays.* Translated by T. Bailey Saunders. Cosimo, Inc., 2007.

Chapter 15

Campbell, Joseph. *The Hero's Journey: Joseph Campbell on His Life and Work* (*The Collected Works of Joseph Campbell*). New World Library, 2003.

Chapter 18

Jung, Carl. *Letters of C. G. Jung: Volume 2: 1951-1961*. Edited by Gerhard Adler and Jaffé Aniela. Translated by R. F. C. Hull. Routledge, 1976.

Chapter 19

Cernuschi, Claude. *Jackson Pollock: Meaning and Significance.* Routledge, 2021.

Rose, Barbara. "Barbara Rose." Artforum, Vol. 47, No. 1 (September 2008) https://www.artforum.com/features/barbara-rose-217294/.

Chapter 29

Minimal Wave. "Richard H. Kirk." Accessed June 18, 2025. https://minimalwave.com/artists/artist/richard-h.-kirk/.

Chapter 34

Bukowski, Charles. *Notes of a Dirty Old Man.* City Lights Books, 2001.

King, Martin Luther, Jr. "Transformed Nonconformist." Speech delivered at Dexter Avenue Baptist Church, Montgomery, Alabama. November 1, 1954. https://kinginstitute.stanford.edu/king-papers/documents/transformed-nonconformist.

Chapter 37

Wilde, Oscar. *Lady Windermere's Fan.* Dover Publications, 1991.

Chapter 41

Epictetus. *The Discourses of Epictetus.* Arkrose Press, 2015.

Chapter 42

Rimbaud, Arthur. *Letter to Paul Demeny, Charleville, May 15, 1871.* University of Warwick. https://my-blackout.com/2019/03/03/arthur-rimbaud-letters-1870-18719-sean-bonney-letter-on-poetics-after-rimbaud/

Chapter 46

Yezzi, David. *Late Romance: Anthony Hecht—A Poet's Life.* St. Martin's Press, 2023.

Chapter 49

Bukowski, Charles. *The People Look Like Flowers at Last: New Poems.* Ecco, 2007.

Chapter 50

Ricard, Rene. *And if you arrive, do you know who you are?* 2012. Oil on linen, glass and wood over a found drawing, unsigned, with label from Cheim & Read, NY. Stair Galleries, Hudson, New York.

Chapter 52

Seneca. *On the Tranquility of the Mind.* Translated by Aubrey Stewart. Lazy Raven Publishing, 2017.

Chapter 58

"banshee." Merriam-Webster.com, 2025, Accessed June 18, 2025. https://www.merriam-webster.com/thesaurus/banshee.

Chapter 60

Jung, C. G. *Collected Works of C. G. Jung, Volume 18: The Symbolic Life: Miscellaneous Writings* (*The Collected Works of C. G. Jung*). Edited by Gerhard Adler. Translated by R. F. C. Hull. Princeton University Press, 2014.

Chapter 65

Jean-Paul Sartre. *Essays in Aesthetics*. Philosophical Labs, 1963.

Chapter 66

Goodreads. "Mateus Williams." Accessed June 18, 2025. https://www.goodreads.com/author/quotes/16659746.Mateus_Williams.

Chapter 67

Pliny the Elder. *Natural History: A Selection*. Penguin Classics, 1991.

Chapter 70

Saint Augustine. *Confessions*. Translated by R. S. Pine-Coffin. Penguin Classics, 1961.

Chapter 73

Euripides, Robin Robertson. *The Bacchae: A New Translation by Robin Robertson*. Ecco, 2014.

Chapter 78

Seneca, Lucius Annaeus. *Letters from a Stoic: Seneca's Moral Letters to Lucilius.* Translated by Richard Mott Gummere. Classy Publishing, 2023.

Chapter 81

Friedrich Nietzsche. *Thus Spoke Zarathustra: A Book for Everyone and No One.* Edited and Translated by R. J. Hollingdale. Penguin Classics, 1961.

Moorjani, Angela and Carola Veit, eds. *Samuel Beckett Today: Samuel Beckett: Endlessness in the Year 2000*. Brill, 2002.

ABOUT THE AUTHOR

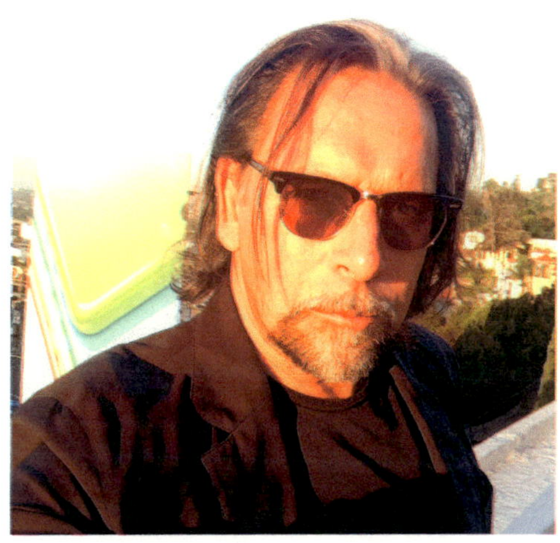

Sante D'Orazio, in a career of more than thirty years, has photographed supermodels, actors, rock stars, and icons for the leading fashion magazines throughout the world, including *Vanity Fair*, *GQ*, Andy Warhol's *Interview*, and the Italian, French, and British editions of *Vogue*. Also a well-exhibited photographer and painter, D'Orazio has shown in museums and galleries throughout the world, and his films have been shown at the Venice Film Festival, Tate Modern, Art Basel, and the Tribeca Film Festival. His previous books include *A Private View, Sante D'Orazio: Photographs*, *Pam: American Icon*, *Gianni and Donatella, Barely Private*, and *Sante D'Orazio: Polaroids*. He lives in New York City.